CONTEMPORARY'S

GED

TEST 2: SOCIAL STUDIES

CONTEMPORARY'S

NEWLY REVISED

GED

TEST 2: SOCIAL STUDIES

PREPARATION FOR THE HIGH SCHOOL EQUIVALENCY EXAMINATION

Reviewers
Alan Kimmel
GED Social Studies Consultant and Editor
Chicago, Illinois

Lynn Schmitz
GED Instructor
Kishwaukee College
Malta, Illinois

CONTEMPORARY
BOOKS
CHICAGO

Library of Congress Cataloging-in-Publication Data

GED test 2: social studies.
      p.   cm.
   ISBN 0-8092-3781-4
   1. Social sciences—Study and teaching (Secondary)—United States—
Problems, exercises, etc.   I. Title.
H62.5.U5G52   1993
300'.76—dc20

93-32445
CIP

Project Editor
Cathy Niemet

Contributing Writers
Karen Scott Gibbons
Virginia Lowe

Published by Contemporary Books, Inc.
Two Prudential Plaza, Chicago, Illinois 60601-6790
Manufactured in the United States of America
International Standard Book Number: 0-8092-3781-4
10   9   8

Editorial Director
Mark Boone

Editorial
Craig Bolt
Loretta Faber
Gigi Grajdura
Eunice Hoshizaki
Lynn McEwan

Editorial Assistant
Maggie McCann

Editorial Production Manager
Norma Underwood

Production Editor
Thomas D. Scharf

Cover Design
Georgene Sainati

Illustrator
Bruce Kerr

Art & Production
Jan Geist

Typography
Terrence Alan Stone

Interior Design
Lucy Lesiak

Cover Illustration
Mark Jasin

 Printed on recycled paper including minimum of 10% post-consumer waste.

Contents

Acknowledgments

Cartoon on page 12 by Jeff Stahler. Copyright 1991 by the *Cincinnati Post*. Used with permission.

Cartoon on page 13 by Mike Keefe, de Pixion Features © 1994. Reprinted with permission.

Excerpt on page 15 from *The Adult's Learning Projects* by Allen Tough, © 1971. Reprinted by permission of OISE Press, The Ontario Institute for Studies in Education, Toronto, Canada.

Illustrations on page 16 from *World Geography* by John Hodgdon Bradley, © 1954. Reprinted by permission of Silver, Burdett & Ginn, Inc.

Cartoon on page 42 by Ken Alexander, from *Best Editorial Cartoons of the Year*, edited by Charles Brooks, © 1978. Reprinted by permission of Ken Alexander, the *San Francisco Examiner*.

Cartoon on page 43 by Rob Rogers, © 1993. Reprinted by permission of UFS, Inc.

Cartoon on page 47 by Guernsey LePelley from Danziger in *The Christian Science Monitor*, © 1977. Reprinted by permission.

Cartoon on page 48 by Sandy Campbell, from *Best Editorial Cartoons of the Year*, edited by Charles Brooks, © 1978. Reprinted by permission of Sandy Campbell, *The Tennessean*.

Cartoon on page 58 by Steve Kelley. Copyright 1985 by Copley News Service. Reprinted with permission.

Cartoon on page 59 by Tom Flannery, from *Best Editorial Cartoons of the Year*, © 1985.

Cartoon on page 65 by Scott Long, © 1977. Reprinted with permission from the *Star Tribune*, Minneapolis.

Cartoon on page 66 by Lou Erickson, from *Best Editorial Cartoons of the Year*, edited by Charles Brooks, © 1978. Reprinted by permission of Mildred Erickson.

Cartoon on page 75 by Karl Hubenthal, from *Best Editorial Cartoons of the Year*, edited by Charles Brooks, © 1978. Reprinted by permission of Hearst Newspapers.

Cartoon on page 76 by Craig Macintosh. Reprinted with permission from the *Star Tribune*, Minneapolis.

Maps on page 112 from *The National Experience: A History of the United States*, sixth edition, by John M. Blum. Reprinted by permission of Harcourt Brace & Company.

Excerpt on page 117 from *Plunkitt of Tammany Hall* by William L. Riordon. Introduction by Arthur Mann. Copyright 1963 by E. P. Dutton and Co., Inc., renewed 1991 by Penguin Books USA Inc. Used by permission of the publisher, Dutton, an imprint of New American Library, a division of Penguin Books USA Inc.

Map on page 143 from *U.S. Map Skills* (IF8552) © 1992. Reprinted by permission of Instructional Fair, Inc.

Cartoon on page 173 by Art Henrikson. Reprinted by permission of Art Henrikson, the *Daily Herald*, Arlington Heights, Illinois.

Cartoon on page 174 by Mike Ramirez. Copyright 1993 by Copley News Service. Reprinted with permission.

Chart on page 174 reprinted with permission from Tribune Media Services.

To the Student

If you're studying to pass the GED Tests, you're in good company. In 1992, the most recent year for which figures are available, over 790,000 people took the tests. Of this number, nearly 480,000 actually received their certificates. Why do so many people choose to take the GED Tests? Some do so to get a job or to get a better one than they already have. Others take the tests so that they can go on to college or vocational school. Still others pursue their GED diplomas to feel better about themselves or to set good examples for their children.

Americans and Canadians alike, from all walks of life, have passed their GED Tests and obtained diplomas. Some well-known graduates include country music singers Waylon Jennings and John Michael Montgomery, comedian Bill Cosby, Olympic gold medalist Mary Lou Retton, former New Jersey Governor James J. Florio, Wendy's Old-Fashioned Hamburgers founder Dave Thomas, Delaware State Senator Ruth Ann Minner, U.S. Senator Ben Nighthorse Campbell of Colorado, motion picture actor Kelly McGillis, Famous Amos Chocolate Chip Cookies creator Wally Amos, *Parade* magazine editor Walter Anderson, NBA referee Tommy Nuñez, and Triple Crown winner jockey Ron Turcotte.

This book has been designed to help you, too, succeed on the test. It will provide you with instruction in the skills you need to pass, background information on key social studies concepts, and plenty of practice with the kinds of test items you will find on the real test.

WHAT DOES GED STAND FOR?

GED stands for the Tests of General Educational Development. The GED Test is a national examination developed by the GED Testing Service of the American Council on Education. The credential received for passing the test is widely recognized by colleges, training schools, and employers as equivalent to a high school diploma.

While the GED Test measures skills and knowledge normally acquired in four years of high school, much that you have learned informally or through other types of training can help you pass the test.

The GED Test is available in English, French, and Spanish and on audiocassette, in Braille, and in large print.

WHAT SHOULD I KNOW TO PASS THE TEST?

The test consists of five examinations in the areas of writing skills, social studies, science, literature and the arts, and mathematics. The chart on the next page outlines the main content areas, the breakdown of questions, and the time allowed per test.

1

THE GED TESTS			
Test	*Minutes*	*Questions*	*Percentage*
1: Writing Skills Part 1: Conventions of English Part 2: The Essay	 75 45	 55 1 topic	Sentence Structure 35% Usage 35% Mechanics 30%
2: Social Studies	85	64	History 25% Economics 20% Political Science 20% Geography 15%* Behavioral Sciences 20%*
3: Science	95	66	Life Sciences 50% Physical Sciences 50%
4: Literature and the Arts	65	45	Popular Literature 50% Classical Literature 25% Commentary 25%
5: Mathematics	90	56	Arithmetic 50% Algebra 30% Geometry 20%

*In Canada, 20% of the test is based on Geography and 15% on Behavioral Sciences.

On all five tests, you are expected to demonstrate the ability to think about many issues. You also are tested on knowledge and skills you have acquired from life experiences, television, radio, books and newspapers, consumer products, and advertising. In addition to the above information, keep these facts in mind:

1. Three of the five tests—Literature and the Arts, Science, and Social Studies—require that you answer questions based on reading passages or interpreting cartoons, diagrams, maps, charts, and graphs in these content areas. Developing strong reading and thinking skills is the key to succeeding on these tests.

2. The Writing Skills Test requires you to be able to detect and correct errors in sentence structure, grammar, punctuation, and spelling. You also will have to write a composition of approximately 200 words on a topic familiar to most adults.

3. The Mathematics Test consists mainly of word problems to be solved. Therefore, you must be able to combine your ability to perform computations with problem-solving skills.

WHO MAY TAKE THE TESTS?

In the United States, Canada, and many territories, people who have not graduated from high school and who meet specific eligibility requirements (age, residency, etc.) may take the tests. Since eligibility requirements vary, it would be useful to contact your local GED testing center or the director of adult education in your state, province, or territory for specific information.

WHAT IS A PASSING SCORE ON THE GED TEST?

Again, this varies from area to area. To find out what you need to pass the test, contact your local GED testing center. However, you must keep two scores in mind. One score represents the minimum score you must get on each test. For example, if your state requires minimum scores of 40, you must get at least 40 points on every test. Additionally, you must meet the requirements of a minimum average score on all five tests. For example, if your state requires a minimum average score of 45, you must get a total of 225 points to pass. The two scores together, the minimum score and the minimum average score, determine whether you pass or fail the GED Test.

To understand this better, look at the scores of three people who took the test in a state that requires a minimum score of 40 and a minimum average score of 45 (225 total). Ann and Willie did not pass, but Ramon did. See if you can tell why.

	Ann	Willie	Ramon
Test 1	44	42	43
Test 2	43	43	48
Test 3	38	42	47
Test 4	50	40	52
Test 5	50	40	49
	225	207	239

Ann made the total of 225 points but fell below the minimum score on Test 3. Willie passed each test but failed to get the 225 points needed; just passing the individual tests was not enough. Ramon passed all the tests and exceeded the minimum score. Generally, to receive a GED credential, you must correctly answer half or a little more than half of the questions on each test.

MAY I RETAKE THE TEST?

You are allowed to retake some or all of the tests. Again, the regulations governing the number of times that you may retake the tests and the time you must wait before retaking them are set by your state, province, or territory. Some states require you to take a review class or to study on your own for a certain amount of time before taking the test again.

HOW CAN I BEST PREPARE FOR THE TEST?

Many libraries, community colleges, adult education centers, churches, and other institutions offer GED preparation classes. Some television stations broadcast classes to prepare people for the test. If you cannot find a GED preparation class locally, contact the director of adult education in your state, province, or territory or call the GED Hotline (800-62-MY-GED). This hotline will give you telephone numbers and addresses of adult education and testing centers in your area. The hotline is staffed 24 hours a day, seven days a week.

WHAT'S ON THE SOCIAL STUDIES TEST?

The GED Social Studies Test consists of 64 multiple-choice questions. About two-thirds of the questions will be based on reading passages of up to 250 words each. About one-third will be based on maps, charts, graphs, or political cartoons. These questions require you to know some of the basic social studies concepts that will be covered in this book. To answer successfully, you will need to

1. understand basic social studies concepts

2. interpret illustrations and reading passages

3. show that you can
   - understand what you read
   - apply information to a new situation
   - analyze relationships between ideas
   - make judgments about the material presented

Actually, you already do all of these different kinds of thinking in daily life. In this book, we will help you apply these skills to social studies materials.

The GED Social Studies Test is broken down into these content areas:

History	25%
Economics	20%
Political Science	20%
Behavioral Sciences	20%
Geography	15%

These subject areas are covered in chapters 5–9 of this book. However, keep in mind that a given question may draw from a number of these subjects. For example, a question on the U.S. Constitution may draw from material covered in both political science and history.

Also remember that you are being tested on your ability to think about certain ideas and concepts. You will be asked to do more than just find an answer that was given in a passage.

These are the thinking skills that will be tested and their percentages of the test:

Understanding Ideas	20%
Applying Ideas	30%
Analyzing Ideas	30%
Evaluating Ideas	20%

Chapters 1–4 of this book provide practice with these thinking skills. Bear in mind that by strengthening your thinking skills in general, you will be able to perform better on any type of test.

TEST-TAKING TIPS FOR SUCCESS

1. **Prepare physically.** Get plenty of rest and eat a well-balanced meal before the test so that you will have energy and will be able to think clearly. Last-minute cramming will probably not help as much as a relaxed and rested mind.

2. **Arrive early.** Be at the testing center at least 15 to 20 minutes before the starting time. Make sure you have time to find the room and to get situated. Keep in mind that many testing centers refuse to admit latecomers.

3. **Think positively.** Tell yourself you will do well. If you have studied and prepared for the test, you should succeed.

4. **Relax during the test.** Take half a minute several times during the test to stretch and breathe deeply, especially if you are feeling anxious or confused.

5. **Read the test directions carefully.** Be sure you understand how to answer the questions. If you have any questions about the test or about filling in the answer form, ask before the test begins.

6. **Know the time limit for each test.** The Social Studies Test has a time limit of 85 minutes.

   Some testing centers allow extra time, while others do not. You may be able to find out the policy of your testing center before you take the test, but always work according to the official time limit. If you have extra time, go back and check your answers.

   For this 64-question test, you should allow a maximum of 1½ minutes per question. However, this is not a hard and fast rule. Use it only as a guide to keep yourself within the time limit.

7. **Have a strategy for answering questions.** You should read through the reading passages, or look over the pictorial materials, once and then answer the questions that follow. Read each question two or three times to make sure you understand it. It is best to refer back to the passage or illustration in order to confirm your answer choice. Don't try to depend on your memory of what you have just read or seen. Some people like to guide their reading by skimming the questions before reading a passage. Use the method that works best for you.

8. **Don't spend a lot of time on difficult questions.** If you're not sure of an answer, go on to the next question. Answer easier questions first and then go back to the harder questions. However, when you skip a question, be sure that you have skipped the same number on your answer sheet. Although skipping difficult questions is a good strategy for making the most of your time, it is very easy to get confused and throw off your whole answer key.

   Lightly mark the margin of your answer sheet next to the numbers of the questions you did not answer so that you know what to go back to. To prevent confusion when your test is graded, be sure to erase these marks completely after you answer the questions.

9. **Answer every question on the test.** If you're not sure of an answer, take an educated guess. When you leave a question unanswered, you will always lose points, but you can possibly gain points if you make a correct guess.

   If you must guess, try to eliminate one or more answers that you are sure are not correct. Then choose from the remaining answers. Remember, you greatly increase your chances if you can eliminate one or two answers before guessing. Of course, guessing should be used only when all else has failed.

10. **Clearly fill in the circle for each answer choice.** If you erase something, erase it completely. Be sure that you give only one answer per question; otherwise, no answer will count.

11. **Practice test taking.** Use the exercises, reviews, and especially the Post-Test and Practice Test in this book to better understand your test-taking habits and weaknesses. Use them to practice different strategies such as skimming questions first or skipping hard questions until the end. Knowing your own personal test-taking style is important to your success on the GED Test.

HOW TO USE THIS BOOK

If you are a student about to prepare for the GED Tests, you are to be admired. You have decided to resume an education that had been cut short. It is never easy to get back on track after you have been derailed, but, while it may not be easy, it will not be impossible. It will require determination and a lot of hard work.

This book will guide you through the types of questions you can expect to find on the Social Studies Test. To answer some questions successfully, you will need to recall facts that you may have heard or read about previously. You may be surprised at what you already know about issues and events in social studies. If you read newspapers, magazines, historical novels, or travel guides, you are already on the road to success. If you do not read very much, now is the time to start. Not only will you improve your social studies skills but you will also set a pattern for lifelong learning.

Before beginning this book, you should take the Pre-Test. This will give you a preview of what the Social Studies Test includes; but, more important, it will help you identify which areas you need to concentrate on most. Use the chart at the end of the Pre-Test to pinpoint the types of questions you answered incorrectly and to determine what skills you need special work in. You may decide to concentrate on specific areas or to work through the entire book. We strongly suggest that you *do* work through the whole book to best prepare yourself for the actual test.

This book has a number of features designed to help make the task of test preparation easier as well as effective and enjoyable:

- A preliminary "warm-up" section of four chapters isolates the four thinking skills—*comprehension*, *application*, *analysis*, and *evaluation*—and provides you with plenty of practice in applying these skills; this section includes a broad sampling of passages, graphics, and cartoons from all five subject areas covered on the Social Studies Test; these sections are indicated by the symbol at the left.

- Skill builders (in the reading chapters only) reinforce social studies skills and concepts; these are indicated by the symbol at the left.

- Content chapters cover the essential social studies concepts you need to know; these are indicated by the symbol at the left.

- A variety of exercise types maintain interest—matching, fill-in-the-blank, true/false, multiple-choice, and short essay questions.

- Writing activities based on thought-provoking issues provide an opportunity to practice critical thinking and writing skills for the essay portion of the GED Writing Skills Test; these are indicated by the symbol at the left.

- Over 400 practice questions strengthen social studies reading and thinking skills.

- An answer key (coded by skill level) for each section explains the correct answers for the exercises; if you make a mistake, you can learn from it by reading the explanation that follows the answer and then reviewing the question to analyze the error.

After you have worked through the five subject areas—U.S. History, Political Science, the Behavioral Sciences, Geography, and Economics—you should take the Post-Test. The Post-Test is a simulated GED Test that presents questions in the format, at the level of difficulty, and in the percentages found on the actual test. The Post-Test will help you determine whether you are ready for the GED Social Studies Test and, if not, what areas of the book you need to review. The Post-Test evaluation chart at the end will be especially helpful for making this decision.

We realize that practice makes perfect. Therefore, we've added a Practice Test as a final indicator of your readiness for the real GED Test. This test is just like the Post-Test in terms of its format, level of difficulty, and percentages found on the real test. After you have completed the Practice Test, you will be able to finally determine whether you are ready to take the GED Test and, if not, what areas you need to review. As with the Post-Test, an evaluation chart is included to help you judge your performance.

Contemporary Books publishes a wide range of materials to help you prepare for the tests. These books are designed for home study or classroom use. Our GED preparation books are available through schools and bookstores and directly from the publisher. For the visually impaired, a large-print version is available. For further information, call Library Reproduction Service (LRS) at (800) 255-5002.

Finally, we'd like to hear from you. If our materials have helped you to pass the test or if you feel that we can do a better job preparing you, write to us at the address on the back of the book to let us know. We hope you enjoy studying for the GED Test with our materials and wish you the greatest success.

The Editors

Social Studies Pre-Test

Directions: Before beginning to work with this book, take this Pre-Test. The purpose of this test is to help you determine which skills you need to develop in order to pass the Social Studies Test.

The Social Studies Pre-Test consists of thirty-two multiple-choice questions. Some of the questions are based on maps, charts, graphs, cartoons, and reading passages.

Answer each question as carefully as possible, choosing the best of five answer choices and blackening in the answer grid. If you find a question too difficult, do not waste time on it. Work ahead and come back to it later when you can think it through carefully.

When you have completed the test, check your work with the answers and explanations at the end of the section.

Use the evaluation chart on page 21 to determine which areas you need to review most. For the best possible preparation for the Social Studies Test, however, we advise you to work through this entire book.

PRE-TEST ANSWER GRID

1 ① ② ③ ④ ⑤	12 ① ② ③ ④ ⑤	23 ① ② ③ ④ ⑤
2 ① ② ③ ④ ⑤	13 ① ② ③ ④ ⑤	24 ① ② ③ ④ ⑤
3 ① ② ③ ④ ⑤	14 ① ② ③ ④ ⑤	25 ① ② ③ ④ ⑤
4 ① ② ③ ④ ⑤	15 ① ② ③ ④ ⑤	26 ① ② ③ ④ ⑤
5 ① ② ③ ④ ⑤	16 ① ② ③ ④ ⑤	27 ① ② ③ ④ ⑤
6 ① ② ③ ④ ⑤	17 ① ② ③ ④ ⑤	28 ① ② ③ ④ ⑤
7 ① ② ③ ④ ⑤	18 ① ② ③ ④ ⑤	29 ① ② ③ ④ ⑤
8 ① ② ③ ④ ⑤	19 ① ② ③ ④ ⑤	30 ① ② ③ ④ ⑤
9 ① ② ③ ④ ⑤	20 ① ② ③ ④ ⑤	31 ① ② ③ ④ ⑤
10 ① ② ③ ④ ⑤	21 ① ② ③ ④ ⑤	32 ① ② ③ ④ ⑤
11 ① ② ③ ④ ⑤	22 ① ② ③ ④ ⑤	

Questions 1 and 2 refer to the following passage.

Psychologists at Rutgers University found that men whose wives worked had lower degrees of self-esteem than men whose wives did not. One explanation that the researchers offered was that the higher living standards made possible by the dual income raised the family's expectations. In the men's minds, the second income became a necessity. As a result, the men believed themselves to be incapable of solely supporting their families in the manner to which they had become accustomed.

Since the year of the Rutgers study, even more women have gotten jobs. Many of the women joined the work force to help keep up with the rising costs of basic family needs. Another similar study about men's attitudes toward their working wives today probably would find that fewer men believe they are failures because their wives have to work.

1. The psychologists at Rutgers University attribute the cause of low self-esteem in men whose wives work to

   (1) the family's high living standards and high expectations
   (2) the fact that their wives' income is higher than their own
   (3) their inability to fulfill the traditional male role of breadwinner
   (4) society's attitude toward men whose wives work
   (5) their wives' inattentiveness and unwillingness to do housework

2. Which of the following expresses the author's opinion about the Rutgers study?

   (1) It was wrong from the start.
   (2) Its results are still valid today.
   (3) Its results would change if done again.
   (4) It is slanted positively toward men.
   (5) It is slanted positively toward women.

Questions 3 and 4 are based on the explanation below.

To a sociologist, your family is not your family; it is your primary group. The purpose of primary groups is to share human intimacies and teach society's ways and norms. You have other primary groups—close friends and confidants—around whom you can "be yourself."

The main purpose of secondary groups is to enable individuals to perform tasks efficiently. Secondary groups are more formal and less relaxed than primary groups. Most work settings involve secondary groups as do most political and community organizations.

3. Which of the following would a sociologist probably call a primary group?

   (1) a supervisor and the employees in her charge
   (2) a parent-teacher organization dedicated to improving its neighborhood school
   (3) next-door neighbors who get together regularly to share gossip
   (4) members of the Young Republicans
   (5) volunteers who work together during a United Way campaign

4. Which of the following would a sociologist probably call a secondary group?

   (1) poker-playing buddies
   (2) members of one's immediate family
   (3) officers of a school's student council
   (4) neighbors who participate in a car pool
   (5) members in a therapy group who meet regularly with their psychotherapist

Questions 5 and 6 are based on the following graph.

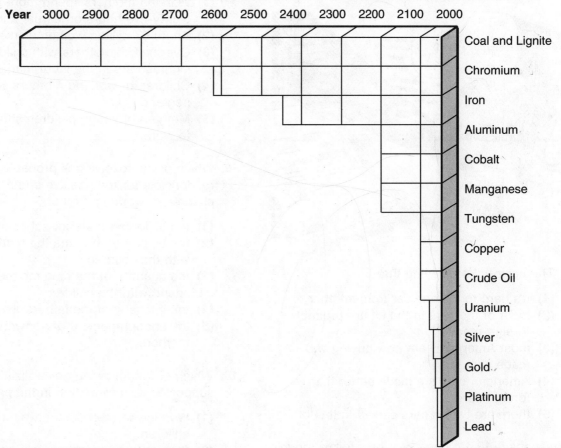

ESTIMATED DATES FOR DEPLETION OF WORLD'S MAJOR MINERAL RESOURCES

5. The information in the graph supports which of the following statements?

   (1) The supply of coal in the U.S. will be in danger by the year 2000.
   (2) There will be a glut in the world's crude oil supply by the year 2000.
   (3) Gold and silver are more scarce than oil and, therefore, are more important resources to be conserved.
   (4) By the year 3000, virtually all the major mineral resources of the world will be gone.
   (5) Manufacturing with iron and aluminum will be possible through the year 3000.

6. In the graph, the artist did not consider that

   (1) there is no limit to the world's resources
   (2) man-made substitutes might extend the supply of scarce mineral resources
   (3) gold is the most scarce of all mineral resources
   (4) all of the world's mineral resources will be exhausted by the end of this century
   (5) coal is the most important of all mineral resources

Question 7 is based on the following political cartoon.

7. The cartoonist is saying that

(1) it's hard to tell one car from another
(2) most of the cars in the lot are probably foreign-made
(3) most Americans are now buying U.S.-made cars
(4) American cars are made better than foreign cars
(5) there are twelve cars parked in the lot

Questions 8–10 are based on the information in the following passage.

In 1991, according to the U.S. Bureau of Labor Statistics, some 57 million American women were employed outside of the home. Also, more than 65 percent of women with children under eighteen years of age were in the labor market, and working mothers spent up to eighty-five hours per week working at two jobs: career and family.

Some people believe that children of working mothers suffer from neglect. But studies have shown that children of working mothers generally do as well at school as children of mothers who stay at home. In fact, many children whose mothers work show better social development. Mothers who work tend to make up for the time away by paying special attention to their children during their time together.

8. Which of the following is a fact stated in the passage?

(1) Working mothers spend more than eighty-five hours on career and family.
(2) About 57 million women worked in 1991.
(3) Over half of mothers with children under eighteen are in the labor market.
(4) Children of working mothers suffer from neglect.
(5) Mothers of young children should not go to work.

9. Which of the following is probably responsible for the positive effect on the children of working mothers?

(1) the children's superior schooling
(2) the quality of the time the mothers spend with the children
(3) the quantity of the time the mothers spend with the children
(4) the intensity of the fathers' involvement
(5) the encouragement of nonworking mothers

10. Which of the following generalizations is supported by information in the passage?

(1) Working women don't have time for their children.
(2) Stay-at-home mothers do a better job than working mothers.
(3) Children of working mothers perform badly at school.
(4) Children of working mothers have poor social skills.
(5) Children of working mothers don't necessarily suffer academically or socially.

Questions 11 and 12 refer to the following quote.

"Justice of this kind is obviously no less shocking than the crime itself, and the new 'official' murder, far from offering redress for the offense committed against society, adds instead a second defilement to the first."

—U.S. Supreme Court Justice Brennan, in a 1975 dissenting opinion on a controversial issue

11. In the quote you just read, the "official murder" refers to

   (1) suicide
   (2) mercy killing
   (3) assassination
   (4) the death penalty
   (5) manslaughter

12. Based on the quote, we can infer that Justice Brennan

   (1) supports pardoning those on death row
   (2) is in favor of life imprisonment for murder
   (3) is against capital punishment
   (4) believes it is the state's responsibility to sentence convicted killers
   (5) supports capital punishment

13. In 1890, the Sherman Anti-Trust Act was passed by the U.S. Congress to prevent monopolies from forming or price-fixing from occurring among producers of similar products. In general, such monopolies are seen as being harmful to the economy. However, the Sherman Anti-Trust Act does not apply directly to certain business activities that are perceived as beneficial to society as a whole. An example would be

   (1) service companies such as gas and electric companies because such competition would lead to waste of natural resources and inefficiency
   (2) such companies as McDonald's and Burger King that get together to set prices for their similar products
   (3) a company such as Kodak that manufactures related products such as cameras, film, projectors, etc.
   (4) a corporation such as IBM that has holdings throughout the world
   (5) a communications corporation such as AT&T that provides a vital service in the communications industry

Questions 14 and 15 are based on the following cartoon.

MODERN ECONOMICS

Reprinted with permission from the *Minneapolis Star and Tribune*

14. The main idea that the cartoonist is expressing is that women

   (1) have equal status with men
   (2) are paid what they are worth
   (3) are joining the workforce in greater numbers than ever before
   (4) are exploited in the media despite their gains in the workplace
   (5) can never compete with men in the workplace

15. With which of the following opinions would the cartoonist most likely agree?

   (1) Women should be able to choose whether to have an abortion or not.
   (2) The "glass ceiling" limiting women's progress in the workplace is a myth.
   (3) Women have a long way to go before true equality is achieved.
   (4) Men who read magazines that exploit women are immoral.
   (5) Censorship violates a basic right guaranteed by the Constitution.

Questions 16–18 are based on the following graph.

DRUG SENTENCES IMPOSED BY ILLINOIS COURTS, 1983-1991

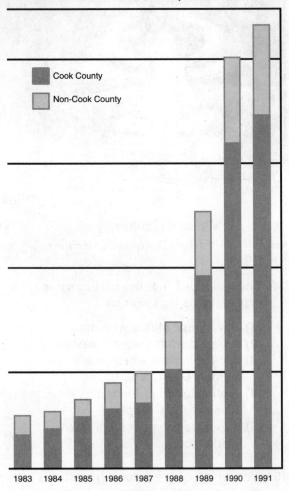

■ Cook County

▨ Non-Cook County

1983 1984 1985 1986 1987 1988 1989 1990 1991

16. According to the information in the graph, the number of drug sentences imposed by Illinois courts has

(1) decreased between 1983 and 1991
(2) remained about the same for a nine-year period
(3) risen sharply since 1988
(4) increased and decreased every few years
(5) increased by the same amount each year

17. Which of the following would probably be hurt the *most* by the increase in the number of drug sentences imposed?

(1) state prosecutors
(2) judges
(3) drug rehabilitation programs
(4) drug traffickers
(5) public defenders

18. Which of the following would be a probable result of the increase in drug sentences?

(1) the overwhelming increase in drug cases for non–Cook County courts
(2) the growth of the population in Cook County jails
(3) a dramatic increase in the number of lawyers defending drug dealers
(4) the increase of drug abuse throughout Illinois
(5) the neglect of other serious crimes

Questions 19 and 20 are based on the following passage.

Crime Stoppers is a private, citizen-run program formed in Lake County, Illinois, in 1981 to encourage residents to get involved in crime prevention. The organization rewards informers with cash, though only 30 to 40 percent of all callers accept the money.

Anonymous callers can call a special phone number to report any information they have about any crime. Though the program has been responsible for over 1,200 felony cases being solved, more than 900 felony arrests being made, and almost $2 million in stolen property and illicit narcotics being recovered, the program may be in jeopardy. A judge of the circuit court dismissed a case against a motorcycle thief because the chief prosecution witness was an anonymous tipster and police had made no attempt to find or identify him.

The Lake County State's Attorney's Office has now appealed the case. Crime Stoppers hopes the ruling of the circuit court judge will be reversed and has stated that not doing so will victimize society.

19. Which of the statements below is an opinion based on the passage?

   (1) Only 30 to 40 percent of the callers to Crime Stoppers accept cash rewards for their information about a crime.
   (2) Callers to the special Crime Stoppers hotline may remain anonymous.
   (3) A judge of the circuit court dismissed a case against a thief because the main witness remained anonymous.
   (4) The ruling of the circuit court judge should be reversed because not doing so will harm society.
   (5) Anonymous callers are accusing their enemies of committing crimes.

20. Crime Stoppers would be likely to support all of the following *except*

   (1) a whistlestop program in which citizens in distress use whistles to alert neighbors
   (2) an armed neighborhood vigilante group that takes the law into its own hands
   (3) a "neighborhood watch" program in which neighbors report any suspicious activity to local police
   (4) a citizens patrol organization in which private citizens patrol the streets looking to report criminal activity
   (5) a local chapter of the Guardian Angels, a volunteer group that supports the police in fighting crime

Question 21 is based on the paragraph below.

"Adults need individualized help particularly in self-planned learning. Indeed, by definition, the self-planner has decided to build his or her own sequence of learning activities, rather than follow a sequence of learning activities determined by a group, by programmed instruction, or by a series of recordings or televised programs."

—Allen Tough, *The Adult's Learning Projects*

21. Based on the information in the paragraph above, which of the tests listed below would be *most* helpful in designing an instructional program for an adult learner?

   (1) Wechsler Adult Intelligence Scale—a test that determines individual intelligence for adults
   (2) Rorschach Inkblot Test—a personality test in which the adult reveals personality characteristics by describing an inkblot
   (3) Vocational Aptitude Test—a test that measures the ability to perform specialized skills required in different jobs
   (4) Kuder Interest Survey—a test that shows a person's values, preferences, and strengths in various areas
   (5) Minnesota Multiphasic Personality Test—a widely used personality questionnaire

PRE-TEST

Questions 22 and 23 are based on the illustrations below.

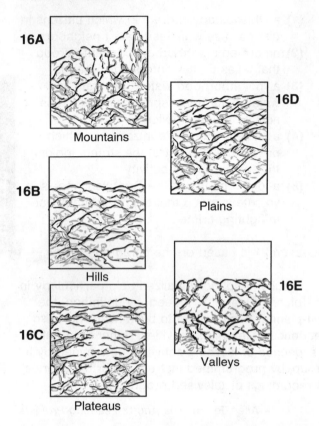

16A

Mountains

16B

Hills

16C

Plateaus

16D

Plains

16E

Valleys

22. The Grand Canyon, a magnificent example of a steep, walled valley, is surrounded by elevations of land that are broad and flat. These land features around the Grand Canyon are called

(1) mountains
(2) hills
(3) plains
(4) plateaus
(5) valleys

23. The terrain of the midwestern region of the United States is

(1) surrounded by mountains
(2) filled with deep valleys
(3) primarily hilly
(4) made up of plateaus of level land raised sharply above adjacent lands
(5) mostly flat, level plains in the rural farmlands

Questions 24–26 are based on the following passage.

The immigrants who came to America at the turn of the century were different from their predecessors. They were Italians, Austrians, Hungarians, Poles, Serbs, and Russians and were either Catholic or Jewish. Their traditions and ways of life seemed strange to more established Americans, and, because they were so different from the northern Europeans, ethnic prejudice became a problem. Years later, for much the same reason, Chinese immigrants to California were hated and feared by the very people who were victims of earlier discrimination.

24. The problems the new immigrants faced at the turn of the century were similar to the problems encountered by

(1) British brides of American soldiers during World War II
(2) American draft dodgers who moved to Canada during the Vietnam War
(3) Russian artists who defected to the U.S. for political asylum
(4) U.S. servicemen living on American bases in Europe
(5) Cuban refugees fleeing to the U.S.

25. The writer of the passage above seems to believe that

(1) the eastern European immigrants are not true Americans
(2) considering their earlier treatment, the eastern European immigrants might have been more tolerant
(3) the eastern European immigrants deserved the treatment given them by established Americans
(4) the Chinese deserved the treatment given them when they settled in California
(5) America is big enough for all people who want to come here

26. According to the passage, immigrants who experienced discrimination at the turn of the century

(1) welcomed later-arriving immigrants
(2) tolerated religious differences
(3) disliked the Poles and the Serbs
(4) learned new traditions
(5) hated and feared later-arriving immigrants

Questions 27 and 28 are based on the information provided below.

In North America, people consume about 3 pounds of meat per person each week. Europeans eat about 2 pounds, South Americans 1½ pounds, and Asians and Africans just ⅓ pound. If all meat were distributed equally throughout the world's population, each person would get about 1 pound per week.

27. Based on the information in the passage, we can conclude that

   (1) Americans eat more than their share of meat
   (2) Europeans do not eat enough meat
   (3) people cannot live on less than one pound of meat per week
   (4) Americans, Canadians, and Mexicans eat more meat than people in other parts of the world
   (5) the world's population could survive without meat in its diet

28. Based on the facts presented in the passage above, we can infer that

   (1) Asians and Africans suffer from malnutrition
   (2) Asians and Africans live only on fish and poultry
   (3) most Asians and Africans subsist on grains and vegetables
   (4) Asians and Africans do not raise cattle for food
   (5) the cattle that normally would supply beef in Asia and Africa are used to plow fields

Questions 29 and 30 are based on the passage below.

As the new immigrants increased their numbers in the U.S., the growth of the cities began displaying its full effects in this country. Tenement houses, lacking safety and health precautions, housed half of New York City's population in 1890. Open drainage gutters polluted water supplies with human and industrial sewage. Working conditions worsened as owners put more money into modern machinery and invested less in comfort and safety measures for employees. Without complaint the new immigrants and the freedmen of the South took any work they could get. As a result, the anger of the more established American workers grew.

29. According to the passage, it was most likely that the established Americans were angry at the new immigrants and blacks because

   (1) they lowered the quality of the products companies sold
   (2) they hadn't earned their jobs
   (3) they were endangering the lives of other workers because of their unfamiliarity with modern machinery
   (4) they protested too much about their living and working conditions
   (5) they were unintentionally hurting working conditions for others by accepting lower pay and poorer working environments

30. The passage illustrates the historic basis for prejudice against minority and foreign-born workers. For largely the same reasons, which of the following immigrant groups is resented by unskilled American workers?

   (1) Filipinos
   (2) Mexicans
   (3) Russians
   (4) Canadians
   (5) Japanese-Americans

Questions 31 and 32 are based on the following table that shows the dollar amounts of personal consumption expenditures at different income levels in 1990.

PERSONAL CONSUMPTION EXPENDITURES					
	Lowest 20%	*Second* 20%	*Third* 20%	*Fourth* 20%	*Highest* 20%
Income level (before taxes)	$ 5,637	$14,115	$24,500	$38,376	$76,660
Expenditures Food and alcohol	2,528	3,309	4,140	5,641	7,681
All housing	4,440	5,866	7,616	9,910	16,619
Clothing	667	961	1,335	1,958	3,391
All transportation	2,041	3,238	4,610	6,463	9,624
Health care	1,012	1,420	1,409	1,560	2,080
Other	2,220	3,131	5,564	8,715	16,016
Personal taxes	83	686	1,822	3,326	8,825
Total expenditures	$12,908	$17,925	$24,674	$34,247	$55,411

31. Expenditures for which of the following change the *least*, even when incomes go up?

    (1) food
    (2) housing
    (3) clothing
    (4) transportation
    (5) health care

32. It can be inferred from the table that the income level at which people can start saving money instead of spending it all is

    (1) the lowest 20 percent
    (2) the second 20 percent
    (3) the third 20 percent
    (4) the fourth 20 percent
    (5) the highest 20 percent

ANSWERS BEGIN ON PAGE 19.

Pre-Test Answer Key

1. (3) The passage states, "As a result, the men believed themselves to be incapable of solely supporting their families in the manner to which they had become accustomed." This means that men felt unable to fulfill the traditional male role of family breadwinner.

2. (3) The author believes that a second study would find a change in men's attitudes about their own roles in their families' finances.

3. (3) A primary group is described as "close friends and confidants around whom you can 'be yourself'"; next-door neighbors are examples of this relationship. The other choices describe secondary groups.

4. (3) Secondary groups are formed to carry out tasks efficiently, a characteristic of work groups. Officers of a school's student council represent a type of work group.

5. (4) Of the fourteen minerals listed, only the line for coal and lignite is shown to extend to the year 3000.

6. (2) Choices (1), (3), and (4) are untrue. Choice (5) is an opinion that cannot be supported by the graph.

7. (2) The man's statement about having the American car implies that most of the other cars in the lot are foreign-made. Also, a Honda (foreign-made car) is shown.

8. (3) The passage states that more than 65 percent of mothers with children under eighteen are in the labor market. Choices 1 and 2 are based on a misreading of the figures given. Choices 4 and 5 are opinions, not facts.

9. (2) According to the passage, working mothers make the time they are able to spend with their children special. The amount of time is less important. There is no mention of the father's role or of influence by nonworking mothers.

10. (5) Children of working mothers "do as well at school as children of mothers who stay at home . . . [and] show better social development." So these children do not necessarily suffer.

11. (4) Of all the choices given, only the death penalty, or capital punishment, means the same as "official murder."

12. (3) Justice Brennan says the "'official' murder . . adds instead a second defilement to the first." This shows his opposition to capital punishment.

13. (1) Gas and electric companies are excluded from anti-trust legislation because competition between them would lead to waste of natural resources. Choice (2) is an example of price-fixing and choices (3), (4), and (5) do not involve monopolies and price-fixing.

14. (4) Based on the woman's thoughts, women have not made enough progress in U.S. society since magazines, such as the swimsuit edition of *Sports Illustrated*, still treat them as sexual objects.

15. (3) The cartoonist depicts a career woman carrying a briefcase as she leaves a magazine stand. In the other corner of the cartoon, a man is reading the swimsuit edition of *Sports Illustrated*. These two facts support the opinion that women have a long way to go before equality with men is achieved.

16. (3) The bars on the graph show a dramatic increase in the number of drug sentences imposed since 1988.

17. **(3)** An increase in sentences for drug charges would hurt drug rehabilitation centers the most because their clients would be in jail instead of receiving treatment.

18. **(2)** The greatest increase of sentencing occurred in Cook County. As the number of people sentenced increased, so would the number going to jail. Non–Cook County courts have not had as dramatic a rise as Cook County. These sentences would not affect other crime.

19. **(4)** The clue word that indicates that an opinion is being expressed is *should*. Choices (1), (2), and (3) are facts stated in the passage, not opinions. Choice (5) is not an opinion.

20. **(2)** The only choice that does not suggest cooperation with the local law enforcement authorities is an armed neighborhood vigilante group.

21. **(4)** The Kuder Interest Survey is the only test instrument shown that includes some element of self-analysis similar to that which is described in the paragraph.

22. **(4)** From the illustration, you can see that plateaus are elevated, broad, and flat.

23. **(5)** The midwestern part of the United States is known mostly for its flat rural farmlands and not the other terrains mentioned.

24. **(5)** Of the choices given, Cuban refugees are the only group that experienced the ethnic discrimination that the eastern European immigrants did.

25. **(2)** The passage states, ". . . Chinese immigrants to California were hated and feared by the very people who were victims of discrimination at the turn of the century." This ironic statement suggests that the eastern European immigrants, having had experiences similar to those of the Chinese, might have been more understanding.

26. **(5)** The passage states that "Chinese immigrants were hated and feared by the very people who were victims of discrimination at the turn of the century."

27. **(4)** The passage compares the amount of meat eaten in different parts of the world. North Americans (Canadians, Mexicans, and Americans) do eat proportionally more meat than people in other parts of the world.

28. **(3)** If Asians and Africans consume the least of the world's meat, we can infer that they depend more on vegetables than the rest of the world. Choices (1), (2), (4), and (5) cannot be supported by the passage.

29. **(5)** The passage says that the established American workers were angry at the new immigrants and freedmen of the South because both groups took any work they could get without complaint. This statement suggests that, in their desperation to find work, the new immigrants and blacks contributed unintentionally to worsened working conditions and pay for established American workers.

30. **(2)** Mexicans are forced to accept unskilled, low-level jobs at the bottom of the pay scale and are perceived as threats by unskilled American workers.

31. **(5)** A comparison of the figures shows that health-care expenses increase only slightly as income rises. The other expenses increase more dramatically.

32. **(4)** A comparison of income level and total expenses shows that expenses exceed income in the first three income groups. Extra money is not available until the fourth group: $38,376 in income versus $34,247 in expenditures.

Pre-Test Evaluation Chart

Use the answer key on pages 19–20 to check your answers to the Pre-Test. Then find the item number of each question you missed and circle it on the chart below to determine the reading skill and content areas in which you need to do the most work. Pay particular attention to areas where you missed half or more of the questions. The reading skills are covered on pages 25–88. The page numbers for each content area are listed below on the chart. Both types of skills are absolutely essential for success on the GED Social Studies Test. The numbers in boldface are questions based on graphics. For those questions that you missed, review the skill pages indicated.

Skill Area/ Content Area	Comprehension	Analysis	Application	Evaluation
U.S. History (pages 91–143)	26	24, 29	13, 30	25
Political Science (pages 145–175)	**7**, 11, **16**	12, **18**, 19	**17**	20
Behavioral Sciences (pages 177–209)	2, 8	1, 9	3, 4, 21	10
Geography (pages 211–231)	28	27	**22**	**23**
Economics (pages 233–255)	**14**	**6**, **32**	**31**	**5**, **15**

CRITICAL THINKING SKILLS IN SOCIAL STUDIES

- **Comprehending Social Studies Materials**
- **Applying Social Studies Concepts**
- **Analyzing Social Studies Materials**
- **Evaluating Social Studies Materials**

1 Comprehending Social Studies Materials

When you ***comprehend*** something, you understand what it means. For example, if you understand football and attend a game with someone who has never seen it before, you should be able to explain the game to that person. The ability to interpret written material or illustrations shows your understanding of the information.

On the Social Studies Test, you will have to show your comprehension of passages, quotes, graphs, charts, maps, and cartoons in at least three ways—by:

- summarizing the main idea
- restating information
- identifying implications

SUMMARIZING THE MAIN IDEA

Summarizing the main idea in social studies materials means finding the key thought. Actually, you often hear lengthy information summarized into one key thought, or main idea. For example, you may have heard the president of the United States give a long speech on television and then later heard a newscaster summarize the speech in just a few sentences.

The main idea of a speech, article, or report is often stated near its beginning or its end, since the speaker or writer wants to give the idea the primary emphasis. Sometimes the main idea is not stated. The author gives the details, but the reader must ***infer***, or read between the lines, to determine the key thought. In some cases, a title may be a clue to identifying the main idea.

Read the passage below and in the question on page 26 circle the choice that best indicates the main idea.

On January 31, 1948, nearly a million people waited in the hot sun of India to mourn the assassination of Mohandas K. Gandhi, a thin brown man of seventy-eight who had died as he had lived—a poor private citizen without official title, position, or academic honors. Yet heads of state from all over the world were there to show respect for this friend of the oppressed, and the United Nations lowered its flag and interrupted its sessions in tribute. Gandhi had demonstrated to the world the effective strategy of nonviolent civil disobedience toward unjust laws. Humanity had lost an international symbol of nonviolence and mourned for itself as much as for the man.

The main idea expressed in the passage on page 25 is

(1) the irony of life in general and one man's life in particular
(2) mankind's loss of a unique activist
(3) that Gandhi never held an official public title or position
(4) that Gandhi died a poor man
(5) a plea for more international understanding and love

In answering this question, it would help to go back to the last sentence of the passage: "Humanity had lost an international symbol of nonviolence and mourned for itself as much as for the man." This concluding sentence summarizes the main idea of the passage, so choice (2) would be the correct answer. All of the other sentences show how unusual and well respected Gandhi was.

EXERCISE 1

Questions 1 and 2 refer to the following passage.

"For a thousand days I would serve as counsel to the president. I soon learned that to make my way upward, into a position of confidence and influence, I had to travel downward through factional power plays, corruption, and finally outright crimes." These are the words of John Dean, who served in President Richard Nixon's administration during the Watergate crisis. His testimony against his employer led to calls for Nixon's impeachment.

President Nixon made his resignation speech on August 8, 1974, after three articles of impeachment had been voted against him by the House of Representatives. Only one other president in history, Andrew Johnson, had ever faced the prospect of impeachment proceedings. No president had ever resigned from office before. Though Richard Nixon was never convicted of a crime or even brought to trial for one, to many people he remains a symbol of abuse of power.

1. The writer's main purpose in this passage is to

   (1) make a case for the elimination of the impeachment process as ineffective and outdated
   (2) compare the corruption of Andrew Johnson's presidency with Richard Nixon's
   (3) show sympathy for former President Nixon
   (4) remind us of the abuse of power in Nixon's administration during his term as president
   (5) point out that John Dean's testimony against Richard Nixon is what led to the former president's resignation

2. *Impeachment* may be defined as

   (1) finding a public official innocent
   (2) convicting a public official
   (3) bringing formal charges against a public official
   (4) executing a public official
   (5) the resignation of a public official

ANSWERS ARE ON PAGE 298.

SUMMARIZING THE MAIN IDEA IN ILLUSTRATIONS

You will work with several major types of materials throughout this text. They are graphs, charts and tables, maps, and political cartoons. Each of these types of illustrations serves a particular purpose.

Graphs make comparisons of numbers or amounts by using lines, bars, circles, or pictures. Graphs show patterns. Line, bar, and area graphs are particularly useful in showing trends at a glance. Circle graphs or pie charts are effective in showing how parts of a thing relate to the whole. Picture graphs, or pictographs, use symbols representing the subject being studied.

Charts and *tables* are concise reference tools. They list information in orderly rows and columns with easily readable headings and captions.

Maps give information about specific geographic areas, highlighting such data as weather, population, politics, and routes for traveling.

Political cartoons express opinions in a humorous and pointed way.

When you read a graph, chart, cartoon, or map, you will need to grasp the main idea of the picture quickly before you can use the information. To do this, you need to translate the picture into words. Look at the example on the left.

This is a circle graph. It looks like a pie that has been cut into pieces. The title of the graph is "Annual Budget Breakdown for School District."

Looking quickly at this graph, you can see that the main idea is that school dollars for this district are used in many ways, the largest amount ($1,200,000) going to teachers' salaries. The next largest amount spent is on books and supplies, followed by administrators' salaries and maintenance of buildings.

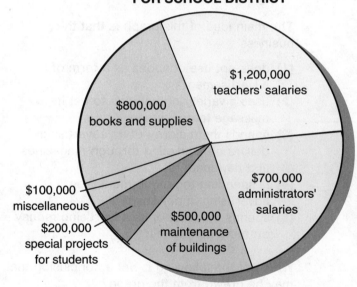

ANNUAL BUDGET BREAKDOWN FOR SCHOOL DISTRICT

$1,200,000 teachers' salaries

$800,000 books and supplies

$700,000 administrators' salaries

$500,000 maintenance of buildings

$200,000 special projects for students

$100,000 miscellaneous

Total = $3,500,000 annual budget

The following Skill Builder is a helpful hint in understanding circle graphs or pie charts. You will find Skill Builders throughout this section to help you strengthen your social studies reading skills.

 **SKILL BUILDER**

Interpreting Circle Graphs or Pie Charts

Pie charts show important pieces of information as parts of a whole. Each segment represents a percentage (or part) of the whole. To understand pie charts, try restating, in a sentence, the figures represented. For example, based on the preceding graph, you could say, "Two hundred thousand (part) of all dollars in the annual budget for the school district (whole) is spent on special projects for students."

 **GED Practice**

EXERCISE 2

Questions 1 and 2 refer to the following circle graph.

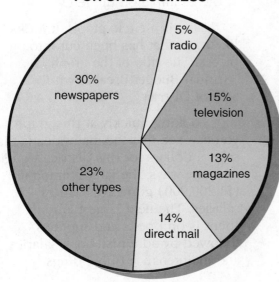

ADVERTISING SPENDING FOR ONE BUSINESS

5% radio
30% newspapers
15% television
13% magazines
23% other types
14% direct mail

1. The main idea of this graph is that this business

    (1) does not use coupons as a form of advertisement
    (2) uses a variety of methods to get its message to consumers
    (3) spends the majority of its advertising dollars on marketing through magazines and newspapers
    (4) is spending too much money on advertising in newspapers
    (5) spends the least of its advertising money on radio commercials

2. Which of the following is *not* a conclusion that may be drawn from the graph?

    (1) Most of the advertising money is spent in the print media.
    (2) Most of the advertising money is spent in the electronic media.
    (3) Less money is spent on television and radio than on newspapers.
    (4) About the same percentage is spent on television, magazines, and direct mail.
    (5) Other forms of advertising account for almost one-fourth of the advertising budget.

ANSWERS ARE ON PAGE 298.

RESTATING INFORMATION

Restating information is "putting it into your own words," or paraphrasing. By paraphrasing the speaker's words, you are showing that you understand what has been said.

One situation in which restating information is useful is in client-centered therapy. Certain psychologists believe that a good way to help troubled patients work through their problems is to restate information that the patient offers. Through this method, the psychologist gives the patient a chance to understand his situation better. A typical dialogue between a doctor and a patient in which information is restated might go like this:

DOCTOR: What is troubling you today? You look worried.

PATIENT: I haven't been sleeping well lately.

DOCTOR: You have had trouble with insomnia.

PATIENT: Well, yes. I'm afraid I'm going to lose my job.

DOCTOR: So, you are fearful of being unemployed. Do you have a reason to be afraid?

PATIENT: Yeah, sorta. I got really mad the other day and told off a couple of people at work. One of them was my boss.

DOCTOR: Oh, you were angry with your supervisor. Can you tell me more about that?

PATIENT: My boss is so hard on me. I don't think he likes me, really, so he picks at everything I do, and I just got fed up.

What do you think this doctor would say next?

DOCTOR: _____

You probably wrote something like *So you feel your boss is too critical of you*. The psychologist would restate the patient's words.

Notice how certain words in the dialogue are restatements of the patient's ideas. When you restate information, the words and phrasing may be different, but the meaning is the same.

Read the passage on the next page and choose the correct restatements that follow.

THE VIRGINIA SPLIT

It is interesting how the geography of an area can influence its culture and politics. The south Atlantic region of the United States provides a good example. There are three important topographical features that were important to the development of the region—the Tidewater, with low-lying land and large rivers; the Piedmont, with gently rolling hills above the falls of the rivers; and the Appalachian Mountains.

The Tidewater and the Piedmont were settled primarily as plantations, but the mountains presented a barrier that was insurmountable for the Virginia gentlemen farmers. The mountains and the valleys west of them were settled instead by a people different from the farmers—in culture, religion, nationality, and economy. So different were they, in fact, that when Virginia seceded from the Union in 1861, western Virginia seceded from Virginia and fought on the side of the small farmers and non-slaveholding owners of the North.

Directions: Based on what you have read, place a check mark before the correct restatements of the ideas from the above passage. As you check off each restatement, underline the words and phrases in the passage that say the same thing.

_____ **(a)** The people who settled what is now West Virginia were from a different social and economic group from those who settled Virginia.

_____ **(b)** The Tidewater is a land of gently rolling hills above the falls of the rivers.

_____ **(c)** West Virginia is largely mountainous whereas Virginia is an area of gently rolling hills and low-lying river basins.

_____ **(d)** Virginia joined the Confederacy in 1861.

_____ **(e)** West Virginia seceded from the Union when the Civil War broke out in 1861.

You should have checked off: (a), (c), and (d). The words that are restatements of (a) are "The mountains and the valleys west of them were settled instead by a people different from the farmers—in culture, religion, nationality, and economy." The words that say the same thing as (c) are "the Tidewater, with low-lying land and large rivers; the Piedmont, with gently rolling hills above the falls of the rivers. . . ." The words that say the same thing as (d) are "when Virginia seceded from the Union in 1861. . . ."

EXERCISE 3

Questions 1–3 refer to the following passage.

The terrorist tactic of hostage taking is becoming all too commonplace around the world, and a primary target is the American citizen. The U.S. Army considers this to be enough of a threat to its servicemen overseas that it has informally set policies to guide soldiers through such an experience. Some of the suggestions that might help ensure a hostage's freedom from captivity and preserve the country's and the victim's own personal dignity are:

● Remain calm, courteous, and cooperative.

● Do not provide any pertinent information to the terrorists or appear capable of giving information that could be used to their advantage.

● Do discuss unimportant personal information with the captors—family, favorite sports, etc.

● Do listen to the terrorists talk about their cause, their beliefs, and their reasons for taking hostages, but do not praise or debate them.

● Form a chain of command among military and civilians present and sustain communication among hostages as much as possible.

1. Which of the statements below best describes a common practice of terrorists who seize hostages?

   (1) Terrorists are usually calm and courteous in such circumstances.
   (2) U.S. military servicemen are always harmed in such situations.
   (3) Terrorists ensure the release of hostages who follow certain guidelines.
   (4) Americans are being sought as hostages.
   (5) Terrorists never release their hostages.

2. Which of the following is recommended as proper behavior for hostages taken by terrorists?

   (1) Do not let the terrorists talk about their ideology to you.
   (2) Make sure to communicate as often as possible with other hostages.
   (3) Do not provide any personal background about yourself to the terrorists.
   (4) Give the terrorists any relevant documents or other information they may need to further their cause.
   (5) Do not cooperate with the terrorists in any way.

3. Which of the following is *not* recommended by the article?

   (1) Appear to be cooperative in unimportant ways.
   (2) Suggest to terrorists that you could provide helpful information if they don't harm any hostages.
   (3) Listen to the terrorists, but don't comment on their views.
   (4) Keep communication lines open among the hostages.
   (5) Discuss family and personal issues with the terrorists.

ANSWERS ARE ON PAGE 298.

RESTATING INFORMATION FROM ILLUSTRATIONS

Giving directions is a form of restating information. Whenever you read road maps on a trip, you are putting the information from the map into words for the driver. Look at the map shown in the example below.

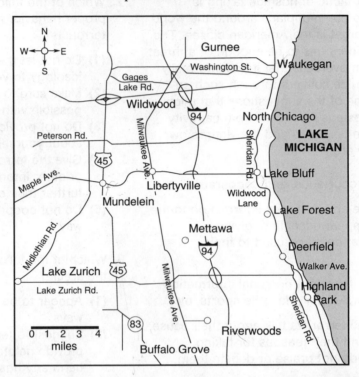

In giving directions to someone driving from downtown Highland Park to the corner of Washington Street and Sheridan Road in downtown Waukegan, you might say, "Take Sheridan Road in Highland Park north to Walker Avenue. Turn left on Walker Avenue to get back on Sheridan Road. Follow Sheridan Road north as it curves into Witchwood Lane and continue north on Sheridan until you reach Washington Street in Waukegan."

In order to give these directions you would have to know the directions north, south, east, and west.

Which direction is Waukegan from North Chicago? _____

Which direction is Lake Bluff from Libertyville? _____

Which direction is Buffalo Grove from Mundelein? _____

On road maps, some streets are heavier and darker than others. On most maps that heavier, darker color indicates a U.S. interstate or state highway.

Name the interstate highway shown on this map. _____

A scale of miles is usually provided in the legend of a road map. A legend explains any symbols that are used in a map. A scale of miles may be shown in inches (one inch = 50 miles) or by marks spaced equally along a line.

According to the scale on the map above, about how many miles is it from

Lake Bluff to North Chicago? _____   From Riverwoods to Mettawa? _____

EXERCISE 4

Directions: Look at the same map and write instructions for the most direct way to get from Lake Zurich to Wildwood.

_____

_____

_____

ANSWERS ARE ON PAGE 298.

IDENTIFYING IMPLICATIONS

So far you have practiced two ways to show your comprehension of passages and illustrations: by summarizing the main idea and by restating information. A third way to show that you understand information is by being able to identify implications.

Implications are ideas that are suggested, or implied but not stated directly. A writer implies ideas; a reader infers meaning from ideas.

Advertisements in newspapers and magazines and commercials on television make suggestions all the time. For example, at election time you may have seen many commercials for political candidates. These commercials often show the candidate in a setting that implies a favorable background. The messages might show a politician at home in a happy family setting. The commercial does not have to state that this candidate is a stable, happy, family man. It implies this fact by showing a smiling family.

Read the following paragraph to identify its implications.

Equality and fairness in the U.S. military are twentieth-century concepts. In fact, it was not until after World Wars I and II were fought and won that technical expertise and a cooperative spirit in leadership were rewarded by promotions through the ranks in the military.

The implication in this paragraph is that the promotion system in the

U.S. military before the twentieth century was _____

_____ .

The author has implied that prior to the twentieth century, promotions in the U.S. military were based on criteria other than technical expertise and a cooperative spirit; therefore, promotions were *unequal* and *unfair*.

The writer states in the first sentence that equality and fairness are new to the military. He then describes the "new" promotion system as an example of fairness and equality.

GED Practice
EXERCISE 5

Questions 1–3 are based on the following passage.

Needs are defined as food, shelter, and clothing. Wants are defined as extras in life—vacations, television sets, jewelry, pleasure boats, etc. Wants and needs can mean different things to different people, but generally social scientists agree that economic groups can be fairly well classified by the amount of money they spend on needs versus wants.

The very poorest people in the world live at a bare subsistence level. At best, they have just enough food and shelter to stay alive. On a rung above this level on the economic ladder are the working poor, those who spend $9 out of every $10 on things they *need* and only $1 out of every $10 on what they *want* out of life. The middle income group spends about $8 out of $10 on needs and the remaining $2 on wants, and the upper income group spends only $4 out of $10 on needs.

1. The implication of the figures listed for needs versus wants in the various economic groups is that

   (1) the wealthier a person is, the fewer needs he or she has
   (2) people at the upper income level want more things than those at the lower end of the economic ladder
   (3) the lower one's income, the more material things one needs to get by
   (4) the middle income group is the only one that is able to keep a sensible balance of needs versus wants
   (5) as one's income goes up, one has more money to spend on wants

2. This author has also implied that some of the very poorest people in the world

   (1) cannot even provide for all their own needs
   (2) are not concerned with providing for their own wants because they have none
   (3) should be given monetary assistance by the government
   (4) are uneducated and unable to deal with money
   (5) are not considered to be in any economic group

3. Philosopher Henry David Thoreau said "Superfluous wealth can buy only superfluities." If *superfluous* means "excess" or "unnecessary," Thoreau was speaking of

   (1) the poorest people in the world
   (2) the working poor
   (3) the middle income group
   (4) the upper income group
   (5) none of the above

ANSWERS ARE ON PAGE 298.

IDENTIFYING IMPLICATIONS IN ILLUSTRATIONS

You can draw implications from illustrations as well as from written materials. Line graphs are particularly effective in showing trends from which we may draw implications. A quick look at a line graph can reveal increases, decreases, uneven movements, or leveling off of numbers.

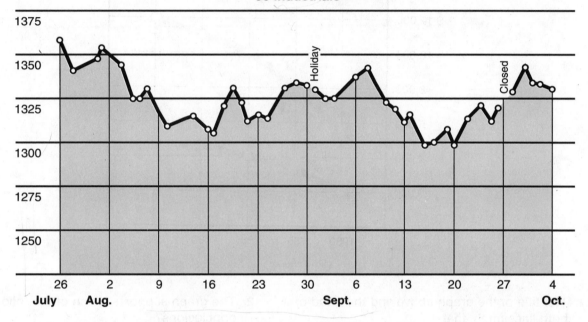

DOW JONES AVERAGE
30 industrials

Notice that the graph has a title, "Dow Jones Average," and a subtitle, "30 Industrials." It has figures going up the vertical axis that represent the number of stocks traded and dates along the horizontal axis that show what period of time the graph represents.

Between July 26 and October 4, the line on this graph fluctuates between 1300 and 1360. The implication is that over a given period of time, the number of stocks traded each day will vary. Looking at the graph, you can see that the line of the graph has moved up and down since early August, so the implication is that it will continue to fluctuate over time.

▨ SKILL BUILDER
Reading Line Graphs

1. The title and/or subtitle indicate the main idea and contents of the graph.

2. The vertical axis contains the information going up the side of the graph.

3. The horizontal axis contains the information going across the bottom of the graph.

4. Trends may be identified by describing the movement of the line from its beginning to its end.

GED Practice
EXERCISE 6

Questions 1 and 2 are based on the following graph.

Here's the average cost of tuition, fees, and room and board for one year at public and private colleges.

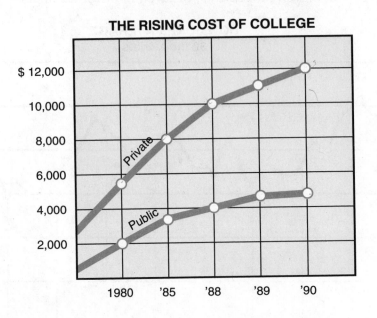

THE RISING COST OF COLLEGE

1. The title of the graph above and the trend of both lines imply that

   (1) institutions of higher education will soon be overcrowded
   (2) in future years, private colleges will most likely continue to cost more than public colleges
   (3) enrollment in private colleges is decreasing
   (4) the number of high school graduates has remained constant
   (5) the average cost of tuition, fees, and room and board has risen at the same rate for public and private colleges

2. The graph supports which of the following conclusions?

   (1) In 1990 the average cost of public colleges was twice the cost of private colleges.
   (2) In 1990 the average cost of private colleges was nearly triple the cost of public colleges.
   (3) The rate of increase for private and public colleges got smaller from 1980 to 1990.
   (4) The rate of increase for public colleges is going down.
   (5) Private colleges are a better bargain than public colleges.

ANSWERS ARE ON PAGE 298.

2 Applying Social Studies Concepts

Have you ever taken a first-aid course and had to use your knowledge to help an injured child, friend, or co-worker? Have you ever taken a driver's education class and then had to apply that knowledge behind the wheel in real traffic and again during the written test for your license? If so, you were applying your knowledge to real situations.

One of the most important ends of learning is an ability to apply what you have learned. On the Social Studies Test you will have to demonstrate this ability by:

- applying given theories, ideas, or facts in a different situation
- applying remembered ideas in a different situation

APPLYING GIVEN IDEAS

When you were in school, a teacher may have given you an explanation of a theory or principle and then asked the class to provide an example.

For instance, the teacher may have explained the economic principle of supply and demand in this way:

> How much a society has of something (the supply) together with how much the people in that society want it (the demand) influences the cost of the product.
>
> If there is a low demand for something but a large supply, the price will be low. On the other hand, if there is a great demand for a product but a small supply, the price will be high.
>
> An initial low price can sometimes influence more people to buy a product. As a result, demand increases and the prices along with it. Also, other factors, such as ease and cost of production, can affect prices. The basic principle of supply and demand, however, is the cornerstone of the U.S. economic system.

The teacher might then ask the class to give some examples of the supply-and-demand principle at work.

Of the statements below, decide which would be correct applications of the principle of supply and demand and which would not. Indicate correct applications by writing *YES* and incorrect applications by writing *NO.*

_____ At the end of a season, when clothing stores have a surplus of stock on hand, they run clearance sales.

_____ Despite the fact that there were very few qualified applicants for the job and the job had to be filled, Henry was not able to get the high salary he wanted.

_____ When Congress set a limit on cars imported, the public's demand for them increased and the prices of Japanese cars went up.

_____ The Cabbage Patch Kids were hard to find and expensive during the Christmas rush but were readily available in July—and cheaper too!

_____ "I've noticed that a lot of companies charge low prices for stuff when it first comes out, but when it gets real popular they jack the prices up."

All of your responses should have been YES except for the second example. In this case, the demand was high (the job had to be filled), the supply was small (there were few qualified applicants), but the price (Henry's salary) would not go up.

EXERCISE 1

Directions: Read the passage below. Indicate a correct application of the Supreme Court ruling by writing *YES* on the line before each statement and an incorrect application by writing *NO.*

In 1954, the Supreme Court of the United States reversed an earlier controversial ruling. In 1896, the Supreme Court had ruled in the case of *Plessy* v. *Ferguson* that separate but equal facilities for blacks and whites were correct and legal. But the decision of 1954, called *Brown* v. *the Board of Education of Topeka*, ruled that blacks had equal rights to the *same* public schools because separate educational facilities were deemed inherently unequal. Public schools were ordered to desegregate "with all deliberate speed."

A correct application of the 1954 ruling would be

_____ **1.** busing children from black inner-city schools to white or racially mixed schools in the same district

_____ **2.** setting up African-American history courses in high schools and colleges

_____ **3.** establishing the United Negro College Fund to send poor, college-bound blacks to black colleges

_____ **4.** using minority quotas in admissions policies at public universities and colleges

_____ **5.** establishing "magnet" schools that attract students of all races

ANSWERS ARE ON PAGE 299.

EXERCISE 2

Directions: Read the passage below and complete the exercise that follows.

Are females usually better with language skills than males? If so, is it because of a natural development of the brain or because of the way the two sexes are raised from infancy?

These questions are often explored and debated by psychologists and sociologists. This debate is often referred to as "the theory of nature versus nurture." Those who believe that nature determines differences in skills believe that males and females are born with inherent differences and these differences become more pronounced as sex hormones change the growing bodies.

Those who believe that nurture plays the most important role in creating differences think that the environment in which a person is raised and nurtured is the determining factor.

For each of the examples below, write *nature* in the blank if the statement is an application of the nature theory of human growth and development and write *nurture* if the statement is an application of the nurture theory.

_____ In an experiment, researchers found that female infants are talked to more than male infants are.

_____ Nurses in a large hospital report that newborn female babies tend to coo, cry, and make other noises much more often than male babies.

_____ Experiments have shown that students who are not expected to do well in school do not do well, and teachers traditionally do not expect males to excel in language skills.

_____ Chemical analyses of male and female brains have shown definite differences between the sexes in the region of the brain that controls language development.

_____ Scientific research indicates that the brain structure of homosexual men differs from the brain structure of heterosexual men. This difference might explain differences in sexual orientation in males.

ANSWERS ARE ON PAGE 299.

=== **GED Practice** ===
EXERCISE 3

Questions 1 and 2 refer to the following passage.

When people hear the word *monopoly*, probably the first thing they think about is the popular board game. A monopoly, however, is the exclusive control over a money-making activity.

In 1890, the U.S. government passed a law called the Sherman Anti-Trust Act that outlawed price-fixing (the agreement between companies to set their prices), underproduction of goods, market sharing, and any other form of monopolizing among producers of a similar product. However, public utilities such as gas, electric power, and water companies are exempted from these restraints. These government-sanctioned monopolies are permitted to exist so that essential services are not duplicated and natural resources are not wasted.

1. According to the Sherman Anti-Trust Act, an example of an illegal monopoly would be

   (1) the existence of only one power company in a city, giving consumers no choice of whom to obtain service from
   (2) a computer company whose growth is well beyond that of any of its competitors
   (3) a hamburger chain's restaurants, all of which belong to the same system of franchises
   (4) the oil refineries in a state agreeing on a minimum price to set for gasoline
   (5) a public university system in a state setting minimum and maximum tuition rates for the schools in its system

2. An example of a *legal* monopoly would be a

   (1) cable television company given the exclusive license to service a particular community
   (2) supermarket chain whose prices undercut its competitor, forcing it out of business
   (3) long-distance telephone company that wins over its competitor's customers
   (4) health-care network that takes over a group of hospitals
   (5) commuter railroad company that takes over three of a region's four competing railroads

ANSWERS ARE ON PAGE 299.

SPECIAL ITEM TYPES

The Social Studies Test will test your ability to apply given ideas in a different situation by using an item type similar to the one on page 41. In this type of item, certain categories are defined and then specific situations are given. You will need to read the categories carefully to understand the differences between them. Then, read the situations to match them up with the information given. If you have trouble with these questions, you might use a process of elimination. In other words, you may go through the categories and decide which ones do *not* fit. In this way, you may be able to narrow your choices.

EXERCISE 4

Questions 1–4 refer to the following information.

Propaganda is a method by which information is provided in such a way as to influence or slant the opinion or feelings of the audience that receives the message. Listed below are five techniques used by propagandists.

name-calling—attaching an unfavorable name to an idea, person, or group of people in order to influence the attitude of the audience against the idea or position

glittering generalities—speaking in high-sounding but general and vague terms to influence positively the feelings of the audience toward a subject

bandwagoning—advising people to do something because "everyone" does it, because it is popular, or because it is the "in" thing to do

transferring—associating the respect, prestige, or power of one person or object with another person so that the audience is influenced favorably

card-stacking—choosing only specific, favorable points that support a cause and ignoring the unfavorable points

1. A manufacturer of laundry detergent introduces a "revolutionary new" product that dissolves grease faster than the "leading product on the market." The propaganda technique described is

   (1) name-calling
   (2) glittering generalities
   (3) transferring
   (4) bandwagoning
   (5) card-stacking

2. A radio commercial suggests that all residents of Rapid Falls, Idaho, should subscribe to the *Rapid Falls Gazette*, since 85 percent of the households there subscribe to the paper. The announcer adds that, "40,000 households can't be wrong." The propaganda technique described is

   (1) name-calling
   (2) glittering generalities
   (3) transferring
   (4) bandwagoning
   (5) card-stacking

3. While campaigning through the South, a candidate for the presidency of the United States appeared in a church on the same platform with a leader of the fundamentalist Christian movement. The propaganda technique described is

   (1) name-calling
   (2) glittering generalities
   (3) transferring
   (4) bandwagoning
   (5) card-stacking

4. During a debate, the Republican candidate for office calls his Democratic opponent a "tax-and-spend liberal" despite the Democrat's record of shown fiscal restraint. The propaganda technique described is

   (1) name-calling
   (2) glittering generalities
   (3) transferring
   (4) bandwagoning
   (5) card-stacking

ANSWERS ARE ON PAGE 299.

APPLYING GIVEN IDEAS IN ILLUSTRATIONS

On the Social Studies Test you also will be asked to apply given ideas or facts from illustrations such as political cartoons.

Look at the cartoon below.

KEN ALEXANDER
Courtesy San Francisco Examiner

"If made into paper it could supply the entire federal government for 16 minutes."

Underline the words in parentheses that best answer each question pertaining to the cartoon.

Based on his statement, what is the ranger's tone? (serious, sarcastic, confused)

This tone may be inferred from the ranger's (understatement, exaggeration, misunderstanding) of the facts about government's use of paper.

The cartoonist seems to think the federal government (has no regard for trees, needs a new source for paper, uses too much paper).

You should have underlined *sarcastic, exaggeration*, and *uses too much paper*.

Organizations like the U.S. government that use large amounts of paper do so because of record-keeping and management systems. The cartoonist thinks that the federal government is a large bureaucracy that uses an excessive amount of paper.

Which of the following systems would this cartoonist likely criticize? Circle the correct answer.

(1) the U.S. Army's insistence on all documents being copied and filed in triplicate
(2) a local grocer's system of having employees post on a chart items that are low in inventory
(3) a government agency's practice of filing its budget on a computer so that it can be readily retrieved and modified
(4) a mortgage company's action to simplify its loan application procedures by consolidating forms
(5) a large corporation's appointment of a chairman to coordinate a United Way Christmas drive

You should have chosen (1) because of the fact that the Army system requires so much paperwork. Choices (2), (3), and (4) are actually systems that reduce paperwork and bureaucracy. Choice (5) has nothing to do with paperwork or wastefulness.

≡ GED Practice ≡

EXERCISE 5

The question below refers to the following political cartoon.

The cartoon is referring to the economic problems in Russia under President Boris Yeltsin (pictured in the cartoon). Which of the following U.S. presidents was similarly blamed for the poor economy of the United States and voted out of office?

(1) Ronald Reagan
(2) Franklin Roosevelt
(3) Herbert Hoover
(4) Richard Nixon
(5) John Kennedy

ANSWER IS ON PAGE 299.

APPLYING REMEMBERED IDEAS

You have practiced applying theories, ideas, and facts in reading passages and illustrations. Now you will apply knowledge you have gained from prior learning or experience rather than from written passages.

For example, if you saw a movie about a Vietnam veteran going back to the site of his worst wartime experiences, you could understand his emotions much better if you had prior knowledge of the horrors of the Vietnam conflict. You could apply that prior knowledge to decide for yourself whether his performance was convincing. If you also had prior knowledge of World War II and its veterans' reactions to their experiences, you would be better able to understand the actions of the Vietnam veterans.

In exercises in this book, you will be expected to apply your prior knowledge of events, people, and ideas to new situations.

In some cases, in this book and on the GED Tests, you may not be familiar with the person, place, or thing being discussed. First of all, keep in mind that the following sections of this book will give you a lot of information on social studies issues. Second, if you cannot recall what is being discussed in a test item, make the most reasonable choice and move on to the next item.

Suppose you read an article with this title: "From Selma to Johannesburg: Americans Are Marching Again, This Time Against Apartheid."

The magazine's editor expects the reader paging through the magazine to read the article because it deals with the issue of apartheid and how Americans are protesting it. The words *Johannesburg* and *apartheid* in the title are clues

that this article is about discrimination in _____.

To fill in the blank above, you must have knowledge of world events and geography. Johannesburg is in South Africa. The fact that the title mentions apartheid may be another clue to that answer, but this again requires the knowledge that apartheid is the system of racial segregation in South Africa.

The title also includes the city Selma. The mention of this city, located in

the state of _____ in the United States, is an attempt to link

the marches against apartheid in South Africa to the _____.

To be able to fill in the blanks, you must have had prior knowledge of the *civil rights marches of the 1960s* in the United States. They took place all over the country, but the site of one of the most famous was Selma, *Alabama*. That march was led by Dr. Martin Luther King, Jr.

EXERCISE 6

Directions: Now try doing an exercise in which you must apply prior knowledge. Circle the number of the choice that best completes each of the following statements.

1. In 1824, John Quincy Adams was elected president of the United States even though he had received fewer votes than his opponent, Andrew Jackson. In 1876, the same situation occurred when Rutherford B. Hayes became president. Historians believe that in both cases these men became president through

    (1) a political deal
    (2) the Supreme Court system
    (3) the House of Representatives

2. A case before the Supreme Court requesting a ruling on whether an Orthodox Jew in the United States Air Force should be allowed to wear the traditional religious skull cap represents another of the many conflicts of

    (1) church vs. state
    (2) national vs. state's rights
    (3) individual vs. state's rights

3. "My mother always used to refer to England as home, although she was born here," said a middle-aged doctor, Ian Prior. "Then, after World War II, it was America we all looked toward. Now perhaps we are starting to feel ourselves a nation that can stand on its own feet. The Maori call it *tutangata*—to stand tall."

Prior knowledge of world history would tell you that the doctor lives, along with the Maoris, in the country of

    (1) France
    (2) New Zealand
    (3) Austria

ANSWERS ARE ON PAGE 299.

APPLYING REMEMBERED IDEAS IN PASSAGES

Read the passage below and choose the best answer to the question that follows on the next page.

Many Americans today complain that we are quickly becoming a bilingual country—the primary and secondary languages being English and Spanish. They resent the concessions made to the non-English-speaking minority. Yet the first European settlers in the New World were Spanish. Christopher Columbus himself was sailing under the flag of Spain when he "discovered" the North American continent in 1492. Saint Augustine, Florida, was founded in 1566 by the Spanish and was the first European settlement in the United States or Canada. As early as 1630, Spanish padres of the Roman Catholic faith established missions in territories now known as the states of California, Texas, Arizona, and New Mexico. Perhaps if more Americans were reminded of this Spanish influence on our country's history, they would be more tolerant of our non-English-speaking minority.

This author would likely agree with the groups who

(1) are trying to get a law passed in the United States to make English the official language of the U.S.
(2) want to ban the use of Spanish in bilingual classes in public elementary and secondary schools
(3) support the use of two languages—French and English—in Canada, where the French played a large role in founding the country
(4) maintain that the Native Americans should be given free land and other special rights as original inhabitants of this part of the world
(5) send teachers of English as a second language all over the world to help those who have the desire to learn our language

You should have chosen (3) because it most closely resembles the situation described in the passage, in which a controversy has developed in a country over the historical justification of officially using two languages. Choices (1) and (2) really express opposite opinions from the author's. Choice (4) does not address the problem of language usage. Choice (5) is on a different topic—the increasing influence of the English language around the world.

GED Practice

EXERCISE 7

The question below refers to the following passage.

Death Valley did not come by its name by whim or chance. Death Valley is an arid desert in southeastern California that was named in 1849 by one of eighteen survivors of an original party of thirty who had attempted to cross it in search of a shortcut to the California gold fields. The Rocky Mountains, too, are well deserving of their title, as are Crater Lake in Oregon and Great Salt Lake in Utah.

In other parts of the world, cities, bodies of water, and land forms have been named for their physical characteristics. The Diamond Coast in southwestern Africa, for instance, gets its name from its valuable resource and Buenos Aires in Argentina for its "fair winds."

Which of the following would this author probably agree was named for its physical attributes as described in the article above?

(1) Cape Horn in Chile, after its first successful navigator's birthplace in the Netherlands
(2) San Juan, capital city of Puerto Rico, named for Saint John by its Spanish founders
(3) the Hwang Ho (Yellow River) of China, for the color it develops as it picks up silt along its course
(4) the city of Philadelphia (City of Brotherly Love) in Pennsylvania, so called by its Quaker founders to reflect their highest hopes for the community
(5) New Delhi, the capital city of India that was built on a site three miles from the original city of Delhi

ANSWER IS ON PAGE 299.

APPLYING REMEMBERED IDEAS TO CARTOONS

You will be expected to apply your knowledge of social studies events, places, and people in other ways on the GED Test than in written form. One of these other methods may be through the use of political cartoons.

Look at the cartoon below.

"It says, 'Negotiations between Israelites, Egyptians, and Philistines are proceeding slowly.' "

The Christian Science Monitor
GUERNSEY LEPELLEY
Courtesy Christian Science Monitor

In the spaces below, fill in the words that best complete each statement. You will need to apply knowledge that you may have gained previously by reading newspapers or magazines, talking with friends, watching television, or going to school.

1. The men in the cartoon appear to be in an _____.

underground cave   Israeli museum   Egyptian tomb

2. The men in the cartoon are probably _____.

archaeologists   politicians   students

3. The cartoonist is implying that war and negotiations to end hostilities between the Israelites and Egyptians have been going on since

_____.

the beginning of this century
the end of World War II
at least ancient Egyptian times

4. The cartoonist wants us to analyze this cartoon and apply our knowledge of today's events to understand his opinion that _____

_____.

hostilities in the Middle East probably will go on forever
interest in ancient Egyptian archaeological findings is increasing
peace in the Middle East will come soon

The blanks should have been filled with

1. *Egyptian tomb* (notice the hieroglyphics on the wall and the mummy in the background)

2. *archaeologists* (notice their appropriate dress and notepads)

3. *at least ancient Egyptian times* (reread the quote and think of where the characters are)

4. *hostilities in the Middle East probably will go on forever* (apply your knowledge of today's events in that part of the world and consider the cartoonist's implication that the war has been going on for thousands of years already)

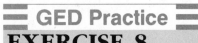

GED Practice
EXERCISE 8

Questions 1 and 2 are based on the following cartoon.

Modern
Leif Ericson Discovers The New World

SANDY CAMPBELL
Courtesy The Tennessean

NORTH SEA SPILLS

1. Leif Ericson is one of several explorers to whom historians attribute

(1) the blame for oil spills in the oceans
(2) the discovery of oil under the ocean floor
(3) the discovery of the New World
(4) the pollution of the New World
(5) the beginning of the environmental conservation movement

2. The cartoonist is implying that were he alive today, Leif Ericson would be

(1) shocked at some of the environmental conditions of modern-day North America
(2) saddened by the pollution near modern-day Norway, his ancestral home
(3) confused by the modern technology used on the North American continent
(4) unhappy about the waste of time and money on underwater oil drills
(5) discouraged by the lack of modern progress along the North Sea coast

ANSWERS ARE ON PAGE 299.

3 📘 Analyzing Social Studies Materials

When you analyze something, you break it down into its basic parts, or elements, to understand better what makes up its whole. For example, if you've ever taken a high school biology course, you probably had to dissect, or take apart, a frog to examine its internal organs.

By analyzing the frog, you were able to understand better the function of each organ and to see how each related to the whole frog. Taking this a step further, you also should have been able to picture the similar placement of these organs in the human body.

In social studies, you must also analyze; however, you look at specific ideas—pieces of information—to understand better the point being made by a writer, graphic artist, or cartoonist. You can analyze information in the field of social studies in a number of ways. On the Social Studies Test, you will be tested on your ability to analyze material in at least five ways:

- identifying cause-and-effect relationships
- distinguishing facts from opinions and hypotheses
- understanding unstated assumptions
- drawing conclusions from supporting details
- drawing inferences from given material

CAUSE AND EFFECT

When we analyze social studies material for causes and effects, we connect important events with the conditions that made them happen. Without thinking about it, you connect causes with effects every day. For example, in recent winters, the U.S. experienced such extremes in temperatures that the frost line reached Florida, damaging the state's orange crop. Many oranges were lost. On the television news, it was predicted that consumers would soon be forced to pay more for orange products at stores.

A number of results stemmed from this single cause: sudden cold temperatures. A couple of them are listed below:

Cause	Effect
1. freezing temperatures	damaged orange crop
2. damaged orange crop	fewer oranges harvested

What effect might come from the cause shown below? Write one.

Cause	Effect
3. fewer oranges harvested	_____

You may have written *higher prices for orange products*, since a short supply of a commodity leads to higher prices. You can probably think of other causes and effects stemming from this event. For example, higher prices for orange products (cause) might mean that fewer orange products will be bought (effect). Also, a damaged Florida orange crop (cause) might mean the sale of more California oranges (effect).

As you see, events can sometimes lead to a chain of cause-and-effect relationships. Analyzing cause and effect helps us to understand everyday events and to plan our actions in accordance with them.

Effects normally follow causes in time. However, sometimes an effect appears in a sentence before the cause, even though the effect follows the cause in time. The statement below is an example of this inverted relationship:

Effect

America finally turned its attention to the exploration of space

Cause

largely because of the Soviet Union's launching of Sputnik in the late

1950s.

 **SKILL BUILDER**

Recognizing Cause-and-Effect Relationships

The cause-and-effect relationship is frequently signaled by key words such as *because, since, therefore, as a result, consequently, accordingly, if . . . then, the reason was, led to, brought about, the outcome was, the end result was,* and *was responsible for.*

EXERCISE 1

Directions: Underline the cause and the effect in each sentence below and write a *C* above the word or words that indicate cause and an *E* above the word or words that indicate effect. Some sentences may include more than one cause or effect.

1. In addition to extreme overpopulation, extended drought has contributed to severe famine in Ethiopia and other parts of Africa.

2. Population growth in the Sunbelt states has come from many companies relocating to that area.

3. The emigration of the first Pilgrims from England to the New World was prompted by religious persecution in their homeland.

4. Unfair employer practices brought about the establishment of labor unions.

ANSWERS ARE ON PAGE 299.

EXERCISE 2

Directions: Read the passage below. Match the effects listed in the column on the right with their causes listed on the left by writing the appropriate letter in the space provided.

Tornadoes, or "twisters," are among the smallest but more violent storms. They are caused by air masses that reach rotational speeds of about 300 miles per hour. Tornadoes often occur in series, like the ones in April of 1965 that caused havoc in Iowa, Wisconsin, Illinois, Indiana, Michigan, and Ohio, killing 271 people and damaging $300,000,000 worth of property. Forty years earlier, in March of 1925, another series had killed 740 persons in Missouri, Indiana, Illinois, Kentucky, and Tennessee.

"Tornado Alley" is a belt that runs through the Great Plains and southeastern portion of the United States. The Chicago area holds the greatest potential for tornado damage because of the combination of its location, its density of population, and its development. However, less-populated southwestern Oklahoma has the highest incidence of tornadoes. Though Chicago has only half the incidence of tornadoes as Oklahoma, the need for disaster aid in Chicago is greater than anywhere else.

Cause

_____ 1. tornado series of 1965

_____ 2. plains location, population density, and development in the Chicago area

_____ 3. rotating air masses of about 300 mph

_____ 4. tornado series of 1925

Effect

(a) 740 people killed in five states

(b) small violent storms

(c) the greatest potential for tornado damage

(d) $300,000,000 in property damage

ANSWERS ARE ON PAGE 300.

☰ GED Practice ☰
EXERCISE 3

Read the two passages below. Circle the letter of the choice that best completes the statements that follow each passage.

A troublesome problem in the American economy has been reduced competitiveness with other industrial nations. This was especially true regarding automobile production and sales between the United States and Japan.

Japanese automakers could produce cars more cheaply than U.S. auto companies could. Also, for many years, the U.S. market was open to Japanese imports. Because of this, car sales for GM, Chrysler, and Ford suffered.

Because of pressure from U.S. government and business, which resulted in protective tariffs, Japan reduced the number of cars exported to the United States. In the meantime, U.S. automakers improved quality, increased automation, and reduced manufacturing costs.

Between 1991 and 1992 the profile of the auto market changed. The average midsize U.S. car sold for $1,500 less than a similar Japanese model. In order to compensate for reduced exports to the United States, Japanese manufacturers had raised the price of their cars. Overall car sales in the United States increased by 1.5 percent, but the Japanese share of the market dropped from 27 million to 25 million.

1. According to the passage, one immediate result of the reduction in Japanese auto exports to the U.S. was that

   (1) American cars became scarce and high-priced
   (2) American auto manufacturers demanded stronger protectionist policies
   (3) Japanese auto prices went down
   (4) The Japanese started buying American cars
   (5) American automakers became more competitive

2. According to the passage, the effect of reduced exports of Japanese cars exported to the United States was

   (1) a reversal in the cost of Japanese and American cars
   (2) more demand for Japanese cars
   (3) an increase in the number of American cars sold in Japan
   (4) a decrease in the cost of Japanese imports
   (5) a renewed effort to improve the quality of Japanese cars

In 1978, voters in the state of California revolted against high taxes by passing Proposition 13. This action severely limited revenue from property taxes that is vitally important in supporting public schools. One result of this was that educational programs in the state suffered. However, after 1978 the federal report *A Nation at Risk* was released. This report focused on the "rising tide of mediocrity" engulfing American schools.

Now, California leads states that have raised taxes to enable schools to improve programs. However, the tax dollars lost since Proposition 13 was passed have contributed to the crisis in education there in the early 1990s.

3. What is suggested as the reason for the change in feeling by the voters of California?

   (1) Homeowners weren't paying their fair share of taxes.
   (2) The public recognized the need for money to improve quality of schools.
   (3) Voters decided property taxes were not the proper source of revenue for schools.
   (4) A federal report convinced citizens that schools misused funds.
   (5) Taxpayers in California were paying a proportionally lower amount for school support than those in any other state.

ANSWERS ARE ON PAGE 300.

CAUSE AND EFFECT IN ILLUSTRATIONS

Graphs, maps, charts, and cartoons can also show cause-and-effect relationships. The illustration below is a pictograph.

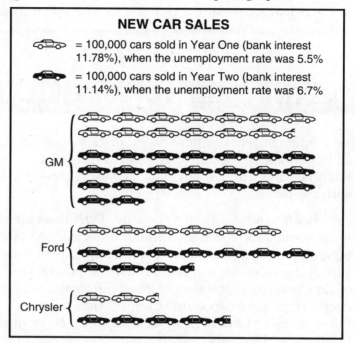

NEW CAR SALES

= 100,000 cars sold in Year One (bank interest 11.78%), when the unemployment rate was 5.5%

= 100,000 cars sold in Year Two (bank interest 11.14%), when the unemployment rate was 6.7%

GM

Ford

Chrysler

What is the topic of the pictograph? _____

Which car companies are being represented? _____

What does each white car in the pictograph represent? _____

What does each black car in the pictograph represent? _____

You should have written that the topic is *New Car Sales*. The cars being compared are *GM*, *Ford*, and *Chrysler*. The white cars represent *the number of cars sold in Year One*; the black cars, *the number of cars sold in Year Two*.

≡ GED Practice ≡
EXERCISE 4

According to the graph above, the drop in interest rates for new-car loans in Year Two

(1) compensated for the rise in the number of Americans no longer able to afford new cars

(2) was enough to stimulate the new-car market

(3) helped sales only for Chrysler

(4) was caused by the drop in car sales

(5) resulted in the drop in car sales

ANSWER IS ON PAGE 300.

▨ SKILL BUILDER
Understanding Pictographs

Pictographs use symbols to stand for the subject being measured. Some common symbols are cars, houses, and dollars. Whole symbols and partial symbols may be used in a pictograph. The title tells us the main topic.

FACTS, OPINIONS, AND HYPOTHESES

Different types of newspaper articles illustrate the difference between facts and opinions. Newspaper and magazine articles are based largely on facts. Editorials and featured columns, however, present a writer's opinions along with the facts.

Facts can be proved to be true. ***Opinions*** are the writer's feelings or ideas about a topic and are influenced heavily by one's background, values, and outlook on life. ***Hypotheses*** are assumptions that are made for the purpose of explaining an event. Hypotheses may be proved or disproved with the passage of time and the acquisition of more information about why or how events occur. Hypotheses, too, are based on facts but also are influenced by one's impressions and hunches about a subject. The examples below show how facts, opinions, and hypotheses differ.

- It is a fact that the West Coast of the United States has several mountain ranges running along it, that it borders the Pacific Ocean, and that it is warmer on the average than the East Coast. These are facts because they can be proved.

- It is an opinion, however, that the West Coast is the best part of the United States in which to live because that is a statement based on a person's values, background, and outlook on life.

- It is a hypothesis that erosion along the coast will make the western coastal area uninhabitable in years to come because more information will be needed to prove or disprove such a hunch.

▚ SKILL BUILDER
Distinguishing Facts from Opinions and Hypotheses

1. Facts can be proved with data.

2. Opinions are beliefs that are influenced by feelings. Opinions can be debated.

3. Hypotheses may be proved or disproved with the passage of time and the acquisition of more information.

Classify each of the following as fact, opinion, or hypothesis, by writing *F*, *O*, or *H* on the line before each statement.

_____ The economic system of the U.S. is basically capitalistic but modified with some aspects of socialism.

_____ If social welfare programs like Medicare were abolished, the economy might perform better.

_____ The socialistic schemes in our system should be removed because they are too expensive for the taxpaying citizens.

The first statement above is a fact, which can be proved by obtaining a definition of capitalism and socialism. The second statement is a hypothesis that could be supported by data and could even be proved to be either true or false in the future. The third statement is an opinion that is based on a person's beliefs.

As the example on page 56 shows, hypotheses provide reasonable explanations for occurrences.

Read the passage below. Then place an *H* on the line next to the hypothesis or hypotheses that explain why the event occurred.

> Over the period of one year, motor vehicle deaths in nineteen states decreased significantly over the previous year's figures. Research has shown that the two most important factors that determine the survival of a victim in a serious traffic accident are (1) whether the victim is restrained in the car and (2) whether medical attention is immediately available.

Based on the information in the above passage, which of the hypotheses listed explain why traffic fatalities were reduced?

_____ **(1)** The states instituted tough drunk driving laws.

_____ **(2)** The states hired more highway patrolmen to catch speeders.

_____ **(3)** The states increased the number of trauma centers and paramedics to handle victims of traffic accidents.

_____ **(4)** The states adopted laws requiring passengers to wear seat belts.

_____ **(5)** The states required more frequent driver examinations for senior citizens and teenagers.

Only (3) and (4) are reasonable explanations of the reduction in motor vehicle fatalities. Both of them address the two criteria upon which survival for victims of traffic accidents is based. None of the other choices have a direct relationship to the immediate access to medical care and the restraint of passengers in the vehicle. Choices (3) and (4) may be proved by comparing the number of motor vehicle fatalities both before and after the number of trauma centers and paramedics were increased and before and after seat belts were required.

SKILL BUILDER
Hints for Identifying Opinions

Phrases like *should be* or *I believe/think/hope/want*, and those filled with emotionally charged words like *evil, wonderful, terrible* often indicate that a writer is presenting his or her opinion.

EXERCISE 5

Questions 1–4 refer to the following passage.

Some jobs are more stressful than others, and air traffic controllers are considered to have one of the most stressful. This belief has been backed up by the fact that controllers have a high incidence of stress-related disorders like chronic anxiety and alcoholism. Many people believe, too, that the reason for the high level of stress is the responsibility that controllers have for the safety of passengers. However, such reasoning does not explain the low rate of stress disorders among airline pilots, who have much more direct responsibility for people's safety.

Recent studies have attempted to explain this discrepancy by naming poor labor-management relations as the main source of the controllers' stress.

Controllers who were interviewed complained that their recommendations for providing safety backups and other measures were not being considered by their employers or the Federal Aviation Administration. Interestingly, too, the studies concluded that the most conscientious of the workers were the ones most prone to experience stress—because of their high level of concern for safety.

1. Which of the following is a hypothesis that may be drawn based on the information in the passage?

   (1) Shortening the hours of air traffic controllers will reduce stress-related disorders.
   (2) Providing proof that management is implementing the controllers' recommendations will reduce stress.
   (3) Providing counseling services for victims of stress will reduce stress levels.
   (4) Ensuring that all planes are no more than twenty years old will lower stress levels among air traffic controllers.
   (5) Reducing the number of daily scheduled flights will reduce stress levels among air traffic controllers.

2. Which of the following is a fact about air traffic controllers that the author could support with data?

   (1) There is a relatively high rate of alcoholism among air traffic controllers.
   (2) There is a low incidence of stress disorders among the controllers.
   (3) Pilots suffer from more anxiety than controllers do.
   (4) The only source of air traffic controllers' stress is poor labor-management relations.
   (5) The controllers are not taken seriously by the Federal Aviation Administration.

3. According to the passage, air traffic controllers have which of the following opinions?

   (1) Some jobs are more stressful than others.
   (2) An air traffic controller's job is more stressful than a pilot's.
   (3) Neither airline company executives nor the FAA is paying attention to controllers' safety recommendations.
   (4) The more conscientious workers experienced the most stress.
   (5) Airline executives have no concern for safety.

4. Recent studies have shown that

   (1) the main reason for air traffic controllers' high level of stress is their concern for passengers' safety
   (2) air traffic controllers should be more conscientious about passengers' safety
   (3) chronic anxiety causes air traffic controllers to become alcoholics
   (4) the negative attitudes of air traffic controllers lead to poor labor-management relations
   (5) the more conscientious air traffic controllers are, the more likely they are to experience stress on the job

ANSWERS ARE ON PAGE 300.

FACTS, OPINIONS, AND HYPOTHESES IN ILLUSTRATIONS
Political Cartoons

The real purpose in a political cartoon is to express an opinion of the cartoonist—a view of a political or social issue as the artist sees it.

Look at the political cartoon at the left. Notice that there are four people in the picture, each representing different groups as shown by their labels. Three of these people (labeled "parents," "teachers," and "courts") are arguing over a book labeled "prayer issue." The boy, labeled "students," is alone at the blackboard, being ignored by the other three, while he is incorrectly doing a math problem. This picture illustrates the opinion that:

Students' education is being _____ while the prayer issue is

being debated by the people who should be helping them to _____ .

The completed statement should read: Students' education is being *ignored* (or *neglected*) while the prayer issue is being debated by the people who should be helping them to *learn*.

▨ SKILL BUILDER
Keys to Understanding Political Cartoons

Political cartoons are often based on politicians or statesmen, shown as caricatures (cartoon figures). The caricatures usually exaggerate a feature of the person being illustrated. For example, Ronald Reagan's dark hair, George Bush's receding hairline, and Bill Clinton's puffy cheeks and rounded nose have been widely caricatured.

Political symbols are often used as well. For example, a donkey represents the Democratic party and an elephant, the Republican party; a bearded man dressed in stars and stripes (Uncle Sam) represents the United States; a dove represents peace and a hawk, war. Often, a family or person is shown to represent how a social problem is affecting the average person. Cartoonists often use humor or sarcasm to express their opinions on important issues.

EXERCISE 6

Circle the numbers that best complete the statements about the cartoon below.

TOM FLANNERY
Courtesy Baltimore Sun

The American Dream House

1. It is the opinion of this cartoonist that the American dream to own a home is

(1) worth the struggle and sacrifice that it demands

(2) threatened by increasingly high costs

(3) becoming less desirable than apartment living

(4) as attractive and as popular as ever

(5) a realistic goal for most people

2. One fact supported by the cartoon is that

(1) the cost of new homes has decreased in the past decade

(2) only two-parent families can afford to buy new homes

(3) the cost of new homes has gone up 100 percent in the past decade

(4) people are buying smaller homes because they are more affordable

(5) owning their own home is only a dream for most Americans

ANSWERS ARE ON PAGE 300.

GED Practice
EXERCISE 7

Look at the pictograph on U.S. Exports to the Major Warring Nations and circle the answer that represents the most accurate hypothesis that may be made.

In April 1917, the U.S. entered the war against the Central Powers. A hypothesis that can be made, based on the graph on the right, is that the U.S. entered the war because

(1) economically, the U.S. had already aligned itself with the Allied Powers

(2) the Central Powers were quite depressed economically and would, therefore, be easy to defeat

(3) the United Kingdom was receiving almost five times as much aid as Czarist Russia

(4) the Central Powers did not need help financially, while the Allied Powers did

(5) the cause of the Allied Powers was more just than the cause of the Central Powers

U.S. EXPORTS TO THE MAJOR WARRING NATIONS

$ = $100 million   c = $10 million

Nations	1914	1915	1916
Major Allied Powers			
United Kingdom	$$$$$$	$$$$$$$$$cc	$$$$$$$$$$$$$$$$$$cc
France	$$	$$$$	$$$$$$ccc
Russia	cccc	cccccc	$$$c
Major Central Powers			
Germany	$$$cccc	ccc	c
Austria-Hungary	cc	c	c
Turkey	c	c	-

ANSWER IS ON PAGE 300.

UNSTATED ASSUMPTIONS

When someone makes an *assumption* about something, that person takes a fact or an idea for granted. In newspaper or television editorials, the writers or speakers often take for granted certain ideas that may or may not be true. By doing this, they attempt to influence your opinion.

For example, in a familiar commercial, an individual with dandruff is shown as a social outcast until he uses a particular shampoo to get rid of the problem. The unstated assumption is that dandruff-free people are popular, while those with dandruff are not. A further assumption is that the use of a certain product will increase your popularity. It is important to be able to know when this kind of subtle persuasion is being used. If you can clearly understand unstated assumptions in what you read or hear, you will be better able to make informed decisions.

Read the statement below carefully to discover the underlying, unstated assumption made by the writer.

All people caught and convicted of DUI (driving under the influence) should be sent to mandatory Alcoholics Anonymous meetings.

The unstated assumption in this statement is that all DUI drivers are _____

_____.

The blank should be filled with the word *alcoholics.* For the writer to state that all DUI drivers should be sent to AA meetings assumes that they are alcoholics. In fact, while they may be drunk at the time they are caught, they may not necessarily be alcoholics.

EXERCISE 8

Directions: Read the statements below. In the space provided, write the underlying unstated assumption behind each one.

1. The United States should use its power to prevent small, developing countries from turning from capitalism to socialism.

   The writer assumes that socialism is _____

   _____.

2. In the televised presidential debates, John F. Kennedy looked better on television than Richard Nixon did. JFK's win in 1960 signaled the beginning of the "media sell" of the U.S. president.

   The writer assumes that Kennedy won the presidency in 1960 because

   _____

   _____.

3. Finally, the people of mainland China can enjoy the benefits of Westernized society and escape, at least partially, the dreariness of their past existence.

   The writer assumes that, before westernization, China _____

   _____.

4. The dress was punk, the music was 50,000 watts, the style was slamdance, but there would be no trouble at this rock concert. This concert was a Christian rock festival.

   The writer assumes that there is usually trouble at _____

   _____.

5. If society would make those on welfare do volunteer work in the community, it would have no more problem with welfare cheats.

   The writer assumes that there are _____.

ANSWERS ARE ON PAGE 300.

EXERCISE 9

Directions: Unstated assumptions are often buried in editorials and newspaper columns. These are types of writing that express a person's point of view. Read the passage below to find unstated assumptions the writer makes and complete the exercise that follows.

Public housing was supposed to be part of the solution, not part of the problem of poverty in the cities. Instead of being a springboard out of unemployment and crime, it has become a breeding ground for the worst of inner-city ills.

The high-rise dwellings are unattractive, dangerous, and, in general, depressing to live in. New units need to be built, with fewer elevators in which to trap victims, with cleaner sewerage systems to keep out disease-carrying insects and rodents, and in areas with good schools to provide better educational opportunities for the youth. Most importantly, drug dealers and pimps must be identified and outlawed from any and all public housing residences.

Check off the statements below that the author has assumed but not directly stated.

_____ **(a)** Public housing breeds inner-city ills.

_____ **(b)** The sewerage systems in public housing units are to blame for the insect and rodent problem.

_____ **(c)** If better facilities are provided, public housing residents will improve their lives.

_____ **(d)** The unattractiveness and uncleanliness of the public housing units is the fault of no one but the dwellers themselves.

_____ **(e)** Drug dealers and pimps are not presently identified and outlawed from public housing residences.

_____ **(f)** No residents have benefited from living in public housing.

_____ **(g)** Public housing residences would be safer if they had more elevators.

_____ **(h)** Inner-city residence problems have been partially solved by providing high-rise dwellings that are safe and attractive.

ANSWERS ARE ON PAGE 300.

EXERCISE 10

Questions 1–4 are based on the following passage.

The Corrections Corporation of America was formed in the early 1980s. It is an investor-owned corporation established to make a profit by running prisons as businesses. Excesses are eliminated, bureaucracy is avoided, employees are trained and paid adequately, and costs are constantly monitored. Though the corporation does not set policy, it runs everything else and manages the facilities toward the goal of turning a profit.

This ever-present concern for the bottom line bothers some of the critics of this bold new idea. Mark Cunniff, executive director of the National Association of Criminal Justice Planners, said pointedly, "The private sector is more concerned with doing well than doing good." For this reason, CCA was expected to be a short-lived company despite the fact that people like former Tennessee governor Lamar Alexander called the idea of a privately run prison "bold" and "impressive." He pointed out that private contractors have been running hospitals for years and have shown they can do it without cost overruns. "If private management is good enough for our sick mothers, it's good enough for our murderers and rapists," he concluded.

1. An unstated assumption made by former governor Alexander is that

    (1) private companies are more concerned about sick people than they are about prisoners

    (2) private corporations are quite capable of setting government policy

    (3) even though private contractors have done a good job of running hospitals, they may not do so well with prisons

    (4) running private prisons would require similar management skills as running private hospitals

    (5) cost overruns are unavoidable in institutions such as hospitals and prisons

2. Mark Cunniff, executive director of the National Association of Criminal Justice Planners, is quoted in the passage. He says, "The private sector is more concerned with doing well than doing good." From the quote it is evident that he thinks that

    (1) private companies are concerned with performing social service

    (2) private companies are more concerned with producing a profit than performing good deeds

    (3) private citizens are more concerned with their own health than that of others

    (4) private citizens are more concerned with having good hospitals than good prisons

    (5) private organizations provide most of the country's social services

3. According to former governor Alexander's statement about Tennessee's prisons, his chief concern seems to be

    (1) untrained employees

    (2) unfair policies

    (3) cost overruns

    (4) overcrowding

    (5) too much red tape

4. According to the passage, how does the Corrections Corporation of America run prisons as businesses?

    (1) It sets fair policies.

    (2) It examines excesses.

    (3) It asks employees to work for less.

    (4) It improves the way bureaucracy is handled.

    (5) It operates facilities in such a way that they can make a profit.

ANSWERS ARE ON PAGE 301.

UNSTATED ASSUMPTIONS IN ILLUSTRATIONS

The information that goes into tables, charts, graphs, and other illustrations is sometimes obtained on the basis of underlying, unstated assumptions. It is a good practice to question how valid or true some data are.

Tables and Charts

A table or chart is an organization of many facts into a small space. Tables and charts are used to keep scores in games, list train schedules, assign work tasks, compare weather reports, and so on.

The chart below reports the results of a survey. The title, "Paying What the Job's Worth," gives us an idea of what the survey was about. Notice that occupations are listed along the left side of the chart and the headings "paid too little," "paid about right," and "paid too much" are on the right. Percentages across from each listed occupation tell us how many of the people surveyed viewed the pay scale for that job as too little, too much, or about right according to the contribution the job makes to society.

PAYING WHAT THE JOB'S WORTH			
843 respondents were asked how they feel "about the amount of income that different kinds of people receive for the contribution they make to society."			
Occupation	*Paid Too Little*	*Paid About Right*	*Paid Too Much*
Movie stars/top entertainers	0.5%	18.8%	80.7%
Professional athletes	2.9%	18.2%	78.8%
Top executives	1.3%	24.3%	74.4%
Physicians	2.4%	27.5%	70.1%
Government officials	4.7%	25.1%	70.2%
Landlords	5.1%	41.8%	53.1%
Skilled blue-collar workers	8.7%	48.3%	43.1%
Union factory workers	14.4%	55.8%	29.9%
Scientists	22.7%	55.8%	21.4%
Middle-level managers	21.1%	69.2%	9.6%
Owners of small business	43.5%	52.5%	4.0%

Source: *American Journal of Public Health*

One assumption the interviewer must have made is that the people responding to the survey knew how much money each job pays. Another assumption the interviewer must have made is that the respondents had some idea of what _____ each job makes to society.

The respondents had to know what *contributions* each job makes to society in order to be able to answer the question effectively in this survey.

◼ SKILL BUILDER
Reading Charts and Tables

1. The title tells the major topic.

2. A caption further explains the data (how it was obtained, who obtained it, when it was obtained, etc.).

3. Columns and rows are arranged so they can be read across or down and are labeled with headings to classify the information in the table.

Political Cartoons

Political cartoonists assume a great deal in representing their ideas in pictures. Such cartoons are usually found on the editorial pages of newspapers because cartoons are really editorials in picture form. Just as a table or chart makes a statement, a cartoon's picture and its few words can be thought-provoking.

Reprinted with permission from the *Minneapolis Star and Tribune*

'GO AHEAD AND OPERATE. JUST DON'T DRAW BLOOD!'

The cartoonist seems to assume that ecology programs adopted to protect our environment will necessarily take a chunk out of the economy, since the cartoon shows a surgeon, labeled _____, about to operate on a patient, labeled _____. The cartoonist also seems to assume that the patient (economy) cannot afford the programs since the patient is asking the surgeon (ecology) not to draw blood.

GED Practice
EXERCISE 11

Questions 1–3 are based on the following cartoon.

LOU ERICKSON
Courtesy Atlanta Journal

1. Which of the following is an unstated assumption made by the cartoonist?

   (1) America started out with too many personal freedoms for its citizens.
   (2) The growth of government in America made it a freer, safer place to live.
   (3) Big government has eroded personal freedoms over the years.
   (4) The security afforded by big government is worth the price of fewer personal freedoms.
   (5) Expansion of the government was an inevitable result of modern problems.

2. The cartoonist is suggesting that America is

   (1) still the world's most powerful nation
   (2) not proud of its history
   (3) not as powerful as it once was
   (4) threatened by the rise of Japan
   (5) incapable of correcting its mistakes

3. An unstated assumption by the cartoonist is that personal freedom should be more highly valued than government security. Which of the following would the cartoonist probably consider government infringement on personal freedom?

   (1) voluntary draft system
   (2) abortion clinics
   (3) voter registration drives
   (4) forced integration of schools
   (5) taxes on luxury items

   ANSWERS ARE ON PAGE 301.

DRAWING CONCLUSIONS

On the Social Studies Test, you will be asked to analyze materials to determine what conclusions the author wants you to draw from the facts supplied. You probably draw conclusions from details every day. If you have ever put together a jigsaw puzzle, you had to draw conclusions. For example, while working a puzzle, you might conclude that the blue pieces fit together, then the brown and white ones, and then the green, until finally the pieces fit together in such a way as to lead you to the conclusion that this is a picture of a snow-capped mountain surrounded by blue sky and green grass.

Read the paragraph below. Draw the necessary conclusion to complete the final sentence.

> In 1977, capital punishment was restored by the legislature in California. By September 1985, the California State Supreme Court had reversed thirty-five out of thirty-eight appealed death penalty convictions and had commuted the sentences to lesser punishments, such as life imprisonment.

This paragraph supports the conclusion that, although the California state legislature supported capital punishment, the state's supreme court questioned the _____ of the death penalty in many cases where it has been applied.

You may have put together the following facts:

a. The state legislature passed the law allowing capital punishment and, therefore, must have supported it.

b. The state supreme court reversed almost all the decisions for the death penalty that had been appealed over an eight-year period of time.

You can draw the conclusion that the courts must have questioned the *legality* of the use of the death penalty.

Like pieces in a jigsaw puzzle, the pieces of information fit together to lead you to a conclusion.

EXERCISE 12

Directions: Read the paragraphs below. Circle the letter of the choice that best indicates the conclusion that may be drawn from the information given.

1. Prior to the 1980s, the U.S. home finance system was stable, easy to understand, and acceptable to lenders and home buyers alike. The basic home loan, or mortgage, was steady for a thirty-year period, during which the rate of interest for the mortgage was fixed and unchangeable. By 1992, lenders were offering home loans for 15-, 20-, or 30-year periods at a maximum 8 percent interest rate. Home buyers were also offered ARMs (adjustable-rate mortgages) that started at a 4.5 percent interest rate for the first year but could change every year during the life of the loan.

A conclusion based on this paragraph is that borrowers looking for a mortgage these days must be prepared to

(1) choose between different mortgage options
(2) settle for a 15-year mortgage
(3) finance the purchase with cash

2. Adults have obligations to the children they bring into this world. Infants are incapable of caring for themselves and will not develop normally without proper love and discipline. Society sets up laws, therefore, to ensure the normal growth of its young. Parental neglect is generally considered to involve the disregard of the physical, emotional, and moral needs of children under the age of eighteen and is punishable in most states by imprisonment, fines, or removal of children from the home.

It can be concluded that this writer thinks that

(1) punishment for adults guilty of parental neglect are too severe
(2) parents have the ultimate responsibility for the proper development of their children
(3) society needs to do more to protect the welfare of its children

3. The creative uses of futuristic computers in such movies as *Star Wars* and *2001: A Space Odyssey* have made many people think about computers' seemingly limitless capabilities. The impact of computers on such industries as grocery stores, banks, gas stations, design and machine shops, and education has been obvious to many. Despite this fact, we are amazed by each new enhancement of computers' capabilities. For example, psychologists and counselors are presently working with programmers to develop a program that will enable computers to perform routine counseling tasks in the areas of career and personal advisement.

We can conclude that in the future computers will be

(1) present in almost all aspects of the workplace
(2) completely replacing psychologists and counselors for career and personal advisement
(3) able to make all our decisions for us

ANSWERS ARE ON PAGE 301.

EXERCISE 13

Questions 1 and 2 refer to the following passage.

In possibly the first action of its kind, a coalition of union, community, and religious groups negotiated an agreement with the city of Vacaville, California, requiring certain employers to give a year's notice of plant closings or major cuts in operations. The agreement was limited to those companies attracted to the city by the offer of tax-supported financial aid.

1. From this paragraph we can conclude that

   (1) when union, community, and religious groups unite, they can demand anything they want from a city

   (2) the city of Vacaville, California, has limited the number of companies that may move there

   (3) cooperation among certain groups in Vacaville, California, has given some employees there a chance to plan their futures

   (4) labor agreements between city and community groups must be limited to companies benefiting from tax breaks

   (5) unions, communities, and religious groups often cooperate with each other to accomplish a common goal

2. Which of the following employers would be subject to this agreement?

   (1) a Vacaville company that loses a big government contract and goes bankrupt

   (2) a Vacaville company that sells shares of stock to employees who eventually become the owners

   (3) a tax-supported Vacaville company that is shut down overnight because of safety and health violations

   (4) a company given tax incentives that merges with a larger company and moves its operations 50 miles away

   (5) a fast-food restaurant in Vacaville that lays off its part-time workers

Questions 3 and 4 refer to the following passage.

Economic researchers at the Federal Reserve and the Internal Revenue Service reported that during the 1980s America's super-rich became even richer. The richest 1 percent of American households (all of them at least millionaires) accounted for 37 percent of private net worth in 1989, up from 31 percent in 1983. In fact, by 1989 the top 1 percent of American households had a greater net worth than the bottom 90 percent of American households. This surge in wealth among the super-rich was the first significant rise in wealth concentration since the Roaring Twenties.

3. We can conclude from this passage that

   (1) the Roaring Twenties were boom years for the super-rich

   (2) during the 1980s most Americans became wealthier

   (3) more households were among the super-wealthy during the 1980s

   (4) Reaganomics' "trickle-down" theory was a success

   (5) the same households have been among the super-wealthy since the 1920s

4. We can infer from the passage that in the late 1980s

   (1) the gap between the super-rich and the rest of the American people grew even wider

   (2) the bottom 90 percent of the American people became poorer

   (3) the tax structure was adjusted to treat rich and poor the same

   (4) more than half of the American people grew richer

   (5) most Americans experienced the same surge in wealth as Americans did in the 1920s

ANSWERS ARE ON PAGE 301.

DRAWING CONCLUSIONS FROM ILLUSTRATIONS

You have seen how conclusions can be drawn from reading a passage. Now let's look at how to draw conclusions from graphs and maps.

Bar Graphs

Look at the bar graph below. Notice that it has a title, "Number of Immigrants to the United States," a horizontal label (across the bottom axis of the graph) of "Years," and a vertical label (up the left axis) of "In Millions." Bars of various heights represent variations in numbers of immigrants throughout the years.

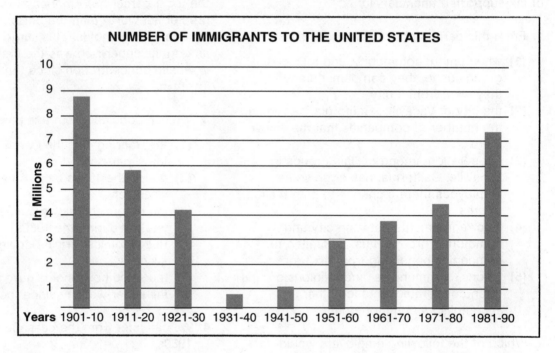

NUMBER OF IMMIGRANTS TO THE UNITED STATES

Place a check next to the correct conclusions that may be drawn.

_____ **(a)** During the 1970s the nationalities of the predominant immigrant groups changed from European to Indo-Chinese.

_____ **(b)** The decades from 1931 to 1950 mark the period when immigration to the U.S. was at its lowest.

_____ **(c)** A 1953 law called the Refugee Relief Act stopped the increasing trend of immigration to the U.S.

_____ **(d)** No significant changes in immigration patterns are foreseen for the coming decades.

_____ **(e)** The post–World War II "baby boom" had no effect on U.S. immigration patterns.

_____ **(f)** Immigration to the U.S. was at its highest during the early twentieth century.

_____ **(g)** In the 1980s, the number of immigrants to the United States was the greatest since the beginning of the twentieth century.

Choice (a) above cannot be concluded logically from the graph because there is nothing in it that indicates the nationalities of the immigrants. Choice (c) would be incorrect because an increasing trend, though slight, seems to be occurring during the 1950s, not a decreasing one. Choice (d) cannot be concluded from the information on this graph. Too many events could occur to change the immigration patterns in the future decades to make a conclusion like this one. Choice (e) is incorrect because it is impossible to conclude from this graph that the baby boom had an effect on immigration.

Choices (b), (f), and (g), however, can be supported by the information in the graph. A look at the bars representing the period from 1931 to 1950 reveals that immigration was at its lowest, the number of immigrants hovering about or just below the 1 million mark, (b). Similarly, a glance at the period from 1901 to 1910 (the early twentieth century) reveals that immigration to the U.S. was at its highest—a figure of nearly 9 million immigrants, (f). The figures for the decade of the eighties (1981–1990) show that immigration was at its highest since the turn of the century (1901–1910), (g).

 ## SKILL BUILDER
Reading Bar Graphs

1. The title tells the main topic.

2. The horizontal axis gives information along the bottom of the graph.

3. The vertical axis gives information up the side of the graph.

4. Bars of differing heights or lengths show how subjects compare in relation to the main topic.

Weather Maps

Maps are other illustrations from which we can draw conclusions. You may have noticed weather maps in newspapers or on television. Maps can give us a variety of information about a place. From the map on page 72, for instance, you can determine what the weather will be like on one day in different regions of the country.

EXERCISE 14

Directions: Look at the map below. Study the symbols for rain, snow, flurries, and showers. Write *Y* for yes before each conclusion listed below that can be based on the map. Write *N* for no before each conclusion that cannot be based on the map.

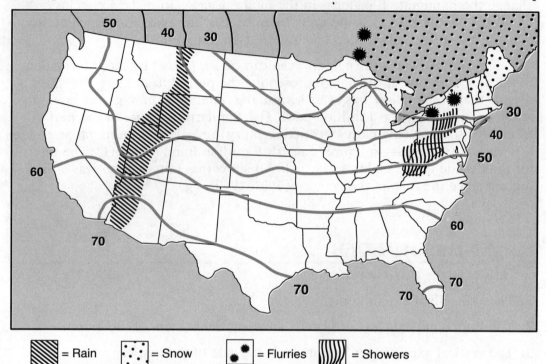

= Rain   = Snow   = Flurries   = Showers

_____ **1.** This was a forecast for a winter day in the U.S.

_____ **2.** Most of the country is free of precipitation on this day.

_____ **3.** As you head south in the U.S., the weather gets warmer.

_____ **4.** There is snow in the Pacific Northwest.

_____ **5.** The East Coast should be prepared for flooding.

_____ **6.** Central Pennsylvania is experiencing periods of showers.

_____ **7.** All of Florida will be in the 70-degree range.

ANSWERS ARE ON PAGE 301.

 SKILL BUILDER
Reading Weather Maps

1. Weather maps can give us temperature ranges, levels of precipitation, or other features of the climate in an area.

2. The title tells us what the map's focus is.

3. Symbols stand for information shown in the map.

4. A key, or legend, explains the symbols.

DRAWING INFERENCES

You draw **inferences**, or figure what is being implied by circumstances, every day. You see a man wearing dark glasses cross the street using a white cane. The man is led by a large dog. You infer that the man is blind.

In making that inference you considered the details that you could see: dark glasses, white cane, large dog. To these details you added knowledge from your past (blind people often use white canes and guide dogs when walking).

You can also infer, or guess, what an author's point of view is by the words he uses.

Read the passage below to infer what the author's attitude is.

By noon the temperature is 118 degrees. By 1:00 P.M. you can't move. The food is monotonous and disease is rampant, but the *professionals* working here wouldn't be anywhere else. This is Ethiopia, and the workers are anthropologists from all over the world searching for hints about prehistoric human existence. Like *skilled detectives*, these *scientists* piece together bits of information about the lives of our earliest ancestors to *increase our knowledge* about mankind.

What is the author's attitude toward anthropologists?

_____

_____

To answer this question, look at the details of the passage. The writer refers to the anthropologists as "professionals," "skilled detectives," and "scientists." He also mentions that they "increase our knowledge."

These details show a *positive, or respectful*, attitude.

EXERCISE 15

Directions: Read each of the following quotations and write an inference that best describes the speaker's attitude toward the subject. Watch for words and phrases that indicate positive or negative feelings.

1. "Either you cry out and act, or you become part of the injustice."

How does this person feel about missionaries who are active in opposing oppressive regimes in Central America?

_____

_____

2. "Efficiency in operations permits the Japanese to price their cars about $1,500 cheaper than their American competitors."

What does this speaker most likely think of Japan's ability to produce cheaper cars?

_____

_____

3. "Thanks to Six Flags Great America Amusement Park, the relatively crime-free village of Gurnee now has the highest crime rate of any town in Lake County, Illinois, and the fourth highest in the entire Chicago region."

How does this person feel about Six Flags Great America Amusement Park?

_____

_____

ANSWERS ARE ON PAGE 301.

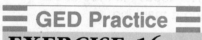
GED Practice
EXERCISE 16

Questions 1 and 2 refer to the following paragraph.

In 1957, Senator Strom Thurmond of South Carolina talked for more than twenty-four hours to purposely delay the vote on the first civil rights law to be proposed since shortly after the Civil War. Fortunately, Thurmond's filibuster did not prevent passage of the bill, and the Civil Rights Act became law that year.

1. What can you infer about the author's point of view on Senator Thurmond's filibuster of 1957?

(1) It was a waste of the senator's valuable time.

(2) It would have been a shame if it had prevented passage of the bill.

(3) It fortunately helped to get the Civil Rights Act passed.

(4) It was a brave and lonely act for the one senator.

(5) It resulted in the unfortunate defeat of the Civil Rights Act.

2. What can you infer to be the meaning of *filibuster*?

(1) a twenty-four-hour delay of a vote to give legislators a chance to discuss a bill

(2) an opportunity to propose a bill on a topic that has been long ignored

(3) a monologue aimed at convincing legislators to vote for passage of a bill

(4) political lobbying to get others to vote either for or against a bill

(5) marathon talking for the sole purpose of delaying the vote on a bill

ANSWERS ARE ON PAGE 301.

DRAWING INFERENCES FROM ILLUSTRATIONS

Most visual materials—graphs, charts, maps, cartoons, etc.—require the use of inference skills in order to get their meanings across. When you see a billboard with a picture of a ruggedly handsome cowboy smoking a cigarette while riding his horse into the sunlit horizon, you infer that this advertisement is trying to influence your feelings about cigarettes. By making it appear that "all-American" individualists like cowboys smoke this brand of cigarette, the advertisers are trying to develop a positive feeling from the public toward their cigarettes. When you see a political cartoon like the one shown below, you should also infer the author's main idea and point of view.

HECK OF A WAY TO RUN A RAILROAD

The people and objects in the cartoon are labeled according to what they symbolize. The engineers who are running the "Social Security" train are labeled "Senate" and "House" to symbolize the U.S. Congress. To the dismay of the elderly couple on the "Social Security" train, this "railroad's" workers are tearing apart the same train that they are trying to keep running.

In drawing such a comparison, the cartoonist is implying that the Social Security system is being _____ by the Congress of the United States and probably will not _____ much longer.

Looking at the expression on the faces of the elderly couple, you can infer that what is happening to the Social Security system is _____ to our senior citizens. If you did not know it already, you could also infer that the elderly _____ on Social Security to support themselves.

You should have inferred that the sentence would be completed this way: ". . . the Social Security system is being *destroyed* (or *dismantled*) by the Congress of the United States and probably will not *last* much longer." In the faces of the older man and woman you can see fright and disbelief, or puzzlement, so you can infer that the situation is *frightening* to them, probably because of how important Social Security is to them financially. You can infer that the elderly *depend* on Social Security for financial support.

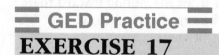

GED Practice

EXERCISE 17

Questions 1 and 2 below are based on the following cartoon.

CRAIG MACINTOSH   Reprinted with permission from the *Minneapolis Star and Tribune*

1. Apparently, the cartoonist thinks that nuclear waste disposal is

   (1) no longer a problem
   (2) being handled carefully by trained technicians
   (3) of concern only in out-of-the-way places
   (4) getting too close for comfort
   (5) the responsibility of all citizens

2. From the way the characters are dressed, you can infer that nuclear waste disposal is

   (1) safe enough to be handled in a person's garage
   (2) handled more easily in cooler weather
   (3) so dangerous that protective suits must be worn when handling it
   (4) no more serious than handling yard waste
   (5) being handled by ordinary citizens

ANSWERS ARE ON PAGE 301.

4 Evaluating Social Studies Materials

When you must make a major purchase—like a car—you often *evaluate* your financial situation and your transportation needs before you shop. Once you are out in the marketplace, you continue to evaluate. You judge the vehicles you see as to how well you can afford them and how well they are made.

In social studies, you also evaluate information. You must be able to judge the value or logic of an idea. You also have to be able to understand how and why people make the decisions that they do. Most important, you need to be able to determine when a decision has been based on sound logic. In this section, you will learn how to evaluate material in social studies in four ways:

- judging the extent to which information satisfies criteria
- recognizing the role that values play in beliefs and decision making
- judging the adequacy of facts
- identifying faulty reasoning

JUDGING INFORMATION

In order to judge the worth or value of something, you must have standards or reference points to go by. A typist's ability is judged by the *criteria* of speed and accuracy. The value of a movie is measured by its entertainment level, its cinematography, its acting and direction. A newspaper article is evaluated by its adequacy of facts, its style of writing, and its objectivity (omissions of opinions or biases of the writer).

If you know and understand the criteria by which something is judged, you are better prepared to evaluate it. For example, if you know the legal requirements for a good and binding contract, then you are better prepared to enter into one. Some of the criteria for a legally binding contract include:

1. a clear written offer by the buyer or buyer's representative
2. a clear written acceptance of the offer by the seller or seller's representative
3. a settlement of the deal that is agreeable and clear to both buyer and seller
4. a clear exchange of something valuable between the buyer and seller
5. no illegal activity involved in the deal by either the buyer or the seller

Judge whether the situation described below constitutes a legally binding contract according to the criteria listed on page 77. If it does, write *YES* in the space next to it. If the situation does not, write *NO* in the space, and write the number of the criterion on page 77 that the case does not satisfy.

_____ A husband and wife both shake hands with a neighbor in an agreement to purchase a used car for $5,995 from him, and the neighbor, in turn, agrees to hand over the title to the automobile upon receipt of the money.

You should have written *NO—1 and 2*. Though an offer to purchase the car is made, and the seller accepts the offer, neither the offer nor the acceptance is in writing. Therefore, no legally binding contract exists.

EXERCISE 1

Directions: In the following cases, judge whether the situation described constitutes a legally binding contract according to the criteria. If it does, write *YES* on the line. If the situation does not, write *NO* on the line. For each *NO* answer write the number of the criterion that the case does not satisfy.

_____ **1.** A private pilot agrees to pick up 100 pounds of marijuana in Mexico and deliver it to a buyer in Texas.

_____ **2.** The attorney of a couple who are selling their home drafts an acceptance to a written offer along with a $5,000 check from an interested buyer.

_____ **3.** After much discussion and haggling over price, an owner of a small bookkeeping business tells a computer salesman that he will seriously consider buying a personal computer only if he can get it for $500 less than the salesman's "final" offer.

_____ **4.** A poor but diligent farmer signs a note promising to feed and house a laborer in his home in compensation for the work the laborer has agreed, in writing, to do on his land.

ANSWERS ARE ON PAGE 302.

EXERCISE 2

Directions: Read the passage below. Be prepared to judge the theory described in the passage.

In 1964, anthropologist Ashley Montagu edited a startling book entitled *The Concept of Race*. In the book, Montagu and nine other writers stated that the concept of race is a myth that leads to the perpetuation of errors.

According to Montagu, skin color and physical features are not necessarily accurate indicators of a person's ancestry. He believes that the term *ethnic group* might be a better term than *race*.

For each of the facts below, write *(1)* in the blank if the fact would help support Montagu's theory, *(2)* if the fact would dispute Montagu's theory, and *(3)* if the fact would have no bearing on Montagu's theory.

_____ **1.** Ashley Montagu is a white man.

_____ **2.** Montagu has supported this theory since at least 1941.

_____ **3.** The use of the term *race* has had a long history and, in fact, is prevalent even today among all levels and aspects of society.

_____ **4.** There are obvious differences among groups of people in the world that seem fairly easy to define and categorize by "race."

_____ **5.** Ashley Montagu is one of America's most distinguished anthropologists, having taught at New York University, Rutgers University, Hahnemann Medical College, and the University of California.

_____ **6.** The book *The Concept of Race* contains contributions from nine other distinguished scientists besides Montagu who all support his theory.

ANSWERS ARE ON PAGE 302.

RECOGNIZING VALUES

What values and beliefs do you hold nearest and dearest to your heart? What would you die for? If you could be doing anything you wanted right now, what would it be? These questions all focus on your personal values.

Your beliefs and values influence the big decisions that you must make in life. In understanding social studies material, you must be able to recognize how an individual's values affect the decisions he or she makes.

For example, former president Jimmy Carter is known to have put great value on human rights during his term in office. Because of his beliefs, he made decisions and statements about Soviet human rights policies during the Strategic Arms Limitation Talks (SALT) with the U.S.S.R. Thus, Carter's beliefs had an influence on his decision making in the area of foreign relations.

Fill in the words that best summarize the values of the person described in the case below.

A senator does not believe that she could ever have an abortion because it is morally repugnant to her. She personally feels that abortion should not be legalized. A survey shows, however, that her constituency overwhelmingly is in favor of a law permitting abortion. The senator votes "yes" on the bill to legalize abortion.

The senator apparently values _____

over _____.

You should have written *her responsibility to her constituency* over *her personal beliefs.* In other words, the feelings of those who elected her override her own personal feelings.

EXERCISE 3

Directions: For each statement, supply the most accurate words that reflect the values of the person described in each case below.

1. A young man wants very much to settle down and save enough money to get married and to buy a home, a good-running car, and some new clothes. However, he has been instilled with a strong belief in the responsibility of every American citizen to serve his country. His decision to join the U.S. Army was

   affected primarily by his sense of _____.

2. A scientist is asked to work on a prestigious project to develop a neutron bomb, a weapon he despises because it is designed to destroy on impact living things, not buildings. When the scientist refuses the project, it shows that he values his

   _____ over his _____.

ANSWERS ARE ON PAGE 302.

EXERCISE 4

Questions 1–4 refer to the following passage.

The derogatory term "Yankee imperialist" has not always been applied to Americans. Prior to the Spanish-American War in 1898, the United States was strongly isolationist and did not concern itself with issues involving other parts of the world.

The Spanish-American War grew out of the American public's growing desire to expand American territory and interests and out of a general "war fever."

Several of the larger American newspapers began to capitalize on the Cuban struggle for independence from Spain, sensationalizing abuses Spanish military forces were committing against the Cubans.

Public outrage reached its peak with the sinking of the battleship *Maine*, which was sent to the Havana harbor to protect U.S. citizens and property in Cuba. Though the cause of the explosion was never discovered, President McKinley approved a congressional resolution demanding immediate Spanish withdrawal from Cuba. A few days later, Spain declared war.

The congressional resolution stated that the U.S. was not acting to secure an empire. However, the terms of the Treaty of Paris that officially ended the war required that Spain cede the Philippines, Puerto Rico, and Guam to the U.S. For good or ill, the U.S. became less nationalistic. It had become a world power, admired by some who felt the U.S. now had an altruistic concern for smaller nations. Others detested the U.S. for what they believed to be imperialistic bullying of countries in its way.

1. According to this writer, what values of Americans most directly triggered the U.S. decision to enter the war against Spain in 1898?

   (1) a desire to help and protect the less economically fortunate in this world
   (2) a belief that democracy is the only fair form of government and that military rule is unjust
   (3) an overriding desire to maintain peace and harmony in the Western Hemisphere
   (4) an abhorrence of social injustice and a belief in their responsibility to the oppressed
   (5) a sense of outrage about dangers to American lives and property abroad

2. What change in American values resulted from the Spanish-American War?

   (1) The public became more wary of electing indecisive candidates for high public office.
   (2) Nationalism increased as Americans found ways to strengthen their internal society and economy.
   (3) The U.S. abandoned a policy of isolationism and became involved in international conflict.
   (4) The U.S. adopted a materialistic policy of acquiring property and increasing capitalistic ventures inside and outside the U.S.
   (5) The public developed a cautious, wait-and-see attitude toward getting involved in further conflicts with other world powers.

3. Those who use the term "Yankee imperialist" against the U.S. would most likely be the same ones who would agree that

   (1) the Peace Corps was established to help Third World countries develop their own independent economic bases
   (2) Puerto Rico should be made a colony of the United States
   (3) the U.S. had no right to invade the island of Grenada in 1983
   (4) the Philippines can blame its economic woes on the U.S. decision to grant it independence in 1946
   (5) the U.S. entered the Vietnam conflict because of its concern for the well-being of Southeast Asia

4. From the information presented in the passage, which was *not* a contributing factor to the start of the Spanish-American War?

   (1) American newspapers' sensationalizing reports
   (2) the sinking of the battleship *Maine*
   (3) the American public's "war fever"
   (4) the U.S. policy of isolationism
   (5) Congress's demand for Spanish withdrawal from Cuba

ANSWERS ARE ON PAGE 302.

JUDGING THE ADEQUACY OF FACTS

Have you ever told one of your favorite jokes to a friend, only to have him appear bewildered after you delivered the punch line? If you considered why the joke failed, you may have learned that you omitted an important detail. Anytime facts are lacking in a story, confusion or misinterpretation of the story is likely to result.

When important facts are omitted, you cannot make an informed decision. Suppose, for example, you overheard a debate about the purchase of a new fleet of buses for your city's transit system. One group supports the buying of American-made buses. These buses cost more than the foreign-made buses that another group wants. To be able to judge how you feel about the issue you need to know all the facts. You need to know:

- the cost of each fleet of buses

- the city's financial situation

- the level of quality of the bus each company manufactures

You may also need to know what impact the purchase of a foreign product over an American product is likely to have on American jobs.

All of these considerations may have some influence on what your final position will be. Similarly, when you read social studies materials, you must be able to determine whether the facts are adequate to support the writer's conclusion or point of view.

Certain information is missing in each case below. On the line provided, indicate what facts are needed to answer each question.

CASE 1

Intelligence (IQ) tests were improved dramatically by French psychologist Alfred Binet when he found a way to measure judgment, comprehension, and reasoning skills. In what ways could Binet have made his test bias-free, also?

_____

You should have written *How are the tests biased?* In order to answer the question, you need to know in what ways the IQ test is biased before you can answer the question.

CASE 2

The number of registered black voters in Leflore County, Mississippi, increased by 50 percent during the last election. However, the defeated black candidate for the U.S. Congress did not benefit directly from this increase in the number of registered voters. In fact, he lost the election by the same margin of votes as he did the last time he ran. Why didn't the candidate get more votes if the number of black registered voters increased by 50 percent?

_____

You should have written the question *How many of the black registered voters in the county actually voted in the election?* The fact that the information tells you the number of registered voters increased by 50 percent does not mean that they voted. The important fact that is missing is the number of black registered voters who actually voted.

EXERCISE 5

Questions 1 and 2 are based on the following passage.

"Equality of rights under the law shall not be denied or abridged by the United States or by any state on account of sex." So reads the Equal Rights Amendment proposed in 1972. Opponents of the amendment insisted, however, that it meant that anti-family, pro-abortion, pro-homosexual, and anti-privacy laws would be passed.

As a result, the amendment was defeated in 1982. Ten years had passed since the first of thirty-five states ratified it. Thirty of these states had approved the amendment within the first year of its proposal. By law, three-fourths of the state legislatures, or thirty-eight states, had to approve it to make it part of the U.S. Constitution.

If there had been more time, the amendment probably would have been ratified. In two major opinion polls just a few weeks before the ERA's defeat, it was reported that the majority of American citizens supported the amendment.

1. Which of the statements in the article is not adequately supported by facts?

   (1) A majority of Americans supported the ERA at the time of its defeat.
   (2) Thirty-eight state legislatures needed to ratify the amendment to make it law.
   (3) The ERA might have passed if there had been more time.
   (4) Its opponents were fearful of the ramifications of the ERA.
   (5) A majority of the states approved of the ERA.

2. Which of the following statements is supported by the information provided in the passage?

   (1) Organizations working for the ERA had more popular support than governmental support.
   (2) As a result of the defeat of the ERA, men are given more consideration in parental custody cases than they were before.
   (3) Since the 1982 defeat of the ERA, single-parent, female-headed families have become more numerous and more poverty-stricken.
   (4) Gay rights groups supported the ERA and worked for its ratification.
   (5) More female citizens were in favor of the ratification of the ERA than males.

ANSWERS ARE ON PAGE 302.

JUDGING THE ADEQUACY OF FACTS IN ILLUSTRATIONS

There are many ways to represent facts in social studies. You have evaluated the adequacy of facts given in written materials. Now you will do much the same thing with maps.

As you have seen, maps are used to represent information visually. They are often the most efficient method to get across certain facts. "One picture is worth a thousand words," says the old expression. Of course, different kinds of maps are used to illustrate different kinds of facts.

Let's look at a map and see how adequately it shows facts about one of the world's continents.

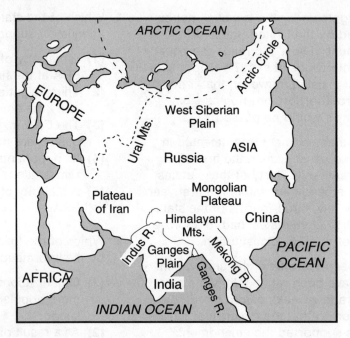

Study this map of Asia. Place an *X* in the space below to indicate whether the information on the map is adequate or inadequate to support each fact. If the information on the map is not adequate, write what kind of map would best show that kind of information. You may refer to the skill builder on page 85 that reviews the types of maps.

Asia is the world's largest continent and covers over one-third of the earth's surface.

__ adequate __ inadequate: _____ map would show this better

You should have marked that the information on the map was *inadequate* and that a *world* map would show this better.

SKILL BUILDER
Review of Types of Maps

1. Topographical maps show geographic land features of an area.

2. Population maps explain distribution of people in an area.

3. Political maps can outline borders between countries or states, show trade relationships among countries, and indicate systems of government.

4. World maps are a type of political map that includes the whole world.

5. Weather maps can show current or forecasted weather as well as climate.

EXERCISE 6

Directions: Use the map of Asia. Answer the following questions in the same way as you answered the question on page 84.

1. The continent of Asia extends north and south of the Arctic Circle.

   __ adequate __ inadequate: _____ map would show this better

2. Asia contains many mountains, plains, plateaus, and river basins.

   __ adequate __ inadequate: _____ map would show this better

3. Some parts of Asia receive more than eighty inches of rain a year.

   __ adequate __ inadequate: _____ map would show this better

4. Asia is bordered by three oceans.

   __ adequate __ inadequate: _____ map would show this better

5. The countries that have the largest population and the greatest land mass are in Asia.

   __ adequate __ inadequate: _____ map would show this better

6. The West Siberian Plain lies in Russia on the continent of Asia.

   __ adequate __ inadequate: _____ map would show this better

ANSWERS ARE ON PAGE 302.

EXERCISE 7

Questions 1 and 2 are based on the following map.

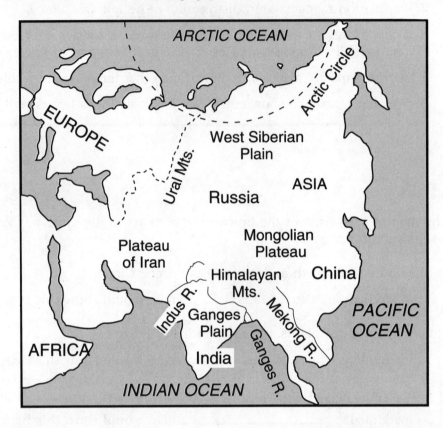

1. Which of the following statements is supported adequately by the data provided by the map?

(1) Russia is located on the continents of Asia and Europe.

(2) The Indus River empties into the Atlantic Ocean.

(3) India and China are unfriendly neighbors.

(4) The Himalayan Mountains are the highest in the world.

(5) India's economic impact on the world is in direct proportion to its size.

2. Which of the following land features is *not* shown adequately by the map?

(1) the location of plateaus in Asia

(2) the range of the Ural Mountains

(3) the size of the Indian peninsula in Asia

(4) the height of the Himalayan Mountains

(5) the course of the Mekong River

ANSWERS ARE ON PAGE 302.

IDENTIFYING FAULTY REASONING

You have practiced drawing conclusions from supporting details in a passage. An extension of that skill is the ability to identify faulty conclusions in arguments. People often make illogical statements; for example:

HUSBAND: I'm late because the traffic was bad. That's all.

WIFE: Two-and-a-half hours late because of traffic! You must think I'm an idiot! I know you stopped at a tavern.

HUSBAND: Now why would I have done that? I never stop at a bar after work. I don't even drink.

WIFE: I know you did because that's why my father used to be so late coming home.

Obviously, the wife is upset and not using her powers of logic. Just because her father used to do something does not mean her husband does the same thing. Her judgment is further shown to be unreasonable by the husband's reply that he does not even drink.

Read the following story. Find two illogical or faulty conclusions.

Marlena Jackson is a typical working wife and mother. She works because she needs to help support her family financially. Her days are very hectic because she has to keep both work *and* home schedules. Marlena shops primarily at one chain grocery store because it sponsors games with prizes for customers. The prizes provide extras for the house, such as towels, cookware, and small appliances.

The food at this grocery store generally costs more than that at a discount store a few miles away. This fact, however, just proves to Marlena that the more expensive store has better food.

Marlena drives an old, gas-guzzling car that is always in need of repair. Her husband, Donnell, knows how to fix it, though, so the repair costs are low. Insurance costs on the car are not high either, so Marlena assumes that the car is safe.

Despite all the money they spend on gas and repairs for the old car, it is still cheaper to keep it than it would be to buy a newer, smaller, more fuel-efficient car.

In the second paragraph above, the faulty conclusion is that *a more expensive store is a better store.* The cost of food can be affected by quality, but it can also be affected by other things, such as more lavish surroundings, higher-paid clerks, or more games and gimmicks that draw in customers.

In the third paragraph, the faulty conclusion is that *lower insurance costs indicate safer cars.* That *could* be a reason for the lower premiums, but other factors, such as lack of comprehensive coverage or lower replacement cost on the vehicle, could also keep the cost low.

GED Practice
EXERCISE 8

Questions 1–3 refer to the following passage.

Some African-Americans can claim ancestors who arrived on the continent before the Pilgrims landed at Plymouth Rock. Unfortunately, this just means that racial bias has always existed in the Americas, for most of the first African arrivals were slaves.

Slavery and indentured servitude were both employed initially because of an acute shortage of labor in the Americas. But there were glaring differences between the two systems from the beginning. Most indentured servants were white, and most served only four or five years. Most slaves were black, and most served for their entire lives. In addition, servile status for slaves was made inheritable through the mother, and intermarriage between slaves and white servants was prohibited by law. The few free Negroes living in those early years had their liberties restricted severely, a practice sanctioned by the law. If it had not been for such laws, white Europeans immigrating to the U.S. would not have become so biased against blacks.

1. Which of the following is an illogical conclusion that is contained in the story?

   (1) Laws restricting the freedoms of the nonslave blacks in the early years of this country fostered the bias against them by the European immigrants.
   (2) Some American blacks can claim ancestry on the continent for many more generations than American whites can.
   (3) Slavery and indentured servitude were both reactions to an economic need in the early development of the U.S.
   (4) The most glaring difference between indentured servants and slaves is that the servants usually served for just four or five years, whereas slaves served a lifetime.
   (5) Intermarriage between blacks and whites was made illegal in the early years of the country because of a fear of the owner that the slave would run away.

2. The conclusion at the end of the passage is illogical because it

   (1) is the opposite of what is shown to be true
   (2) compares events of different generations
   (3) is not based on facts to support it
   (4) is unrelated to the topic being developed
   (5) is true for only a limited number of cases

3. The *chief* difference between indentured servitude and slavery was that

   (1) indentured servitude was for life; slavery was for a limited period
   (2) indentured servitude preceded slavery in America
   (3) indentured servitude was for a limited period; slavery was for life
   (4) indentured servitude was for whites only; slavery was not
   (5) indentured servitude was inheritable; slavery was not

ANSWERS ARE ON PAGE 302.

UNDERSTANDING SOCIAL STUDIES

- ■ U.S. History
- ■ Political Science
- ■ Behavioral Sciences
- ■ Geography
- ■ Economics

5 U.S. History

"Those who cannot remember the past are condemned to repeat it," said the philosopher George Santayana. Was he right?

World War I was supposed to be "the war to end all wars," but, of course, it was not. Twenty-one years after it ended, World War II began.

A no-win situation in a limited, undeclared war in Korea apparently was not reminder enough to keep the U.S. from becoming involved in Vietnam.

Today, many people believe that the U.S. will never again get involved in such an unwinnable war in a foreign land because of what we learned from Vietnam. Yet, others see evidence of such involvement all over the world.

The United States went to war again in 1991. The Persian Gulf War lasted only a few days. But television footage of U.S. air attacks on Iraq introduced Americans to the power of modern warfare as no other war had in recent years.

We study history to help chart our future by studying the past. Sometimes we learn from our mistakes, but many times we do not. In this chapter, you will study U.S. history. As you read, try to keep in mind events today that parallel those of yesterday. You may find that, indeed, history repeats itself.

A NEW NATION IN A NEW WORLD
EXPLORATION, DISCOVERY, AND COLONIZATION

Nothing has changed about what Christopher Columbus accomplished, but the way we think about it has changed over the years. In some ways Christopher Columbus can be considered a failure. He originally set sail in 1492 to find a new, easier passage to the Far East to make trade cheaper and more convenient. However, he did not find that route or any riches in the New World. And America was named for Italian explorer Amerigo Vespucci, who journeyed to the New World later and wrote a very good account of that trip.

But Columbus was a great success in other ways. He believed that the world was round, and he undertook a journey based on that idea. What he did find was a territory full of natural resources and new opportunities. He is also credited with starting the first colony that established Europe's ties to the New World, on the island now made up of Haiti and the Dominican Republic.

Recently, many people have protested the celebration of Columbus Day. Rightly or wrongly, many believe that Columbus was responsible for the exploitation and subjugation of many native populations.

LAND CLAIMS IN
THE NEW WORLD 1689

English

Spanish

French

Claimed by France and England

Portugese

Dutch

Unclaimed

COLONIAL AMERICA
IN 1763

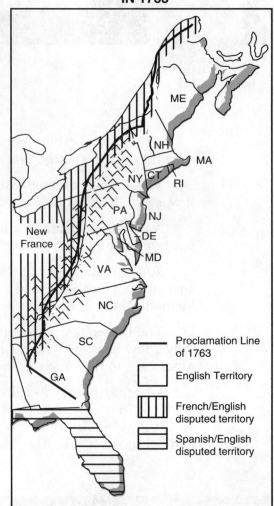

ME

NH

MA

NY CT

RI

PA

NJ

DE

MD

New
France

VA

NC

SC

GA

Proclamation Line
of 1763

English Territory

French/English
disputed territory

Spanish/English
disputed territory

Once word of Spain's discovery spread, it was no longer the only European country interested in the New World. The map above shows the division of territory as it stood in 1689.

In claiming land in the New World, Spain was interested primarily in finding gold and sending in Christian missionaries. The French were interested especially in the seemingly endless abundance of furs in the interior territories of North America. However, the English who came were interested mainly in finding a new homeland. Many were persecuted for their religious beliefs back in England, and the British king was glad to let them leave.

In the mid 1700s, the French and English clashed again and again over claims of land "ownership." At the same time, English settlers were fighting the continent's natives over the rich farmland beyond the Appalachian Mountains. In a treaty of lasting significance, the French and the English agreed to divide the land of North America as shown in the map above. The Appalachian Mountains marked the Proclamation Line of 1763, separating French from English territory. In this Proclamation, the British king forbade white settlers to go beyond the line shown on the map. However, the Proclamation of 1763 later proved to be meaningless.

GED Practice
EXERCISE 1

Questions 1–4 are based on the maps and written information on page 92.

1. According to the map of the New World and the information that follows it, which of the following conclusions can be drawn about the years from 1492 to 1689?

   (1) Spain became uninterested in the resources and possibilities of the New World.
   (2) France and England became rivals in the establishment of some settlements in the New World.
   (3) The Dutch were consistently driven out of areas that they tried to colonize in the New World.
   (4) Portugal's fortunes dwindled in the financing of exploration of the New World.
   (5) Much of North America was unclaimed by anyone.

2. Which European nation had claimed the largest area of land in North America by 1689?

   (1) Spain
   (2) England
   (3) the Netherlands
   (4) France
   (5) Portugal

3. According to the map of colonial America in 1763 and the information that follows it, what was the result of the treaty between France and England in 1763?

   (1) Spain and England went to war over the competition for land in the New World.
   (2) The English became allies with the Spanish and Russians.
   (3) The Spanish gave up their search for gold in the New World.
   (4) The English gave up power in the New World.
   (5) The French lost virtually all claim to territory in the thirteen colonies.

4. Why was the Proclamation Line of 1763 called a "paper fence"?

   (1) It was a good idea but didn't work on paper.
   (2) It looked good on paper but was unenforceable.
   (3) It made governing colonials easier for England.
   (4) It was respected because the British king put it in writing.
   (5) It showed that England was insensitive to colonial interests.

ANSWERS ARE ON PAGE 303.

THIRTEEN ENGLISH COLONIES

The English were not the first to establish a colony in the New World, but when they came, they came in earnest. In 1607 Jamestown, Virginia, was settled as a business venture, and the colonists soon made a profit on tobacco. The Pilgrims and the Puritans came later for religious and political reasons and developed governing bodies soon after their arrival.

The English settled along the eastern coastline in three distinct geographic regions. The chart below highlights the characteristics of the regions.

THIRTEEN COLONIES IN THREE GROUPS
New England Colonies Territory—Massachusetts, New Hampshire, Rhode Island, Connecticut Founding Purpose—religious freedom Land Features—dense forests; good harbors and rivers; rocky soil
Middle Colonies Territory—New York, New Jersey, Pennsylvania, Delaware, Maryland Founding Purpose—fur trade and grain farming Land Features—coastal plains and river valleys; fertile farming soil; large, convenient harbors
Southern Colonies Territory—Virginia, North Carolina, South Carolina, Georgia Founding Purpose—large-scale farming Land Features—fertile soil; abundant rainfall; warm climate; long growing season

EXERCISE 2

Directions: Check off the statements that are supported by the chart above.

_____ **(1)** The New England colonies had less desirable farmland than the Middle and Southern colonies.

_____ **(2)** The Middle colonies tended to be most closely tied to the British.

_____ **(3)** Colonists who sought religious freedom settled only in New England.

_____ **(4)** Both the climate and the founding purpose of the southern settlers laid the basis for a plantation economy.

ANSWERS ARE ON PAGE 303.

THE REVOLUTIONARY WAR

> ### KEY WORDS
>
> **duty**—a tax, usually placed on imported goods
> **sovereign nation**—a nation free from outside control

War is expensive. So, soon after the end of the French and Indian War in 1763, England needed to finance its huge war debt. As a result, the British Parliament and King George III passed the Stamp Act of 1765 and the Townshend Acts of 1767. The Stamp Act required all official documents in the colonies to bear a purchased British stamp. The Townshend Acts placed large duties on glass, lead, and tea.

By September 1774, the colonists had had enough. However, the first Continental Congress did not ask Britain for independence for the colonists; it demanded only their rights as British subjects. The purpose of the congress was to demand representation in the British Parliament so that colonists could have a say in what taxes they would have to pay. But by the time of the second Continental Congress in May 1775, hostile encounters had already taken place between the English soldiers and the colonists.

In the battles of Lexington and Concord, British soldiers had been surprised by the diligence and unorthodox tactics of the American militia. George Washington was named commander-in-chief of the colonists' army, and he immediately began reorganizing and strengthening his troops.

On July 4, 1776, the second Continental Congress adopted the Declaration of Independence, and thereafter the Americans fought as citizens of a sovereign nation who were expelling a foreign power, not as British rebels against their own king. This was important not only to boost their own morale but also to elicit the sympathetic support of the world for their fight.

Second Continental Congress, July 4, 1776

GED Practice
EXERCISE 3

Choose the *one* best answer for each statement or question below.

1. The purpose of the first Continental Congress was to

   (1) ask the British king for the colonies' independence
   (2) demand the colonists' rights as British citizens
   (3) form a militia to fight the British soldiers
   (4) name George Washington as commander-in-chief of the militia
   (5) write the Declaration of Independence from Great Britain

2. Actual battles between the British and the colonists began

   (1) after George Washington was named commander-in-chief
   (2) before the second Continental Congress
   (3) after the Declaration of Independence was written
   (4) on the same day that the Declaration of Independence was written
   (5) before George III became king

3. The fight of the American colonists against Great Britain can be compared to which anticolonialist event of the twentieth century?

   (1) the attempted takeover of Europe by Hitler
   (2) the struggle of India for its independence from Great Britain
   (3) the attack on Pearl Harbor by the Japanese in 1941
   (4) the return of the Panama Canal to the country of Panama
   (5) the growth of communism in Latin America

4. The purpose of the Stamp Act of 1765 and the Townshend Acts of 1767 was to

   (1) stop the unorthodox tactics of the American militia
   (2) expel foreign powers from England
   (3) supply needed money to Great Britain after the French and Indian War
   (4) stop hostile encounters between colonists and British soldiers
   (5) give colonists representation in the British Parliament

ANSWERS ARE ON PAGE 303.

 # WRITING ACTIVITY 1

The American Revolution set the stage for many revolutions that followed. Revolutionaries in Haiti, France, and Vietnam were inspired by the American Declaration of Independence.

Why do you think the American Revolution captured the imagination of people around the world? Write two or three paragraphs explaining why the American Revolution was so inspirational.

ANSWER IS ON PAGE 303.

SPLITTING INTO POLITICAL GROUPS

Great Britain recognized its former colonies as the United States of America on September 3, 1783. For more than five years afterward, the new nation struggled with heavy war debts and a weak central government operating under the Articles of Confederation, which had almost no authority over the separate states.

In 1786 and 1787, Daniel Shays, a former captain during the American Revolution, led a group of poor, debt-ridden farmers in violent rebellion against high taxes and an unjust legal system. The rebellions highlighted the need for a strong central government that could keep the peace when the country was not at war and could govern the states uniformly.

In 1787, a Constitutional Convention was called to strengthen the Articles of Confederation, but it did not take long before the delegates realized that the articles would have to be thrown out and a new constitution drawn up. The articles were lacking too many vital ingredients for effective unification. They did not empower the national government to collect taxes, defend the new country, pay the war debt, or even regulate trade and commerce.

But drawing up a new constitution that all the representatives would agree to was no easy task. A split soon developed between the Federalists, who wanted a strong central government with authoritative control over the states, and the anti-Federalists, who were afraid that the individual person and the individual states would lose their freedom and flexibility under one central government. Other disputes over how the new government should be set up arose. These arguments and the compromises that settled them are highlighted in the chart on page 98.

Despite all the disagreements among the states, the Constitution of the United States was ratified by the required ninth state in July of 1788 and by all thirteen by May of 1790, a year after the new government had already started operating.

COMPROMISES AT THE CONSTITUTIONAL CONVENTION

Dispute: Should the states be governed by a strong central government (Federalists' view)?

or

Should the new government be based on the sovereignty of the states (anti-Federalists' view)?

Compromise:
1. President is elected by electoral college, the Senate by the state legislatures (this was later changed by the Twelfth Amendment, adopted in 1804), and House of Representatives by the people.
2. Bill of Rights—first ten amendments were added to the Constitution later to guarantee individual rights.

Dispute: Should the makeup of Congress be based on each state's population (large states' view)?

or

Should all states have equal representation (small states' view)?

Compromise: bicameral legislature (two houses in Congress)
1. Members of House of Representatives are based on each state's population.
2. Senate consists of two delegates from each state. This was called the "Great Compromise."

Dispute: Should slaves be counted in the population (southern slave states' view)?

or

Should slaves be excluded from the population count (northern industrialized states' view)?

Compromise:
1. Slave importation would be allowed until at least 1808.
2. Slaves would be counted as three-fifths of the population only for the purposes of representation and for assessing taxes; however, they were not permitted to vote.

EXERCISE 4

Directions: Read the quotes shown below. Write *F* (for Federalist) in the space provided if the speaker favors Federalism and *A* (for anti-Federalist) if the speaker advocates states' rights.

_____ **1.** "The territories themselves should determine whether slavery should exist."

_____ **2.** "I need assurance that my money will have value in Georgia as well as in New Jersey."

_____ **3.** "If this nation is to prosper, trade among states must be regulated uniformly."

_____ **4.** "We need our own local standing militia to put down uprisings in the states' own territories."

_____ **5.** "What right does Massachusetts have to make treaties with other nations?"

ANSWERS ARE ON PAGE 303.

≡ GED Practice ≡
EXERCISE 5

For questions 1–4, choose the answer that best completes each statement.

1. Alexander Hamilton stated that it would be impossible to govern one nation through thirteen separate sovereign states. It can be assumed that Hamilton was

(1) a Federalist
(2) an anti-Federalist
(3) from a large state
(4) from a northern industrialized state
(5) a southern slave owner

2. The "Great Compromise" of the Constitutional Convention involved

(1) the settlement of trade laws across the states
(2) the mutual agreement by North and South on how to count slaves in the population
(3) the addition of a Bill of Rights to guarantee personal freedoms for the states' citizens
(4) the creation of a two-house federal legislature to allow for fairness in state representation
(5) the establishment of an electoral college so that the people could not directly elect the president of the country

3. Counting slaves as only three-fifths of the population penalized the southern states in

(1) determining the number of seats for the House of Representatives
(2) deciding on the number of senators to represent those states
(3) figuring property taxes
(4) establishing trade laws between the North and South
(5) setting a date to abolish slavery in the nation

4. Why was the Bill of Rights such an important addition to the Constitution, especially for the anti-Federalists?

(1) It guaranteed the end of slavery by a certain date.
(2) It set the rules for the process of amending the Constitution.
(3) It would end the abuse of personal liberties many colonists had experienced.
(4) It determined a fair process under which the president of the U.S. would be elected.
(5) It gave the states supreme rights over the federal government.

Question 5 refers to the following quote.

"It appears to me, then, little short of a miracle, that the Delegates from so many different States (which States you know are also different from each other), in their manners, circumstances, and prejudices, should unite in forming a system of National Government, so little liable to well-founded objections."

—George Washington to Marquis de Lafayette, February 7, 1788

5. From this quote we can assume that George Washington believed ratification of the Constitution by the United States

(1) would be quick and easy
(2) would be hampered because of the southern states' resistance
(3) would be a long, tedious process, taking many years
(4) would never take place
(5) looked more likely than one would expect from such a diverse group of states

ANSWERS ARE ON PAGE 303.

WRITING ACTIVITY 2

The chart on page 98 cites the position of the southern and northern states about counting slaves as part of the population. Write a paragraph telling why you think the South wanted slaves counted and the North did not.

ANSWER IS ON PAGE 304.

DOMESTIC AND FOREIGN POLICY

THE WESTERN FRONTIER

KEY WORDS

Manifest Destiny—the drive to extend the U.S. borders to the Pacific Ocean

implied powers—authority suggested in the Constitution that is not specifically spelled out

Next to buying Manhattan Island from the Indians for $24 worth of kettles, axes, and cloth, the Louisiana Purchase was probably the United States' best bargain. The United States paid only $15 million to purchase the Louisiana Territory from France in 1803. This acquisition doubled the size of the country, expanding its territories from the Mississippi River westward to the Rocky Mountains. Moreover, the Louisiana Purchase fortified the nation's wealth and position in the world, intensified the expansion westward, and set a precedent for the president's use of implied powers. Implied powers represent authority a president has that is not specifically spelled out in the Constitution.

Because he was afraid of setting a precedent of going beyond constitutional powers, President Thomas Jefferson was at first opposed to the Louisiana Purchase. He thought a constitutional amendment would be necessary to make such a move possible, but time did not permit the long amendment process, and, besides, the idea of the "destiny" of expansion to the Pacific Ocean was already becoming a popular one in the U.S.

In 1804, Jefferson sent Meriwether Lewis and William Clark on an expedition to explore the newly purchased territory, which was virtually a mystery to its new owner. The two men started in St. Louis, went northwest toward the present-day Dakotas, and there took on the Indian guide Sacajawea. They eventually reached the Pacific Ocean and then journeyed back to St. Louis. They did not find an all-water route to the West as they had sought, but they did find several passes through the Rockies, establish friendly relations with the Indians in the West, and gather invaluable information about the life and resources in the new territory.

By 1853 the boundaries of the continental U.S. were set as they are now. "Manifest Destiny" had become a rallying cry in America and shaped the history and culture of the country. Manifest Destiny was the drive to expand the territory of the United States into the undeveloped areas of the West and South. It led directly to the annexation of Texas in 1845 and the acquisition of the Oregon territory in 1846. By 1848, the area comprising California, Nevada, Arizona, Utah, and New Mexico became part of the United States as the nation's boundaries stretched from the Atlantic to the Pacific.

GED Practice
EXERCISE 6

For questions 1–3, choose the statement that best answers each question.

1. Which of the following expresses an opinion of Thomas Jefferson regarding the Louisiana Purchase?

   (1) It doubled the size of the U.S. territory and increased its wealth.
   (2) It helped increase the movement of settlers to the West.
   (3) It was not a move allowed by the Constitution as written.
   (4) It would start a cultural ideology known as "Manifest Destiny."
   (5) Its purchase and exploration would provide invaluable information to the country.

2. In what way did the American belief in "Manifest Destiny" shape the history of the U.S.?

   (1) The relationship between the settlers and the Indians improved greatly.
   (2) The Constitution of the U.S. was amended to allow for more purchase of land for expansion.
   (3) Rivers became an important method of traveling and formed boundaries between states and territories.
   (4) The settlement of the West became more rapid.
   (5) The U.S. soon obtained its first colonial territory in the Pacific.

3. Which of the following statements is best supported by evidence presented in the reading above?

   (1) President Jefferson's commissioning of the Lewis and Clark expedition was foolish considering the waste of time and money to the U.S.
   (2) The Louisiana Purchase and the Lewis and Clark expedition both detracted from President Jefferson's prestige at home and abroad.
   (3) The movement of settlers westward after the Louisiana Purchase raised hostilities between white men and the Indians.
   (4) Jefferson's authorization of the Louisiana Purchase established the idea that a president has powers not stated directly in the Constitution.
   (5) The Louisiana Purchase enabled the U.S. to buy all of the territory to the Pacific Ocean.

ANSWERS ARE ON PAGE 304.

THE WAR OF 1812

KEY WORD

nationalism—pride in one's country, especially the elevation of one nation or group of people above all others

---

Had the Americans been successful in the War of 1812, Canada would now be part of the U.S. The takeover of Canada was a major aim of the American forces once they had decided to declare war against Great Britain. The War of 1812 was declared, in part, because the Americans blamed their motherland for interfering with trade with other nations and for inciting Indian uprisings in the West. In addition, there was proof of the British forcing American men into the British navy during the Napoleonic Wars.

Tecumseh, chief of the Shawnee Indian tribe, along with his brother Tenskwatawa, had worked tirelessly in the early 1800s to unite the North American Indians in a confederation against white customs, dress, products, and land encroachment. During the War of 1812, Tecumseh and his followers joined forces with the British. It was the great Indian warrior's death in this war that marked the end of the united Indian resistance in most of the Midwest and South of the United States.

Despite the fact that the U.S. did not really win this war, impressment of American men had stopped, the Indian/British alliance had been undone, and the U.S. dependence on Europe was broken. A new sense of nationalism soon developed as America entered the Era of Good Feelings and turned its focus inward.

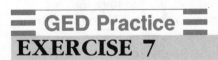

GED Practice
EXERCISE 7

For questions 1–4, choose the statement that best answers each question.

1. Which of the following British actions of which the colonists had proof contributed to America's declaration of war in 1812?

(1) the passage of the Townshend Acts
(2) the forcing of American seamen to join the British navy
(3) the British attempt to regain control of the former thirteen colonies
(4) Britain's attempt to gain control over Canada
(5) Britain's responsibility for America's economic depression

2. Which event that occurred during the War of 1812 had the most direct effect on its outcome?

(1) the takeover of Canada
(2) the impressment of American men into the British navy
(3) the death of the British ally Tecumseh
(4) the economic depression in the American West
(5) the incitement of Indian uprisings

3. Which of the following accounts for America's new sense of independence from Europe after the War of 1812?

  (1) The war had forced the U.S. to learn to do without Europe's economic and political help.

  (2) The end of the war had brought peace between the white settlers in the U.S. and the Indians.

  (3) The war proved that the American military could win a war against a larger, more experienced army.

  (4) The Treaty of Ghent that ended the war gave the U.S. its legal freedom from British rule.

  (5) Europeans shunned the U.S. after the war and forced Americans to depend on themselves for their needs.

4. Which of the following is a hypothesis that *can't* be proved?

  (1) Great Britain forced American men into its navy.

  (2) Tecumseh and his forces aligned with the British against America.

  (3) If the United States had won the War of 1812, Canada would be part of our nation today.

  (4) Great Britain is considered to have won the War of 1812.

  (5) The United States became less dependent on Europe.

ANSWERS ARE ON PAGE 304.

THE MONROE DOCTRINE

> ### KEY WORDS
>
> *colonization*—the act of establishing colonies
> *Monroe Doctrine*—a statement of U.S. foreign policy that prohibits foreign intervention in the Western Hemisphere

The feelings of nationalism that arose at the end of the War of 1812 were heightened by a "hands-off" policy initiated in 1823 by President James Monroe. The Monroe Doctrine announced to the world that the U.S. would no longer tolerate European intervention or colonization in the Americas and that the U.S. would not interfere in any political affairs in Europe. It was issued to further America's security from foreign governments. Monroe believed that if European countries continued to seek colonial power, and if Russia tried to extend its boundaries in North America, the safety of the United States would be threatened.

The map on page 104 illustrates the boundaries on which the Monroe Doctrine was based.

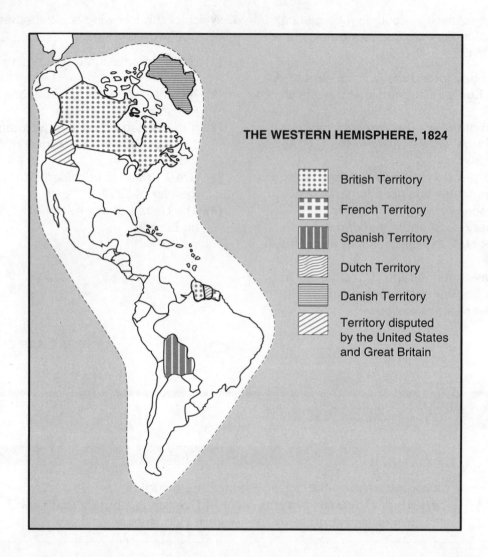

THE WESTERN HEMISPHERE, 1824

British Territory

French Territory

Spanish Territory

Dutch Territory

Danish Territory

Territory disputed by the United States and Great Britain

EXERCISE 8

Directions: Place a check mark before each situation below that represents an attempt to enforce the principles of the Monroe Doctrine.

_____ **(1)** the dispatch of American soldiers to Grenada in the Caribbean to protect American citizens during an internal conflict

_____ **(2)** the opposition of the United States to Spanish domination of Cuba in the late nineteenth century

_____ **(3)** the sending of arms to Nicaraguan Contras in Central America to fight the Sandinistas who took over the government

_____ **(4)** the American blockade of Cuba to prevent Soviet ships from entering and establishing missile bases

_____ **(5)** the sending of U.S. arms to El Salvador in Central America to fight the rebels who fought against their own government

ANSWERS ARE ON PAGE 304.

TIMES OF INTERNAL STRIFE

SECTIONALISM AND SLAVERY

> ### KEY WORDS
>
> ***abolitionist***—one who strongly favors doing away with slavery
> ***secession***—the breaking away of a part of a country to form its own nation

Though the nation had developed a sense of national pride and identity after the Monroe Doctrine was announced, sectional loyalty throughout the U.S. persisted. The first U.S. president elected to office as a result of these sectional differences was Andrew Jackson, a southerner. Jackson was considered to be a ***populist***, a man who claimed to represent the interests of the common people. He opposed the establishment of a national bank because he feared eastern merchants and industrialists would control it. As the country expanded its borders and its population, resentments grew. New Englanders saw the West as an irresistible lure for the youngest, ablest, and most energetic of their population. The South was offended by the other sections' criticism of its dependence on slavery as a part of its economy and society.

As new territories were added to the U.S., the debate over slavery continued. Southern plantation owners believed that they should be able to run their businesses as they thought best, while some northerners believed slavery was wrong and should not be allowed in the new territories and states. However, these northerners did not believe that slavery should be prohibited from areas where it was already the established practice. It was only the abolitionists who believed slavery was evil and demanded that it be banned throughout the country. Compromises were attempted, but none resulted in a lasting solution to the problem of slavery in the country.

SECESSION AND STATES' RIGHTS

"This government cannot endure, permanently half slave and half free," President Abraham Lincoln proclaimed as he openly campaigned against the spread of slavery into the new territories.

Talk of secession from the Union started among influential southerners and came to a climax when Abraham Lincoln was elected president in 1860.

Almost immediately after the election, South Carolina withdrew from the United States. By February of 1861 six more states—Georgia, Florida, Alabama, Mississippi, Louisiana, and Texas—had also seceded. Jefferson Davis became president of these new Confederate States of America, and Montgomery, Alabama, was chosen as their capital. Soon, four more states—Virginia, Arkansas, North Carolina, and Tennessee—joined the Confederacy, and the capital was moved to Richmond, Virginia.

VOTE ON SECESSION IN THE SOUTH

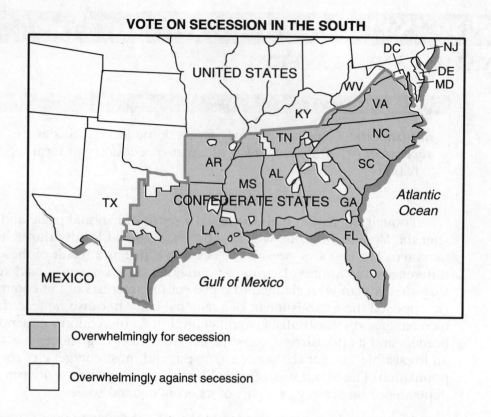

☐ Overwhelmingly for secession

☐ Overwhelmingly against secession

EXERCISE 9

Directions: Refer to the map above. Write the letter of the description on the right that matches the state listed on the left.

_____ **1.** Virginia

_____ **2.** Texas

_____ **3.** Kentucky

_____ **4.** Mississippi

_____ **5.** Maryland

(a) As a "border state," it remained in the Union despite being a slave state.

(b) As a solid southern slave state, this one voted overwhelmingly to secede from the Union.

(c) This state split in two over the issue of secession, with the western part loyal to the Union.

(d) The entire state seceded from the Union despite the fact that only its eastern part voted to do so.

(e) This border state is located too closely to the nation's capital to have been lost to the Confederacy.

ANSWERS ARE ON PAGE 304.

EXERCISE 10

For questions 1 and 2, choose the best answer to each question.

1. Delaware, Maryland, Kentucky, and Missouri were "border states" that remained with the Union in spite of the fact that that they were slave states. Which of President Lincoln's positions at the beginning of the Civil War was most probably influenced by the status of these four states?

   (1) his request that Robert E. Lee become chief strategist for the North
   (2) his reluctance to issue an order for the emancipation of slaves throughout the country
   (3) his call for volunteers for the Union to fight the rebels
   (4) his reluctance to draft young men into military service
   (5) his agreement with Congress to raise taxes to pay for the war effort

2. The Emancipation Proclamation applied only to slaves held in certain designated Confederate states. Which of the following states did it *not* apply to?

   (1) Florida
   (2) Louisiana
   (3) Missouri
   (4) Tennessee
   (5) Arkansas

ANSWERS ARE ON PAGE 304.

BROTHER AGAINST BROTHER

> **KEY WORD**
>
> *emancipate*—to free from bondage

The Union underestimated the Confederacy's zeal even after the South had captured Fort Sumter in South Carolina in April of 1861. Initially, President Lincoln had ordered 75,000 untrained volunteers to stop the "rebellion" of the Confederates.

On July 21, 1861, nearly 28,000 ill-prepared Union soldiers followed by picnic basket–toting spectators marched from the North toward the Confederate capital at Richmond. At Bull Run, Virginia, they met with nearly 33,000 equally unskilled Confederate soldiers. After five hours, 2,900 Union soldiers were dead, wounded, captured, or missing and 2,000 Confederate casualties were recorded.

After this confrontation, the status of the conflict changed from a rebellion to a civil war. The war lasted four years—four years of state fighting against state, friend fighting against friend, and often brother fighting against brother.

The South had a greater familiarity with battle sites, a burning desire to win, and strong leadership from outstanding generals like Robert E. Lee, a graduate of West Point and former officer in the U.S. Army. His superior military ability, however, was overcome by the Union's larger population, its abundance of natural resources, and its excellent transportation system.

In 1862, President Lincoln issued the Emancipation Proclamation. The document ordered the freeing of all slaves in certain designated areas of the Confederate states. As a result of this proclamation, the Union Army's ranks were swelled by 180,000 former slaves who fought against the Confederacy.

In 1863, Congress approved a law to begin drafting males into the military to maintain its ranks. Although riots broke out in protest, the North overcame this and other setbacks.

Women stepped into many work settings as the army took the men away to fight. Expenses for the war effort were financed through war bonds, taxes, duties on imports, and the printing of paper money. A network of government agencies was established to support the Union Army, and private industry changed and grew to meet the demands of these new agencies.

In the South, however, changes were not as quick or as successful. Since there were not as many businesses and industries, selling bonds and taxing profits were not as rewarding as in the North.

Cotton and tobacco farming were the big industries of the South, and they required lots of land and manpower. Because these crops were not as important to the war effort as food was, the region's two biggest industries were nearly abandoned. The southern economy ground to a halt because the slaves who had not left to join the Union army refused to work. As the men went off to fight, the women took over the plantations. These conditions contributed to the end of the institution that had built the South.

Confederate general Robert E. Lee surrendered to Union general Ulysses S. Grant at Appomattox Court House, Virginia, on April 9, 1865. By this time, the people of the South were bitter and alienated. The severe difficulties and changes they had experienced made readmission into the Union difficult.

EXERCISE 11

Directions: In the spaces below, write *N* if the description applies to the North, *S* if it applies to the South, and *B* if it applies to both based on the passage above.

_____ **1.** greater population

_____ **2.** outstanding field generals

_____ **3.** burning desire to win

_____ **4.** abundance of natural resources

_____ **5.** cash crops abandoned in favor of food crops

_____ **6.** better transportation network

_____ **7.** forces boosted by Emancipation Proclamation

_____ **8.** women assumed bigger role as men went to war

_____ **9.** war debt financed in creative ways

_____ **10.** greater familiarity with battle sites

ANSWERS ARE ON PAGE 304.

GED Practice
EXERCISE 12

Question 1 is based on the information on page 108.

1. The effect of the Emancipation Proclamation on the outcome of the war was that

   (1) the South gained a reliable source of soldiers in the freed slaves
   (2) the border states that held slaves joined the Confederacy
   (3) it officially ended the war, since the question of slavery was no longer an issue
   (4) it made President Lincoln one of the most unpopular presidents in American history
   (5) it gave the Union a military advantage, since many former slaves fought on the side of the North

Questions 2 and 3 are based on this quote.

"It is clear enough that the Civil War was a watershed experience for America. . . . To understand that part of our past we need to understand the present, because today we are grappling with the commitment that was made for us a century ago. The ultimate meaning of that war depends on what we do now. We are still involved in it. When we move to make a living reality out of the great ideal of the equality of all Americans; when we take our stand anywhere in the world for freedom, and for just dealing between all races and conditions of man; when we work for an enduring unity among human beings, whether at home or abroad—when we do any of these things we are simply trying to meet the obligation that was laid upon us a century ago at a price higher than any other price we ever paid."

—Bruce Catton, Civil War historian

2. Based on the quote, it is likely that Bruce Catton would support the actions of which group in recent years?

   (1) the Ku Klux Klan of the fifties
   (2) the civil rights workers of the sixties
   (3) the anti-ERA demonstrators of the seventies
   (4) the Vietnam War protestors of the seventies
   (5) the antiabortionists of the eighties

3. It is the opinion of Bruce Catton that

   (1) the Civil War was the most important event in U.S. history
   (2) the Civil War experience obligates us to promote freedom throughout the world
   (3) the cost of the Civil War in lives and money was too high
   (4) the Civil War could and should have been avoided
   (5) writing about the Civil War is his obligation

_____

4. The Civil War forced women to become equal partners in the work force. What other event in U.S. history led to a similar adaptation?

   (1) the Vietnam War
   (2) World War II
   (3) the Great Depression
   (4) the Women's Suffragist Movement
   (5) Prohibition

ANSWERS ARE ON PAGE 305.

RECONSTRUCTION AND HEALING

KEY WORDS

carpetbaggers—northerners who moved to the South during Reconstruction to take advantage of business and political opportunities

impeachment—the bringing of charges against a public official for misconduct

Reconstruction—the reestablishment of the Confederate states as part of the Union after the Civil War

scalawags—white southerners who supported the efforts of the North in rebuilding the South

After the Civil War, the South was faced with the difficult task of picking up the pieces and rebuilding. Strangers from the North who moved to the South to work in business and politics were called carpetbaggers by the southerners. They were despised by the former Confederates, who believed that these men came to exploit the region and its citizens. Even more hated were the scalawags, southern citizens who were perceived as helping the carpetbaggers.

The Freedmen's Bureau was set up in 1865 to provide food, schooling, and work for many former slaves and poor whites. The same year, Lincoln announced his "Ten Percent Plan," by which Confederates could become U.S. citizens again by taking an oath of loyalty to the Union. States could reenter once 10 percent of their citizens had taken the oath. One month later, however, Abraham Lincoln was assassinated by a Confederate sympathizer.

Vice President Andrew Johnson succeeded Lincoln as president. Johnson, a Tennessean, was the only southern senator not to join the Confederacy. Although Lincoln had trusted him, many in Congress believed him to be pro-South.

In 1867, Congress authorized federal army generals to head the policing of the South, which was divided into five military districts. It then demanded that the states set up new constitutions that would give blacks the right to vote and to hold office.

The same year, Congress passed the Tenure of Office Act to protect a certain member of Johnson's cabinet from being fired for agreeing with Congress's ideas on Reconstruction. When Johnson dismissed the cabinet member, Congress reacted by voting to impeach the president. Johnson, thus, was the first president to be impeached. He was acquitted by just one vote.

In 1868, Ulysses S. Grant was elected president, and in 1870 the Fifteenth Amendment guaranteed the right to vote to blacks and former slaves. It is viewed by many as a great victory for civil rights in general and Radical Reconstruction in particular.

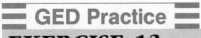
EXERCISE 13

Questions 1–3 refer to the following definitions.

Thirteenth Amendment—abolished slavery

Fourteenth Amendment—gave full citizenship to freed slaves

Fifteenth Amendment—guaranteed voting rights to all races

Freedmen's Bureau Act—provided food, education, and work in the reconstructed South

Ten Percent Plan—proposed a plan by which confederate states could reenter the Union

1. Which is sometimes regarded as the authorization for the nation's first federal welfare system?

    (1) the Thirteenth Amendment
    (2) the Fourteenth Amendment
    (3) the Fifteenth Amendment
    (4) the Freedmen's Bureau Act
    (5) the Ten Percent Plan

2. Which of the following is used as the basis for abolishing discrimination in voting requirements?

    (1) the Thirteenth Amendment
    (2) the Fourteenth Amendment
    (3) the Fifteenth Amendment
    (4) the Freedmen's Bureau Act
    (5) the Ten Percent Plan

3. Which of the following was a direct result of the Emancipation Proclamation?

    (1) the Thirteenth Amendment
    (2) the Fourteenth Amendment
    (3) the Fifteenth Amendment
    (4) the Freedman's Bureau Act
    (5) the Ten Percent Plan

ANSWERS ARE ON PAGE 305.

THE RISE OF INDUSTRIAL AMERICA

THE INDUSTRIAL REVOLUTION

> **KEY WORD**
>
> ***industrial revolution***—the change in the economy from a manual means of production to a mechanical one

The U.S. emerged from the Civil War only to experience another major upheaval in the nation's way of life. America and the rest of the Western world entered an industrial revolution in which the economy relied less on animal power and more on machinery to produce goods.

As industries were founded, cities grew up around them. Mechanization of farming jobs caused some people to lose their jobs and move from farm to town. However, more commonly, the potential to earn more money and obtain modern conveniences lured workers to the cities. Jobs in industry paid much higher wages than farmhand work, and these wages bought luxuries never before dreamed of on the farm. The maps on page 112 illustrate the amazing growth of American cities over a short thirty-year period.

GED Practice
EXERCISE 14

For questions 1 and 2, choose the best answer for each statement or question.

1. Eli Whitney's idea of using interchangeable parts for mass production was important to the industrial revolution because

   (1) it encouraged the invention of products that would have been impossible before
   (2) guns could be produced on a larger scale than before
   (3) purchasers of products could then assemble them themselves
   (4) the quality of workmanship was no longer as important
   (5) many industries took advantage of its application to the factory system

2. By 1899, the U.S. had more miles of railroad than all of Europe and Russia combined. By the same year, the U.S. had been recognized as the industrial leader of the world. Which of the following implications may be drawn from this fact?

   (1) The railroad was a symbol of power and prestige.
   (2) The railroad system became the biggest industry in the U.S.
   (3) Industrialization is not possible without a large railroad system.
   (4) Industrialization depends on factories for mass production of goods.
   (5) Dependable transportation is a key to the mass production and sale of goods.

For questions 3 and 4, refer to the maps below.

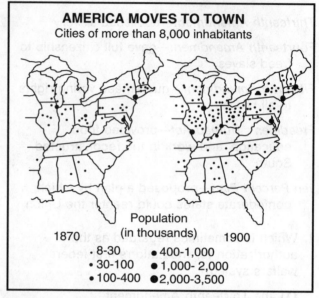

AMERICA MOVES TO TOWN
Cities of more than 8,000 inhabitants

1870   Population (in thousands)   1900

• 8-30   ● 400-1,000
• 30-100   ● 1,000- 2,000
• 100-400   ● 2,000-3,500

3. With regard to the period 1870–1900, which of the following statements is supported by the data provided in the maps and in the paragraphs on page 111?

   (1) The U.S. experienced the loss of much of its farming areas.
   (2) There was more industry in the northern states than in the southern states.
   (3) There was a great influx of immigrants to the U.S.
   (4) There was a population loss in many areas.
   (5) There was a bigger move to the South than in any other direction.

4. From the maps it appears that industries and the big cities that grew up around them were usually established near

   (1) the middle of the country
   (2) national boundaries
   (3) mountains and hills
   (4) bodies of water
   (5) farming areas

ANSWERS ARE ON PAGE 305.

GROWTH OF BIG BUSINESS

> **KEY WORDS**
>
> **laissez-faire**—a government policy of noninterference in the affairs of business
>
> **urbanization**—the shift of population from the country to the city

In this climate of rapid expansion, big business grew without restrictions. The U.S. government observed a policy of laissez-faire, or "letting business alone" to do what it knows best. This policy often resulted in economic and social abuse as power became concentrated in the hands of a few.

Consolidation became a key to big business and industrial growth and power. Such men as Andrew Carnegie (Carnegie Steel), J. P. Morgan (U.S. Steel), and John D. Rockefeller (Standard Oil) created industrial empires through takeovers and trusts. These men became known as **robber barons** because of their unscrupulous business practices.

Several of these newly rich businessmen justified their prosperity as the result of "survival of the fittest," termed social Darwinism. Social Darwinism held that the rich were richer because they were smarter than the poor.

As industrialization expanded, more and more people were lured to the cities, a process that became known as urbanization. The cities and factories became overcrowded and unhealthy. However, the social Darwinists held that those conditions were due to the inferiority of the poor and not due to their exploitation by the wealthy factory owners.

EXERCISE 15

Directions: Place a check mark before each of the following actions that represents economic activity without government intervention.

_____ **(1)** Major airlines engage in a price war, setting competitive prices for air fares.

_____ **(2)** A state does not have a usury law, a law that sets the maximum interest rate that can be legally charged for a loan.

_____ **(3)** A government commission determines the maximum wage increases for certain jobs.

_____ **(4)** Kansas wheat farmers are paid by Washington not to grow wheat on certain tracts of land.

_____ **(5)** Banks charge whatever rate of interest the market will bear on passbook savings accounts.

ANSWERS ARE ON PAGE 305.

EXERCISE 16

Questions 1 and 2 are based on the information on page 113.

1. Which of the following is a conclusion that is supported by the information?

   (1) Sociologists do not understand business theories.
   (2) Big business grew in the U.S. at the expense of the welfare of the public.
   (3) Governments should not try to regulate private business.
   (4) Only the best businessmen survived industrialization in the U.S.
   (5) Congressmen received special favors to sponsor legislation favorable to big business.

2. Why were Carnegie, Morgan, and Rockefeller referred to as robber barons?

   (1) They stole from the rich to improve the working and living conditions of the poor.
   (2) They bought out their competitors, fixed prices, and made millions of dollars through unfair business practices.
   (3) They each bought their companies at bargain prices.
   (4) They were among the richest men in America at that time.
   (5) They controlled the lion's share of big business during their lifetimes.

ANSWERS ARE ON PAGE 305.

THE "NEW AMERICANS"

The chance to escape oppressive conditions in their homeland lured an unprecedented number of immigrants to America in the late 1800s. These new immigrants from eastern and southern Europe were different from their predecessors. The Italians, Austrians, Hungarians, Poles, Serbs, and Russians were Catholic or Jewish rather than Protestant. Their customs and ways of life were foreign to naturalized Americans, and, as a result, prejudice based on the immigrants' ethnic background became a problem.

This great influx of immigrants gravitated toward the cities where the jobs were, presenting new problems for the young nation. In 1890, half of New York City's population lived in tenement houses. Open drainage gutters polluted water supplies with human and industrial sewage. Working conditions worsened as owners put more money into modern machinery and invested less in comfort and safety measures for the employees. At the same time, the "new Americans" competed with established Americans for jobs, a competition that caused increasing friction in the workplace.

EXERCISE 17

Questions 1–3 are based on the following bar graph.

SOURCES OF IMMIGRATION TO THE U.S., 1871-1910

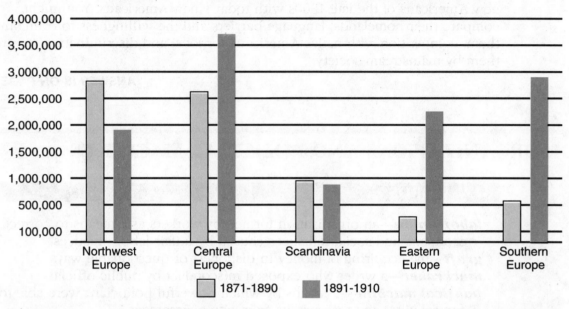

1871-1890   1891-1910

1. According to the bar graph, the trend at the beginning of the twentieth century was for immigrants to the U.S. to come here

   (1) in much fewer numbers than during the 1870s and 1880s
   (2) in about the same numbers as during the 1870s and 1880s
   (3) from eastern, central, and southern Europe in greater numbers than twenty years earlier
   (4) from northwest and central Europe in greater numbers than twenty years earlier
   (5) from northwest and central Europe more so than from eastern and southern Europe

2. Of the regions listed below, which one experienced the greatest reduction in the numbers of immigrants coming to the U.S.?

   (1) Scandinavia
   (2) Central Europe
   (3) Northwest Europe
   (4) Eastern Europe
   (5) Southern Europe

3. Which region *not* represented on the graph is the source of the largest number of immigrants to the United States today?

   (1) Northern Africa
   (2) Western Europe
   (3) Southeast Asia
   (4) South America
   (5) Australia

ANSWERS ARE ON PAGE 305.

WRITING ACTIVITY 3

How do today's new Americans compare to the new Americans of the nineteenth century? Do we naturalized Americans accept immigrants more readily than did our ancestors? Write two or three paragraphs comparing these new Americans of the late 1800s with today's new Americans. You might compare their homelands, language barriers and the willingness to overcome them, competition with native Americans for jobs, and discrimination toward them by mainstream society.

ANSWER IS ON PAGE 306.

LABOR ORGANIZATIONS AND POLITICAL MACHINES

> ### KEY WORDS
>
> ***labor union***—an organization formed by workers as a means to correct economic and social injustices caused by unfair labor practices
> ***graft***—the acquiring of money in dishonest or questionable ways
> ***muckraker***—a writer who exposed misconduct by public officials
> ***political machine***—a means by which powerful politicians were able to control votes and reap profits from city government

Friction also surfaced between the employers and the employed. Workers formed labor unions as a means to fight unfair employer practices. One of the first was the Noble and Holy Order of the Knights of Labor, founded in 1869.

In 1881, the American Federation of Labor (AFL) was founded to represent skilled workers who were organized by specific crafts. These workers readily acknowledged the need for strikes and boycotts. By 1904 there were over a million laborers in the AFL under the leadership of Samuel Gompers.

Efforts to organize workers and labor disputes often resulted in violence. One of the most famous was the Haymarket Square riot in Chicago in 1886 in which seven policemen and ten workers were killed and 117 people were hurt.

Another phenomenon that grew out of the industrialization of the cities was the political machine. "Political bosses," controllers of machines, commonly offered jobs for votes. Many of these politicians came from the ranks of the immigrants and sought to help their brethren even as they profited from them.

The most notorious of the city bosses was Boss Tweed of New York. Boss Tweed was often caricatured by the famous political cartoonist Thomas Nast. Nast and other political writers were called muckrakers because of their ability to scrape up dirt about political corruption. These writers helped to formulate the attitudes and methods of the middle-class reformers of what came to be known as the Progressive Era in U.S. politics.

EXERCISE 18

Questions 1–3 are based on the following information and quote.

The quote below is from George Washington Plunkitt, who was a ward boss for the corrupt political machine in New York City known as Tammany Hall.

"Everybody is talkin' these days about Tammany men growin' rich on graft, but nobody thinks of drawin' the distinction between honest graft and dishonest graft. There's all the difference in the world between the two. Yes, many of our men have grown rich in politics. I have myself. I've made a big fortune out of the game, and I'm gettin' richer every day, but I've not gone in for dishonest graft—blackmailin' gamblers, saloonkeepers, disorderly people, etc.—and neither has any of the men who have made big fortunes in politics.

"There's an honest graft, and I'm an example of how it works. I might sum up the whole thing by sayin': 'I seen my opportunities and I took 'em.'

"Just let me explain by examples. My party's in power in the city, and it's goin' to undertake a lot of public improvements. Well, I'm tipped off, say, that they're going to lay out a new park at a certain place.

"I see my opportunity and I take it. I go to that place and I buy up all the land I can in the neighborhood. Then the board of this or that makes its plans public, and there is a rush to get my land, which nobody cared particular for before.

"Ain't it perfectly honest to charge a good price and make a profit on my investment and foresight? Of course it is. Well, that's honest graft."

—from *Plunkitt of Tammany Hall*

1. Which of the following judgments could be made based on the passage?

    (1) There is a real difference between "honest" and "dishonest" graft.
    (2) Taking advantage of an opportunity is not the same as graft.
    (3) Graft is the "American way" in big-city politics.
    (4) He who does not take advantage of an opportunity is a fool.
    (5) Political bosses appeared to have no sense of right and wrong.

2. Another name for "honest" graft as described by George Washington Plunkitt might be

    (1) accepting bribes
    (2) appointing friends and relatives to political office
    (3) demanding payoffs from gamblers
    (4) profiting from inside information on government purchases
    (5) blackmailing tavernkeepers

3. Which of the following does Plunkitt describe as "dishonest" graft?

    (1) rushing to buy land that will soon become valuable
    (2) listening to tip-offs about public improvements
    (3) making a fortune by gambling
    (4) backmailing tavern owners
    (5) grabbing political power and becoming rich

ANSWERS ARE ON PAGE 306.

PROGRESSIVE REFORM

KEY WORDS

progressivism—a reform movement demanding governmental involvement to bring about economic and political improvements for the poor and disadvantaged

capital—money, machinery, or any other resource used to produce goods

---

In response to the abuses that resulted from rapid industrialization and urbanization, the Progressive Era flourished during the first fifteen years of the twentieth century. The goal of this reform movement was to stamp out political corruption and improve the quality of life for Americans.

President Theodore Roosevelt was considered the embodiment of Progressive reform. Only forty-two when he became president, he brought energy and adventure to the office. He used the implied powers of the presidency to establish our national policy of conserving the nation's natural resources.

During the Progressive Era, the government abandoned its laissez-faire policy of noninterference in the affairs of business and produced legislative reforms that have an impact on Americans today. Some of these reforms are highlighted in the following chart:

PROGRESSIVE REFORMS

The Sherman Anti-Trust Act, which outlawed monopolies

The Hepburn Act, which gave the Interstate Commerce Commission increased authority to regulate the nation's railroads

The Pure Food and Drug Act, which set standards for the production and sale of foods and drugs

The U.S.D.A. (United States Department of Agriculture), which was authorized to inspect meat

Child labor laws, which prohibited child labor

Many well-known journalists wrote about the corruption and poverty that rapid industrialization had caused. They were also known as muckrakers because they attacked these conditions in their columns and books. Among these writers were Lincoln Steffens, Edward Bellamy, Jane Addams, Jacob Riis, and Upton Sinclair. In his book *The Jungle*, Sinclair exposed the unhealthy conditions in the meat-packing industry and is credited with helping to get the Pure Food and Drug Act passed.

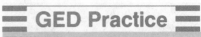
EXERCISE 19

Questions 1–5 refer to the following passage.

In 1890, the journalist Jacob Riis published a book titled *How the Other Half Lives,* which contained photographs and detailed descriptions of the deplorable life in New York's tenement district. About this problem Riis wrote: "The remedy that shall be an effective answer to the coming appeal for justice must proceed from the public conscience. Neither legislation nor charity can cover the ground. The greed of capital that wrought the evil must undo it, as far as it can now be undone."

1. According to Riis, New York's tenements in 1890 could *best* be improved by

    (1) enacting new legislation
    (2) appealing to charity
    (3) changing capitalistic greed
    (4) demanding justice
    (5) asking more questions

2. With which of the following positions on today's poverty and discrimination would Riis likely agree?

    (1) Each individual should pull himself up by his own bootstraps.
    (2) Government's funding for social programs should be cut.
    (3) The states themselves must pass legislation to correct the problem.
    (4) A booming, growing economy will automatically solve the problem.
    (5) Private industry is morally responsible for helping to correct social problems.

3. Based on the values expressed in the quote, to which of the groups below would Riis likely have given support?

    (1) New York's "Four Hundred," the self-appointed social elite
    (2) machine politicians who have the power to give jobs
    (3) private citizens who established the cities' settlement houses
    (4) a lobbying group to pass antipoverty legislation
    (5) businessmen who believed in the theory of social Darwinism

4. Which statement *best* summarizes what Progressives believed?

    (1) Big business was part of the solution and not the problem.
    (2) Industry leaders treated workers fairly.
    (3) Governmental and big-business policies needed improvement through legislation.
    (4) Women should not try to compete for men's jobs.
    (5) Industrialization resulted in better living conditions and employment for working-class Americans.

5. Which of the following does *not* adhere to the beliefs of the Progressive Movement?

    (1) decreasing the number of monopolies
    (2) allowing businesses to act without governmental constraint
    (3) demanding fair child-labor laws
    (4) setting standards for production of prescription medicine
    (5) authorizing meat inspection

ANSWERS ARE ON PAGE 306.

THE U.S. AS A WORLD POWER

FROM ISOLATIONISM TO IMPERIALISM

KEY WORDS

imperialism—one nation extending its authority over other territories or nations

isolationism—the policy of noninterference in world affairs

jingoism—extreme nationalism marked by the frequent use of warlike rhetoric

American warships against the Spanish fleet in Santiago, Cuba

Immediately after the Civil War, as the U.S. entered the industrial revolution, the nation pursued a foreign policy of isolationism. America's rapid industrialization, however, soon forced the country to seek foreign markets for its manufactured goods, a cheaper labor supply to produce those goods, and new sources of raw materials. These three goals became accessible as the U.S. moved toward a policy of imperialism.

The new technology of the industrial revolution made many products, including newspapers, more readily available. Newspaper "wars" erupted among publishers. The "yellow press" emerged with exaggerated stories and became popular with the reading public.

When Cuban rebels revolted against Spain's presence on the island, the belligerent "jingo press" played a big part in stirring up anti-Spanish sentiment in the U.S. And, when it was reported that Spain sunk the U.S. battleship *Maine* in Havana Harbor, the U.S. declared war in 1898, handily winning the Spanish-American War four months later. Conceded to the U.S. under the terms of the Treaty of Paris were the territories of Guam, Puerto Rico, and the Philippines. This acquisition, along with President McKinley's annexation of Hawaii, positioned the U.S. well as a world power.

These moves, however, were criticized by anti-imperialists such as Mark Twain, former president Grover Cleveland, and Andrew Carnegie, who believed that the U.S. had no business controlling nations overseas. Defenders of American imperialism maintained not only that it was good for commercial and military reasons but also that it was America's "burden" to bring Christianity to "heathen" lands. The debates between the imperialists and the anti-imperialists that began in the aftermath of the Spanish-American War continue today.

GED Practice

EXERCISE 20

Choose the one best answer for each statement or question below.

1. Which of the following is an example of American imperialist policy?

   (1) sending food and medical assistance to drought-stricken Ethiopia
   (2) the purchase of Alaska from the Czar of Russia in 1867
   (3) blockading Cuba to prevent Soviet ships from entering the Western Hemisphere
   (4) controlling most of the Panama Canal Zone until 1979
   (5) the bombing of Libya in retaliation for terrorist acts

2. President Grover Cleveland refused to annex Hawaii to the U.S. after learning that a majority of the natives preferred being ruled by their queen, Liliuokalani. In making this decision, he was abiding by the the principle of rule by "consent of the governed" put forth by

   (1) the Declaration of Independence
   (2) the Monroe Doctrine
   (3) the Treaty of Ghent
   (4) the Emancipation Proclamation
   (5) the idea of Manifest Destiny

ANSWERS ARE ON PAGE 306.

WORLD WAR I

The rivalry between William Howard Taft and Theodore Roosevelt for president in 1913 helped elect Democrat Woodrow Wilson. One of Wilson's first moves was to pass the Federal Reserve Act in 1913. The law remedied many of the ills in American banking at the time. The Wilson presidency is probably better known, however, for the United States's entrance into World War I.

In Europe, the assassination of Austrian Crown Prince Ferdinand, by a Serbian nationalist, touched off a war between the rival Central Powers, which included Germany and Austria-Hungary, and the Allied Powers—Great Britain, France, and Russia.

The United States tried to remain neutral during the early years of the war but was angered by the German submarine attack on the passenger ship the *Lusitania.* Other threats to U.S. neutrality drew the U.S. into the war. On April 6, 1917, the United States declared war on Germany and joined the Allied Powers.

The U.S. servicemen played a vital role in World War I. They arrived just as the Europeans were tiring on all fronts. As the Allies broke through the German lines, the Germans conceded defeat.

President Wilson capitalized on Europe's exhaustion from four years of war and on November 11, 1918, proposed a "peace without victory." The fourteen-point plan presented at the Paris peace conference was not accepted in its entirety, and the harsher Treaty of Versailles ended the war.

Wilson's attempt to establish a League of Nations to prevent war did succeed. However, isolationist sentiment in the U.S. Congress prevented the U.S. from joining, thus contributing to the organization's decline.

EXERCISE 21

Directions: Place a check mark before the events that directly contributed to the United States' entering the war on the Allied side. You may check more than one.

_____ **(1)** the assassination of the Austrian prince

_____ **(2)** the arrest of the Serbian nationalist

_____ **(3)** the involvement of its old ally, Great Britain

_____ **(4)** Germany's attack on the passenger ship the *Lusitania*

_____ **(5)** threats to U.S. neutrality

ANSWERS ARE ON PAGE 306.

THE ROARING TWENTIES

RETURN TO NORMALCY

> ### KEY WORDS
>
> ***free enterprise***—freedom of private businesses to organize and compete without unnecessary government interference
> ***individualism***—a belief that the interests of the individual should prevail

The United States had just experienced an exhausting world war, and weary Americans overwhelmingly supported President Harding's "return to normalcy."

The twenties were anything but normal, however, as Warren Harding's administration became tainted by the Teapot Dome scandal. This bribery scandal disgraced the Harding Administration and characterized it as one of the nation's most corrupt presidencies.

Under President Calvin Coolidge (Keep Cool with Cal), the country prospered as it never had before. Business efficiency experts, advertising executives, and public relations people replaced the reformers of the Progressive Era as America's spokespersons of the twenties.

In 1929, Herbert Hoover won the presidency on the promise that good times would continue under the Republicans. He praised protective tariffs, Prohibition, individualism, and free enterprise. He won easily over Al Smith, a Catholic and big-city liberal politician, in spite of the fact that Smith polled twice as many votes as had the Democratic candidate in the previous election. It became obvious that changes in attitudes were developing slowly and that the voices of labor, immigrants, and minorities were demanding to be heard. The Democratic party, if it were to be successful, would have to embrace these groups.

Also, during the twenties taxes were cut, especially for the rich, with the belief that the remaining capital would "trickle down" in wages and other benefits to the poorer segments of society. Social programs were similarly cut, again hurting the poor and middle class to the benefit of the wealthy. Agencies that had been established by the Progressives were rendered ineffective by the appointment of antagonistic individuals to lead them.

WRITING ACTIVITY 4

How does today's social and economic climate compare to that of the twenties? Write two or three paragraphs comparing the twenties to the eighties in the areas of tax cuts or social programs. How are the eighties different from the twenties? How are they similar?

ANSWER IS ON PAGE 306.

THE JAZZ AGE AND THE LOST GENERATION

> ### KEY WORD
>
> ***prohibition***—the outlawing of the manufacture, sale, and transportation of alcoholic beverages

The twenties could not be described as "normal" in other areas as well. It was an era marked by the glorification of youth. Young men and women thumbed their noses at conventional American behavior. This defiance of accepted behavior was expressed frequently in dance and music. Jazz emerged as the medium that best expressed this youth worship and alienation from the larger society.

Prohibition, which took effect in 1920, was largely ignored as speakeasies offered illegal liquor along with freewheeling fun. Many were run by members of organized crime who trafficked in drugs as well as prostitution.

In reaction to what many of them considered to be smugness and an emphasis on the material in American life, American writers such as Ernest Hemingway and F. Scott Fitzgerald retreated to Paris and became members of the "lost generation."

F. Scott Fitzgerald

Ernest Hemingway

EXERCISE 22

Directions: Read the passage about one writer's opinion of the Jazz Age. Then check off the statements listed below that reflect assumptions by the writer of the piece.

A new breed of Americans is emerging in our cities. Were I not so frightened by this phenomenon, I might be amused.

1920s "flappers"

Young people are throwing all caution to the wind; their only interest seems to be outdoing one another in outlandish behavior, dress, and dance. The so-called "flappers"—women whose outrageous antics exceed the men's—are the worst offenders.

"Jazz" seems to be the "music" for this younger generation, and it certainly expresses a disdain for American conventions. It is sensuous, spontaneous, and startling. Some are blaming it for an increase in sexual promiscuity, an increase in divorce rates, and a breakup of families.

In reaction to this obvious breakdown in the American moral fabric, our best writers are retreating to Paris to escape their social responsibility for decrying this ugly aspect of American life. As if the Jazz Age's scornful sneering at American ideals were not enough, we are being deprived of our most imaginative minds when we need them the most.

_____ **(1)** The "lost generation" could have reversed the negative effects of the Jazz Age if it had chosen to do so.

_____ **(2)** Their art was more important to the "lost generation" than concern about its country's moral climate.

_____ **(3)** American society was benefited when young artists and writers flocked to Paris.

_____ **(4)** Young people's striving for individuality and self-expression is a positive sign for our society.

_____ **(5)** Writers have a social responsibility that outweighs their responsibility to themselves as creative artists.

ANSWERS ARE ON PAGE 307.

THE CRASH AND RESULTING DEPRESSION

> ### KEY WORDS
>
> ***speculation***—buying or selling with the expectation of profiting from a change in market conditions
>
> ***conservatism***—the belief that the existing order should be maintained and that any change should be gradual
>
> ***depression***—a low period of economic activity marked by high unemployment

"I have no fears for the future of our country. It is bright with hope." These were the words of Herbert Hoover at his inauguration in 1929. But a decade of tax breaks for the rich, antagonism toward labor unions, high protective tariffs, and laissez-faire policies intensified the problems developing in the stock market.

Speculative buying had reached sky-high limits, and much of it had been financed by loans. When the banks called the loans in, the borrowers could not pay. The prices of stocks fell rapidly. Though the stock market had wavered for two months, no one was prepared for the frenzied selling of October 23, 1929.

President Hoover's conservative policies did not help. His policy of noninterference in business affairs would not allow the drastic measures the country needed.

Investments fell at a staggering level. Banks closed their doors to shut out customers demanding their money.

The number of unemployed workers rose from 4 million in 1930 to 11 million in 1932. Depression was an apt word for the country's economic condition, for it described not only the financial situation but also the mood of the country.

 **GED Practice**

EXERCISE 23

The following questions refer to the above information.

1. Based on the preceding reading, which of the following was *not* a cause of the Great Depression?

   (1) the enforcement of high protective tariffs
   (2) speculative buying financed by loans
   (3) Hoover's pursuit of conservative policies
   (4) the unemployment of 11 million workers by 1932
   (5) the steep decline in investments

2. Which of the following presidents was most similar to Herbert Hoover in his enactment of governmental policies?

   (1) Jimmy Carter
   (2) Bill Clinton
   (3) Ronald Reagan
   (4) Franklin Roosevelt
   (5) John Kennedy

ANSWERS ARE ON PAGE 307.

THE THIRTIES AND FORTIES

THE NEW DEAL

The election of 1932 gave the Democrats the chance to come back, and they did so in full force. Elected president in 1932, Franklin Delano Roosevelt promised Americans a "New Deal." Four days after his inauguration in March 1933, he presented a draft of banking legislation that passed the Senate and House in just eight hours.

Within his first hundred days in office, Roosevelt used his executive authority to get Congress to approve an unprecedented number of bills to deal with the nation's economic crisis. Roosevelt's legislation created an "alphabet soup" of agencies, many of which remain part of the federal government today.

Frequently criticized for abuse of his executive powers, Roosevelt, through his actions, reversed the economic and emotional climate of the country. Voters showed their approval by reelecting the president by the largest margin (up to that time) in U.S. history.

During Roosevelt's second term, the nation's priorities shifted away from New Deal politics to the brewing trouble in Europe. The social revolution of the New Deal, however, had altered the lives of Americans in every corner of the nation.

 **GED Practice**

EXERCISE 24

Read the passage and answer the questions that follow.

Early in his presidency, Ronald Reagan was frequently compared to former president Franklin D. Roosevelt. In the passage below, the writer discusses both men.

During the presidential campaign of 1980, Ronald Reagan lauded Franklin Delano Roosevelt as his political hero. On the face of it, this fact is hard to believe, given the sharp political differences between the two.

President Roosevelt, a liberal Democrat, founded the social security system to provide a worry-free retirement for the nation's elderly. President Reagan, a conservative Republican, was criticized for trying to weaken the program. President Roosevelt's New Deal legislation provided for the regulation of banks and other financial institutions; under the Reagan administration these institutions were greatly deregulated. President Roosevelt's administration set the minimum wage law; President Reagan's administration favored changing it. Labor organizations were encouraged under the Roosevelt administration and thrived; labor organizations were weakened and threatened under the Reagan administration.

Despite these differences, there are striking similarities between the two men. Roosevelt, an extremely popular leader, became president in the midst of economic despair. Reagan, an equally popular leader, became president when the country was suffering from a malaise and economic problems. Roosevelt was a persuasive politician and a strong communicator; Reagan's nickname is the "Great Communicator" because of his skill in handling the media. Both men were reelected to the presidency after huge landslides. The legislation of the New Deal affected the lives of many Americans, and we now see that the "Reagan Revolution" has had a profound effect on the lives of many Americans.

Roosevelt, a man from a wealthy background who became a champion of the "little people," is considered one of America's few great presidents. Will Ronald Reagan, a man from a modest background who became the "champion of big business," be accorded the same honor throughout history? Opinions are sharply divided.

1. The purpose of the passage is to

   (1) show how President Reagan and Roosevelt are alike
   (2) show how Reagan and Roosevelt are different
   (3) compare and contrast two modern American presidents
   (4) prove that history repeats itself
   (5) persuade the reader that Reagan was a better president than Roosevelt

2. The author expresses the opinion that

   (1) it is mere coincidence that Reagan's rise to power parallels Roosevelt's
   (2) Reagan and Roosevelt have less in common than most people think
   (3) Roosevelt was a better president than Reagan was
   (4) Reagan deliberately patterned his presidency after Roosevelt's
   (5) the verdict is still out on Reagan's stature as president

3. From the passage it is obvious that the author is

   (1) impartial
   (2) an admirer of Roosevelt's policies
   (3) an admirer of Reagan's policies
   (4) a critic of Roosevelt's personal style
   (5) a critic of Reagan's personal style

ANSWERS ARE ON PAGE 307.

WRITING ACTIVITY 5

Why did the American people choose two such different men for president in times of national hardship? Choose either Franklin Roosevelt or Ronald Reagan and write two or three paragraphs telling why you think that individual appealed to American voters.

ANSWER IS ON PAGE 307.

WORLD WAR II

A month before FDR's second inauguration, Adolf Hitler, chancellor of Germany, was on a collision course with Britain and France as he sought to expand his power in western Europe.

Japan, too, displayed military aggression, especially toward China. Elsewhere in Europe, Spain was experiencing a bloody civil war, and Italy had invaded Ethiopia.

The U.S. attempted to remain neutral, but Roosevelt knew that the nation could not remain neutral forever.

By 1940, Italy and Germany had joined forces as the Axis powers in an effort to control the rest of the continent.

The Pacific was anything but peaceful during this time. The Chinese government, under Chiang Kai-shek, had been resisting the Japanese invasion. By 1941, the U.S. imposed an embargo on essential materials for Japan and entered into negotiations to avoid armed conflict. Later in the same year, Japan, now an Axis power, intensified its invasion of Indochina and on December 7, 1941, bombed American bases at Pearl Harbor. The U.S. declared war, joining the Allied forces, which included Great Britain, France, and the Soviet Union. The Allied forces made the decision to stop Hitler in Europe before dealing with Japan in the Pacific.

On June 6, 1944, the Allies landed on the beaches of Normandy, France, and soon spread throughout the country. In August, Paris was liberated from German control, and in September the Allied Powers crossed the German border, eventually forcing Germany's surrender.

The Allies turned their attention to the Pacific. By this time, Japan had captured Guam, Wake Island, Hong Kong, Singapore, Indonesia, and the Philippines in addition to maintaining its stronghold in China.

The Pacific was primarily an American concern and therefore an American responsibility. Japan's defenses lay chiefly in its numerous fortified islands. American General Douglas MacArthur devised a plan to weaken Japan's defense by "leapfrogging," or attacking selected islands. Weakened by these attacks, Japan was warned to surrender. Japan's failure to respond quickly was taken as a refusal. In an unprecedented action, Harry S Truman, Roosevelt's successor, gave the go-ahead to drop the atomic bomb on the city of Hiroshima. It devastated the city, killing almost 80,000 people. The aftereffects of nuclear warfare were just beginning to become fully measurable when a second bomb was dropped at Nagasaki. On September 2, 1945, Japan surrendered.

As a result of World War II, the United Nations was formed. The purpose of the organization is to arbitrate international disputes in an effort to maintain world peace.

EXERCISE 25

Directions: Write *T* in the space if the statement is true, *F* if it is false.

_____ **1.** Territorial aggression by the Axis powers was the leading cause of World War II.

_____ **2.** The Axis powers were Great Britain, France, and the U.S.

_____ **3.** Japan's bombing of Pearl Harbor ended the United States's neutrality.

_____ **4.** The U.S. did not use negotiation to avoid war with Japan.

_____ **5.** The United Nations is a league of nations determined to defend its members in the face of war.

ANSWERS ARE ON PAGE 307.

GED Practice
EXERCISE 26

Questions 1–3 are based on the following passage.

"The SS had given the order to destroy us and burn the camp. April 11, 1945: We were to be shot at 3 P.M.; the British arrived at 11 A.M."

The writer of these words, Fania Fenelon, was a survivor of the German concentration camp at Auschwitz-Birkenau. She was one of the lucky European Jews of World War II. Six million others were slaughtered by the Nazis for no other reason than that they were Jewish and thus considered to be racially inferior to Germans. The dimensions of this Holocaust were not fully understood until after the invasion of Germany by the Allied forces. The shock waves caused by such a revelation of man's inhumanity to man are still being felt today.

1. The above passage describes which belief of the Germans taken to the extreme?

    (1) isolationism
    (2) imperialism
    (3) progressivism
    (4) jingoism
    (5) racism

2. The author of this piece exhibits which of the following?

    (1) racism
    (2) humanitarianism
    (3) nationalism
    (4) sectionalism
    (5) materialism

3. According to the passage, the author's life was spared because of

    (1) sudden SS intervention
    (2) the fact that she was not German
    (3) the timely arrival of the British
    (4) a Nazi officer's sympathy toward her
    (5) shock about former Holocaust murders

Questions 4–6 are based on the brief passage below.

Two days after Japan attacked Pearl Harbor, FDR made the following statement: "In the past few years and most violently in the past few days, we have learned a terrible lesson. We must begin the great task that is before us by abandoning once and for all the illusion that we can ever again isolate ourselves from the rest of humanity."

4. In the above statement, Roosevelt is expressing the ideas of

    (1) an isolationist
    (2) an imperialist
    (3) a jingoist
    (4) an internationalist
    (5) an anti-imperialist

5. By trying to remain neutral while the Allied forces fought against the Axis powers, the United States was expressing which of the following policies?

    (1) progressivism
    (2) imperialism
    (3) jingoism
    (4) internationalism
    (5) isolationism

6. From reading Roosevelt's statements, you can infer that he possessed which of the following traits?

    (1) idealism
    (2) violence
    (3) humanity
    (4) realism
    (5) terror

ANSWERS ARE ON PAGE 307.

WRITING ACTIVITY 6

Was President Truman justified in permitting the atomic bomb to be dropped on Hiroshima? Some believe that his action was justified because it saved American lives. Others maintain that the massive civilian casualties and the use of nuclear weapons can never be justified. Write two or three paragraphs defending your position.

ANSWER IS ON PAGE 307.

THE ATOMIC AGE

THE TRUMAN ERA

KEY WORD

Cold War—the term applied to the breakdown in U.S.-Soviet relations fueled by the threat of nuclear war

While relations with Germany and Japan improved as the 1940s waned, President Truman quickly saw that alliances with the Soviet Union were deteriorating.

The Soviets' goal to become a world power became apparent as they established footholds in such eastern European countries as Poland, Czechoslovakia, and Rumania.

The perceived threat to take over Greece and Turkey, however, led to the historic Truman Doctrine, in which Truman announced to the world that the United States would support free peoples who resist attempted control by armed minorities or outside pressures. Thus, a U.S. policy on containment of communism was put into words, and Truman granted military and economic aid to those European countries he believed to be threatened by Soviet domination.

By 1951, the Marshall Plan, proposed by Secretary of State George C. Marshall, was adopted to help western European countries resist Soviet oppression.

In response, the Soviets tried to force the Western powers out of Berlin by blockading the city. The West circumvented the blockade. After this success, in 1949, the U.S., Britain, France, Italy, Belgium, the Netherlands, Denmark, Norway, Portugal, Luxembourg, Ireland, and Canada formed the North Atlantic Treaty Organization (NATO), an alliance of nations that promised to unite in defense if one of its member nations was attacked. The U.S. took immediate steps to build up its military strength. The Cold War between the U.S. and the Soviet Union had begun.

Though Truman led the country through perilous times in foreign policy, he was not favored to win the 1948 election. But to the amazement of the political pundits, he defeated his opponent, Thomas Dewey, in one of the narrowest victories in American presidential politics.

EXERCISE 27

Directions: Place a check mark before each modern-day situation below that represents an attempt to enforce the principles of the Truman Doctrine.

_____ **(1)** sending American troops to prevent a communist takeover of South Vietnam

_____ **(2)** providing weapons to Afghanistan, enabling it to protect itself against Soviet domination

_____ **(3)** the U.S. blockade of Cuba to prevent ships of its ally, the Soviet Union, from entering the Western Hemisphere

_____ **(4)** ordering American troops into South Korea to repel the advances of communist North Korea

_____ **(5)** the U.S. pressuring Jean-Claude "Baby Doc" Duvalier to leave Haiti

ANSWERS ARE ON PAGE 308.

THE KOREAN WAR

The Korean War was the world's first example of a Cold War that heated up. The thirty-eighth parallel had been set after World War II as the dividing line between U.S. and Soviet interests in Korea. By 1949, the U.S. had helped establish the Republic of South Korea and withdrawn from the country.

At the same time, the Soviet Union set up its own North Korean government and in 1950 sent its troops across the thirty-eighth parallel.

President Truman made the decision to commit U.S. troops to help the South Koreans and also asked for UN troop support.

When the UN troops, under General Douglas MacArthur, crossed the thirty-eighth parallel, the Chinese forces drove them back. President Truman, deciding that this was "the wrong war, at the wrong place, at the wrong time, and with the wrong enemy," advised MacArthur to stick to the original objective of regaining South Korea up to the thirty-eighth parallel. When MacArthur publicly advocated an attack on Red China, he was relieved of his command.

The Korean War era also ushered in a period of anticommunist activity in the United States. In the early 1950s, a little-known senator from Wisconsin, Joseph R. McCarthy, charged that many communists were employed by the State Department. Though his charge was unfounded, the atmosphere of fear created by the Korean conflict allowed him to carry his crusade to extremes.

President Truman declared, "Liberty can be endangered by the 'Right' as well as by the 'Left.'" Nonetheless, the Korean conflict, the question of communism, and the suspicion of corruption within the administration forced him to withdraw from consideration as a 1952 candidate for president.

THE EISENHOWER YEARS

The voters chose World War II hero General Dwight D. Eisenhower as president over Democrat Adlai E. Stevenson. The United States, under President Eisenhower, signed an armistice ending the Korean War on July 27, 1953. By that time, more than 23,000 Americans had lost their lives in battle. Communism had been contained in Korea, and the strength and authority of the United Nations had met the challenge. However, the Cold War between the United States and the Soviet Union escalated.

During the early years of his administration, Eisenhower believed that communism could be contained only by threats of military retaliation against the Soviet Union. At home, domestic issues demanded attention as inflation rose, driving prices up, and economic growth declined as the country experienced a recession.

Above all other issues, however, loomed the problem of segregation. President Truman had tried to push through a civil rights program in 1948 but was unsuccessful. The NAACP (National Association for the Advancement of Colored People) bypassed the executive and legislative branches and took the issue to the courts. On May 17, 1954, the Supreme Court ruled, in *Brown* v. *the Board of Education of Topeka*, that "separate educational facilities are inherently unequal." Resistance to this decision climaxed in Little Rock, Arkansas, in 1957 when Eisenhower sent federal troops to the high school to allow black students to enter the building. Subsequently, the Civil Rights Act of 1957 established the Civil Rights Commission to investigate violations of voting rights on the basis of race, color, national origin, or religion.

Traumatic as the civil rights conflicts were, however, other events signaled the end of the Eisenhower era. Relations with nations such as Japan and Venezuela reached such a low that American leaders were warned not to visit. The Batista regime in Cuba was overthrown in 1958 and 1959, and Fidel Castro came to power. Scandals in the highly regarded administration became known to the shocked public. Voters were ready for a change.

EXERCISE 28

Questions 1–4 are based on the information on pages 131–132.

1. The undeclared war in Korea most closely resembled the situation in

   (1) World War I
   (2) World War II
   (3) the Spanish-American War
   (4) the Vietnam War
   (5) the Civil War

2. The decision in *Brown* v. *the Board of Education of Topeka* is significant today because

   (1) it sanctioned segregated schools
   (2) it allowed Eisenhower to send troops to Little Rock
   (3) it serves as the legal basis for school busing to achieve desegregation in some cities
   (4) it permitted blacks to attend private schools
   (5) it helped to increase Eisenhower's personal popularity

3. Which of the following hypotheses best explains Dwight Eisenhower's great popularity?

   (1) He was a war hero who represented American strength.
   (2) He established the Civil Rights Commission.
   (3) His policies started a recession.
   (4) His administration was free of scandal.
   (5) He defeated Adlai Stevenson for the presidency.

4. Which event did *not* influence the end of the Eisenhower era?

   (1) rising inflation
   (2) overthrow of communism
   (3) civil rights legislation
   (4) poor relations with Japan and Venezuela
   (5) scandals in the administration

ANSWERS ARE ON PAGE 308.

THE NEW FRONTIER

John F. Kennedy, the youngest man and the first Roman Catholic to be elected president, was indeed a change for the country. No president since Roosevelt had so roused the country with his enthusiasm, vigor, and idealism.

Kennedy's challenge to the nation is best summed up by the quote delivered at his inauguration: "Ask not what your country can do for you, ask what you can do for your country."

Youth rallied to his call by joining his newly established Peace Corps. He declared war against poverty, illiteracy, and ill health among the nation's poor and elderly. The space program added excitement to this period, as the Mercury Seven astronauts ushered in the era of U.S. manned space flights. Thus, the rivalry between the U.S. and the Soviet Union shifted to another arena.

The political situation in Vietnam became increasingly troublesome, and JFK sent military advisors there in 1961. These advisors sent home glowing reports of American successes, but these proved later to be untrue. By 1963, the tiny Asian country was in turmoil.

In April of 1961, tensions between the United States and Cuba worsened as Cuba, under communist leadership, developed friendly relations with the Soviets. In October of 1962, President Kennedy quarantined the waters around Cuba to prevent Soviet shipments of nuclear missiles to Cuba. He demanded the dismantling of the missile site already established and the removal of the missiles, warning that any attack on the U.S. from Cuba would be considered a Soviet attack. After a week of international tension, the Soviet Union removed the bases and missiles.

During the Kennedy years, executive action toward guaranteeing civil rights that began during the Eisenhower era continued. In 1962 the president sent federal troops to protect the right of James Meredith, a black student, to attend the University of Mississippi. A civil rights commission appointed in 1963 found that the citizenship of blacks was seriously hampered in the U.S. by the illegal denial of the right to vote. The same year Dr. Martin Luther King, Jr., led a series of nonviolent protests through the South, culminating in the march on Washington that August.

Legislation to support blacks was to be the triumph of a different president, however, as was legislation providing for Medicare, aid to education, and other social programs. On November 22, 1963, John Fitzgerald Kennedy was killed in downtown Dallas, Texas, by a sniper's bullet. Americans eventually would recover from the shock, but the country had lost the innocence and the youthful optimism that the Kennedy years had brought.

GED Practice
EXERCISE 29

Questions 1 and 2 are based on the information on pages 133–134.

1. The Kennedy administration was characterized by

   (1) a return to conservative politics
   (2) growing commitments at home and abroad
   (3) a loss of national optimism and idealism
   (4) illegal denial of the vote to black Americans
   (5) the passing of legislation to provide Medicare to the elderly

2. From reading the section "The New Frontier," it may be assumed that

   (1) the Soviet Union sought to control Cuba
   (2) the Soviet Union planned an attack on the U.S. from Cuba
   (3) Cuba and the U.S. enjoyed friendly relations
   (4) Cuba, a communist nation, was an ally of the Soviet Union
   (5) Cuba planned to attack the U.S.

ANSWERS ARE ON PAGE 308.

WRITING ACTIVITY 7

Was President Kennedy justified in quarantining the waters around Cuba? Why or why not? Defend your position in two or three paragraphs.

ANSWER IS ON PAGE 308.

THE GREAT SOCIETY

Lyndon Baines Johnson had quite an act to follow, but he pursued the course of fulfilling his predecessor's dreams. LBJ was a skillful politician and legislator whose influence pushed bills through Congress in numbers that had not been seen since the New Deal.

The Economic Opportunity Act of 1964 was the chief weapon in the "war on poverty" envisioned by Truman, reformulated by Kennedy, and finally carried out by Johnson.

The war on poverty was directed toward urban areas where most Americans then lived. The Head Start program provided early education to urban preschoolers, a Job Corps helped high school dropouts, Upward Bound brought bright but poor youth to college, and VISTA (Volunteers in Service to America) connected energetic middle-class workers with the cities' poor.

The Civil Rights Act of 1964, Johnson's most noteworthy achievement, forbade racial discrimination in circumstances where federal funds were used. Johnson also established the Equal Employment Opportunity Commission.

In 1965, voting rights were enhanced by law, federal aid to education and Medicare were enacted, immigration laws were liberalized, and the National Foundation on the Arts and Humanities Act was passed.

In foreign policy, Johnson was not so successful. Decisions on action in Latin America undid all the trust building so carefully constructed by Roosevelt's Good Neighbor policies and Kennedy's Alliance for Progress. And the Vietnam War, an inherited problem, was escalated in 1965.

In that year, American combat troops were committed for the first time, and by 1967 the number of soldiers there reached half a million. The administration justified the action as a response to the larger threat of the spread of Chinese communism. Critics argued that the war was essentially a civil war in which outsiders did not belong. As a result of the winless war in Vietnam, Lyndon Johnson chose not to seek reelection in 1968, and his former vice president, Hubert Humphrey, lost to Republican Richard Nixon.

GED Practice
EXERCISE 30

Questions 1 and 2 are based on the information on page 135.

1. President Johnson's chief contribution to society was

   (1) the active pursuit of world peace
   (2) a commitment to social justice for blacks and the disadvantaged
   (3) the successful containment of communism throughout the world
   (4) the attainment of economic prosperity for all Americans
   (5) the withdrawal of troops from Vietnam

2. Which of the following explains why Johnson decided *not* to seek reelection in 1968?

   (1) his failure to fully carry out all the provisions of the Civil Rights Act of 1964
   (2) his failure in foreign policies toward Latin America
   (3) his reversal of Roosevelt's Good Neighbor policies
   (4) his discontinuance of Kennedy's Alliance for Progress
   (5) his inability to win a clear victory in the Vietnam War and America's questionable involvement in the war

Questions 3 and 4 are based on the following passage.

   By 1967 over 10,000 young Americans had died in the small land so far away, and they had died for a cause that no one seemed to understand. In the midst of great poverty and problems at home, $20 billion had been spent on the unpopular war in 1967 alone.

   In ever-increasing numbers, senators, statesmen, and citizens opposed U.S. involvement in the war. Protest marches, demonstrations, sit-ins, and love-ins continued through the sixties and into the seventies.

   "Make love, not war" became a favorite slogan of American youth. The thoughtful criticism of the Kennedy years had soured into an open confrontation between generations and a complete disaffection with modern American society. Experimentation with drugs, avoiding the military draft, and exploration of mystical religions were some of the ways in which American youth reacted against the Vietnam War.

3. The purpose of the passage is to

   (1) defend American involvement in Vietnam
   (2) compare the nation's mood under the Kennedy and Johnson administrations
   (3) pay tribute to those who died in the Vietnam War
   (4) explain why the war was unpopular
   (5) show how an unpopular war disrupted American society

4. Which of the following statements is best supported by the evidence in the passage above?

   (1) The Vietnam War was the most unpopular and expensive war America ever fought.
   (2) The American government should not have wasted money and lives in Vietnam.
   (3) Most elected officials were afraid to speak out against the war lest they lose their jobs.
   (4) The Vietnam War had repercussions that went well beyond Vietnam itself.
   (5) America's purpose in Vietnam was clear and well supported by the American people.

ANSWERS ARE ON PAGE 308.

THE NIXON ERA

The Vietnam War was still extremely unpopular in the U.S. when President Richard Nixon took office. His ordering troops into Cambodia and other military moves did not help his personal popularity. But he did gradually withdraw troops and negotiated a pullout by the end of March 1973. The war did not end officially until the fall of Saigon in 1975. It was not a victory, but the war was over after two decades of U.S. military and monetary support, the loss of 56,000 young American lives, and the deaths of countless Vietnamese, Cambodians, and Laotians.

Riding the crest of popularity after the Vietnam pullout, Nixon was at the peak of his political career. *Détente*—the easing of tensions between nations—with the Soviet Union was more successful than it had ever been. Friendly relations with the People's Republic of China had been established for the first time in many years, and President Nixon visited there in 1972. In the Middle East, the U.S. had become a major peacekeeping influence. Four vacant Supreme Court slots had been filled by Nixon with justices who held his conservative philosophy.

Nixon won the 1972 election with one of the largest margins in modern history. But the illegal break-in of the Democratic National Committee Headquarters at the Watergate Hotel in June of 1972 and the subsequent attempt at a cover-up forced him from office in August 1974. Thus, former president Richard Nixon became the only U.S. president to have resigned from office to escape impeachment. Vice President Gerald Ford succeeded Nixon and finished his term. In his reelection bid, Ford lost to Democrat Jimmy Carter in 1976.

GED Practice

EXERCISE 31

Questions 1 and 2 are based on the above information.

1. Which of the following opinions is best supported by the evidence presented above?

   (1) Political spying is a common practice in American politics.
   (2) Nixon's military strategy brought about victory in Vietnam.
   (3) Nixon's aides broke the law for the good of the country.
   (4) A serious character flaw cost Nixon the presidency.
   (5) The president of the United States is not above the law.

2. Of President Nixon's foreign policy initiatives, for which will history likely credit him most?

   (1) the ordering of troops into Cambodia
   (2) negotiating peace in the Middle East
   (3) reestablishing relations with the People's Republic of China
   (4) the bombing of Hanoi to end the war
   (5) ending the Cold War with the Soviet Union

ANSWERS ARE ON PAGE 308.

CLOSING THE TWENTIETH CENTURY

CARTER AND THE MIDDLE EAST

The nation's distrust of Washington government officials created a thirst for honest leadership. The American people found it in a little-known peanut farmer from Georgia, James Earl (Jimmy) Carter, who ran on an anti-Washington platform.

Jimmy Carter had been a successful governor of Georgia from 1971 to 1975, but he was virtually unknown nationally when he won the presidency in 1976. He used his obscurity to an advantage in the years when the American people were wary of politicians. He promised decency, honesty, and humanitarianism in Washington, and voters welcomed his smiling face and small-town handshake.

He was not so welcome in Washington, however. He surrounded himself with Georgia friends. He advocated restraint in the use of natural resources, emphasis on education for personal and national betterment, and the safeguard of human rights and peace throughout the world. He was also a driving force in establishing full diplomatic relations with mainland China, concluding a second SALT (Strategic Arms Limitation Talks) treaty with the Soviet Union, relinquishing U.S. control of the Panama Canal, and framing a peace treaty between Egypt and Israel.

Carter was less successful with his domestic policy, however. He could not reform the nation's tax structure or simplify the unwieldy federal civil service system. He was also unable to quell the raging inflation rates.

Carter's biggest disappointment, however, was his frustrated attempts to bring fifty-two American hostages home from Iran. These foreign service employees were seized at the American Embassy in Iran on November 4, 1979, to punish the U.S. for welcoming the exiled shah of Iran. After 444 days, the hostages were released on January 20, 1981—the day Ronald Reagan took his oath of office.

REAGAN AND THE NEW CONSERVATISM

At the age of sixty-nine, Ronald Reagan was the oldest man to be elected president of the United States. Reagan was a conservative Republican who had twice served as governor of California.

Ronald Reagan won the election against Carter on the platform of making America strong again and improving the inflation-wracked economy. At the time Reagan took office, the inflation rate was at a high of 13 percent a year. To make matters worse, about 1 out of every 14 workers was unemployed.

Under the Reagan administration, conservatism became a national drive in many areas of American life. The Democratic spending policies of the sixties were blamed for the predicament of the American economy. To reduce federal spending, President Reagan cut many of the social programs implemented during the sixties. The "Reagan Revolution" soon became as well known for cutting social programs as Roosevelt's New Deal had been for establishing them.

American foreign policy focused on anticommunism as the administration supported the efforts of anticommunists in El Salvador, Nicaragua, and elsewhere throughout the world.

BUSH AND THE "NEW WORLD ORDER"

Vice president under Ronald Reagan for eight years, George Bush was elected president in 1988. Bush promised to carry on many of Reagan's conservative policies and made a "no new taxes" campaign pledge that later proved impossible to keep.

Bush became known as a "foreign-relations president." It was during his administration that communism collapsed in Eastern Europe (in 1989) and in the Soviet Union (in 1991), giving rise to Bush's phrase "a new world order." The apparent end to the Soviet empire forced the United States to rethink its Cold War policies.

Foreign relations again became paramount during the 1990–1991 crisis in the Persian Gulf, when Iraq's Saddam Hussein invaded neighboring Kuwait. Along with the United Nations, the United States used economic sanctions and then military force to oust Iraqi troops from Kuwait. The ground war, known as Operation Desert Storm, lasted a mere 100 hours—from February 23 to February 27, 1991. Saddam's troops were overthrown, although Saddam himself remained in power in Iraq. During the Persian Gulf War, President Bush's popularity was at an all-time high.

Economic troubles in the United States soon affected Bush's public-approval rating, however. As the economy dipped into recession in the early 1990s, the public began to feel that Bush was paying too much attention to foreign affairs and ignoring the nation's domestic problems. The deepening recession became a major issue in the 1992 presidential campaign.

The "fix-it-if-it's-broken" approach of independent presidential candidate Ross Perot and Democrat Bill Clinton's promise of economic reform resulted in the Republicans' losing their hold on the presidency for only the second time in twenty-four years. Perot, a self-made Texas billionaire businessman, appealed to Americans' growing discontent with traditional politicians. His grass-roots campaign drew many votes away from the two major parties, but Clinton, who stressed the importance of developing jobs and reducing health-care costs, won the election. Americans were more worried about their own dwindling resources than about the state of the world.

≡ GED Practice ≡
EXERCISE 32

Questions 1–4 are based on the information on pages 138–139.

1. For which of the following actions will Jimmy Carter probably be remembered most favorably?

   (1) formally recognizing the African nation of Zimbabwe
   (2) establishing a friendship with the shah of Iran, who was accused of human rights violations by his people
   (3) negotiating for peace between Egypt and Israel
   (4) providing support for Nicaraguan dictator Anastasio Somoza Debayle during a bloody civil war against him
   (5) failing to gain the release of the fifty-two American hostages from Iran

2. Which of the following actions exemplifies the main thrust of Reagan's foreign policy?

   (1) giving aid to anticommunist rebels in Nicaragua, Angola, and Afghanistan
   (2) setting up summit talks with former Soviet leader Mikhail Gorbachev
   (3) refusing to intervene in the Philippines' election of 1986 between dictator Ferdinand Marcos and his opponent, Corazon Aquino
   (4) helping dictator Jean-Claude "Baby Doc" Duvalier to flee from Haiti
   (5) initiating the "Star Wars" strategic defense system

3. Which of the following statements is best supported by the evidence in the section about Bush?

   (1) The public should not blame the president for economic problems.
   (2) The president should not react to public opinion polls.
   (3) The performance of the economy has a major effect on the president's popularity.
   (4) The president should focus on domestic issues first.
   (5) Breaking a campaign promise will hurt the president's approval rating.

4. What did Carter, Reagan, and Bush all have in common?

   (1) They fared better in dealing with foreign policy matters than with domestic issues.
   (2) They were all conservative members of their political parties.
   (3) They all implemented programs that greatly improved the economy.
   (4) They were all able to decrease taxes for the middle class.
   (5) They were all virtually unknown when they took office as president.

ANSWERS ARE ON PAGE 309.

BILL CLINTON—THE FIRST "BABY BOOM" PRESIDENT

William Jefferson Clinton had been the governor of Arkansas for twelve years before he was elected president of the United States. At the age of 46, Clinton and his 44-year-old vice president, Albert Gore, were the first of the Baby Boom generation to hold the nation's highest offices. The song "Don't Stop Thinking About Tomorrow," by the 1970s rock group Fleetwood Mac, became the campaign theme song.

Clinton's victory marked the third time in five elections in which an incumbent president was defeated. Also, for the first time in recent memory, both the president and vice president were from the South. Clinton's campaign centered on the issues of a stagnant economy, growing unemployment, and a faltering health-care system. He promised to stimulate the economy without placing an additional tax burden on the average American. He also stressed the need for government to become more involved with protecting the environment and, like President Kennedy, supported the idea of a civilian service corps.

Within the first 100 days of office, Clinton was faced with more problems than he had expected. Controversy arose around the selection of an attorney-general, his plan to end discrimination against homosexuals in the military, and the appointment of his wife, Hillary Rodham Clinton, to head a health-care advisory committee. On the domestic front, his economic promises proved difficult to move through Congress. Weak in foreign policy experience, Clinton also had to make tough decisions about continued trouble with Iraq, aid to financially troubled Russia, and intervention in the Bosnian civil war.

GED Practice

EXERCISE 33

Questions 1 and 2 are based on the passage above.

1. What does Clinton's initial time in office suggest about the presidency?

   (1) Former governors make the best presidents.
   (2) The presidency is more complex than candidates expect.
   (3) Presidents don't need to know about foreign affairs.
   (4) There are few surprises for a newly elected president.
   (5) The presidency is overrated by the American people.

2. With which of the following statements would Clinton be most likely to agree?

   (1) The American public is easy to please.
   (2) Women have no place in government.
   (3) Economic recovery is easy to achieve.
   (4) The hardest part of being president is getting elected.
   (5) Thinking about tomorrow's problems is easier than creating today's solutions.

ANSWERS ARE ON PAGE 309.

GED Practice
U.S. HISTORY

Questions 1 and 2 are based on the following passage.

The short-lived American Party had its beginnings as a secret society in the 1840s. Early members were called "Know-Nothings" because when asked about their politics, they said they knew nothing. The group had organized in reaction to the large number of German and Irish immigrants entering the United States. The Know-Nothings were sure that these immigrants would accept low wages and take jobs away from Americans. As a political party, the group supported only the candidacies of people who were Protestant and American-born.

Abraham Lincoln said of this group that, "As a nation, we began by declaring that 'all men are created equal.' . . . When the Know-Nothings obtain control, it will read: 'All men are created equal except Negroes, foreigners, and Catholics.' "

1. Which of the following effects did President Lincoln foresee if the American party were to come into power?

   (1) Immigrants would get all the good-paying jobs.
   (2) A Catholic president would be elected.
   (3) The principles of the Declaration of Independence would be undermined.
   (4) All Americans would be able to live as equals.
   (5) African Americans would support the Know-Nothing party.

2. If the Know-Nothings were active today, with which of the following statements would they most probably agree?

   (1) America is open to all who need help.
   (2) Undocumented aliens must be kept out of the country at all costs.
   (3) Immigration laws should be relaxed to allow more people to enter the country.
   (4) Immigrants should not be turned away if they are HIV-positive.
   (5) America is strong because of its diversity of peoples.

Questions 3 and 4 are based on this passage.

Andrew Jackson's election as president in 1828 gave new meaning to the idea of democracy. Jackson, a poor orphan from South Carolina, became a tough soldier and later a self-educated lawyer in Tennessee. To ordinary voters, he represented the common man. He believed in equal economic opportunity and allowing people to make their own decisions. The right to vote had been given to people who did not own property only a few years before Jackson's candidacy. The new Democratic Party drew its strength from the working class and the developing middle class. Jacksonian Democracy was seen as government by and for the "plain people." Its goal was reform based on mass participation.

3. According to the passage, Jackson was elected because he

   (1) followed the old party line
   (2) was an aristocrat
   (3) spent a lot of money on his campaign
   (4) was a true patriot
   (5) had the support of average Americans

4. Which of the following conclusions is supported by information in the passage?

   (1) Jackson was a good president because he was a true "man of the people."
   (2) The United States was not a democracy until 1828.
   (3) Jacksonian Democracy helped broaden the base of American politics.
   (4) Jacksonian Democracy was an unwelcome change in American politics.
   (5) Jackson will be remembered as one of the nation's least important presidents.

Questions 5–7 are based on the following map.

NATIVE AMERICAN TRIBES AND CULTURAL AREAS IN 1492

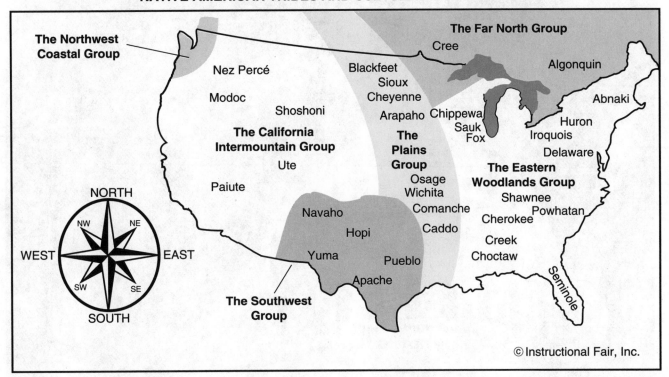

5. Which of the following information *cannot* be found on the map?

(1) the date
(2) the names of tribes
(3) the names of cultural areas
(4) the location of tribes
(5) population figures

6. According to the map, the Sioux were in which group?

(1) Far North
(2) Eastern Woodlands
(3) Plains
(4) Southwest
(5) California-Intermountain

7. The information on the map best supports which of the following conclusions about America in 1492?

(1) The land was heavily forested.
(2) Most of the land was unoccupied.
(3) Native American culture was well established throughout the land.
(4) Native Americans were primarily hunters and gatherers.
(5) Native Americans lived in only a few areas.

ANSWERS ARE ON PAGE 309.

6 Political Science

"Man is by nature a political animal," said Aristotle more than two thousand years ago, and it is just as true today. As long as humans feel the need to live in groups, organization will be necessary for order and efficiency. Organization requires formal rules. Rules determine the basis for forms of government.

The form of government a society adopts has to fit the needs of its people, or it will not last long. Many different types of government have been tried throughout civilization. **Political scientists** study the different forms of government and the process by which governments operate.

TYPES OF GOVERNMENT

KEY WORDS

democracy—a system of government in which "the will of the majority" rules; citizens elect representatives in free elections

dictatorship—a system of government in which one person has absolute authority to govern

monarchy—a system of government in which a single person rules by inherited power

oligarchy—a system of government in which a small group of people exercise total control

MONARCHY

A king or queen is at the head of government in a monarchy. If his or her position is severely limited by a constitution or other system of laws, it is called a **constitutional monarchy**, as exists in Great Britain today.

A ruler who has the absolute and final say in governmental decision making is called an **absolute monarch**, a rarity today. In the past, many absolute monarchs claimed their authority was bestowed upon them by God. This belief was called the doctrine of **divine right**.

In either case, the monarch rules for life and passes the power to someone within his or her family, usually the oldest male child.

DEMOCRACY

The leader of a democracy is elected by the people that he or she directs. All power to govern comes from the people, and decisions must meet their approval. The equality of all citizens is a principle that forms the basis of a democratic government, too.

Often, when a democracy is established within a country that once had been governed by a monarch, the new government is structured as a **parliamentary democracy**. In a parliamentary democracy, an elected legislature, a cabinet of executives, and a prime minister replace the absolute power of the king or queen. The king or queen maintains ceremonial authority as head of state and is considered to be a figurehead.

Most democracies today are representative, not direct or pure, democracies. Only nations or states with very small populations can let *all* the citizens make *all* the decisions. For this reason, a nation such as the United States, with more than 260 million people, must function as a representative democracy, in which we elect others to represent us.

DICTATORSHIP

In a dictatorship, only one person has total control of the government. For this reason, it is often called a **totalitarian government**. Total control means the complete domination of the citizens' lives as well as the sole power to govern. The most basic of citizens' rights are taken away in order to guarantee absolute authority to one person. A dictatorship begins and ends by a violent overthrow of the government.

OLIGARCHY

Though in *theory* communist countries are governed by the workers, or **proletariat**, in *practice* they are governed by a few party leaders. Such a "government by few" is called an oligarchy and is similar to a dictatorship in that government officials are not elected and often come to power after a coup, or violent overthrow, of the existing government.

EXERCISE 1

Directions: In the space provided, write *M* if the situation describes a monarchy, *DE* if it describes a democracy, *DI* if it describes a dictatorship, and *O* if it describes an oligarchy.

_____ **1.** The People's Republic of China claims that this system is most efficient and fair, since decisions are made by a few top men in the government's only political party.

_____ **2.** Fidel Castro rules Cuba with a system of complete control, having overthrown his predecessor, Batista, in 1959.

_____ **3.** King John of England and his predecessors ruled by this system for many generations before the Magna Carta changed it to more democratic ways.

_____ **4.** In the 1930s, Adolf Hitler ruled Germany with absolute power in a system of strong centralized government.

_____ **5.** Canada patterns its system after the British one, with a prime minister who heads a cabinet and an elected parliament.

_____ **6.** The tiny kingdom of Tonga believes that this system works well because it retains respect and power for a ruler who claims to have inherited his throne by the will of the gods.

_____ **7.** Generalissimo Franco used this system because it gave him absolute control over the country of Spain after a bloody takeover.

ANSWERS ARE ON PAGE 309.

BLUEPRINT FOR A NEW NATION

A SEPARATION OF POWERS

KEY WORDS

federalism—a system of government in which the states yield supreme authority to a central government
republic—a government in which voting citizens delegate to elected representatives the authority to govern

The U.S. Constitution is the "law of the land," or the base upon which all laws in the United States rest. It is the oldest written constitution still in effect, and republics throughout the world have modeled their own constitutions after it.

The U.S. Constitution is based on the principle of federalism. It provides for a central government made up of three branches: the *legislative*, which makes the laws; the *executive*, which carries out the laws; and the *judicial*, which interprets the laws.

This separation of powers was proposed to keep each center of power in check and to prevent the abuses that the former colonies experienced under British rule.

THE LEGISLATIVE BRANCH: MAKER OF THE LAWS

Article One of the Constitution concerns the legislative branch of the national government. The legislative branch, called **Congress**, is comprised of two houses: the House of Representatives and the Senate.

In the House of Representatives, each state's number of representatives is based on its population; in the Senate, each state is equally represented with two senators each.

Representatives are chosen by popular election and serve for two years. Senators are chosen by popular election also, although under the original constitution they were chosen by the state legislatures. Senators serve six-year terms. Some of the important powers of Congress are:

- to levy and collect taxes
- to borrow money
- to regulate commerce
- to coin money
- to declare war

- to approve presidential appointments
- to provide and maintain an army and navy
- to ratify treaties (Senate only)
- to impeach the president (House only)
- to admit new states to the union

In addition to the powers of Congress that are stated specifically, the framers of the Constitution allowed for powers not spelled out. The **elastic clause** allows the legislative branch to make all laws "necessary and proper" to execute the powers granted by the Constitution. This clause enables Congress to stretch its authority to meet the needs of a changing nation without having to go through the laborious process of amending the Constitution.

EXERCISE 2

Directions: Based on the reading above, write *C* if the action below is an example of a power stated in the U.S. Constitution. Write *E* if it is an example of an application of the elastic clause that gives Congress certain necessary and proper powers.

_____ **1.** Congress declared war on Japan in 1941.

_____ **2.** The Senate approved Nixon's appointment of John Mitchell as attorney general in 1969.

_____ **3.** Congress established the United States Air Force in 1947.

_____ **4.** The House of Representatives impeached Andrew Johnson in 1868.

_____ **5.** In 1986 Congress enacted the law moving the beginning of Daylight Savings Time from the last Sunday in April to the first Sunday in April.

_____ **6.** Congress approved economic sanctions against South Africa.

_____ **7.** Congress annexed Alaska as the forty-ninth state of the Union.

ANSWERS ARE ON PAGE 310.

EXERCISE 3

Directions: Based on the facts and the definition of gerrymandering below, check off logical conclusions that could be drawn from the map of three congressional districts in suburban Chicago.

Gerrymandering takes place when the political party in power redraws congressional district boundaries to its advantage and to the disadvantage of the opposing party. To prevent this political abuse, the Supreme Court ruled (in the case of *Baker* v. *Carr* in 1962) that redrawn legislative districts must be kept as proportional to population as possible.

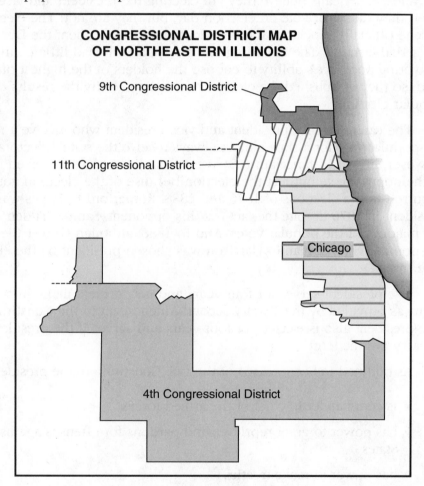

CONGRESSIONAL DISTRICT MAP OF NORTHEASTERN ILLINOIS

9th Congressional District

11th Congressional District

Chicago

4th Congressional District

_____ **(1)** The 9th Congressional District is the most densely populated of the three districts shown on the map.

_____ **(2)** Suburban districts are more politically desirable than urban districts.

_____ **(3)** If these districts had been drawn to equalize land area, population apportionment would not have been fair.

_____ **(4)** The 4th Congressional District has more voters from the political party in power than the other two districts shown.

_____ **(5)** The 9th Congressional District is too small.

ANSWERS ARE ON PAGE 310.

THE EXECUTIVE BRANCH: ENFORCER OF THE LAWS

KEY WORDS

electoral college—a body of electors who elect the president and vice president of the United States

precedent—an earlier action that serves as a justification for a later action

---

Most Americans believe they are electing the president and vice president when they cast their vote on election day, but they are not! The electoral college officially proclaims the president and vice president the December *after* the actual election. The Founding Fathers apparently had little confidence in the voting populace's ability to choose the holders of the highest office in the land, so they established the electoral college to certify the results of the popular election.

The candidates for president and vice president who receive a majority of the popular vote for a state almost always receive the state's electoral votes. However, in two instances in U.S. history candidates have received the majority of the popular vote but lost the election because of the electoral vote. This occurred in the elections of 1876 and 1888. Rutherford B. Hayes was chosen president in 1876 despite the fact that his opponent, Samuel Tilden, received the majority of the popular votes. And in 1888, although Grover Cleveland won the popular vote, Benjamin Harrison was chosen president by the electoral vote.

The president serves for four years and may serve a maximum of two terms as provided by the Twenty-second Amendment to the Constitution. The vice president also is elected for four years and serves if the president is unable to carry out the term.

As outlined in Section Two of the U.S. Constitution, the president:

- is commander-in-chief of the armed forces

- has power to grant reprieves and pardons for offenses against the United States

- has power to make treaties

- may appoint judges to the U.S. Supreme Court and ambassadors

- may nominate and appoint major executive officers

- may veto bills sent by Congress

In executing the nation's laws, presidents have often established precedents not specifically provided for in the Constitution. For example, President Jefferson entered into the Louisiana Purchase even though such an initiative was not written specifically into the Constitution. This exercise of implied powers is discussed on page 100. Other cases involving the establishment of a precedent based on the use of implied powers include:

- George Washington's setting up a cabinet of advisors
- James Polk's ordering U.S. troops into action before Congress had declared war against Mexico
- Abraham Lincoln's acting to free the slaves during the Civil War
- Theodore Roosevelt's mediating labor and international disputes

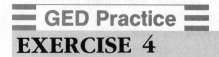

EXERCISE 4

For questions 1 and 2, choose the word or words that best complete each statement.

1. The Constitution originally specified that the president's term would be for four years, but it did not specify how many terms a president could serve. Until FDR's administration, each president followed Washington's example and stepped down after completing two terms. Doing something because a previous president did it is known as following a presidential

   (1) proclamation
   (2) pardon
   (3) precedent
   (4) amendment
   (5) priority

2. Under the Kennedy and Johnson administrations, the executive branch of the government underwent an increase in the number of bureaucratic agencies. Based upon what you have read in the U.S. History section, this increase in the number of agencies was probably due to a precedent set by President

   (1) George Washington
   (2) Harry S Truman
   (3) Franklin Roosevelt
   (4) Theodore Roosevelt
   (5) Grover Cleveland

ANSWERS ARE ON PAGE 310.

EXERCISE 5

Directions: Match the presidential precedent with the subsequent action of a later president by writing the correct letter in the space provided.

Presidential Precedent

____ 1. Polk's activation of troops in Mexico without waiting for Congress to declare war

____ 2. Lincoln's expansion of executive power during a national emergency

____ 3. Teddy Roosevelt's mediation between two other disputing countries

Subsequent Action

(a) Carter's role in the Camp David accords between Egypt and Israel

(b) Johnson's military buildup in the undeclared Vietnam war

(c) FDR's establishment of agencies during the Depression and World War II

ANSWERS ARE ON PAGE 310.

GED Practice

EXERCISE 6

Based on the information below, choose the *one* best answer to the question.

"Strong" presidents have been described as dominating the legislative branch and making the office of the presidency self-directing. "Weak" presidents have made the office more reliant on and subordinate to the legislature. Which of the following early presidents best fits the description of a "strong" president?

(1) President Madison, a statesman who declared war on Britain in 1812 only after popular demand called for it

(2) President John Adams, who believed that the governing representatives should be "the rich, the well-born, and the able"

(3) President Thomas Jefferson, who opposed the Louisiana Purchase and the First Bank of the United States on the grounds that the Constitution did not provide for them

(4) President James Monroe, who advanced the idea of the Monroe Doctrine on the advice of his secretary of state John Quincy Adams

(5) President Andrew Jackson, who made unprecedented use of his veto power and who relied little on Congress and his cabinet in making his decisions

ANSWER IS ON PAGE 310.

WRITING ACTIVITY 1

Should the president and vice president of the United States be elected by direct popular vote or by the electoral college system, as is currently the case? Write one to two paragraphs defending your point of view.

ANSWER IS ON PAGE 310.

THE JUDICIAL BRANCH: INTERPRETER OF THE LAWS

KEY WORD

judicial review—the ability to decide on the constitutionality of a law

That the U.S. Constitution is a living document can be proved by the performance of the Supreme Court, which can and does reverse itself. On page 38, you read that in 1896 the Supreme Court ruled that separate but equal facilities for blacks in the South were correct and legal. In 1954, however, the court reversed the earlier decision and ruled the opposite. This action by the court illustrates how this branch of government changes with the times.

Article Three of the Constitution describes the Supreme Court. The function of the Supreme Court is to decide whether certain laws are in keeping with the spirit of the Constitution. This ability to decide on the constitutionality of a law is called *judicial review*.

The Supreme Court is composed of nine justices appointed for life by the president. The head of the Supreme Court is called the *chief justice*.

The federal court system consists of the Supreme Court, eleven Circuit Courts of Appeal scattered throughout the country, and approximately ninety federal District Courts. In addition to the federal system of courts, each state has its own system. The diagram below illustrates the organization of the federal court system.

FEDERAL COURT SYSTEM

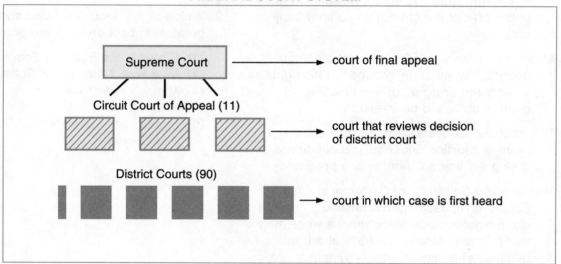

Some of the powers vested in the Supreme Court are the powers to rule on:

- cases involving a state and citizens of another state
- controversies between two or more states
- cases between citizens of different states
- cases between a state and a foreign state

The Supreme Court does not have the last word on all legal cases in the country. Only when a provision of the Constitution, an act of Congress, or a right guaranteed by federal law is involved does the Supreme Court have the authority to rule on a state court's decision. Appellate (appeals) courts' cases are reviewed only when they involve the national interest.

GED Practice
EXERCISE 7

Questions 1 and 2 refer to the following definitions.

Listed below are five landmark Supreme Court decisions made in the last thirty-five years.

Brown v. *Board of Education of Topeka*, 1954, held that separate facilities for the races were not equal and therefore were unconstitutional.

New York Times Co. v. *Sullivan*, 1964, guaranteed that freedom of the press protected a newspaper from liability for defamation of a public official if it did not do so knowingly or recklessly.

Miranda v. *Arizona*, 1966, ruled that a person under arrest must be informed of his rights as an accused criminal, or any resulting confession would be invalid.

Roe v. *Wade*, 1973, stated that states could not prohibit abortion under certain conditions during the first six months of a pregnancy.

Rights of the University of California v. *Allan Bakke*, 1978, decided that reverse discrimination took place when a white man was refused entrance to medical school because of a minority quota system.

1. In each of the five landmark decisions described above, the Supreme Court assumed the role of

   (1) checking the powers of Congress
   (2) checking the power of the president
   (3) extending Congress's authority
   (4) defending civil liberties
   (5) limiting personal freedoms

2. Which of the decisions listed above had the greatest impact on local law enforcement?

   (1) *Brown* v. *the Board of Education of Topeka*
   (2) *New York Times Co.* v. *Sullivan*
   (3) *Miranda* v. *Arizona*
   (4) *Roe* v. *Wade*
   (5) *Rights of the University of California* v. *Allan Bakke*

ANSWERS ARE ON PAGE 311.

WRITING ACTIVITY 2

One example of a president's use of implied powers is the replacement of retiring Supreme Court justices with judges sympathetic to the appointing president's political views. For example, presidents Reagan, Bush, and Clinton all appointed justices to the Supreme Court who agreed with their political philosophy. Do you approve of this practice? Write two or three paragraphs defending your point of view.

ANSWER IS ON PAGE 311.

EXERCISE 8

Questions 1–3 are based on the following list of U.S. government actions.

Brown v. *the Board of Education of Topeka* decision (1954)—separate educational facilities declared inherently unequal by the Supreme Court

Central High School, Little Rock, Arkansas (1957)—federal troops sent by the president to escort black students into a previously all-white school

U.S. Commission on Civil Rights (1957)—by authority of the president's office, allowed the U.S. attorney general to enforce voting rights in the states

Civil Rights Act (1964)—outlawed racial discrimination in public accommodations and by employers, unions, and voting registrars

Voting Rights Acts (1965, 1970)—stopped the use of literacy tests for voter qualification and gave greater power to the federal government to protect citizens' voting rights

1. Which of the following federal actions was primarily the work of the judicial branch?

   (1) *Brown* v. *the Board of Education of Topeka* decision
   (2) the dispatch of federal troops to Central High School in Little Rock
   (3) the enforcement of voting rights
   (4) the outlawing of racial discrimination in public accommodations
   (5) the prohibition of literacy tests to qualify people to vote

2. Which of the following federal actions *most directly affected* the voiding of a New York state law requiring voters to be able to write in English?

   (1) the *Brown* v. *the Board of Education of Topeka* decision
   (2) the dispatch of federal troops to Central High School
   (3) the passage of the Civil Rights Act
   (4) the founding of the U.S. Commission on Civil Rights
   (5) the passage of the Voting Rights Acts

3. Which of the following federal actions led to greater opportunity in the workplace and at the ballot box?

   (1) *Brown* v. *the Board of Education of Topeka* decision
   (2) dispatch of troops to Little Rock, Arkansas
   (3) establishment of the U.S. Commission on Civil Rights in 1957
   (4) passage of the Civil Rights Act of 1964
   (5) passage of the Voting Rights Acts of 1965 and 1970

ANSWERS ARE ON PAGE 311.

SYSTEM OF CHECKS AND BALANCES

The Founding Fathers understood that the powers of the three branches had to be balanced so that no one center of power dominated the other two. To prevent this from happening, the U.S. Constitution allows the president to refuse approval of (veto) a bill sent to him by Congress.

Congress, however, can still pass the bill into law by a majority vote of its members. This procedure is called ***overriding a veto***. Finally, if the law is brought to the Supreme Court, the court can declare it unconstitutional if the justices feel the law contradicts the principles of the Constitution.

The diagram below shows how a bill is enacted into law.

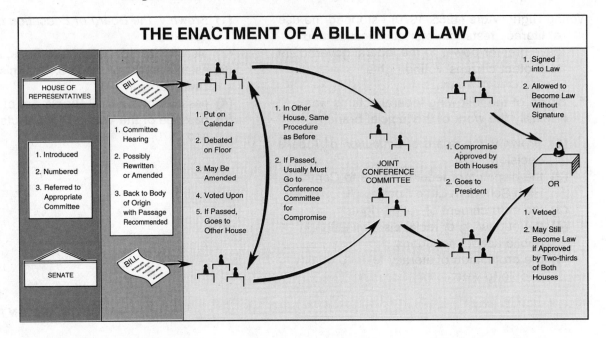

THE ENACTMENT OF A BILL INTO A LAW

HOUSE OF REPRESENTATIVES

SENATE

BILL

1. Introduced
2. Numbered
3. Referred to Appropriate Committee

1. Committee Hearing
2. Possibly Rewritten or Amended
3. Back to Body of Origin with Passage Recommended

1. Put on Calendar
2. Debated on Floor
3. May Be Amended
4. Voted Upon
5. If Passed, Goes to Other House

1. In Other House, Same Procedure as Before
2. If Passed, Usually Must Go to Conference Committee for Compromise

JOINT CONFERENCE COMMITTEE

1. Compromise Approved by Both Houses
2. Goes to President

1. Signed into Law
2. Allowed to Become Law Without Signature

OR

1. Vetoed
2. May Still Become Law if Approved by Two-thirds of Both Houses

EXERCISE 9

The following question is based on the flowchart on page 156.

Which of the statements below is best supported by the chart?

(1) Bills justified by the elastic clause in the Constitution must be introduced directly by the president.

(2) Before being sent to the president, a bill must be approved in identical form by both houses of Congress.

(3) A filibuster on certain bills may not take place in either house.

(4) A bill introduced in the Senate may be changed by the House, but not the other way around.

(5) The president must sign all bills in order for them to become law.

ANSWER IS ON PAGE 311.

EXERCISE 10

Directions: In column I below, write the branch of government that *exercises* the power described on the left. In column II, write the branch of government that is *checked* by the use of the power. The first one is done for you.

Power	I Who exercises power?	II Who is checked?
1. to appoint federal judges	executive	judicial
2. to impeach the president		
3. to approve appointment of judges		
4. to override a veto		
5. to rule a law unconstitutional		
6. to veto a bill		

ANSWERS ARE ON PAGE 311.

AMENDING THE CONSTITUTION

As pointed out in the section on the judicial branch, the U.S. Constitution is often described as a living document because of its ability to adapt to changes in American society.

The means by which the Constitution adapts to changes is the amendment process. Article Five describes this two-step process:

1. An amendment first must be proposed by either two-thirds of both houses of Congress or by a national convention requested by the legislatures of two-thirds of the states.

2. It must be ratified (approved) by three-fourths of the state legislatures.

There are only twenty-six amendments to the U.S. Constitution after more than two hundred years of changes in society. This is not only a credit to the Founding Fathers' farsightedness in writing the original document but also a testimony to how difficult the amendment process is. The last proposed amendment to follow the procedure outlined above was the Equal Rights Amendment, which was defeated in 1982 because the required majority of state legislatures failed to ratify it.

THE BILL OF RIGHTS

The first ten amendments to the Constitution are called the *Bill of Rights*. The Founding Fathers added these guarantees of personal liberties after it became obvious that the states would not ratify the Constitution without them. The Bill of Rights allayed the fears of those who were afraid that the new government would threaten individual freedoms. The following amendments constitute the Bill of Rights:

1. guarantees the freedom of religion, speech, the press, and assembly

2. guarantees the right to belong to a state militia and keep weapons

3. prohibits the government from housing soldiers in civilian homes without the owners' permission

4. requires a warrant before property can be searched or seized

5. guarantees the right to remain silent; establishes a grand jury to hand down indictments for a crime; also safeguards individuals from having to testify against themselves and forbids government seizure of property without compensation

6. guarantees the right to a trial by jury after being informed of charges against oneself, the right to hear and see witnesses against oneself, and the right to a lawyer

7. permits the privilege of a jury trial in most lawsuits

8. forbids excessive bail or cruel and unusual punishment

9. requires the government to increase the list of personal liberties if necessary

10. gives the states and the people any rights not specifically denied them by the Constitution

═══ GED Practice ═══
EXERCISE 11

Questions 1 and 2 are based on the information on pages 158–159.

1. When an arresting officer reads an accused man his "rights" and gives him a quarter to make one telephone call, the policeman is referring to which amendments?

   (1) the Seventh and Eighth Amendments
   (2) the First and Second Amendments
   (3) the Fourth and Fifth Amendments
   (4) the Fifth and Sixth Amendments
   (5) the Sixth and Seventh Amendments

2. "Your rights exist as long as they don't affect the well-being of others . . . in other words, you don't have the right to yell 'Fire!' in a packed theater." This quote refers to the

   (1) Tenth Amendment
   (2) Second Amendment
   (3) First Amendment
   (4) Sixth Amendment
   (5) Ninth Amendment

ANSWERS ARE ON PAGE 311.

WRITING ACTIVITY 3

In recent years, the First Amendment right to freedom of the press has been a controversial issue at several universities and high schools across the U.S. Student newspapers have come under attack for printing items considered to be racist, sexist, or intolerant of religious differences. School administrators assert that these ideas contradict the open-minded tenets of their institutions.

If school administrators take action against the publication of certain articles, are they violating the student journalists' right to freedom of the press? Write two to three paragraphs defending your position.

ANSWER IS ON PAGE 311.

THE U.S. POLITICAL SYSTEM

POLITICAL PARTIES

Although it has existed for two hundred years, the political party system is not provided for in the U.S. Constitution. Political parties evolved out of necessity and have become an integral part of the American political process. The two major political parties in the United States are the Democrats and the Republicans.

Political parties are beneficial to the American system of government because they:

- help to determine which of a large number of possible candidates will run for office

- help pay for the burdensome costs of the candidates' campaigns

- present the issues and the party's stand on them

The differences between the major political parties have become blurred in recent years. However, over the years, each party has taken a definitive stand on certain issues. The issues often involve economic, social, and foreign policies and form the basis for party loyalty for most Americans.

Voters may change political parties if they feel that the party to which they belong no longer reflects their positions on a number of issues. Although party affiliation in the U.S. is to some extent influenced strongly by ethnic and family heritage, a growing number of voters classify themselves as independents. *Independents* do not follow strict party lines in voting but consider the candidate's stand on the issues before casting their vote.

Party leaders are responsible for keeping the party platform in line with the thinking of the at-large membership in order to maintain party loyalty.

Both parties maintain national party headquarters and staffs. Each holds a national convention every four years to nominate a presidential candidate. The convention participants are delegates from each of the fifty states. A testimony to the control of our political system by two major parties is that the Democrats and the Republicans have controlled the presidency since 1900.

The chart below shows party control of the presidency from 1900 to 1997.

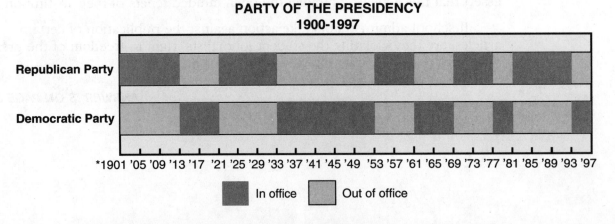

PARTY OF THE PRESIDENCY
1900-1997

Republican Party

Democratic Party

*1901 '05 '09 '13 '17 '21 '25 '29 '33 '37 '41 '45 '49 '53 '57 '61 '65 '69 '73 '77 '81 '85 '89 '93 '97

◼ In office ▨ Out of office

*Dates indicate time from inauguration to expiration of term of office

EXERCISE 12

Directions: Answer the following questions based on the chart shown on page 160.

1. Which party controlled the presidency for the longest continuous stretch of time?

_____

2. Which party controlled the presidency for the greatest number of terms over the eighty-eight years shown on the graph? (Remember that presidential terms are four years long.) _____

3. Which party is in control of the presidency at this time? _____

ANSWERS ARE ON PAGE 312.

WRITING ACTIVITY 4

Do you think a third political party will ever gain control of the U.S. presidency? Write two to three paragraphs explaining why or why not.

ANSWER IS ON PAGE 312.

POLITICAL LABELS

Traditionally, the voting populace has been viewed as holding a range of political positions. These political positions are illustrated below as one of five segments of a continuum. The segments are generally referred to as political labels.

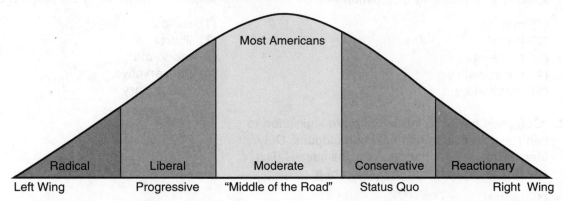

THE POLITICAL CONTINUUM

| Radical | Liberal | Moderate | Conservative | Reactionary |
| Left Wing | Progressive | "Middle of the Road" | Status Quo | Right Wing |

In order to win an election, each political party must obtain the majority of votes cast. Since the majority of American voters occupy the middle of the continuum, both political parties must appeal to this group of voters to win an election. For this reason, you probably have heard candidates speak about representing "middle America," or you may have heard a candidate described as being a "middle-of-the-roader."

GED Practice
EXERCISE 13

Questions 1–5 are based on the following definitions of the five political labels shown in the diagram on page 161 and on the paragraph below.

radical—advocates sweeping changes in laws and methods of government with the least delay

liberal—advocates political change in the name of progress, especially social improvement through governmental action

moderate—believes in avoiding extreme changes and measures in laws and government

conservative—advocates maintaining the existing social order

reactionary—resists change and usually advocates a return to an earlier social order or policy

A controversial issue that has dominated American life in recent years is gun control. Handguns seem to be increasingly accessible and are one of the leading causes of death in the United States. Americans have varying opinions about crime and handgun control. Read the quotes below and identify them with the correct label.

1. "Everybody should arm himself with a gun like people did in the Old West. Then you wouldn't have to worry about crime in the streets." The speaker is expressing the opinion of a

   (1) radical
   (2) liberal
   (3) moderate
   (4) conservative
   (5) reactionary

2. "Congress needs to introduce more legislation to ban the possession and sale of handguns. Only then will senseless handgun deaths cease." The speaker is expressing the opinion of a

   (1) radical
   (2) liberal
   (3) moderate
   (4) conservative
   (5) reactionary

3. "The Second Amendment gives American citizens the right to bear arms. To deny this basic right is an infringement on our personal liberties. The law should remain the way it is." The speaker is expressing the opinion of a

   (1) radical
   (2) liberal
   (3) moderate
   (4) conservative
   (5) reactionary

4. "There's no need to enact new laws or to abolish existing laws on gun control. All that's needed is the enforcement of the current laws on the books." The speaker is expressing the opinion of a

   (1) radical
   (2) liberal
   (3) moderate
   (4) conservative
   (5) reactionary

5. "The time to enforce gun control is *now*. Not one more murder should be committed because guns are so readily available. Let's stop the manufacture of guns *today*." The speaker is expressing the opinion of a

   (1) radical
   (2) liberal
   (3) moderate
   (4) conservative
   (5) reactionary

ANSWERS ARE ON PAGE 312.

THE IMPACT OF THE MEDIA

Another significant force in the modern American political process is the media. Television, radio, newspapers, and magazines are all part of the media. But television, by far, has the greatest influence on the American voter. It is estimated that 97 percent of U.S. households own television sets.

Huge sums of campaign money are spent on television commercials each election year as politicians capitalize on the power of this medium.

Sometimes campaigns are won or lost on the basis of a candidate's media campaign. Political observers attribute John Kennedy's 1960 victory over Richard Nixon to the favorable image Kennedy projected on the television screen to voters.

PRESSURE GROUPS

KEY WORDS

pressure group—an independent organized group that seeks to influence public opinion, policies, and actions
lobbying—conducting activities to influence public officials

Along with the media, pressure groups influence government also. Pressure groups are organized groups, not associated with any political party, that actively seek to influence public opinion, policies, and actions. This attempt to influence legislation is called lobbying.

While members of pressure groups ordinarily do not seek political office they do support candidates sympathetic to their causes. Two types of lobbies are economic lobbies and social lobbies. Examples of economic lobbies are trade and professional associations, such as the American Bankers Association, the American Medical Association, and the AFL-CIO. Examples of social lobbies are the National Education Association, the American Legion, and the National Welfare Rights Organization.

Through advertisements, meetings, mailings, and telephone calls, these pressure groups get their message out to the public and to the government.

Some political influencing is done more directly. For example, Political Action Committees (PACs) contribute to legislators' campaign funds in return for favorable votes on legislation important to the committees. Articles in law journals can also influence judicial decisions about cases. These tactics, however, are not without critics, who believe that such groups ultimately have a negative effect on the political process.

Public opinion is a third political force that affects politics in America. American citizens have unlimited sources of information upon which to form their opinions. These public opinions are the basis for surveys on a variety of topics. The results of these surveys are published in newspapers and magazines and are aired on television. Often, the media take polls, or surveys, of people's opinions on current events. Polls A and B below asked voters whom they would vote for in the election of 1948. The results of the 1948 election are also recorded below.

PUBLIC OPINION POLLS AND 1948 VOTE RESULTS			
	Democrats (Truman)	Republicans (Dewey)	Others*
Poll A	44.5%	49.5%	6.0%
Poll B	37.5%	53.0%	9.5%
Actual Vote	49.5%	45.1%	5.4%

*Dixiecrat party and Progressive party candidates

EXERCISE 14

Directions: Look at the chart above. Notice that there was a big difference between what the polls predicted and how the 1948 election turned out. Put an *H* in front of each statement that could be a reasonable hypothesis explaining this discrepancy. Since these are hypotheses, or possible explanations, more than one could be true.

_____ **(1)** Many voters changed their minds between the time of the surveys and the time of the election.

_____ **(2)** Dewey supporters were not as committed to him as pollsters were led to believe.

_____ **(3)** Poll A was conducted less scientifically than Poll B.

_____ **(4)** The people doing the surveys did not ask either enough people or the right people.

_____ **(5)** These public opinion polls were done by people in favor of Dewey.

ANSWERS ARE ON PAGE 312.

EXERCISE 15

Questions 1 and 2 are based on the following passage.

Some people say that public opinion polls should not be taken close to an election because the results might influence the voters. For example, during the 1980 election, the outcome was predicted by television networks before the polls closed. Informal surveys, *exit polls*, were being conducted outside the voting areas and vote percentages for each candidate were projected from them. These exit polls showed candidate Ronald Reagan with a substantial lead over incumbent Jimmy Carter. In fact, former President Carter lost the 1980 election to Ronald Reagan.

1. Which of the following best explains how the televised poll results could have affected the election's outcome?

    (1) Carter's supporters who had not yet voted did not bother to when they saw the lopsided poll results.
    (2) When it became known that Carter was trailing Reagan, more of Carter's supporters rushed out to vote than would have otherwise.
    (3) Backers of Reagan who had not yet voted did not think it necessary to vote since he was far ahead.
    (4) Happy about the obvious victory, Reagan supporters came out in even greater numbers to vote.
    (5) Voters who were undecided before finally decided to join the winning team and vote for Reagan.

2. Based on the passage, public opinion polls

    (1) have no effect on election results
    (2) help incumbents win elections
    (3) should not be shown on television until after voting areas have closed
    (4) are the best informed survey of voters' interests
    (5) should be conducted outside voting booths

Question 3 is based on the passage below.

In the 1988 election, 50 percent of women voters polled reported voting for George Bush and 49 percent for Michael Dukakis. In 1992, 36 percent voted for George Bush, 17 percent voted for Ross Perot, and 46 percent voted for Bill Clinton. Exit polls for both years also reveal that in 1988 the men's vote was 57 percent for Bush and 41 percent for Dukakis; and in 1992, 37 percent for Bush, 41 percent for Clinton, and 21 percent for Perot.

3. Clinton won the election because of a shift in

    (1) the women's vote toward Bush
    (2) the women's vote toward Clinton
    (3) the men's vote toward Clinton
    (4) the men's vote toward Bush
    (5) men's and women's vote toward Perot

ANSWERS ARE ON PAGE 312.

WRITING ACTIVITY 5

Do you agree with the television networks' practice of predicting the outcome of an election before all of the votes are cast? Write two to three paragraphs explaining why you agree or disagree with this practice.

ANSWER IS ON PAGE 312.

STATE AND LOCAL GOVERNMENTS

STATE GOVERNMENTS

Unlike the Articles of Confederation, the U.S. Constitution did not provide for state sovereignty. In fact, it spelled out, in Section Ten of Article One, exactly what the states could *not* do. Other prohibitions are stated in amendments to the Constitution. The Constitution prohibits the states from:

- making treaties with other countries
- manufacturing paper money or coins
- giving out titles of nobility
- imposing taxes on imports or exports
- making agreements with other states without federal approval
- waging war
- taking away privileges and rights of American citizens
- denying life, liberty, or property to anyone without due process
- depriving anyone of the right to vote because of race or sex

Since the Constitution was not specific about the powers of the states, the Supreme Court has played a major role in defining states' rights.

Some of the powers of the states include the establishing of most criminal codes, laws for contracts, and other regulations concerning the operation of business. Property and marriage and divorce laws also are the responsibility of the states, as is public education.

All fifty states have constitutions, and many are based on the U.S. model. Like the U.S. Constitution, they all have a system of checks and balances based on three branches of government: legislative, executive, and judicial.

THE LEGISLATIVE BRANCH

> ### KEY WORDS
>
> *initiative*—a procedure that enables the voters to propose a law and present it to the legislature and other voters for approval
> *referendum*—a procedure that allows the voting public to approve or disapprove of a measure enacted or proposed by the legislature
> *recall*—the procedure of removing a public official by popular vote

All but one state (Nebraska) have two-house legislatures. Most even call these legislatures by names similar to those used by the U.S. Congress. Most of their work is done by committee also.

Determining the distribution of state money is one of the most important functions of state legislatures, as this determines the state's spending priorities each year. Much of the revenue that a state takes in comes from taxes it imposes. Some money also is allocated to the states by the federal government.

Since the early citizens of the states feared powerful legislatures, they built into the state governments certain powers held by the voters. These powers serve as checks and balances at the state government level.

An initiative is a type of check in which the people can propose a law and sometimes even get it passed. Another type, a referendum, permits the voters to approve of or reject a law or proposal made by the legislature. In most states the voters can also recall, or remove, an official from office by vote.

THE EXECUTIVE BRANCH

KEY WORDS

pardon—the excusing of a public offense
reprieve—a delay in punishment of a person convicted of a crime

The chief executive at the state level is the governor. Like the president, the governor has strong veto power. But limits on the governor's power have been carefully set, too.

In some states, either governors cannot succeed themselves or they serve very short terms. In others, the lieutenant governor (the equivalent of a vice president) can be from a different political party and can serve as the loyal opposition. This provides another opportunity to check the power of the executive officer.

The attorney general (the chief law enforcement officer in the state) is sometimes from a different party, too. The attorney general is not always elected by the people, however. Sometimes attorney generals are chosen by the legislature and are often given much power as legal guardians of the states' affairs. In six of the fifty states, this officer is appointed by the governor.

Like a strong president, a strong governor is a leader in proposing legislation, preparing budgets, and influencing public opinion. Governors usually have many departments and agencies under them through which much of the state's work gets done. The governor also commands the state militia (the National Guard) but has less authority over other law enforcement agencies.

In most states, too, the governor can override a judicial decision by a pardon or a reprieve for a convicted criminal. A pardon is a full release from punishment, as if the crime were never committed. A reprieve is a delay in punishment, but it sometimes gives a lawyer for the accused enough time to gather evidence for a new trial. These powers often give the governor the final word in a state's criminal justice system.

≡ GED Practice ≡
EXERCISE 16

Questions 1 and 2 are based on the information on pages 166–167.

1. Which of the following would be an action *not* allowed a state by the Constitution?

   (1) establishing a state income tax
   (2) setting a residency requirement for a person to be allowed to vote
   (3) forbidding a news editor to criticize the governor
   (4) denying a convicted criminal the right to vote
   (5) depriving aliens the right to vote

2. What is the most likely reason that the writers of the U.S. Constitution found it necessary to forbid the states to grant a title of nobility?

   (1) Royal governors had used that power for their own benefit.
   (2) It would make the states more powerful than the federal government.
   (3) It contradicted the principle that "all men are created equal," a cornerstone of our democracy.
   (4) Clear standards had not been set for granting titles.
   (5) The states might become too powerful.

ANSWERS ARE ON PAGE 313.

EXERCISE 17

Directions: In the space provided, write *S* if the power belongs to the states, *F* if it belongs to the federal government, and *B* if it belongs to both.

_____ **1.** vetoing a bill by the chief executive

_____ **2.** passing laws that provide for the welfare of its citizens

_____ **3.** declaring war against a foreign country

_____ **4.** setting import quotas and duties

_____ **5.** establishing a legal age for marriage

_____ **6.** setting up guidelines for chartering a business

ANSWERS ARE ON PAGE 313.

THE JUDICIAL BRANCH

The federal and state court systems have been kept separate, with the U.S. Supreme Court intervening only when a matter is clearly of national interest. The state courts use magistrates or justices of the peace for minor criminal and civil cases. Also at this level are lower courts—traffic courts and juvenile courts are examples. Most are conducted without trial or jury.

The next level includes circuit courts, county courts, district courts, and superior courts. They handle more serious criminal cases and civil cases that involve bigger fines, more punishment, and greater monetary rewards. Juries are available at this level, if desired.

Appellate courts review the decisions made by circuit, county, district, and superior courts. They are usually divided into two classes—intermediate and supreme. Supreme courts, like their federal counterparts, have the last say on the cases they hear. In appellate courts, judges decide the cases.

Judges are very powerful in state judicial systems. In most states they are elected by the people, but in some they are appointed by the governor or the legislature.

GED Practice

EXERCISE 18

Questions 1 and 2 are based on the above information.

1. In which court is a case involving a personal injury suit likely to be heard first?

    (1) federal Supreme Court
    (2) federal district court
    (3) state circuit court
    (4) appellate court
    (5) state supreme court

2. An Ohio man is convicted of murder and is given the death penalty. After the trial, new evidence is uncovered that can prove the man's innocence. Which court will likely hear the case?

    (1) a state lower court
    (2) the federal Supreme Court
    (3) a circuit court
    (4) a state appellate court
    (5) a state district court

ANSWERS ARE ON PAGE 313.

LOCAL GOVERNMENTS

The level of government that most affects the daily lives of its citizens and the one that could be affected most by the actions of its citizens is the one usually given the least attention. Few Americans know who is taking care of local business—who are the mayor, the town council and the county board members, the sheriff, the highway commissioner, etc. Few even know how local government is structured.

The next level of government after the state system is the county (in Louisiana, the parish; in Alaska, the borough).

COUNTIES

Counties were not defined or provided for in the U.S. Constitution. The county system of government began in Virginia and originally was established to govern sprawling, rural areas. Counties usually act as agents for the state, carrying out the powers of the state at a local level.

One important function of counties is gathering revenue to provide services, usually through property taxes. The ***property tax*** is a percentage tax on real estate owned in the city or county. It yields a great amount of money and can be raised to provide more revenue when needed. Additional money is raised through special taxes on cigarettes or liquor, for example.

The way the money is appropriated and spent depends on the needs of the population of the individual area. The most expensive item in the local budget is education. Local government also offers road building and repair, police and fire protection, sanitation and sewage services, and public welfare services.

The majority of counties in the fifty states have a system of government in which the administrative authority is shared by members of a board or commission. These members are elected by the voters of the county. This organizational plan is called the ***plural-executive plan***.

This plural-executive plan has been criticized often for inefficiency and lack of individual accountability. For this reason, some counties have changed to a county-manager plan, in which one person is hired to manage the county's day-to-day operations.

≡ GED Practice ≡
EXERCISE 19

Questions 1 and 2 are based on the following pie charts.

COUNTY EXPENDITURES

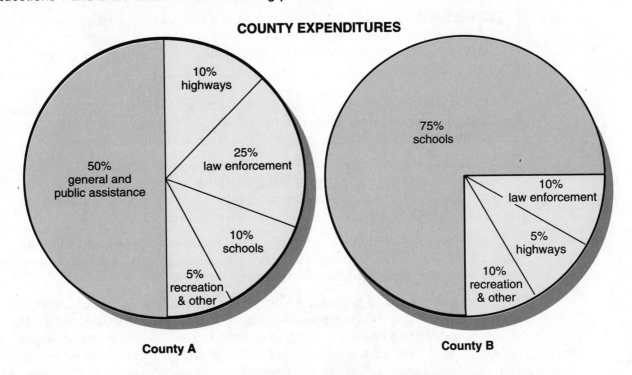

County A

County B

1. Which of the following can you infer about the makeup of Counties A and B?

    (1) County A has a greater concentration of children.
    (2) County A has more crime.
    (3) County A is smaller than County B.
    (4) County B has a greater concentration of children.
    (5) Counties A and B are both the same size.

2. Which hypothesis would best explain the difference between the two counties' expenditures for law enforcement?

    (1) It is more difficult to enforce the law in County B.
    (2) County A has a better law enforcement system.
    (3) Police officers are not needed in County B.
    (4) There is a greater need for law enforcement services in County A.
    (5) Too little money has been set aside for law enforcement in County B.

ANSWERS ARE ON PAGE 313.

TOWNSHIPS AND MUNICIPALITIES

> **KEY WORDS**
>
> *incorporation*—a legal process by which a town, city, or village sets up a plan under which it will operate
>
> *charter*—a written instrument that establishes a city, village, or town

Below the county form of local government are the township and municipal levels. The township, like the county, acts as an agent for the state and carries out many of the functions of the state at the local level.

Municipalities are established generally through incorporation, a legal process in which the town, city, or village sets up a charter under which it will operate. The charter provides a system for administering police and fire protection, libraries, paved streets, water, sewage disposal, etc.

Once incorporated, a community can raise its own money and share in state and county taxes. Without incorporation, a community is dependent upon the county government to provide necessary services.

The government of a village, town, or city can take a variety of forms: the mayor-council form, the commission form, and the council-manager form. The most commonly used form of city government in the U.S. today is the mayor-council plan. Under such a plan, either the mayor may wield the most power (strong mayor-council plan) or the council of aldermen may wield the most power (weak mayor-council plan). The least commonly used plan is the commission form in which members of a governing board share authority.

 WRITING ACTIVITY 6

In a paragraph, describe the type of local government your town or city has.

ANSWER IS ON PAGE 313.

PROBLEMS OF THE CITIES AND SUBURBS

In recent decades, the cities, particularly in the Northeast and Midwest, have been experiencing such problems as flight of the white, upper, and middle classes to the suburbs, rising in crime rates in the inner cities, loss of tax bases as urban industries die off, and a drop in educational achievements in the older city schools.

Despite their problems, the cities represent a crucial component of our economic and social life. One of the challenges facing America in the last part of the twentieth century is the revitalization of our large urban areas.

EXERCISE 20

Directions: Look at the following cartoon and fill in the blanks below with the appropriate words.

The bundled-up people are sitting in **(1)** _____.

They are talking to a man who is looking for **(2)** _____.

The season of the year is **(3)** _____.

ANSWERS ARE ON PAGE 313.

≡ GED Practice ≡
EXERCISE 21

Questions 1 and 2 are based on the cartoon above.

1. What is the cartoonist implying about America's suburbs?

   (1) America's suburbs have no housing problems.
   (2) The homeless should move to the suburbs.
   (3) Lack of affordable housing in America's suburbs is leading to a homeless population.
   (4) People looking for affordable homes can get good advice from the homeless.
   (5) City streets are getting colder.

2. You can infer from the cartoon that the problem of homelessness has

   (1) become centered in the suburbs only
   (2) been solved by providing affordable housing
   (3) decreased in the cities
   (4) gone beyond the cities and spread to the suburbs
   (5) been talked about too much

ANSWERS ARE ON PAGE 313.

GED Practice

POLITICAL SCIENCE

Questions 1 and 2 are based on the following cartoon.

Entitlements are government-funded programs such as Medicare and Social Security that provide financial assistance to individual Americans.

1. Which of the following best expresses the main idea of the cartoon?

   (1) The government has decided to cut funds for entitlement programs.
   (2) The government has decided to increase funds for entitlement programs.
   (3) The government has decided to create new entitlement programs.
   (4) The government has decided not to touch entitlement programs.
   (5) The government has no authority over funding for entitlement programs.

2. Which of the following best expresses the cartoonist's opinion?

   (1) Government has too much money.
   (2) Entitlement programs are overfunded.
   (3) Entitlement programs are underfunded.
   (4) The future of America depends on funding entitlement programs.
   (5) Entitlement programs deserve support.

Questions 3 and 4 are based on the following pie charts.

THE CHANGING FACE OF CONGRESS

The 103rd Congress that convened Jan. 5, 1992 was the most diverse ever. There were more women, and members were younger and more racially mixed.

More Women
Women made record gains in the House and Senate, but they still made up only about 10 percent of Congress.

Women in House	
freshmen elected	24
incumbents	24
total	48

Men 387 | 48 Women
Total 435

Women in Senate	
freshmen elected	4
incumbents	2
Total	6

Men 94 | 6 Women
Total 100

Sources: Congressional Quarterly, Congressional Black Caucus, news reports

---

3. Which of the following statements is best supported by the information in these charts?

   (1) Women prefer working in the House to working in the Senate.
   (2) There is a great imbalance in the number of men and women representatives in Congress.
   (3) All the freshmen in Congress are women.
   (4) All the women who ran for office were elected.
   (5) African-American women were among the freshman representatives.

4. According to the charts, how many women are there in the 103rd Congress?

   (1) six
   (2) four
   (3) twenty-four
   (4) forty-eight
   (5) fifty-four

Questions 5 and 6 are based on the following passage.

The Declaration of Independence states, "We hold these truths to be self-evident, that all men are created equal, that they are endowed by the Creator with certain inalienable rights, that among these are Life, Liberty and the pursuit of Happiness. That to secure these rights, Governments are instituted among Men, deriving their just Powers from the consent of the governed."

When Thomas Jefferson wrote these words in 1776, he made one of the most powerful political statements of all time. The principles outlined in the Declaration of Independence shaped the American political structure. Specific examples of rights were later added to the U.S. Constitution in the form of Amendments.

5. Which of the following is an opinion expressed by the author of this passage?

   (1) The quotation is from the Declaration of Independence.
   (2) Thomas Jefferson was the author of the quotation.
   (3) The Declaration of Independence was one of the most powerful political statements ever written.
   (4) The Declaration of Independence was written in 1776.
   (5) Specific rights are described in Constitutional amendments.

6. According to the Declaration of Independence, which of the following principles did Jefferson most value?

   (1) the survival of the fittest
   (2) the natural rights of the individual
   (3) the power of government
   (4) freedom of religion
   (5) telling the truth

Questions 7 and 8 are based on the following information.

Three well-known federal agencies often get confused in the public mind. The *Central Intelligence Agency* was designed to collect information about the activities of foreign governments. The CIA is responsible only to the president and can keep its operations secret from Congress. The *Federal Bureau of Investigation* is part of the Justice Department and investigates suspected violations of federal laws, including espionage and treason. The *Secret Service* was founded to prevent counterfeiting. Since 1901, this agency has also protected U.S. presidents and, more recently, the vice president, the president's family, and major presidential candidates.

7. Which of the following situations would be investigated by the Secret Service?

   (1) the discovery of fake $20 bills circulating in Tampa
   (2) a person suspected of selling U.S. military secrets
   (3) a revolution in Central America
   (4) a suspected drug ring operating in St. Louis
   (5) the kidnapping of a U.S. senator's son

8. Which of the following situations would be investigated by the CIA?

   (1) the discovery of fake $20 bills circulating in Tampa
   (2) a person suspected of selling U.S. military secrets
   (3) a revolution in Central America
   (4) a suspected drug ring operating in St. Louis
   (5) the kidnapping of a U.S. senator's son

ANSWERS ARE ON PAGE 313.

7 Behavioral Sciences

To a biologist, a person is a living body of bones, muscles, tissues, and cells whose existence depends on the physical health of those parts. To an anthropologist, a person is a member of a unique culture. To a sociologist, a person is a member of a society who contributes to or detracts from the health of that society through interaction with others. And to a psychologist, a person is defined by his personality, intelligence, and behavior.

Biology is a natural science. All the others are ***behavioral sciences***, because they study the behavior of people rather than their physical makeup.

THE SCIENTIFIC METHOD

The behavioral sciences did not exist as separate fields of study before the 1800s. But, of course, long before then people wondered why human beings behaved as they did. In fact, the ancient Greek philosophers Plato and Aristotle knew the importance of understanding oneself and others. Both developed theories about the human mind and its relationship to the physical body. But these theories were highly speculative, were explained by "human nature," and thus were not based on the scientific method applied universally today.

The scientific method that both natural and social scientists use involves the following steps:

1. observing a problem

2. developing a theory (hypothesizing) about that problem

3. designing an experiment or carrying out research to prove or disprove the theory

4. carrying out the experiment and summarizing the findings

5. drawing conclusions from the findings and verifying the conclusions through more experiments

Only by following the steps described above can a scientist arrive at objective conclusions about how humans behave.

EXERCISE 1

Directions: Complete each of the sentences below by filling in the blank with the type of scientist the statement describes: *anthropologist, biologist, sociologist,* or *psychologist.*

1. The scientist who discovered that the brain produces a chemical that helps it defend itself when under attack was most probably a(n)

_____.

2. A scientist who studies the effects of pressure on Israel's society while it is under constant threat of war would most likely be a(n)

_____.

3. A person who is tracing the development of India's culture from ancient times to this day would be called a(n)

_____.

4. A scientist who tries to discover the effects of stress on the personality and mental capabilities of individual children is a(n)

_____.

ANSWERS ARE ON PAGE 314.

EXERCISE 2

Directions: Number the steps below (1–5) in the order of the scientific method. Refer to the scientific method on page 177.

_____ giving the questionnaire to students in high school and college classes and tabulating their answers

_____ hypothesizing that women can reverse sex roles more easily than men because men's roles have higher status and men are unwilling to give up the status associated with their roles

_____ finding that men are less willing to take the responsibility for housework and childcare than women; planning to survey adults by phone next

_____ observing that men cannot reverse sex roles as easily as women

_____ developing a questionnaire that asks men and women about their interest in reversing sex roles

ANSWERS ARE ON PAGE 314.

WHAT IS ANTHROPOLOGY?

"May I have the pleasure of introducing you to yourself? Please meet *Homo sapiens*, meaning 'man of the wise,' the most interesting creature on the face of the earth."

When writer Ashley Montagu began one of his books this way, he summed up the attitude of the professional anthropologist. The anthropologist is interested in many aspects of that fascinating creature the human being. Anthropologists specialize in either cultural or physical anthropology.

CULTURAL ANTHROPOLOGY

Cultural anthropologists compare and contrast the different cultures of man today and of societies in the past. They study the art, religions, governments, and languages of a culture as well as the customs or practices that make it unique.

The primary interest of cultural anthropologists is in primitive and ancient cultures, and many of their investigative techniques are used by sociologists in their study of modern peoples today.

PHYSICAL ANTHROPOLOGY

Physical anthropologists study the origin and development of human physical characteristics and how they vary from human to human, society to society, and race to race. Their job is as much related to biology as it is to the social sciences. They have categorized humans into races and have found similarities between man and the apes. Their work includes a range of activities, from assembling bone fragments to reconstructing buildings from lost civilizations.

Anthropologists live with their subjects for long periods of time, read extensive writings by and about a culture, or dig up what is left of dead-and-gone societies. The diggers, called archaeologists, require specialized training to be able to recognize the cultural significance of such findings as broken pottery, bone fragments, primitive stone weapons, and parts of old tools.

EXERCISE 3

Directions: Fill in each blank below with the term that best fits the anthropologist described below.

1. Colin Turnbull lived among the Pygmies of the Congo, in Africa, to study every aspect of their unique life in the rain forest.

   Mr. Turnbull is a _____.

           (cultural anthropologist)   (physical anthropologist)

2. Louis and Mary Leakey have made many significant discoveries about ancient, primitive man through their analysis of skeletal remains dug up in Africa.

   The Leakeys are _____.

           (cultural anthropologists)   (physical anthropologists)

ANSWERS ARE ON PAGE 314.

THE EVOLUTION OF CULTURE

> **KEY WORDS**
>
> *civilization*—a classification of cultures by how they farm, domesticate animals, produce goods, and use oral and written language
> *clan*—a group that believes its members are all biologically related
> *evolution*—the gradual development of something into a more complex form
> *tribe*—a social group whose members share a distinct culture and language

Physical anthropologists have found much evidence that man is a close relative of the ape. Man and apes share the characteristics of a complex brain; efficient vision; relatively flat face; flexible hands, feet, and forearms; and even internal biological makeup, including reproductive capabilities. Their young are cared for by adults for longer periods of time than is the case with other animals.

Many scientists believe that the process of evolution has gradually distinguished the apes from other animals and has distinguished humans from the apes. Moreover, most anthropologists believe that man's culture has evolved from a simpler to a more complex form as human beings themselves became more complex. The passage below illustrates how civilizations changed from a simple to a more complex form.

EXERCISE 4

Directions: Read the passage and then number each event in the order in which it occurs in the passage.

After thousands of years, humans abandoned hunting of big game as their primary means of obtaining food and clothing, and they turned to farming and domesticating of animals to meet their survival needs.

This change led to the establishment of clans and tribes and the organization of work and responsibilities. This organization created the need for rules for people to live by.

As people prospered and focused less on basic survival, they had more time for leisure. Out of this leisure, they crafted items of handiwork, art, and other trappings that reflected their unique culture.

These goods created a demand that contributed to the development of villages and towns around trading centers. Increasing trade demanded the efficiency of a written language for the purposes of communication. Through this evolutionary process, what anthropologists call "civilization" emerged.

_____ Farming and domestication of animals is learned.

_____ Arts and crafts become a part of society.

_____ Big game is hunted as a source of food and clothing.

_____ Clans and tribes are established.

_____ Written language is created.

_____ Towns grow out of trading centers.

_____ Organized rules are set for society.

ANSWERS ARE ON PAGE 314.

GED Practice
EXERCISE 5

Questions 1–3 are based on the passage on page 181.

1. Art was created primarily because

   (1) a wealthy class emerged to support artists
   (2) the people desired some form of beauty in their harsh environment
   (3) artists from other advanced communities exposed primitive people to it
   (4) the people had the leisure time in which to create art
   (5) the rulers established a class of artists

2. Which of the following led directly to the creation of written language?

   (1) the abandonment of hunting in favor of farming and domestication of animals
   (2) the establishment of clans and tribes
   (3) material prosperity, which led to more time for leisure
   (4) the development of trade between villages
   (5) the emergence of civilization

3. Of the following statements, which is supported by the passage?

   (1) Society developed rules and laws to encourage the domestication of animals.
   (2) The growth of leisure time led to disorder and chaos.
   (3) Tribes and clans preferred hunting to domesticating animals.
   (4) Tribes and clans developed written language so that they could write down their laws.
   (5) The production of goods led directly to the establishment of villages as trading centers.

ANSWERS ARE ON PAGE 314.

WRITING ACTIVITY 1

What differences in culture have you observed among Americans of ethnic groups other than yours? Choose one group with which you are familiar and write two paragraphs describing a cultural difference in the area of dress, family relationships, child rearing, or any other aspect with which you are familiar.

ANSWER IS ON PAGE 314.

ETHNOCENTRISM AND CULTURAL RELATIVITY

KEY WORDS

cultural relativity—judging another culture objectively
ethnocentrism—using one's culture as the standard by which to judge another culture

Often, we assume that our culture is the "right" one and is superior to others in the world. We might describe other cultures as being heathen, backward, savage, or barbarian. Such attitudes show our ethnocentrism. Ethnocentrism is the act of judging another culture on the basis of one's own cultural values.

To avoid being ethnocentric, anthropologists strive to be objective in their assessments of the cultures they observe. By practicing cultural relativity, anthropologists are able to appreciate and understand the customs of the diverse cultures of the world.

GED Practice

EXERCISE 6

Questions 1 and 2 are based on the above information.

1. Which of the following situations illustrates the concept of ethnocentrism?

   (1) Filipinos forcing into exile Ferdinand Marcos, whom they believed abused his power
   (2) the criticism of the U.S.S.R. by Russian dissident Andre Sakharov
   (3) the refusal of devout Catholics to eat meat on Fridays during the season of Lent
   (4) a nonsmoker agreeing to smoke a peace pipe during a Native American ritual
   (5) an American woman's description of European women who refuse to shave their legs as "masculine"

2. In India, Hindus dispose of their dead's remains by building a funeral pyre and cremating the body during a public ceremony. At Indian prime minister Rajiv Gandhi's cremation, his oldest son applied the torch. Which of the following attitudes of an American tourist reflects the concept of cultural relativity?

   (1) Cremation is a barbaric way to dispose of a person's remains.
   (2) The human body is sacred and therefore should not be burned.
   (3) The Hindu rite of cremation can be a religious experience.
   (4) Burial is the only Christian way to dispose of a person's remains.
   (5) Cremation is better than burial because it is cheaper, efficient, and conserves land.

ANSWERS ARE ON PAGE 314.

CULTURAL DIFFUSION

KEY WORD
cultural diffusion—the spreading of cultural elements to different societies

The saying "It's a small world" is probably truer today than in any other period in human history. Many conveniences of the modern world, such as air travel and telecommunications, have bridged the distances between people. The result is that there is hardly any corner of the world that has not been explored by man.

Wherever humans travel, they bring their culture with them. For example, even in the remotest regions of the world, an American can obtain a Coke or a McDonald's hamburger and thus feel right at home. When one culture adopts cultural elements from another, the process is called cultural diffusion.

According to anthropologists, cultural diffusion has both advantages and disadvantages to the culture that accepts the changes.

The passage below illustrates the process of cultural diffusion as it applies to the Pygmies in central Africa.

GED Practice
EXERCISE 7

Questions 1–7 are based on the following passage.

The Pygmies of central Africa were most probably an isolated tribe thousands of years ago. Pygmies rely very much on hunting and gathering for their basic needs, and such techniques are considered the most primitive for a human society. Although they still live in the thick, sunless rain forest, today they do much business with the Bantu, an African tribe that is more "civilized" in its culture.

In Pygmy society, as in other "primitive" societies, many rituals and religions are tied closely to food gathering. However, many of these institutions have begun to change. Since rituals and religions reinforce group solidarity and dependence on one another, the group is weakened when the rules begin to bend or are ignored.

Food-gathering techniques, rituals, and religions are not the only aspects of the culture that are changing, however. The use of environmental materials in traditional house building is being replaced by the use of prefabricated materials such as tin roofs and cement blocks.

Crude stone and wooden tools are becoming scarce as ready-made hammers and screwdrivers are becoming available to the previously secluded natives. Handicrafts are produced less for use by home and society than for sale to tourists.

Once "primitives" come into contact with the outside world, an innocence and unquestioning contentment is lost. A visible example of this can be seen in the way they dress. For Pygmies and other African tribes who live in warm areas, modesty is not innate. Most wear few articles of clothing, if any, until they learn to feel ashamed by tourists from more "advanced" cultures.

Anthropologists understand that the disappearance of "primitive" peoples from this earth would mean a loss to human culture in general, since we have much to learn from them.

1. Based on the above passage, which of the examples listed below illustrates the process of cultural diffusion?

   (1) the Pygmies' policy of trading with the Bantu
   (2) the Pygmies' use of prefabricated materials to build their houses
   (3) the Pygmies' reliance on hunting and gathering to meet their basic needs
   (4) the weakening of tribal bonds among the Pygmies
   (5) the Pygmies' production of handicrafts for use by home and society

2. The author of the passage apparently feels that the effect of cultural diffusion in central Africa

   (1) has had a good effect on the Pygmy society
   (2) has had no observable impact on Pygmy society
   (3) has had a negative impact on Pygmy society
   (4) did not really take place in Pygmy society
   (5) had a greater effect on Bantu society than Pygmy society

3. The words *civilized*, *advanced*, and *primitive* are in quotations in the passage. In emphasizing these words, the author is

   (1) being ethnocentric—judging Pygmy society according to his own values
   (2) emphasizing how cultural diffusion works in some societies
   (3) suggesting that the Bantu tribe is more advanced and civilized than any other African tribe
   (4) implying that the descriptions *civilized*, *advanced*, and *primitive* should never be used
   (5) suggesting that those cultures described as *civilized*, *advanced*, and *primitive* may not be what we think they are

4. The author of the passage believes that the Pygmies

   (1) prefer to remain isolated
   (2) are not open to changes suggested by more "advanced" cultures
   (3) are more civilized than the Bantu
   (4) have held on to their innocence
   (5) produce handicrafts more for sale to outsiders than for their own use

5. The author of the passage attributes weaknesses in the Pygmies' group solidarity to

   (1) changes in rituals and religions that affect their dependence on one another
   (2) changes in dress that cause arguments among the tribe members
   (3) housing that separates group members from one another
   (4) new food-gathering techniques
   (5) disagreements about the need for hunting and gathering

6. After contact with more "advanced" cultures, the Pygmies have

   (1) learned new art techniques
   (2) preserved their ancient tool-making methods
   (3) retreated further away from modern society
   (4) become embarrassed about their manner of dressing
   (5) given up their former religious beliefs

7. Which area of Pygmy culture has *not* been affected by recent changes?

   (1) type of housing
   (2) choice of dress
   (3) practice of rituals
   (4) religious beliefs
   (5) reliance on hunting and gathering

ANSWERS ARE ON PAGE 315.

EXERCISE 8

Directions: Study the map of the Ituri Forest below. Then place an *X* next to the statement(s) that can be concluded from the information on the map.

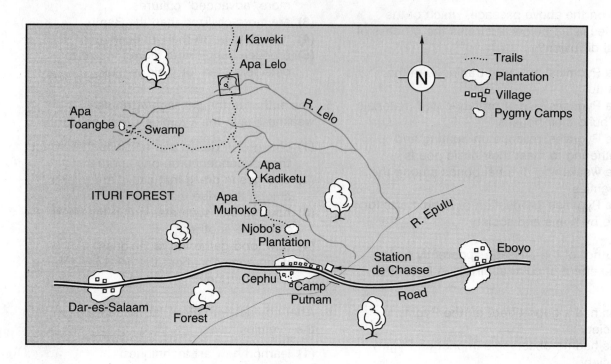

_____ **(1)** The Pygmy camps are smaller than plantations.

_____ **(2)** Apa must mean "camp" or "tribe" in Pygmy language.

_____ **(3)** The Ituri Forest is a rain forest in central Africa.

_____ **(4)** The villages are located inside plantations.

_____ **(5)** Most Pygmy camps range from east to west in the Ituri Forest.

ANSWERS ARE ON PAGE 315.

WHAT IS SOCIOLOGY?

KEY WORDS

group—two or more people who interact because of certain shared characteristics or interests

primary group—a group in which the members share highly personal relationships

secondary group—a group in which the members work together for a common purpose but do not share close personal relationships

Sociologists attempt to understand today's society and its organization by observing people's behavior in groups and by studying the rules that govern group behavior.

According to sociologists, a group is two or more people who interact with one another. A load of passengers on an airplane is not a group unless the members have something in common: if, for instance, they are professional football players on their way to a game, or senior citizens on a charter flight to a distant city, or even a group of businessmen and tourists suddenly bonded together by the fate of a hijacking.

Basically, sociologists study two types of groups: primary and secondary. Primary groups include your family and personal friends with whom you share close relationships. Secondary groups include your work team, classmates, church members, or any group in which your relationship with the members is more impersonal than with a primary group.

Society today is placing more emphasis on secondary groups than ever before in history. Frequently, this is because of the widening geographic distance between families, a growing feature of modern American life. For example, when a young single parent has to work these days, she may have to seek a professional daycare center (a secondary-group relationship) instead of relying on her mother or other relatives (a primary-group relationship).

Some sociologists believe that this distancing of families may be beneficial to society at large. As a widely diverse society, we are getting to know people who differ from us in many ways. As a result, sociologists feel Americans are becoming more tolerant of differences among people than before.

EXERCISE 9

Directions: Indicate whether the examples below represent primary or secondary groups by writing *P* in the space for a primary group and *S* for a secondary group. Remember that primary group members share close personal relationships while secondary group members work together for a common purpose.

_____ **1.** members of an Elvis Presley fan club

_____ **2.** all the members of a large fraternity

_____ **3.** members of the Democratic party

_____ **4.** your child's closest playmates

_____ **5.** players on the Chicago Bears football team

_____ **6.** employees of the Acme Screw Company

_____ **7.** members of the Brotherhood of Electrical Workers

_____ **8.** your grandparents and great grandparents

_____ **9.** senior citizens on a charter flight to Hawaii

_____ **10.** members of a household

ANSWERS ARE ON PAGE 315.

 **WRITING ACTIVITY 2**

Write a paragraph describing the primary and secondary groups to which you belong. What makes these groups primary and secondary in your life?

ANSWER IS ON PAGE 315.

SOCIAL INSTITUTIONS

An ***institution*** is a system organized by society to provide for its members' important needs. The function of many institutions is to teach citizens a society's appropriate customs and behaviors.

In complex societies like the United States, five major institutions exist: family, religious, political, economic, and educational. The most important of these, however, is the family.

THE FAMILY

To most Americans, a family consists of a husband, a wife, and their children, if they have any. There is close interaction among the members of this family. Sociologists call this the nuclear family.

In other countries, and in some cultures within the United States, however, the family is said to be extended because it contains not only the husband, wife, and children, but also other blood relatives among whom there is close interaction. An extended family might include the nuclear unit plus the husband's or wife's mother and father, brothers and sisters, and the husbands, wives, and children of those brothers and sisters.

The establishment of a new family or a new branch of a family begins in most cultures with a marriage. Every society sets its own norms or accepted practices for such a union. For example, in the U.S. a husband may have only one wife and vice versa. Therefore, marriage in the U.S. is described as monogamous. Other cultures, however, permit its members to have more than one spouse. Marriage in these cultures is described as polygamous.

Other cultures may differ according to who selects the mate and where the couple will live. In the U.S., the individuals themselves usually choose the person whom they want to marry. In other cultures, the parents may choose the mate for their son or daughter. The matter of where to live is left up to the married couple in the U.S.; in some other societies the newlyweds don't have such freedom of choice. Sometimes they are required to live near the family of either the husband or the wife.

EXERCISE 10

Directions: Write *N* in the space if the situation below describes a nuclear family, and write *E* if it describes an extended family.

_____ **1.** An engaged couple heed the advice of friends who warn them that if they want to be happy, they should move far away from their in-laws after marriage.

_____ **2.** A tribal law requires a husband and wife to maintain a home in the same compound as his relatives.

_____ **3.** A woman depends on her brothers for help in raising her children, while her husband takes care of his sister's children.

_____ **4.** In Japan, a married couple with children is still responsible for housing and supporting their elderly parents.

_____ **5.** The typical family in the United States is changing. This is causing an increase in single-parent households with mothers raising children alone.

ANSWERS ARE ON PAGE 315.

▄▄ GED Practice ▄▄
EXERCISE 11

Questions 1 and 2 refer to the following paragraph.

"The Seminole are organized into matrilineal clans. Inheritance and descent are through the mother's side of the family. The mother is head of the household. When a man marries he lives with his wife's family. In clan functions, a boy receives instruction from his mother's brother, who is in his clan, rather than from his father. Marriage inside one's clan once was forbidden, but this rule is no longer observed strictly."

—from *Vanishing Tribes* by Roy Pinney

1. In the Seminole tribe, the mother's brother rather than her husband may be more of a father figure to her sons because

(1) the uncle lives with them, and the father does not

(2) the uncle is part of the mother's blood family, and the father is not

(3) the brother is the true biological father, not the husband

(4) the father of the son is more important to the clan than is the uncle

(5) the uncle is the head of the mother's clan

2. Which of the following would be a likely hypothesis about Seminole matrilineal clans, based on the information in the paragraph?

(1) Women are not the central figures in their own nuclear families but are the central figures in the extended family.

(2) Women are central figures in both the nuclear and extended families.

(3) Women are not the central figures in either nuclear or extended families.

(4) Women are more concerned with the care of children than men are.

(5) Women are less concerned with the care of children than men are.

ANSWERS ARE ON PAGE 315.

WRITING ACTIVITY 3

Write a paragraph describing your family structure—its members, the amount and degree of interaction, its living arrangements. Can your family be described as nuclear or extended?

ANSWER IS ON PAGE 316.

ROLES AND STATUS

KEY WORDS

role—the behavior that goes with one's position
ascribed status—the position in society one inherits through birth or attains with time
achieved status—the position one attains through individual effort

Your role in society is the behavior that is expected of you because you occupy a certain position. For example, the role of a parent requires a different pattern of behavior from one of an employee. Closely related to role is *status*. Status is the position you hold in society.

In Japan, a common expression is translated to mean "nothing is as unimportant as a Japanese woman." This expression communicates clearly the traditional status of the female in that culture. And, in fact, the Japanese woman's traditional role as a meek, obedient wife supports the statement.

In recent years, however, in Japan as in many Westernized nations, women are beginning to adopt roles that have been considered traditionally male. This phenomenon is called *role reversal*.

Role reversal has been encouraged for females in the United States. Examples include girls being allowed to participate in traditionally male sports and women taking on such jobs as telephone installers and engineers. Role reversal is generally not encouraged for males. Sociologists theorize that females are positively rewarded for role reversal and males are not because the male role is one of higher status in U.S. culture.

Roles based on gender are not the only ones dictated by our society. Within our jobs we play certain roles. Our marital status also determines how we behave in certain settings, as do our economic status and our ethnic background.

Because we are born into one sex or the other, sociologists say the status that comes with the role is ascribed. That is, society assigns a particular status to being male or female, regardless of individual qualities. Also, age gives one a unique status in many societies. For example, the elderly often are respected because of their age and teenagers looked down on because of theirs.

On the other hand, when we attain a certain status through our own effort, be it through educational or professional training, the status is achieved.

In countries like the U.S., where more opportunities for occupational choices exist, an individual has more chances to gain an achieved status. However, in any society, your position is affected by ascribed status, as you can never completely escape the category society places you into at birth.

EXERCISE 12

Directions: Male and female roles have been changing rapidly during the twentieth century. Indicate role reversal in each of the situations below by writing the correct name in the spaces.

1. Debra and Claude are married and have two preschool-age children. Presently, both parents work, but _____ has decided to quit soon to stay home with the kids during the day because of the lack of good daycare facilities.

2. Dr. Scott has been working for three years with Nurse Davis, whom many consider to be the most warm and caring R.N. in the hospital. Their mutual respect has not been affected by the fact that _____ is a woman and _____ is a man.

3. Betty Sue and Jimmy are given the opportunity to choose an elective class their senior year of high school, so _____ chooses home economics and _____ chooses auto mechanics.

ANSWERS ARE ON PAGE 316.

EXERCISE 13

Directions: Identify each of the following as ascribed (given by birth or attained by age) or achieved (earned) status.

_____ **1.** being a member of the mongoloid race

_____ **2.** becoming a policeman

_____ **3.** retiring from the work force at age sixty-five

_____ **4.** obtaining a GED certificate

_____ **5.** inheriting a royal title

ANSWERS ARE ON PAGE 316.

SOCIAL CLASSES

> ### KEY WORDS
>
> *social class*—a ranked level of social status in a society
> *stratification*—the categorizing of people into different social classes

Closely related to status is social class. Your social class is where you stand in relation to other members of the larger society. The importance of social class was shown humorously in an episode of a popular sitcom. A single, working mother is given a mink coat under an improbable set of circumstances. She finds that when she wears the mink she is treated differently.

At a French restaurant, she does not have to wait for service, she is treated formally and politely, and it is assumed that she has a wealthy background and a high position at her job. In other words, she is taken to be a member of the upper class. The mink coat indicated that she had money. And, while money may not be the only determination of class position in our society, it is the most important one.

Social class indicates an attitude and a way of life. It takes a lot of money to be considered a member of the upper class, but is an unemployed factory worker automatically considered to be a member of the upper class after winning several million dollars in a lottery? No, according to sociologists. The lottery winner's children or grandchildren might achieve upper-class status after the money has been in the family for a couple of generations. However, the "newly rich" generally do not possess and exhibit the appropriate lifestyle of the upper class. Nor do the "nouveau riche" understand the customs that set the upper class apart from the lower class.

Obviously, money is not the only criterion that determines status in our society. College professors, for example, are accorded high social status and rank by most people but earn less money per year than skilled tradesmen, who have much less prestige in a community. This contradiction may be explained by the fact that the degree of formal education also contributes to social status in America.

Social classes are neither unique to the U.S. nor to Western society. They develop out of the division of labor. The more jobs and divisions that exist in a society, the more flexible the structure of the job market and the greater the *social mobility*, or movement between classes.

In the U.S., there is much social mobility, especially for members of the middle class. The ease of movement between classes in the U.S. compared to other societies is part of the reason that one cannot distinguish easily between members of one class and another.

GED Practice
EXERCISE 14

Questions 1 and 2 are based on the information on page 193.

1. Which of the statements below is supported by the information?

   (1) Money is the sole criterion for determining status in the U.S.
   (2) When you have money, you are automatically accepted by members of the upper class.
   (3) A combination of money and amount of formal education contributes to social status in the U.S.
   (4) The poor have no status in the U.S.
   (5) It is impossible to improve your status in the U.S.

2. Based on the information, which of the following might be considered to have the highest status in American society today?

   (1) a newspaper journalist
   (2) a professional basketball player
   (3) a brain surgeon
   (4) a university professor
   (5) a television actress

ANSWERS ARE ON PAGE 316.

EXERCISE 15

Directions: Read the passage below. Place an *X* before each conclusion that logically can be drawn from the passage.

"The school was small, the families mostly Jewish and Catholic, and were well up in the middle economic class, happy with their simple escape from the troubles of the city.

"Now, in the short time of six years, the population of the suburb has doubled. The original settlers who could afford it have moved on down the road, onto newly excavated, paved, and wired hillsides. The city moved out to replace them. Their replacements were more often working class, spoke more Spanish, were darker, more occasionally black, had more children, fewer dads, collected more welfare, and took achievement tests less well."

—from *The Way It Spozed to Be* by James Herndon

_____ (1) There are more Hispanics and blacks in the working class than in the middle class.

_____ (2) The working class lives primarily in the city and has little hope of escaping.

_____ (3) The social mobility of the classes can be proved by their ability to move from one location to another.

_____ **(4)** Children of working-class parents do not do as well in school, on the average, as middle-class children.

_____ **(5)** Receiving welfare from the state is more common among the working class than the middle class.

_____ **(6)** When the working class moves to the suburbs, its attitudes and lifestyles become more like the middle class.

ANSWERS ARE ON PAGE 316.

WRITING ACTIVITY 4

There is a lot of controversy about exactly how much social mobility there is in American society. The "American Dream" is that anyone who works hard can succeed economically in this country. Is the American Dream being realized? If not, why not? Write two to three paragraphs defending your position on this question. Be sure to include specific examples to support your position.

ANSWER IS ON PAGE 316.

WHAT IS PSYCHOLOGY?

PSYCHOLOGICAL THEORIES

KEY WORDS

behaviorism—a field of psychology that focuses mainly on the treatment and study of behavior

psychoanalysis—a method of treating emotional disorders that emphasizes early childhood experiences

psychiatry—a branch of medicine that specializes in the diagnosis and treatment of mental illness

A psychologist is a scientist whose aim is to explain, predict, and control the behavior of individuals. Psychology is related to psychiatry; however, psychiatry is not a behavioral science. It is a branch of medicine that specializes in the diagnosis and treatment of mental illness. Although many theories of psychology have been developed, two that probably have had the greatest impact on the field are psychoanalysis and behaviorism. Behaviorists and psychoanalysts have very different approaches to correcting behavioral disorders.

PSYCHOANALYSIS

> **KEY WORDS**
>
> ***id***—the part of the personality that is unconscious and represents instinctual needs and drives
>
> ***ego***—the part of the personality responsible for conscious decision making
>
> ***superego***—the part of the personality that represents socially accepted values; the conscience

Sigmund Freud (pronounced "Froyd"), an Austrian, developed the theory of psychoanalysis. According to psychoanalytic theory, much of human behavior is motivated by unconscious instinctual drives. We are unaware of these drives because they are hidden from us. Many of these drives are linked to childhood experiences, so psychoanalysts probe this area of a patient's life.

Freud believed that the sex drive also has great influence on human motivation, and his pioneering work in this area of the unconscious made him unpopular with some of his contemporaries.

According to psychoanalytic theory, the human subconscious may be divided into three parts: the id, the ego, and the superego.

The id consists of all the basic drives and instincts that we are born with. According to Freud, the id provides our life force—the energy that keeps us going. The id is basically pleasure seeking and can cause trouble for us in its drive to satisfy the needs for food, water, sex, and self-protection.

The ego acts as a check on the id's never-ending search for pleasure. It is the ego that keeps us from having "too much of a good thing." The ego is the center of thought, reasoning, and common sense.

The superego acts as the conscience. It determines the difference between morally right and wrong behavior and stops us from doing things that may satisfy the id but hurt society.

People who are considered to be emotionally healthy and behaviorally normal have an id, an ego, and a superego that work in cooperation. When one or another of these three components has gone out of control, a person may go to a psychologist or therapist to restore the balance. People with problems, of course, do not usually recognize this imbalance. It is when their behavior constantly causes problems for themselves or others that they seek professional help.

EXERCISE 16

Directions: Read the situation below and answer the questions that follow.

Lenny loves cookies. One day, he is hungry and can't wait for dinner. He robs the cookie jar and takes five cookies. Although there are still many cookies left in the jar, he takes only five to avoid getting sick from eating too many. After he has eaten the cookies, he feels guilty because he knows he is not supposed to eat sweets before a meal.

1. What drive represents the id in this case? _____

_____

2. What action represents the functioning ego? _____

_____

3. What represents the superego for Lenny? _____

_____

ANSWERS ARE ON PAGE 316.

BEHAVIORISM

> ### KEY WORDS
>
> ***conditioning***—the means by which an animal or human learns a pattern of behavior
> ***positive reinforcement***—in the conditioning process, the act of rewarding an individual for a correct response
> ***negative reinforcement***—in the conditioning process, the act of punishing an individual for an incorrect response

Methods for changing human behavior are studied and applied by a group of psychologists called ***behaviorists***. The process of changing human behavior is called ***behavior modification***.

B. F. Skinner and many other American psychologists have done much experimentation to learn methods of changing behavior. One such method is termed conditioning.

Conditioning involves the use of positive or negative reinforcement to encourage or discourage a certain behavior. In positive reinforcement, the subject is given a reward for demonstrating an appropriate behavioral response. In negative reinforcement, a subject is punished for exhibiting inappropriate behavior. After repeated rewards or punishments, the subject is conditioned to exhibit an appropriate behavior.

Russian physiologist Ivan Pavlov was the first to experiment with such conditioning. In Pavlov's experiments, he first observed that when dogs saw meat they automatically salivated. By presenting meat simultaneously with the ring of a bell, he found that the dogs produced saliva when they heard the bell and saw no meat. Thus, the dogs were conditioned to respond to the sound of the bell.

Conditioning of human behavior often happens by chance. Many young parents have discovered how easy it is to condition a baby to expect to be picked up, cuddled, diapered, or fed whenever it cries! While opinions may differ as to whether this reinforcement by the parents produces a spoiled child or a secure one, almost everyone agrees that reinforcement has encouraged more of the same behavior.

GED Practice
EXERCISE 17

Questions 1 and 2 are based on the information on pages 195–198.

1. In business, a well-known philosophy for managing employees is called the "carrot and stick" approach. According to this belief, people really are not motivated to work; they have to be supervised closely, threatened with some kind of punishment or rewarded before they will perform. The psychological basis for this management attitude lies in

   (1) human nature
   (2) psychoanalytic theory
   (3) conditioning
   (4) negative reinforcement
   (5) positive reinforcement

2. A parent is trying to encourage a child to do better in school. Which of the following is an example of the use of positive reinforcement?

   (1) grounding the child until his grades improve
   (2) suspending his allowance until the grades improve
   (3) having periodic discussions about study habits
   (4) buying the child a desired gift if grades improve
   (5) meeting with the school guidance counselor to get the child placed in easier classes

ANSWERS ARE ON PAGE 317.

EXERCISE 18

Directions: In each of the cases below, write *B* in the blank if behaviorist theory is illustrated and *P* if psychoanalytic theory is shown.

_____ **1.** Kevin exhibits very stubborn behavior as an adult. His therapist suggests that it may be because he was over three years old when he finally was toilet trained.

_____ **2.** David hates to go to bed at night and will not get up when called in the morning. His mother bought him an alarm clock that rings loudly. Now that he is forced to awaken by the alarm clock, David goes to bed and rises on time without the clock's going off.

_____ **3.** Lillie is overweight because of her compulsive eating. She has tried every type of diet. Finally, she joins Weight Watchers and is losing steadily now that each weight loss is applauded by other members each week.

_____ **4.** Al has been trying to quit smoking but without success. Even when he is without cigarettes, he finds himself chewing on pens or pencils. His therapist suggests that Al didn't have enough oral stimulation as a baby.

_____ **5.** Johnny is learning to use the computer in math class. Each time he correctly completes a problem on the computer, a "smiley face" appears on the screen and a new problem appears for him to solve.

ANSWERS ARE ON PAGE 317.

WRITING ACTIVITY 5

Based on your experience, which is likely to be the most effective—positive reinforcement (rewarding desired behavior) or negative reinforcement (punishing undesired behavior)? Write two to three paragraphs explaining your position. Be sure to provide examples to support your point of view.

ANSWER IS ON PAGE 317.

FRUSTRATION AND CONFLICT

> ### KEY WORDS
>
> ***approach-approach conflict***—a conflict in which a person is attracted to two different, desirable goals
>
> ***avoidance-avoidance conflict***—a conflict in which a person is caught between two undesirable choices
>
> ***approach-avoidance conflict***—a conflict in which a person is both attracted to and repelled by the same goal

According to psychologists, ***frustration*** is the response that occurs when a goal is not reached or a need is unfulfilled. Most commonly, however, frustration develops over conflicts between goals and desires. Psychologists have identified three basic types of conflicts that people encounter in life. They are approach-approach conflicts, avoidance-avoidance conflicts, and approach-avoidance conflicts. An example of each is illustrated below.

Approach-Approach Conflicts

Brenda and Cliff were recently married. Brenda wants to work in order to help pay bills and to fulfill her desire to have a career. However, she also wants desperately to have a child. Brenda's situation illustrates an approach-approach conflict because both of her alternatives are attractive to her and she experiences some degree of frustration in trying to satisfy both of them. In order to resolve the conflict, Brenda has to either satisfy one goal first or give up one goal for the other.

Avoidance-Avoidance Conflicts

Brenda decides to accept a full-time bank job that she grows to dislike. She can't quit because Cliff depends on her income to help pay the bills they have accumulated, some of which he incurred before they were married. Although she dislikes her job, Brenda can't quit because the job market is tight and she knows she'll have trouble landing another job.

Brenda's situation now reflects an avoidance-avoidance conflict. She faces the undesirable choices of staying on a job she dislikes and losing her income if she quits. Whatever choice she makes, she has to suffer the consequences of it. Avoidance-avoidance conflicts are common in everyday life.

Approach-Avoidance Conflicts

Brenda grows to resent the fact that she has to work when she wants to start a family. This resentment has begun to affect her marriage. Linc, the bank president's son, is interested in Brenda, and she likes him. They go out to lunch frequently. Brenda realizes that if she left Cliff and married Linc, she would no longer have to work and could start the family she's been wanting. But hers would be the first divorce in her family and would cause a scandal once her parents learned the facts.

Now Brenda is experiencing an approach-avoidance conflict. She is attracted to Linc, but the possibility of divorce repels her. There is no way out of this situation unless Brenda changes basic values that were instilled in her as a child. For this reason, approach-avoidance conflicts often are the most difficult to solve.

EXERCISE 19

Directions: In each case below, identify the conflict as approach-approach, avoidance-avoidance, or approach-avoidance.

1. José has a sore tooth and does not want to go to the dentist, but he knows he must or the tooth will just get worse.

   _____

2. Keisha is asked by popular, handsome Lionel to go out Saturday night, but she has already promised her best friend she would help her celebrate her birthday that night.

   _____

3. Hal needs to buy a new car but does not want to go further into debt to do so.

   _____

4. Kim and Lee have put a deposit on their dream vacation they want to take next month, but they just found out that Kim's parents are celebrating their anniversary on the weekend they planned to leave for Hawaii.

   _____

5. Tina is overweight and unhappy about her appearance, but she doesn't want to go on another diet that promises weight loss but just makes her feel deprived of the foods she loves to eat.

   _____

ANSWERS ARE ON PAGE 317.

WRITING ACTIVITY 6

We all have frustration and conflicts in our lives. Think of a conflict you had recently. Was it an approach-approach, avoidance-avoidance, or approach-avoidance conflict? Write a paragraph or two describing the conflict and identifying which kind of conflict it was. Also, explain how you resolved the conflict.

ANSWER IS ON PAGE 317.

EXERCISE 20

Directions: Some conflicts are summed up in everyday common sayings. Match the conflict on the right with the correct saying shown on the left. Some of the terms on the right may be used more than once.

_____ **1.** between the devil and the deep blue sea

_____ **2.** honey's sweet, but the bee stings

_____ **3.** caught between a rock and a hard place

_____ **4.** no rose without a thorn

_____ **5.** having your cake and eating it too

(a) approach-approach

(b) avoidance-avoidance

(c) approach-avoidance

ANSWERS ARE ON PAGE 317.

DEFENSE MECHANISMS

In each of the three situations Brenda found herself in, she had to cope, or to make some adjustment. She could cope directly by changing either herself or the situation. Human beings use many methods to deal with their frustrations. **Defense mechanisms** are ways in which people reduce frustration.

The use of defense mechanisms can be healthy for an individual. Sometimes they are the only methods by which an individual can deal with an unbearable situation. We all use them. In fact, those people who are diagnosed as mentally disturbed often have not learned to use defense mechanisms to their benefit. As a result, the stress of everyday life becomes too much for them to bear. Listed below are five common defense mechanisms illustrated by an example.

rationalization—disguising the reason for one's failure to reach a goal

Julian cuts classes to play cards in the student lounge. When he flunks all of his classes, he complains that they were boring anyway.

repression—keeping unpleasant thoughts that cause anxiety hidden in one's subconscious; temporarily "forgetting"

Fred "forgets" to pay his rent because it will leave him flat broke.

projection—assigning a bad trait or problem of one's own to another person

> Gertrude is terrified to leave her house for fear that she will be attacked by a stranger.

displacement—transferring one's frustrations to a person or object that did not cause them

> Susie has a baby brother who is now the center of her parents' attention. She is jealous and wants to hurt the baby but knows that it would be wrong. Instead, she takes her frustration out on her doll and succeeds in completely destroying it.

reaction-formation—behaving in a way opposite to one's beliefs and feelings

> Deep down, Walt hates cats, but whenever he visits his grandmother he lets her Siamese sit in his lap and strokes the cat lovingly.

GED Practice
EXERCISE 21

Questions 1–3 refer to the five defense mechanisms listed on pages 202–203.

1. A dishonest politician accuses her opponent of not being truthful with the voters. The defense mechanism used is

   (1) rationalization
   (2) repression
   (3) projection
   (4) displacement
   (5) reaction-formation

2. A man who, deep down, enjoys watching X-rated films, joins a campaign to have them banned from the local theater. The defense mechanism used is

   (1) rationalization
   (2) repression
   (3) projection
   (4) displacement
   (5) reaction-formation

3. In the cartoon at the right, the defense mechanism the bowler is using is

   (1) rationalization
   (2) repression
   (3) projection
   (4) displacement
   (5) reaction-formation

(Roir, Ben Roth Agency)

ANSWERS ARE ON PAGE 317.

WRITING ACTIVITY 7

Choose one of the defense mechanisms described on pages 202–203 and write a paragraph describing a situation in which you or someone you know used it.

ANSWER IS ON PAGE 318.

NEUROSES

> ### KEY WORDS
>
> ***anxiety***—uneasiness of mind or fearful concern
> ***neurosis***—a personality disorder in which a person is unusually anxious or miserable in his or her work or relations with others
> ***phobia***—an irrational fear

Have you ever been so depressed you couldn't work? So restless you couldn't sleep? So afraid you couldn't breathe? If so, you have had a glimpse of the world of the emotionally disturbed.

Psychologists like to classify the mentally ill by type of disorder and by degree of illness. Generally, the less severe disorders come under the heading of neurosis. Neurotics usually function well on a day-to-day basis. But every now and then they experience anxiety that makes it difficult to perform tasks or to relate to others. The six case studies below describe a variety of neuroses. Read each case and be prepared to answer the questions at the end of this section.

PHOBIC PHIL

Phil has a phobia. He has such a paralyzing fear of small, closed-in places (claustrophobia) that he does not ride airplanes, use elevators, or go very far in automobiles. He is successful in avoiding those situations, so most of his co-workers and acquaintances do not know of his problem.

Most psychologists believe that such phobias are linked to a biological trait developed in humans during evolution but triggered by an unpleasant experience. Phil may have been frightened by something when he was in his small crib as an infant, or he may have been left there for long periods of time.

Other such phobias that psychologists believe have a biological base are acrophobia (fear of high places), nyctophobia (fear of the dark), and ophidiophobia (fear of reptiles).

It is easy for us to understand such fears, but few of us go to the extremes a neurotic does to avoid them.

COMPLAINING CLAUDE

Claude has a different problem. He is normal in almost every regard, but he constantly complains and worries about being physically ill. His physician has decided that Claude is a **hypochondriac**. In other words, Claude feels sick but has no real symptoms beyond his voiced complaints.

Sometimes hypochondriacs, and otherwise healthy people, do develop real biological problems after long periods of anxiety and its resultant stress. Ulcers, migraine headaches, asthma, high blood pressure, and heart conditions have all been found to be the results of psychological disorders for some people. Such diseases are called **psychosomatic** (they are caused by the mind) and are considered to be a conversion-reaction to an emotional problem. That is, the emotional problem is converted into a physical symptom.

IMMACULATE ISABEL

Isabel likes her home to be neat, clean, and orderly. In fact, Isabel is obsessed with cleanliness. She does nothing much all day every day except scrub, polish, dust, vacuum, pick up, put away, and rearrange. She compulsively follows her family around, cleaning up after them.

Isabel has a disorder described by psychologists as obsessive-compulsive. Many psychologists would theorize that some childhood experience involving the need for approval triggered Isabel's neurosis.

DOWN-IN-THE-DUMPS DOLLIE

Dollie responds to her failures and disappointments more severely than most people. When she fails a test, loses a job, or gives a boring party, she gets extremely depressed. She cannot sleep, eat, or do much of anything. She is sad and apathetic, blames herself entirely, and feels worthless—for days, weeks, or months at a time. Psychologists say she is experiencing a neurotic depression, or depressive reaction.

ANXIOUS ANNA

At least Dollie knows why she is depressed. Anna, on the other hand, feels anxious much of the time but cannot figure out why. She cannot relax for days at a time. She is uneasy, restless, and apprehensive, and she does not know why. Psychologists often can help people like Anna with their anxiety neuroses by connecting their anxiety to a source (repressed feelings of anger or sexual desires, for example).

WANDERING WAYNE

Wayne's case is even more dramatic. He works two jobs to support his wife and four children. He has left home a couple of times and been found many miles away some time later, leading a less stressful, less responsible kind of life. He does not remember leaving home, starting a new life, and making the decisions he made. Psychologists call Wayne's disturbance a fugue state, for upon recovering Wayne cannot recall this recent period in his life. He does not really have a multiple personality because he keeps the same basic personality traits when he goes into his fugue states.

EXERCISE 22

Directions: In the blanks below, write *behaviorist* if the case describes the behaviorist theory of psychology and *psychoanalytical* if the case describes the psychoanalytical theory.

1. The cases of Phobic Phil and Immaculate Isabel are similar in that the causes can be linked to childhood experiences. The _____ theory of psychology best explains Phil's and Isabel's actions.

2. If Complaining Claude needs attention and receives it only when he complains about being ill, his behavior is said to be conditioned. In this case, the _____ theory of psychology would best explain his actions.

ANSWERS ARE ON PAGE 318.

═ GED Practice ═
EXERCISE 23

Questions 1–3 are based on the following definitions.

You play psychologist. Diagnose each of the following patients. The neuroses are redefined below:

phobia—a crippling fear

conversion-reaction—an emotional problem converted into a physical symptom

obsessive-compulsive—a reaction characterized by an obsession (a preoccupation with an idea) and a compulsion (an irresistible impulse to perform an act)

depressive reaction—a reaction characterized by mental depression

fugue state—a reaction in which a person consciously performs an act but upon recovery does not remember it

1. George cannot function without excessive order in his life. Even his record albums must be kept in special groupings on the shelf or he becomes upset. George's neurosis may be described as

(1) a phobia
(2) conversion-reaction
(3) obsessive-compulsive
(4) depressive reaction
(5) fugue state

2. After Sylvia had been missing for six months, she was found living on the streets like a "bag lady," though she had a husband, children, a nice home, and an important job with a great deal of responsibility. When found, Sylvia did not remember ever having left her home and family. Sylvia's neurosis may be described as

(1) a phobia
(2) conversion-reaction
(3) obsessive-compulsive
(4) depressive reaction
(5) fugue state

3. Lavonna's husband is very good to her, but she realizes she doesn't love him anymore. She had an affair with a friend of her husband's not too long ago and now is experiencing severe stomach cramps that no doctor can find a physical cause for. Lavonna's neurosis may be described as

(1) a phobia
(2) conversion-reaction
(3) obsessive-compulsive
(4) depressive reaction
(5) fugue state

ANSWERS ARE ON PAGE 318.

WRITING ACTIVITY 8

Do you know someone whose behavior might be considered neurotic? Write a two-paragraph paper describing this person and his or her neurosis.

ANSWER IS ON PAGE 318.

PSYCHOSES

> ### KEY WORD
>
> **psychosis**—a mental or personality disorder, more severe than a neurosis and often requiring institutionalized treatment

A psychosis is a more serious personality disorder than a neurosis. Psychotics cannot think, feel, or behave in a manner appropriate to reality.

Some forms of psychosis are displayed by extremely inappropriate moods and emotions. Katherine, for example, acts severely depressed and apathetic one day and uncontrollably excited, talkative, outgoing, and confident the next. She is a **manic-depressive**, and neither of her moods is ordinarily triggered by anything in particular in the real world.

Schizophrenia is probably the most publicized form of psychosis. People suffering from this type of disorder fantasize and hallucinate and often retreat into their own worlds.

Psychiatrists generally handle these personality disorders. In addition to psychotherapy, they may use a variety of methods ranging from electric shock therapy to medication in treating these severe behavioral problems.

GED Practice
EXERCISE 24

The question is based on the following paragraph.

Schizophrenia is believed to have some biological basis. "For every twisted thought there is a twisted molecule" is how some psychologists put it. Which of the statements below best supports this theory?

(1) Both members of a set of identical twins will not necessarily develop schizophrenia.

(2) Cases of both identical twins being schizophrenic are much more common among sets that have been raised together in the same environment.

(3) Both members of a set of identical twins are much more likely to be schizophrenic than two non-twin brothers or sisters.

(4) A member of a set of fraternal twins (nonidentical) is likely to be schizophrenic if the other twin is.

(5) Families that produce schizophrenics often display patterns of individual isolation or excessive closeness to one another.

ANSWER IS ON PAGE 318.

=== **GED Practice** ===
BEHAVIORAL SCIENCES

Questions 1–3 are based on the following passage.

Differences in the general psychological makeup of men and women can affect behavior in unexpected areas.

"Women play a greater part in farm marketing decisions than typically thought, and their influence tempers the opportunistic and risk-taking views that men are more likely to take. . . .

"The results come from a study by Bonnie Lindemann. . . . Lindemann studied 559 men and women who responded to a survey. She said half of the respondents reported that women share in the decision to market farm products, even though it's the men who usually arrange the sale.

" 'This suggests that one reason women's participation has been underestimated in the past is that their contributions are not visible to others,' Lindemann wrote. 'They are less active in collecting information and dealing with sales agents than they are in monitoring the process within the operation.'

"She said the study also shows that women are more security-conscious than men. 'They may be a little more objecting about making marketing decisions and not so competitive as men are,' she said.

"She said the research shows men and women approach problems from different perspectives. 'In most cases the wives were much more likely to make comments that suggested they were considering the costs or risks involved,' she said. 'The language they used is very security-focused where the men tended to focus on opportunities, on chance for the big gain, maybe the price will go higher, hope for the future, those sorts of things. I don't know that by itself either one of the focuses is complete,' she said."

—from "Women's Hidden Farm Role," in *The Rural American* magazine (Spring 1993)

1. Which of the following *best* describes the attitudes of the women Lindemann studied?

   (1) careful
   (2) aggressive
   (3) passive
   (4) hesitant
   (5) unrealistic

2. According to Lindemann, the marketing decisions made by men are influenced by the high value they place on

   (1) taking chances
   (2) security
   (3) moderation
   (4) their wives' opinions
   (5) their sales agents

3. Which is the most logical argument for considering the views of both men and women in making farm market decisions?

   (1) Both men and women need to feel useful.
   (2) Their opposing outlooks can help create a balanced decision.
   (3) Men are more self-confident than women.
   (4) Women are more responsible than men.
   (5) Sales agents feel more secure when dealing with a couple.

Questions 4–6 are based on the following cartoon.

DAVID DONAR
Courtesy Macomb Daily (Miss.)

BIG MAN ON CAMPUS

4. Which of the following statements *best* expresses the main idea of the cartoon?

  (1) Drinking is not allowed on college campuses.
  (2) Drinking is very popular on college campuses.
  (3) Very few college students drink.
  (4) Drinking on campus went out with raccoon coats.
  (5) College students should be free to drink as they please.

5. Which of the following *best* explains why college students might drink too much?

  (1) They don't have good family values.
  (2) They are worried about flunking out.
  (3) They want to protest school regulations.
  (4) They feel pressure from other students to "have a good time."
  (5) Their parents were alcoholics.

6. Which of the following topics would you expect this cartoonist to address if he wanted to make a similar point?

  (1) drug abuse in high schools
  (2) hazardous experiments in science
  (3) student-teacher conflicts
  (4) computers as a teaching tool
  (5) the high cost of education

Questions 7 and 8 are based on the following passage.

Even an anthropologist can experience culture shock. Conrad Kottak told about his initial reactions when he went on his first field trip to Brazil. He described himself as being "an urban boy . . . with little experience with rural life in my own country. . . ."

To Kottak, everything smelled different, tasted different, and looked different from what he was used to. He was also unsettled by what seemed like a lack of privacy. Children in Arembepe looked into his windows to see what the strangers were doing.

Kottak had expected trouble speaking Portuguese. But he remembers two things he had to become accustomed to. The only toilet paper he could afford felt like sandpaper. And Kleenex wasn't available for anyone who needed to wipe a drippy nose.

7. According to the passage, part of culture shock occurs because people make which of the following assumptions?

  (1) The language will be easy to learn.
  (2) The ordinary things people take for granted will still be available.
  (3) The cooking will take some getting used to.
  (4) Most cultures are primitive.
  (5) Rural lifestyles are simpler than urban lifestyles.

8. Which of the following would most likely cause culture shock for an average American?

  (1) riding a double-decker bus in London
  (2) seeing a McDonald's in Paris
  (3) seeing elephants in a wildlife preserve in Kenya
  (4) finding that the fish served in a Kyoto restaurant is still alive
  (5) finding a shopkeeper in a small Brazilian town who speaks excellent English

ANSWERS ARE ON PAGE 318.

8 Geography

Where do you live? To begin, you live within the universe, in which lies a huge galaxy of stars, the Milky Way. To be more specific, you live within the solar system, within which the planet Earth moves.

Earth is comprised of the oceans, seas, and seven continents. You live on the continent of _____.

The continents are further divided into nations. The nation to which you belong is _____.

The nation you live in is divided into regions—the North, South, East, and West. These regions are further divided into the Northeast, Northwest, Southeast, Southwest, and Midwest. The region of the country you live in is _____.

These broad regions are composed of the fifty states. The state you live in is _____.

The next largest division within a state is the county (in Louisiana, parish; in Alaska, borough). The county in which you live is _____.

Counties are divided further into townships. Your township if you have one is _____.

Townships are divided into towns, villages, boroughs, and cities. Your town, village, borough, or city is _____.

Residents of large cities live in neighborhood communities. If you live in a large city, your neighborhood community is called _____.

Your neighborhood is made up of a street that may run north and south or east and west. Your house number and street determine your address, which finally pinpoints your location—unless you are studying for the GED Tests away from home!

In this explanation, you could see your relationship to the world, from the broad perspective of a terrestrial being living on the planet Earth to the specific perspective of a member of a neighborhood community.

WHAT IS GEOGRAPHY?

The **geographer** is interested in the places where human beings live and their relationships with the part of the world they live in. The location of people is important because so much of their culture is affected by it.

What we eat is determined by the climate and soil conditions. The kind of clothing we wear and the types of homes we build are dictated by the climate. Location even determines what kind of recreation is available.

The geographer studies locations by visiting and reading about them. Herodotus, a Greek who lived during the fifth century B.C., is sometimes credited with being the first geographer. He traveled to places such as Italy, North Africa, and Persia and recorded in detail what he observed. Though the people of his time learned much from his writings, they were still limited by the points of view held by Herodotus and society in general. Most people believed that the earth was flat, that the Mediterranean Sea and Black Sea were at the center of this world, and that a mysterious, unnamed ocean totally surrounded the lands and seas. Christopher Columbus later proved them wrong, of course, but not before many centuries worth of misinformation had been passed along.

Though very little of the earth's surface remains unexplored, geographers are still noting natural and man-made changes in the earth's composition, striving for accuracy in mapmaking, and recording population shifts.

The questions on page 213 are based on the map below. Study the map and answer the questions that follow.

THE WORLD ACCORDING TO HERODOTUS

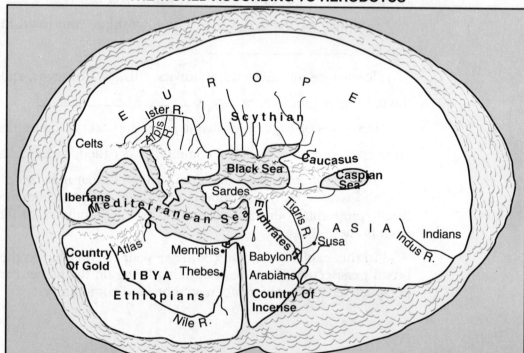

According to the map of the world, as Herodotus and his contemporaries saw it, did the country of your birth exist? _____

How many continents did the ancient Greeks think there were? _____

What were their names? _____

_____

If you are a native American, the country of your birth could not have existed according to the map of the world as Herodotus saw it. The continents on the map of the world are written in all capital letters; therefore, the ancient Greeks thought there were three continents—*Europe*, *Asia*, and *Libya*.

EXERCISE 1

Questions 1–4 are based on the map on page 212.

1. During Herodotus's day, explorers believed that the center of the world existed where they lived. If this was the case, you could infer that Herodotus was a citizen of

    (1) Thebes
    (2) Sardes
    (3) Caucasus
    (4) Babylon
    (5) Euphrates

2. Which of the concepts studied in the Anthropology section most closely describes the above viewpoint held by Herodotus and others like him?

    (1) cultural diffusion
    (2) cultural relativity
    (3) ethnocentrism
    (4) primitivism
    (5) racism

3. Which factor *most* influenced Herodotus and other people of his time about their view of the world?

    (1) Christopher Columbus's discoveries
    (2) population shifts
    (3) people's relationships with one another
    (4) their belief that the earth was flat and that the Black Sea and the Mediterranean Sea were located in the world's mid-point
    (5) the mysterious oceans that surrounded their lands

4. According to Herodotus's map of the world, the largest body of water was the

    (1) Indus River
    (2) Black Sea
    (3) Tigris River
    (4) Mediterranean Sea
    (5) Nile River

ANSWERS ARE ON PAGE 318.

THE TOOLS OF THE GEOGRAPHER

KEY WORDS

map—a flat representation of the surface of a region
globe—a spherical representation of the surface of the earth
projection—the way in which the round earth is represented on a flat surface
scale—the proportion used to show distance on a map
legend, or *key*—the explanatory description of how to read a map or chart

We have known for almost five hundred years that the earth is not flat; rather, it is round—shaped like a sphere. So we use globes in classrooms and libraries and in some homes when we want to locate a particular place. It is difficult to carry a globe with us when we take a trip by car, however; so we still use flat maps.

But when we use a flat map to show the round world, we get a distorted picture in which natural relationships are misrepresented. For example, some countries may appear smaller or larger than their true size, some land masses may appear to be shaped differently from how they actually are, or some distances between regions may appear to be greater or smaller than they really are. Therefore, the type of projection mapmakers choose depends on what information is most important for them to highlight.

TYPES OF PROJECTION

Two types of projection mapmakers generally use are Mollweide and Mercator projections. The differences between the two can be seen in the illustration below.

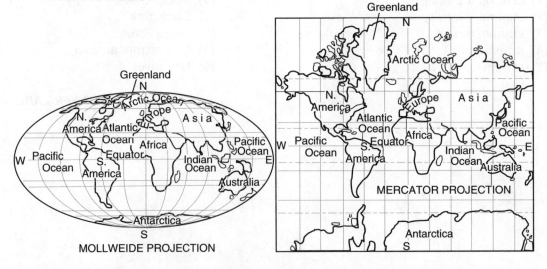

MOLLWEIDE PROJECTION

MERCATOR PROJECTION

Notice the apparent difference in size between the Mollweide and Mercator projections of Greenland (located northeast of North America) and Antarctica. The Mollweide shows a relatively accurate depiction of land sizes, but the Mercator does not; yet the Mercator is used more often. This is because the Mercator does not distort the shape of the more populated areas far from the North and South Poles (top and bottom of the earth), and it represents true and constant directions on a compass used by navigators to travel the vast oceans.

On which map is the area of the oceans likely to be shown most accurately? _____

Because the Mollweide projection shows land sizes more accurately, it must also show the sizes of the oceans more accurately than the Mercator projection.

SHOWING DISTANCE ON A MAP

Distance is another important factor to someone planning a journey by using a map. Naturally, great distances have to be shown smaller on a map, but they still must be proportional. As you read on page 32, the legend, or key, on a map often contains a scale that shows that proportion.

On this map, one inch represents about five hundred miles. You can measure with a ruler or with your finger to approximate any number of distances shown by the scale. You should be able to see that the United States covers about three thousand miles from coast to coast.

LATITUDE AND LONGITUDE

KEY WORDS

equator—the imaginary line that circles the earth, dividing it into the Northern and Southern Hemispheres

hemisphere—a half of the earth, east or west, north or south

latitude—a system of imaginary lines measuring distance north or south of the equator

longitude—a system of imaginary lines measuring distance east or west of the prime meridian

prime meridian—the imaginary line that divides the world into the Eastern and Western Hemispheres

grid—the pattern on a globe or map formed by the intersecting lines of latitude and longitude

The equator touches such exotic places as Cayambe, in Ecuador, South America; Pontianak, in Indonesian Borneo; and Entebbe, in Uganda, Africa. These places are located on a line that divides the world into two hemispheres, north and south. Distance from the equator is measured on a map by degrees of latitude. Latitude is a system of parallel lines measuring distance north or south of the equator. The equator is at 0 degrees latitude, and the poles are at 90 degrees north and 90 degrees south.

Most of the continental United States, including Alaska, lies between 25 and 50 degrees north latitude. Lines of latitude are shown in the diagram below.

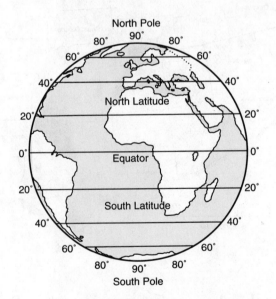

The U.S., in addition to other countries north of the equator, lies within the Northern Hemisphere. All places south of the equator are said to lie in the Southern Hemisphere.

Longitudinal lines run north and south and measure distances east and west of the prime meridian. The Greenwich meridian, or prime meridian, is another name for the 0-degree line of longitude. There are 180 degrees east of the prime meridian and 180 degrees west of it, for a total of 360 degrees around the circular earth. Most of the continental U.S., including Alaska and Hawaii, lies between 65 and 125 degrees west longitude. Lines of longitude are illustrated in the diagram below.

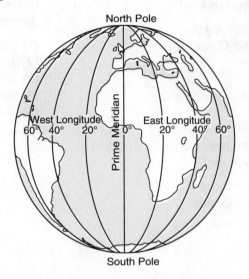

The lines of latitude and longitude cross each other to form a grid. To locate a particular place on a globe or map, find the point where these two lines intersect.

In the diagram below, eastern Spain is located at approximately 40 degrees north latitude and 0 degrees longitude. A grid is shown in the diagram below.

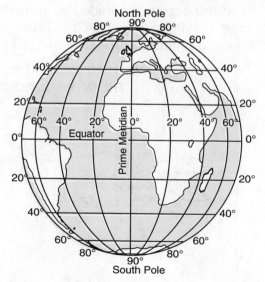

Based on the above grid, what continent is found at 20 degrees south and 60 degrees west? _____

You should have answered *South America*. The point where the 20-degree-south line of latitude meets the 60-degree-west line of longitude is on the continent of South America.

EXERCISE 2

Questions 1–3 are based on the grid on page 217.

1. Which of the following is the location of 20 degrees north, 20 degrees east?

    (1) The north Atlantic Ocean
    (2) The south Atlantic Ocean
    (3) North Africa
    (4) South Africa
    (5) Northern Europe

2. If you traveled westward 50 degrees from the above location (20 degrees north, 20 degrees east), where would you be?

    (1) the North Atlantic Ocean
    (2) the South Atlantic Ocean
    (3) North Africa
    (4) South Africa
    (5) Northern Europe

3. Which of the following countries is located nearest 40 degrees north latitude and 60 degrees west longitude?

    (1) Nigeria
    (2) the United States
    (3) Chile
    (4) Argentina
    (5) Greenland

ANSWERS ARE ON PAGE 319.

THE INTERNATIONAL DATE LINE

The 180-degree longitude line runs through the middle of the Pacific Ocean and is directly opposite the prime meridian. It marks the approximate location of the international date line, which shows where a new day begins.

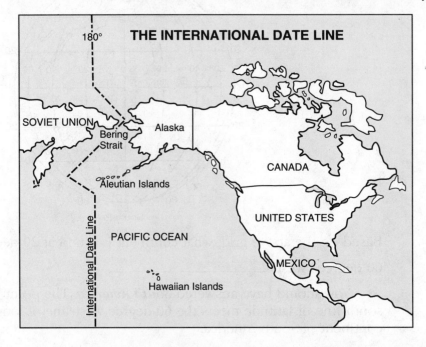

Notice how the international date line zigzags from the 180-degree mark. The line zigzags so that there are not two different dates in one country.

As travelers proceed westward across the date line, they move into the next day. For example, if people on a westward cruise across the Pacific Ocean reached the line at 3:00 P.M. Tuesday, the day and time would change to 3:00 P.M. Wednesday when they crossed the date line. They would have "lost a day." Travelers going eastward would "gain a day." For example, they would go back to 3:00 P.M. Monday if they crossed the line at 3:00 P.M. Tuesday.

TIME ZONES

KEY WORD

time zone—an area within imaginary boundaries that uses one uniform clock time across its whole region

There are 24 hours in a day. By dividing the earth (which totals 360 degrees) into 24 one-hour-long sections, 15 degrees are equivalent to each hour of the day. So, as people travel west they move into an earlier time zone for every 15 degrees that they travel. For example, travelers completing their journey west through the eastern time zone in the U.S. at 5:00 P.M. would have to move their watches to 4:00 P.M. as they crossed over into the next time zone, central time.

TIME ZONES ACROSS NORTH AMERICA

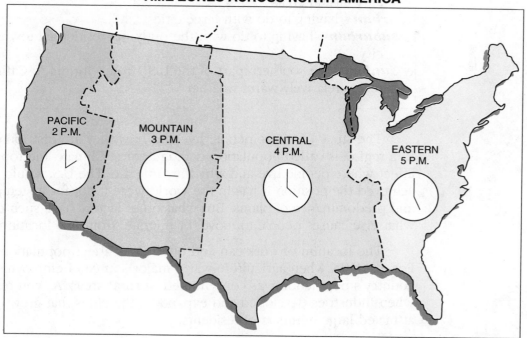

Based on the map above, in what time zone is the city where you live?

EXERCISE 3

Questions 1 and 2 are based on the map on page 219.

1. According to the time zones map, what time is it in San Francisco when it is midnight in Chicago?

(1) 9:00 A.M.
(2) 10:00 P.M.
(3) 11:00 P.M.
(4) 1:00 A.M.
(5) 2:00 A.M.

2. What time is it in New York when it is midnight in Salt Lake City?

(1) 5:00 A.M.
(2) 10:00 P.M.
(3) 2:00 A.M.
(4) 1:00 A.M.
(5) 9:00 P.M.

ANSWERS ARE ON PAGE 319.

POPULATION DISTRIBUTION AND MIGRATION

KEY WORDS

population demographics—the statistical study of the numbers and locations of people in a region
migrate—to move from one region in order to settle in another
rural—having to do with small towns and country living, especially near agricultural areas
urban—having to do with large cities
suburban—having to do with the outlying, residential towns around a city
Sunbelt—the southern part of the U.S., from Virginia to California, known for its relatively warm weather

The study of where people live and how they are distributed or spread out in a region is called population demographics. Climate and topography clearly affect where people live and why they migrate. The U.S. would not have achieved the position it has in the world were it not for its temperate climate and predominance of plains. But what other factors have such effects? And what else causes people to move, or migrate, from one location to another?

The location of work can and often does affect population distribution. For example, when agriculture was a major source of employment, our country's population was concentrated in rural areas. As you read in Chapter 5, when industries developed and expanded, the cities that grew up around them attracted large numbers of residents.

Today, this trend seems to apply to the suburbs, especially in the U.S. Suburbs have become more desirable places than big cities in which to live and to build businesses. This is largely because of their relative safety from crime as compared to the big cities, their newness and cleanliness, their wider spaces, and their better educational systems.

Another trend in the U.S. today is the decline of heavy manufacturing jobs and a rapid growth in the service industries. As a result, the midwestern and eastern cities are no longer the industrial centers they once were.

Fast-growing industries such as computer technology and financial planning depend less on the availability of natural resources than they do on the availability of human labor and skills.

States like Georgia, California, and Arizona, described as Sunbelt areas, have especially benefited from the relocation of high-tech industries there.

EXERCISE 4

Questions 1 and 2 are based on the following map.

1. Iowa is one of the flattest states in the U.S. Based on the information in the map on the right, which of the following inferences can be made about population distribution in Iowa?

   (1) Farming is still a major industry and influence in the state of Iowa.
   (2) Lowlands allow for an even distribution of population.
   (3) Iowa is being drained of its population by the Sunbelt.
   (4) Iowa is one of the most heavily populated states.
   (5) There are few big cities on the plains of the U.S.

2. Which of the following states would be most unlike Iowa in terms of population distribution?

   (1) Kansas
   (2) Nebraska
   (3) West Virginia
   (4) Ohio
   (5) Indiana

POPULATION DISTRIBUTION IN IOWA

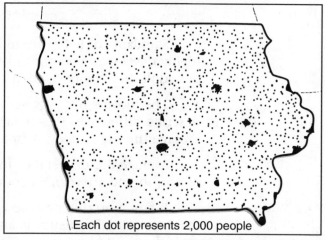

Each dot represents 2,000 people

U.S. Bureau of the Census

ANSWERS ARE ON PAGE 319.

WRITING ACTIVITY 1

Describe in two to three paragraphs the population distribution in your state. Is it densely or sparsely populated? Why? Is your state gaining or losing residents? Why?

ANSWER IS ON PAGE 319.

STANDARDS OF LIVING AROUND THE WORLD

> ### KEY WORDS
>
> ***standard of living***—measurement of quality of life based on certain indicators
> ***demographics***—statistics that describe a population
> ***average life expectancy***—the length of time, on the average, a baby born in a certain place can be expected to live
> ***infant mortality rates***—the frequency of deaths among babies of a region
> ***population growth***—the rate at which the population of an area is increasing or decreasing

Standards of living are most tied to income per person in the country. In highly developed countries like the U.S. and Sweden, this is over $4,000 a year per adult. In underdeveloped countries, it is less than $750 a year per adult.

The income per year per person is just one of the demographics that describe differences in standards of living across the world. Others include average life expectancy, infant mortality rates, and population growth.

Average life expectancy in developed countries is more than seventy years of age; in underdeveloped countries it is only fifty years of age.

Infant mortality rates account for some of that difference. The rate of children dying in infancy is less than 25 deaths for every 1,000 children in most developed countries; it is over 250 deaths for every 1,000 children in many underdeveloped ones. Population growth in developed countries is less than 1 percent per year; in underdeveloped countries it is more than 2.5 percent per year.

The growth rate in a country is significant because overcrowding often contributes to a poor standard of living. Natural resources, jobs, and money have been spread thin in some countries like India that have large populations and large growth rates.

There are examples like Japan, of course, that are densely populated but are not underdeveloped. Such countries have overcome the handicap of large people-to-land ratios through a wise use of natural resources and human ingenuity. A traditional emphasis on education and technological manufacturing has helped in that regard.

Japan and other developed countries as densely populated have also made a concentrated effort to keep their birthrate down. Through family-planning programs, such countries have managed to keep growth rates low.

Whether standards of living can be raised significantly and quickly by organized family planning in underdeveloped countries is a theory still being tested. But one thing that is certain is that the people of those countries are becoming increasingly aware of how their standard of living compares to that in developed countries. Being more aware has made them more desirous of material goods and their benefits. Natural resources have not been distributed evenly throughout the world, however, and that fact alone may keep some countries underdeveloped for generations to come.

EXERCISE 5

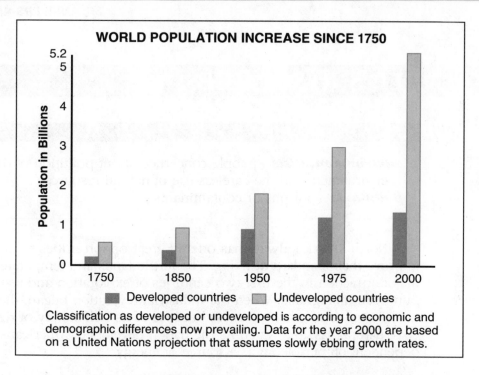

WORLD POPULATION INCREASE SINCE 1750

Classification as developed or undeveloped is according to economic and demographic differences now prevailing. Data for the year 2000 are based on a United Nations projection that assumes slowly ebbing growth rates.

Directions: In the space provided, write *YES* next to each of the following statements that can be supported by information on the graph and *NO* next to those that cannot.

_____ **1.** The populations of developed countries far exceeds that of undeveloped countries.

_____ **2.** Populations of undeveloped countries are growing at a faster rate than developed ones.

_____ **3.** By the year 2000, the world's population will be over five times the population of 1750.

_____ **4.** The population of developed countries has represented a minority of the world's population since at least 1750.

ANSWERS ARE ON PAGE 319.

GED Practice
EXERCISE 6

Choose the one best answer for each statement below.

1. A nation of over a hundred million people that has a problem with large growth rates similar to that of India would be

    (1) Canada
    (2) Brazil
    (3) Germany
    (4) Australia
    (5) France

2. A European country that is most similar to Japan in terms of population density and heavy industrial development would be

    (1) Spain
    (2) England
    (3) France
    (4) Italy
    (5) Ireland

ANSWERS ARE ON PAGE 319.

THE WORLD'S RESOURCES

KEY WORDS

environmentalists—people concerned about pollution of the environment and the careless use of natural resources
pollutants—poisons or contaminants

North America always has offered great opportunities to people wanting to improve their standard of living. The fertile lands and temperate climate were a major attraction in the first two centuries of exploration and settlement by European immigrants. When the industrial revolution began, the continent contributed to America's success because of its rich supply of resources such as coal, natural gas, and water. As the nation developed, Americans became dependent on petroleum as a source of energy.

COAL

Coal remains an important resource because of its importance in producing electricity. But reliance on coal also causes safety and environmental problems that threaten our quality of life.

Underground mines are vulnerable to cave-ins, explosions, and gas leaks. Strip, or surface, mines create large areas of gaping, exposed holes from which rains wash pollution into the lakes and streams. Besides these problems, coal is also criticized by environmentalists as a dirty fuel because it emits pollutants into the air when burned.

PETROLEUM

Petroleum is a source of fuel that is becoming increasingly vital to industrial and personal use. In its natural state, it is used to produce heat and light; in its refined state, it is used to make gasoline and other products.

Petroleum is another "dirty" fuel that pollutes the environment when it is burned or spilled into the oceans. Fires on offshore oil rigs also pose dangers. However, the importance of petroleum as a fuel is growing rather than diminishing. Petroleum-poor nations like the U.S., which uses huge quantities of petroleum, must depend on oil-rich Middle Eastern countries for their supply. In 1960, the Organization of Petroleum Exporting Countries (OPEC) was founded to counteract falling petroleum prices. Skyrocketing oil prices in the 1970s have established many of these countries as oil-rich.

NATURAL GAS

Natural gas is found together with or separate from oil deposits. The vapor, or dry gas, that we use as fuel for heat and cooking in our homes is taken from natural gas after liquid fuels such as butane, propane, and gasoline are removed. Besides its use as a fuel in homes and business, gas is used in the manufacture of important products such as plastics, drugs, and dyes.

WATER

Although all of the world's natural resources are of limited and decreasing supply, the resource of most critical scarcity is water. It is absolutely necessary to the survival of humanity: each person on earth requires at least two or three quarts per day.

In the U.S., the standard of living demands fifty gallons a day for every man, woman, and child. Water is not as easily transported over long distances as are other commodities like coal and natural gas.

The supply of ocean water is large but presently of limited use for drinking. In order to make ocean water drinkable, the salt must be removed. While desalination plants have the capability of making ocean water potable, they are very costly to build. Fresh water is distributed unevenly around the world. To correct this problem, icebergs have been towed from the polar regions and water has been piped from mountain ranges, but at great trouble and expense. In addition, pollution of the lakes, rivers, and streams has affected the existing supply of fresh water, mainly for those areas that lack facilities to purify it.

The graph in the exercise on page 226 predicts the water shortage that will occur in the U.S. in future decades. In the graph, two-child families are compared to three-child families.

≡ GED Practice ≡
EXERCISE 7

Questions 1–3 refer to the following graph.

The graph below predicts the water shortage that will occur in the U.S. in future decades. In the graph, the artist compares what might happen if families continue to have an average of two children with what might happen if families average three children.

PREDICTED U.S. WATER SHORTAGES BASED ON FAMILY SIZE (in billion of gallons)

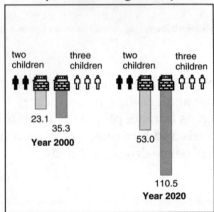

1. The artist has failed to consider which of the following?

   (1) Three-child families use more water than two-child families.
   (2) Water shortages will continue to increase with either two-child or three-child families.
   (3) The faster the increase in population, the greater the degree of water shortage.
   (4) No new technologies for finding, processing, or transporting fresh water supplies will be found by 2020.
   (5) Technologies that will help find, process, and transport fresh water supplies will help lessen the shortages by 2020.

2. What would likely be the outcome if the population growth pattern projection through the year 2020 was reduced from two-child to one-child families?

   (1) The amount of water available to the general population would triple.
   (2) The amount of water available to the general population would hold steady.
   (3) The amount of water available to the general population would decrease.
   (4) The water shortage for the general population would be reduced.
   (5) There would be enough water for all Americans, in all regions of the country.

3. Based on what you know about the geography and climate regions of the U.S., which region would you infer to have the most limited supply of water?

   (1) the Northeast
   (2) the Middle West
   (3) the Northwest
   (4) the Southeast
   (5) the Southwest

ANSWERS ARE ON PAGE 319.

WRITING ACTIVITY 2

Is our dependence on nuclear-energy plants to produce electrical power worth the risk they pose to human life? Write a three-paragraph essay defending your point of view. Include facts to support your position.

ANSWER IS ON PAGE 320.

NUCLEAR AND SOLAR ENERGY

KEY WORDS

nuclear energy—energy released through atomic reactions
solar energy—energy from the sun's rays

Because of the environmental hazards of burning coal and petroleum, alternative sources of energy are being explored and applied. The most important and most controversial of these is nuclear energy.

Problems associated with atomic power include the disposal of radioactive wastes and the accidental release of radioactive particles into the atmosphere. Both the 1979 accident at Three Mile Island in the U.S. and the 1986 incident at Chernobyl in the former Soviet Union dramatized the potential dangers of nuclear energy.

Solar energy is a clean, safe alternative source of power. Solar "batteries" have been invented that capture the sunlight and store it for long-term use.

The exercise on page 228 is based on the following map.

NUCLEAR POWER REACTORS IN THE U.S.

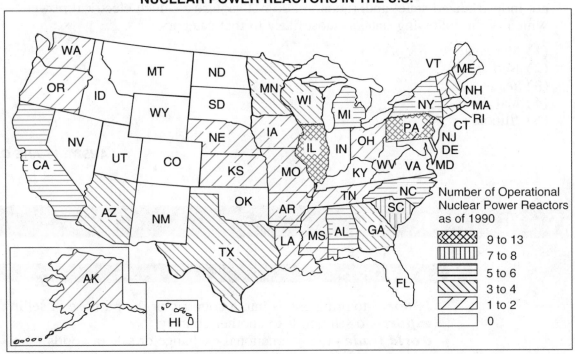

Number of Operational Nuclear Power Reactors as of 1990

▩	9 to 13
▥	7 to 8
▤	5 to 6
▨	3 to 4
▧	1 to 2
☐	0

EXERCISE 8

Directions: Study the map on page 227 and then choose the one best answer for each question or statement below.

1. According to the map, which of the following states has the greatest number of nuclear-power plants?

   (1) Illinois
   (2) California
   (3) New York
   (4) Florida
   (5) Texas

2. Which statement may you infer about the states that have the greatest number of nuclear-energy plants?

   (1) They have few coal reserves.
   (2) They are all located in the East.
   (3) Most have large populations and are high-energy users.
   (4) They have no other alternatives for energy.
   (5) Most have expanses of land far from human habitation.

3. Some states have not had to turn to nuclear-energy production because they are not industrialized states and, therefore, do not require as much electrical power. Which of the following states is most likely in that category?

   (1) Montana
   (2) Nebraska
   (3) Texas
   (4) Maryland
   (5) Illinois

ANSWERS ARE ON PAGE 320.

WORLD TRADE

KEY WORDS

import—to bring goods into a country for the purpose of selling them
export—to sell goods to another country
world trade—the international exchange or sale of goods
cartel—an agreement among countries to control the price of a natural resource on the world trade market

The U.S. has a wealth of natural resources, but it must import many goods, such as rubber, tin, chrome, sugar, coffee, and petroleum.

In turn, the U.S. exports many manufactured goods—cars, canned foods, computers, and plastics. Importing and exporting goods among nations is called world trade, and without it, nations with few natural resources, such as Japan, would not have been able to develop into major industrial powers. Without world trade, an oil-glutted nation like Saudi Arabia would be stuck with an oversupply of crude petroleum that could not feed its people or provide clothing or shelter.

Generally, the poorest countries of the world are not involved in the world trade market except as sources of cheap labor. Developing nations are involved in exporting raw materials and importing manufactured goods and services. The most highly developed nations import more raw materials than manufactured goods and export large numbers and varieties of man-made products and services.

Developing countries may improve their standard of living by using their own natural resources to produce goods and services within their own borders. They could, therefore, avoid the high cost of some imports and possibly produce enough to export for profit. They could also charge higher prices for their raw materials in the world trade market. Many countries have been able to raise prices by forming cartels; OPEC, formed in 1960, is an example of a cartel. Member nations of OPEC agreed to set prices for exported petroleum to oil-dependent countries like the U.S. To some extent, the prices we pay at the gas pump are a direct result of this price-setting policy.

EXERCISE 9

Directions: In the spaces provided below, write the name of the country—*the U.S.,* *Japan,* or *Saudi Arabia*—that correctly completes the statements.

1. Great Britain's rise to power in the world trade market most resembled

_____'s in that it had few natural resources but imported what it needed to manufacture goods to sell for high prices elsewhere.

2. South Africa must import many goods necessary for its population but can afford such an imbalance in trade since it has accumulated wealth from the international sale of its large supply of gold. In this regard, South Africa is much

like the country of _____.

3. The former Soviet Union had an abundance of mineral resources that helped develop its manufacturing capabilities and resultant position as a world power.

Thus, the Soviet Union was like _____ in this respect.

ANSWERS ARE ON PAGE 320.

≡ GED Practice ≡
GEOGRAPHY

Questions 1 and 2 are based on the following bar graph.

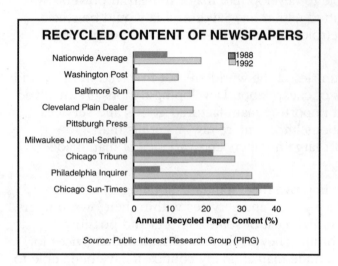

RECYCLED CONTENT OF NEWSPAPERS

■ 1988
□ 1992

Nationwide Average
Washington Post
Baltimore Sun
Cleveland Plain Dealer
Pittsburgh Press
Milwaukee Journal-Sentinel
Chicago Tribune
Philadelphia Inquirer
Chicago Sun-Times

0   10   20   30   40
Annual Recycled Paper Content (%)

Source: Public Interest Research Group (PIRG)

1. According to the graph, which of the following is true about the amount of recycled fiber content used in the eight papers listed?

   (1) It had increased from 1989 to 1992 in all the papers.
   (2) It had increased from 1989 to 1992 in only five of the papers.
   (3) It had increased from 1989 to 1992 in all but one paper.
   (4) It had decreased from 1989 to 1992 in all but one paper.
   (5) It had decreased from 1989 to 1992 in three of the papers.

2. The environmental trend suggested by the graph is most similar to which of the following?

   (1) the cleanup of PCB-contaminated soil
   (2) the ban on dumping of hazardous waste
   (3) the increase of reforestation programs
   (4) the use of recycled plastic bottles in automobile bumpers
   (5) the decrease in use of styrofoam packaging

Question 3 is based on the following passage.

The mining of coal in various parts of the country has resulted in some well-publicized problems such as air pollution and the creation of "dead land" by strip mining. A less well known and unexpected effect concerns the land above abandoned underground mine sites.

Mine subsidence occurs when the roofs of mine tunnels gradually collapse. The areas where supporting pillars of unmined coal were left remain more stable but also tend to sink slowly because of settling in the surrounding earth. Coal companies rarely left records of the exact location of shafts and supporting pillars.

The tiny village of Stiritz, in southern Illinois, almost disappeared when the Franco Mine was abandoned in 1938. Store owners moved to larger towns and cities. The land along Stiritz Road became a residential area. Thirty years later, the homeowners found that something else was disappearing—their backyards. Along the south side of Stiritz Road, yards had started to sink two to six feet lower than the houses. During heavy rains and spring thaws, residents could look out on spaces that looked more like swimming holes than lawns. The homes had been built close to the road, and the yards extended back over what once had been mine shafts. On the north side of the road, where the tunnels had not been dug, the land remained flat.

3. Homeowners in mining areas can get insurance against mine subsidence. But many insurance companies require proof that land sinkage is due to mine subsidence. Which of the following is wrong with this requirement?

   (1) It wrongly places blame on former mine owners.
   (2) It fails to account for other causes of land sinkage.
   (3) It falsely assumes homeowners can provide records that never existed.
   (4) It falsely assumes homeowners are lying.
   (5) It fails to account for damage done by land sinkage.

Questions 4 and 5 are based on the following passage.

The population of Washington State has changed from the 1960s to the 1990s. The state's total population has grown from 2,853,214 to an estimated 5,018,000. Back in 1960, the population of Seattle, Washington's largest city, was 557,087, and the population of Spokane was 181,608. By 1990, Seattle had 516,259 residents and Spokane had 177,196. Two small cities near Seattle also have changed. The population of Bellevue has increased from 12,809 people to 86,874, and Renton's population has more than doubled.

4. Which of the following *best* explains the shift in population distribution?

(1) People have been leaving Washington State in droves.
(2) People have been moving from large cities to smaller ones.
(3) People have been moving from large cities to farms.
(4) People have been moving from rural areas to large cities.
(5) Spokane has become more popular than Seattle.

5. The information in the passage supports which of the following conclusions?

If the shift in population distribution continues in this pattern,

(1) Seattle will grow and Spokane will lose residents
(2) Seattle will lose residents and Spokane will grow
(3) both Seattle and Spokane will lose residents
(4) the population of Washington will decrease
(5) Renton will soon become larger than Bellevue

Questions 6 and 7 are based on the map below.

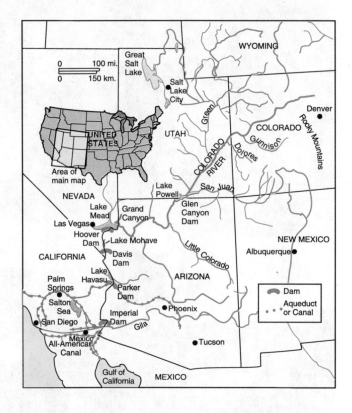

6. According to the map, which of the following groups of states receives water from the Colorado River?

(1) Colorado and Utah only
(2) Utah, Nevada, and Arizona only
(3) Arizona and California only
(4) Colorado, Utah, Arizona, and California only
(5) Colorado, Utah, Nevada, Arizona, and California

7. Recently, experts have warned that the Colorado River is in trouble. Its once-raging waters have been reduced to a trickle by the time they reach the Gulf of California. Which of the following situations *best* explains the cause of the problem?

(1) the drying up of parts of the Gila River
(2) overuse of Lake Mead and Lake Mohave
(3) drainage into the Little Colorado and San Juan rivers
(4) erosion in the Grand Canyon
(5) drainoff by dams and aqueducts

ANSWERS ARE ON PAGE 320.

9 Economics

The Green Thumb is a small company that produces indoor and outdoor plants that it distributes through home parties. Its sales personnel visit people's homes to show them the plants, explain how to grow and care for them, and convince the people to be buyers, or consumers, of the plants.

The plants are **goods**; the selling of them is a **service**. The people who took the risk to establish the business are **entrepreneurs**. They are attempting to fill a need in society. If they succeed, their activity will pay off, or return a profit for the money they invested in the business.

In the production of the plants, raw materials, called **natural resources**, are used. **Human resources**, or labor, are the gardeners, the salespeople, and the office workers of The Green Thumb. **Capital**, which includes the greenhouse, gardening tools, grow lights, and money, is also invested in the effort.

The study of the process of producing and distributing these plants and how it relates to buying, selling, and making a profit in a society is the interest of the economist.

Additionally, economists explore the role of the government in regulating such business activity and examine how the government gathers money for its own needs.

EXERCISE 1

Directions: Based on the reading above, match the terms on the left with the descriptions on the right by writing the correct letter in the space provided.

_____ **1.** producers

_____ **2.** distributors

_____ **3.** consumers

_____ **4.** goods

_____ **5.** service

(a) interior designers and homemakers who buy Green Thumb plants

(b) the different varieties of plants Green Thumb sells

(c) the trucks that deliver the nursery-grown plants to Green Thumb outlets

(d) what the Green Thumb salespeople give potential buyers

(e) Green Thumb and other companies like it

ANSWERS ARE ON PAGE 320.

ECONOMIC SYSTEMS

KEY WORDS

capitalism—an economic system that is based on the private ownership of property and the resources of production

communism—an economic and social system in which private ownership of property is not permitted

socialism—an economic system under which a country's major industries and services are owned publicly and cooperatively

free enterprise—an economic system based on private ownership and operation of businesses with little or no government control

As much as people try to distinguish politics from economics, it is difficult to separate them totally. A nation's political system often determines the type of economic system that the nation operates under.

The world's three major types of economic systems are capitalism, socialism, and communism. How each operates is illustrated below.

CAPITALISM

The Happy House Painters, Inc., is a small company run by individual investors for their own private profit and is allowed to operate with few government restraints. The company is located in a capitalist country. Capitalism is an economic system that works on the theory that under free enterprise, resources and income are most fairly distributed. Free enterprise means little or no government involvement in business practices.

Under capitalism, investment decisions are made mainly by the individual rather than by the government. The production, distribution, and prices of goods and services are determined by competition in a free market. The government intervenes only when necessary to protect the public interest. The economy of the United States is based on the economic principle of capitalism.

Over time, the U.S. economic system has evolved to permit more government control than is the ideal of free enterprise. The degree of government involvement in the economy changes with each political administration although, generally, the Democratic party favors more involvement and the Republican party favors less.

SOCIALISM

A socialist does not attempt to separate politics from economics. For example, in a country whose economic system is based on socialism, the Happy House Painters would have to answer to the government on many issues. The government might be the sole owner of the oils out of which the paint is made. Or it might run the transportation system that distributes the paint to its final destination or the electric company that provides the lights and power to accomplish the work. The number of hours that employees work or the amount of wages they earn might be regulated by the government. Health and welfare benefits would be provided for the workers by the state, which would get much of the money for such efforts by taxing companies.

Socialists believe that the entire country benefits from such government ownership and control, that there is more efficiency in industrial output, and that wealth is distributed more equally and fairly. Elements of socialism exist today in democracies such as Great Britain, Sweden, and Germany.

COMMUNISM

Under communism, all property is owned by the people and regulated by the state. The state is run by one political party that controls more than just the economy.

In a communist country, even the name of the company might be regulated by the state. The Happy House Painters might be the State Decorating Company—or perhaps a name would not be designated at all, since under communism there is no competition among companies. In fact, if the state determined that painting houses was no longer necessary, the company would not exist at all. The People's Republic of China and Cuba are two countries that operate under communist economies today.

MIXED ECONOMICS

None of the three economic systems described above exists in pure form in any country. That is, no *completely* capitalist, socialist, or communist economy exists in the modern world. In its operation, each of the economic systems incorporates some aspect of the other. Each economic system is modified to meet the needs of the nation it serves.

For example, though the U.S. has a capitalist economy, government agencies regulate, to some extent, the practices of certain businesses. The Federal Trade Commission's responsibility is to eliminate false advertising and to prevent the formation of monopolies. The Food and Drug Administration can remove from the market any food, drug, or cosmetic it deems to be dangerous to the public. The Department of Agriculture inspects and grades meats, dairy products, and produce bought and sold across state lines.

EXERCISE 2

Directions: Fill in each description below with the appropriate word: *capitalist,* *socialist,* or *communist.*

1. Vladimir Lenin carried the beliefs of Karl Marx to an extreme that many believe Marx himself would not have agreed with. Lenin led the Russian Revolution against a system wherein the peasants had been exploited by a few aristocrats. He replaced that system with one in which the state owned and controlled all

   enterprises. Lenin may be described as a _____.

2. Adam Smith wrote a book called *The Wealth of Nations*, in which he introduced the theory of a free market that could prosper without government interference.

   Adam Smith is thought of as the first _____ theorist.

3. Eugene Debs ran for the presidency in the United States in 1912 and included in his platform the economic ideas that wealth should be distributed more evenly throughout the population and that the government should have more say in

   accomplishing that. Debs may be described as a _____.

ANSWERS ARE ON PAGE 321.

WRITING ACTIVITY 1

Thoreau, in paraphrasing Emerson, is quoted as saying, "The government that governs least, governs best." However, others point out that without governmental involvement, unscrupulous individuals or companies would take advantage of people.

Each of the questions below asks whether government should involve itself in a certain activity. Choose one and write one or two paragraphs to support your view.

1. Should cigarette manufacturers be permitted to advertise?

2. Should pornographic magazines be sold?

3. Should the government require inflatable airbags on all new cars?

ANSWER IS ON PAGE 321.

SUPPLY AND DEMAND

KEY WORDS

demand—the desire and ability of consumers to buy a product or service
supply—the quantity of goods and services available for sale at all
  possible prices
surplus—a situation in which the supply of a product far exceeds the
  demand for it
equilibrium—the price at which supply equals demand

The American free enterprise system is based on the interplay between supply and demand. Supply is the quantity of goods and services available for sale at all possible prices. Demand is the desire to buy a product or service and the ability to pay for it. Producers or suppliers provide a supply of goods and services. Consumers who are willing and able to buy these goods and services create a demand.

The amount of production of an item and the price for it depend on the cost of production and the demand in the marketplace. If there is a great enough demand for a product, a high price can be charged for it, the cost of production can be covered, and a profit can be made.

For example, the owners of the Happy House Painters, Inc., went into business when they discovered that no company existed that painted houses within a ten-mile radius of their location, and yet there were many busy families seeking such a service. The entrepreneurs who founded Happy House Painters, Inc., also learned that paint could be bought at low cost, workers could be hired at low hourly wages, high prices could be charged, and a good profit could be made.

THE DYNAMICS OF SUPPLY AND PRICE

In general, the higher the price, the greater the number of competing companies that supply the product or service. This is because a high-priced item or service that yields a good profit for a business will attract many producers who will compete with one another for a share of the market. As a result, the Happy House Painters soon found themselves in competition with four other similar companies within their ten-mile working radius.

When too many producers compete for business, the supply of a product or service becomes so great that supply exceeds demand. A surplus results when the supply of a product far exceeds the demand for it. Under such a condition, the price is driven down. Often, competing businesses cannot make a profit and therefore are forced out of business. The graph below illustrates the supply curve. (In the graphs below and on pages 239 and 240, the lines appear straight because the numbers were simplified for clarity. The actual figures would appear as a curve.)

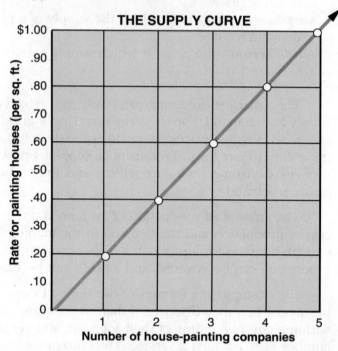

THE SUPPLY CURVE

Rate for painting houses (per sq. ft.)

Number of house-painting companies

In the graph, as the rate (price) per square foot for house painting goes up, the number (supply) of house-painting companies increases. In this graph, at a rate of $.20 per square foot, only one house-painting company exists. As the rate rises to $.80 per square foot, four companies compete for the business.

According to this graph, what would happen to the number of house-painting companies if the price reached $1.00 per square foot?

_____

By locating $1.00 per square foot on the graph, you can see that *there would be five house-painting companies* competing for business.

THE DYNAMICS OF DEMAND AND PRICE

Just as the price of a product or service affects supply, price also affects demand. In general, when prices go down, demand goes up; conversely, as prices go up, demand goes down. For example, if the homeowners in the area felt that the Happy House Painters, Inc., and their competitors charged too much to paint houses, the homeowners might paint their houses themselves or put off painting their homes. As a result, the number of house-painting companies would decrease, since the demand for the service would fall off. The following graph illustrates the demand curve.

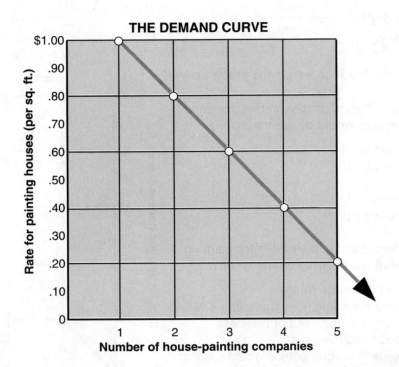

In the graph above, as the rate for house painting goes down, the number of house-painting companies goes up (the demand for the service increases). At $1.00 per square foot, only one company is needed to satisfy demand. If the rate were lowered to $.40 per square foot, four companies would be needed to satisfy the increased demand. According to the graph, if the price were lowered to $.20 per square foot, would demand (and the number of companies needed to satisfy demand) increase or decrease? By how many?

According to the graph, if the price were lowered to $.20 per square foot, *demand would increase to five companies.*

Does this seem confusing? Does it seem like two contradictory things are occurring here? Acutally, the supply and demand curves are based on economists' theories. In real life, supply, demand, *and* price are all interrelated. To understand how these components work together, we have to understand what economists call equilibrium.

SUPPLY, DEMAND, AND EQUILIBRIUM

In order to service exactly the number of customers who need their homes painted, producers must determine at what point supply equals demand. Economists call this point the equilibrium. Equilibrium occurs when the supply of a product or service equals the demand for it. This establishes the market price for a product or service. When the price is greater than the equilibrium point, demand falls, and there is more of a product or service than people need. This is called a surplus. When the price falls below the equilibrium point, demand increases, and a shortage in the product or service exists.

GED Practice

EXERCISE 3

Questions 1 and 2 are based on the graph below.

1. According to the graph, the market price for painting houses would be approximately

   (1) $1.00 per sq. ft.
   (2) $.80 per sq. ft.
   (3) $.70 per sq. ft.
   (4) $.60 per sq. ft.
   (5) $.20 per sq. ft.

2. If companies lowered their rates for painting houses, what would likely be the result?

   (1) Demand would decrease.
   (2) All of the house-painting companies would lose money and go out of business.
   (3) Demand would increase.
   (4) House-painting companies would expand their market area.
   (5) All of the house-painting companies in the area would enjoy record profits.

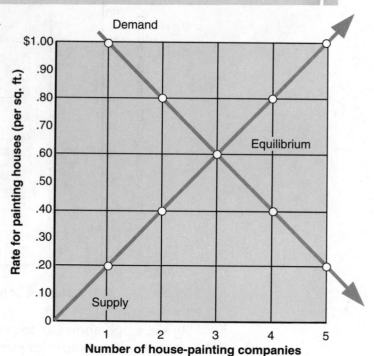

Questions 3 and 4 on page 241 are based on the following paragraph and table.

When the business of the Happy House Painters, Inc., began to increase, the company had to hire more workers. At a certain point, the company should have stopped hiring painters and, instead, should have accepted fewer jobs because it was no longer cost-efficient to take on more jobs. Thus, the company had not heeded the law of diminishing returns, and it began losing money. This table illustrates the productivity of the Happy House Painters, Inc.

Number of Painters	Number of Houses That Can Be Painted Each Day
2	1
4	3
6	5
8	5
10	6
12	7

3. In the situation described in the passage on page 240, the company failed to heed the law of diminishing returns. Which explanation below best defines the law of diminishing returns described in the passage?

The law of diminishing returns is the point at which

(1) the amount of money invested is less than the return on the investment

(2) the amount of money invested on equipment diminishes and the investment in labor increases

(3) the return on investment fails to increase in relation to the additional investment in labor

(4) profit far exceeds the additional labor costs

(5) profit and the labor costs are exactly equal

4. At a certain point, adding more workers did not result in a substantial increase in the number of houses painted. According to the table, at what point did this occur?

(1) 4 painters for 3 houses
(2) 12 painters for 7 houses
(3) 10 painters for 6 houses
(4) 8 painters for 5 houses
(5) 6 painters for 5 houses

ANSWERS ARE ON PAGE 321.

WRITING ACTIVITY 2

During the summer of 1986 the members of OPEC voted to reduce the amount of oil drilled in order to boost the price of petroleum exported to other nations. The U.S. imports one-third of the petroleum it uses. Write one paragraph from the oil-producing nations' point of view. Why do they think they should be able to raise prices? Write another paragraph from the consumer's point of view. How might this action affect the supply and price of oil and gasoline to the consumer?

ANSWER IS ON PAGE 321.

MONEY AND MONETARY POLICY

Money is a medium of exchange accepted by a society in payment for goods and services. Before money appeared, many methods of exchange were used, including barter. **Barter** is an item-for-item trade that is still used in some societies. Under the barter system, for example, you could exchange the extra tomatoes you had grown in your garden for some of your neighbor's spare lettuce.

In most purchases today, however, we use money as the medium of exchange because money works more efficiently than barter. Money has a standard value that both buyers and sellers recognize and readily accept. How many tomatoes are a fair exhange for a head of lettuce—and what about the varying sizes of each? Fifty cents a pound or seventy cents a head are much clearer values to all parties concerned.

FINANCIAL INSTITUTIONS

The establishment of financial institutions was a natural outgrowth of a monetary system of exchange. People needed a safe place to secure their paper and coin currency.

Financial institutions attract deposits and make money by lending their savers' deposits for a fee, called *interest*. These institutions keep, as income, part of the interest received from loans and pay part of it to the depositor. The most common financial institutions in the U.S. are banks, savings and loan associations, and credit unions.

Commercial banks are the most numerous of all financial institutions in the U.S. They make their money by lending to businesses. The interest rate they charge to their best customers is known as the *prime rate*.

ESTABLISHMENT OF THE FEDERAL RESERVE SYSTEM

KEY WORDS

Federal Reserve System—the nation's central banking system, which regulates banks and influences the flow of money and credit
monetary policy—the regulation of the nation's supply of money and credit by the Federal Reserve Board
reserve ratio—the percentage of nonlendable deposits that financial institutions must set aside
discount rate—the interest rate that the Federal Reserve charges banks that borrow from it

The need for the establishment of a national bank in the United States was recognized early in the country's history, and in recognition of this need the Bank of the United States was founded in 1791. The constitutionality of the Bank of the United States was questioned, however. It failed, as did a second national bank that was founded in 1816 but was opposed by President Andrew Jackson.

It was not until 1913 that the permanent Federal Reserve System was set up. The main purpose of the system is to regulate the nation's money supply and to provide a source of credit (serve as the central bank) for the nation's banks. Most of the nation's banks are required to be members of the Federal Reserve System. Without a central banking system, the supply of money fluctuates (goes up and down) too easily, and the entire economy becomes unstable.

The Federal Reserve (the Fed) stabilizes the economy by regulating the supply of money and credit. This process is known as establishing monetary policy. One method by which the Fed regulates the money supply is by setting the reserve ratio for banks. Banks are required to set aside a certain amount of money that is deposited in them. This amount cannot be loaned out. The

Federal Reserve sets the percentage that cannot be loaned out. This is the reserve ratio. The diagram below shows the effect on the economy of raising and lowering the reserve ratio.

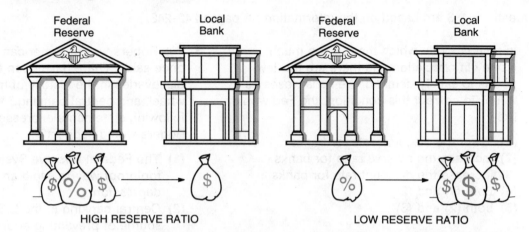

By raising the percentage, the Fed is able to decrease the amount of funds banks are able to lend. By lowering it, the Fed is able to increase the amount of money in circulation.

Another method by which the Fed controls the money supply is by regulating the discount rate. The discount rate is the interest rate it charges banks that borrow money from it. When the discount rate is raised, banks can borrow less money, charge higher interest rates to their customers, and make fewer loans. This is described as a tight money policy. When the discount rate is lowered, banks can borrow more money, charge lower interest rates to their customers, and make more loans. This is described as a loose money policy.

Another service of the Federal Reserve System is to act as a clearinghouse for most checks written on checking accounts from most banks across the country.

EXERCISE 4

Directions: Circle *T* if the statement below is true based on the reading above, or *F* if it is false.

T F 1. The chief role of the Fed is to lend the U.S. government money when it needs it.

T F 2. The Fed's lowering the discount rate for banks results in more money in circulation.

T F 3. The interest rate the Fed charges member banks to borrow from it is called the prime rate.

T F 4. Two ways by which the Federal Reserve influences the money supply are coining money and setting the prime rate.

T F 5. When the Federal Reserve System lowers the reserve ratio, consumers can borrow more money.

ANSWERS ARE ON PAGE 321.

▤ **GED Practice** ▤
EXERCISE 5

Questions 1–3 are based on the information on pages 242–243.

1. In a situation in which there is too much money in circulation and there are too few goods to satisfy demand, the dollar loses its value. To correct this condition, the Fed would likely

   (1) lower the discount rate for banks
   (2) increase the reserve ratio for banks
   (3) increase the discount rate for banks
   (4) both (1) and (2)
   (5) both (2) and (3)

2. In a situation in which there is too little money in circulation and there are too many goods to satisfy weak demand, the dollar gains in value. To correct this condition, the Fed would likely

   (1) lower the reserve ratio for banks
   (2) lower the discount rates for banks
   (3) increase the reserve ratio for banks
   (4) both (1) and (2)
   (5) both (2) and (3)

3. Will Rogers was an American humorist who once said, "There have been three great discoveries in the history of man: fire, the wheel, and central banking." Which of the following statements expresses an opinion that Rogers would support?

   (1) The Federal Reserve System presents a foolproof way to avoid an economic depression.
   (2) Central banking in the U.S. has been the source of preventing economic disaster since colonial times.
   (3) A national banking system gives the federal government a means to keep the economy steady during shaky times.
   (4) The federal banking system has been a success since the beginning of human civilization.
   (5) A central banking system has not been very successful in preventing economic catastrophe.

Question 4 refers to the following cartoon.

4. The U.S. military budget is funded and approved by the Congress. In the cartoon, the artist shows that government money has been

   (1) well spent
   (2) spent only on necessities
   (3) watched over carefully by Congress
   (4) used to keep unnecessary military bases open
   (5) wasted through excessive payments for goods

ANSWERS ARE ON PAGE 321.

GOVERNMENT AND FISCAL POLICY

KEY WORDS

fiscal policy—governmental use of its taxing and spending powers to influence the nation's economy

deficit spending—an economic condition in which the government spends more money than it collects in taxes

"In this world nothing is certain but death and taxes," said Benjamin Franklin. We still recognize that taxes are unavoidable, for there is no other way to pay public officials, to build roads, to provide for defense, or to care for the poor and homeless among the population. However, there will probably always be debate over who should pay taxes, how much they should pay, and how the money should be collected.

Like the Federal Reserve Board, the national government exerts some influence on the nation's economy; however, the government's influence is more indirect than the Federal Reserve's. The federal government affects the nation's economic condition through its fiscal policy. Fiscal policy involves the government's taxing and spending measures.

In establishing fiscal policy, the president proposes an annual budget to Congress. As Congress determines which programs are needed, it must consider how these programs are to be funded. Levying taxes is the answer. By increasing government spending, money is taken out of the hands of consumers. By decreasing spending, taxpayers' purchasing power is increased. Thus, the government indirectly influences the nation's supply of money and credit.

When the government spends less than it receives in taxes, a **budget surplus** is the result. Conversely, when the government spends more than it takes in, the condition is described as deficit spending. A **balanced budget** results when the income from taxes equals the money spent on programs.

In 1985, the U.S. Congress passed the Gramm-Rudman-Hollings Act, which required that the federal government have a balanced budget by 1991. Despite this law, the federal budget continued to reflect a deficit—$200 trillion in 1990 alone. The struggle to balance the budget revolves around these issues:

1. Should the federal government cut its programs or raise our taxes?

2. If programs are cut, where should the emphasis be? Military spending? Government waste? Social programs for the poor and needy? Maintenance of federal highway, water, and environmental programs?

EXERCISE 6

The question refers to the following passage.

The nation's budget deficit created a controversy that demanded much newspaper coverage and television air time during the 1980s and 1990s. Many politicians and voters expressed the opinion that either more taxes should be collected or government spending should be cut to reduce the national debt. Many others felt, however, that the debt was unavoidable in complex times like ours and that, indeed, national security and economic stability depend on just such a debt.

Which of the following statements supports the opinion described in the last sentence of the passage: ". . . the debt was unavoidable in complex times like ours and that, indeed, national security and economic stability depend on just such a debt"?

(1) The Department of Defense's budget demands, needed to carry out the modernization of its programs, were a major cause of the growing national debt of the 1980s.

(2) The Department of Defense could provide for national security on much less than the sum of money it received during the 1980s.

(3) Though the Department of Defense spent huge sums of money during the 1980s, national security suffered rather than improved.

(4) The Federal Reserve Board was able to bring down inflation during the 1980s despite its relatively small outlay of funds.

(5) The Federal Reserve Board was unable to control inflation during the early 1980s despite the great expenses it laid out to try.

ANSWER IS ON PAGE 322.

 ## WRITING ACTIVITY 3

Some critics of the congressional legislation to cut the budget deficit complain that the budget is being balanced "on the backs of the poor." This means that federal programs implemented to help the needy are being cut in order to reduce government spending. Do you believe that the poor are carrying an unfair burden in the government's budget reduction efforts? State your position in one or two sentences and write two or three paragraphs defending your point of view.

ANSWER IS ON PAGE 322.

MEASURES OF ECONOMIC ACTIVITY

KEY WORDS

gross national product (GNP)—the amount of all goods and services a nation produces in one year

inflation—an increase in the supply of money and credit, accompanied by an increased demand for fewer goods, resulting in reduced purchasing power

business cycles—regular economic trends in businesses

depression—a severe decline in economic activity accompanied by falling prices and increased unemployment

recession—a period of reduced economic activity characterized by rising unemployment

When you buy a new car, or clothing, or a ticket for a seat on an airline, you are contributing to the gross national product (GNP) of the country. When a business invests in some new machinery or in a new warehouse, it too is contributing to the GNP. The GNP is one of the most important measurements of economic growth. It represents the total amount of all goods and services produced by a nation in one year.

Many economists believe that to truly understand the GNP one must understand the effects of inflation. Inflation occurs when the prices of goods rise faster than the dollar's purchasing power. As a result, the dollar loses value.

Even after adjustment for inflation, the GNP figure is to be interpreted as a general guideline with far from perfect accuracy. Nonetheless, it is a guide to how well the economy is doing, in general, throughout the country. It is computed four times a year and reflects trends, or business cycles, of the nation as a whole.

A falling GNP indicates a slowdown in business activity. When the slowdown results in unemployment, the economy experiences a recession. The U.S. economy experienced severe recessions in the mid-1970s, the early 1980s, and the early 1990s, when unemployment rates climbed and business growth and investment fell. If a recession is prolonged and extreme, a depression results such as the U.S. experienced during the late 1920s and early 1930s.

Depressions and recessions are characterized by high unemployment and falling prices that develop into patterns difficult to change, even through the nation's fiscal or monetary policies. In the late 1970s and early 1980s economists were faced with a new problem—high unemployment combined with inflation, which resulted in the coining of a new word, *stagflation*.

THE CONSUMER PRICE INDEX

In the U.S., the rate of inflation is measured by the **Consumer Price Index** (CPI). The CPI is the measure of change in prices of a group of goods or services that a typical consumer would purchase.

Using 1982–84 as base years (100 percent), the CPI figures other years' prices as percentages in comparison to it. For example, in 1990 an item that cost $130.70 would have cost an average of $100.00 between 1982 and 1984. Based on those dollar figures, the CPI for 1990 was 130.7.

≣ GED Practice ≣
EXERCISE 7

Questions 1 and 2 are based on the following table.

1. Based on the data in the CPI, what was the effect of the 49 percent increase in oil prices from 1979 to 1980?

   (1) a sharp increase in the CPI
   (2) a sharp decrease in the CPI
   (3) a 2 percent increase in the CPI
   (4) a 2 percent decrease in the CPI
   (5) none

2. What has been the general trend of consumer prices in dollars since 1970?

   (1) unpredictable rises and falls
   (2) predictable up-and-down cycles
   (3) a general rise in prices
   (4) a constant fall in prices
   (5) a tendency to remain the same

CONSUMER PRICE INDEX, 1970–1991

Year	Consumer Price Index in Dollars (1982–84 = 100)	Percent Change from Previous Year
1970	38.8	5.7
1971	40.5	4.4
1972	41.8	3.2
1973	44.4	6.2
1974	49.3	11.0
1975	53.8	9.1
1976	56.9	5.8
1977	60.6	6.5
1978	65.2	6.3
1979	72.6	11.3
1980	82.4	13.5
1981	90.9	10.3
1982	96.5	6.2
1983	99.6	3.2
1984	103.9	4.3
1985	107.6	3.6
1986	109.6	1.9
1987	113.6	3.6
1988	118.3	4.1
1989	124.0	4.8
1990	130.7	5.4
1991	136.2	4.2

Questions 3 and 4 are based on the cartoon.

EUGENE PAYNE
Courtesy WSOC-TV, Charlotte

Inflation hasn't slowed travel

3. Based on the information in the cartoon, the artist would likely agree with which of the following statements?

　(1) Americans' spending is greater than it's ever been.
　(2) Americans' spending has fallen off because of inflation.
　(3) Americans' spending is supported more and more by credit.
　(4) Americans' spending far exceeds the spending of foreign consumers.
　(5) Americans' spending habits are going to drive the economy into a tailspin.

4. By comparing a credit card to a flying carpet, the artist is suggesting that Americans

　(1) are riding high on consumer debt
　(2) expect a free ride
　(3) put trust in their financial future
　(4) are as rich as Arabian sheiks
　(5) use credit cards to purchase carpets

ANSWERS ARE ON PAGE 322.

UNEMPLOYMENT AND ECONOMIC ACTIVITY

> ### KEY WORDS
>
> ***unemployment***—the lack of jobs for all those who want to and are able to work
>
> ***cyclical unemployment***—unemployment caused by recession or other unstable economic times
>
> ***dislocated (or displaced) workers***—workers who have lost their jobs due to the relocation of an industry
>
> ***structural unemployment***—unemployment caused by a rapid change in the character of the economy

The nation's unemployment rate is another important measurement of economic activity. Unemployment may be described as a lack of jobs for all of those who want to and are able to work. The unemployment rate is released during the first week of each month, and economists and government officials await its release to spot trends in the economy. Government economists believe that an unemployment rate of less than 4 percent is acceptable for a healthy economy.

Different categories of unemployment are observable in an economy, as illustrated in the passage below.

> During the decade of the 1960s, many businesses, including the Pleasure Boat Corporation, were enjoying healthy economic times. Unemployment rates were low, people had plenty of extra money to spend, and pleasure boats sold well all over the country.

> During the mid-1970s, however, various events caused the economy to take a turn for the worse. The one that affected the Pleasure Boat Corporation the most was the OPEC oil embargo. It resulted in increased prices on many fuel-dependent items, including cars, planes, buses, and boats. Fewer people took long trips in cars or short excursions in boats. As a result, fewer boats were manufactured, and many people at the Pleasure Boat Corporation lost their jobs.

> Soon the country entered a recession, with widespread unemployment. The Federal Reserve System can fight such cyclical unemployment by adopting a monetary policy of lowering reserve ratios for its member banks and lowering interest rates. The federal government itself can adopt a recession-fighting fiscal policy of increased spending, or it can decrease taxes to increase consumer spending. But each of these methods takes a long time to change an economic trend. Thus, the 1970s closed without a significant improvement in the nation's economic condition.

> The 1980s saw a gradual improvement in the economy, but by then the Pleasure Boat Corporation had been bought out by a larger corporation that had made the decision to relocate south, where lower wages could be paid to a much less unionized work force.

The employees who were left behind in the Midwest were labeled dislocated (or displaced) workers and were offered the chance to be retrained by the federal government for a different or more technologically advanced field. Unemployment caused by rapid change in the character of the economy is called structural unemployment by economists, and it, too, is difficult and slow to change.

Given the rapid rate of economic and technological change, it may be that massive unemployment is here to stay. Only creative, long-range solutions can help the economy and our people cope with this problem.

≡ GED Practice ≡
EXERCISE 8

Questions 1–3 refer to the following definitions.

cyclical unemployment—unemployment caused by recession or other unstable economic times

structural unemployment—unemployment caused by a rapid change in the character of the economy

frictional unemployment—unemployment caused by workers quitting jobs for reasons of dissatisfaction

seasonal unemployment—unemployment caused by a change from one season or time period to another

normal unemployment—the level of unemployment that is considered acceptable for a healthy economy (usually less than 4 percent)

1. Construction workers are often out of work for long periods of time during the winter in the North and Midwest of the U.S. Theirs is said to be

   (1) cyclical unemployment
   (2) structural unemployment
   (3) frictional unemployment
   (4) seasonal unemployment
   (5) normal unemployment

2. The increasing importance of computers in various business and industry settings has most likely caused

   (1) cyclical unemployment
   (2) structural unemployment
   (3) frictional unemployment
   (4) seasonal unemployment
   (5) normal unemployment

3. The number of new housing starts is an important indicator of the health of the nation's economy. Under a slow economy, the number of housing starts decreases and construction workers are laid off. When the economy picks up again, these workers are rehired. This type of unemployment is

   (1) cyclical unemployment
   (2) structural unemployment
   (3) frictional unemployment
   (4) seasonal unemployment
   (5) normal unemployment

ANSWERS ARE ON PAGE 322.

GED Practice
EXERCISE 9

Questions 1–5 are based on the bar graph below.

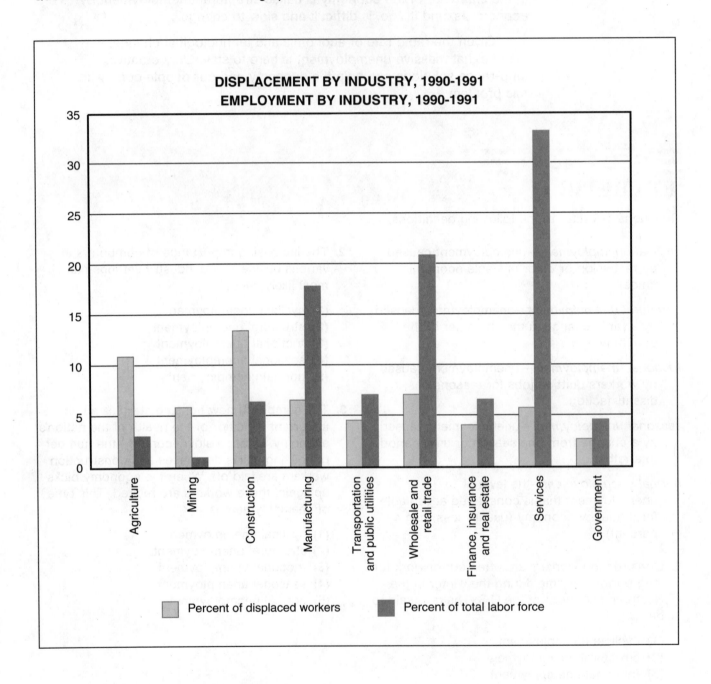

DISPLACEMENT BY INDUSTRY, 1990-1991
EMPLOYMENT BY INDUSTRY, 1990-1991

Legend: ▢ Percent of displaced workers ▮ Percent of total labor force

1. Based on information in the bar graph, which industry had the greatest amount of worker displacement during 1990–1991?

   (1) construction
   (2) manufacturing
   (3) wholesale and retail trade
   (4) services
   (5) government

2. According to the graph, which industry had the highest total employment?

   (1) agriculture
   (2) mining
   (3) manufacturing
   (4) wholesale and retail trade
   (5) services

3. Based on information in the bar graph, which industry had the smallest percent of displaced workers during 1990–1991?

   (1) agriculture
   (2) services
   (3) construction
   (4) manufacturing
   (5) government

4. According to the employment bars, which industry was the smallest in the United States from 1990 to 1991?

   (1) government
   (2) transportation and public utilities
   (3) mining
   (4) construction
   (5) manufacturing

5. Which of the following statements is supported by the graph?

   (1) Employment in the transportation and public utilities industries went up between 1990 and 1991.
   (2) The mining industry had the lowest rate of increase in worker displacement.
   (3) Worker displacement affected the major U.S. industries during 1990 and 1991.
   (4) Government workers were unaffected by the recession in the early 1990s.
   (5) Agriculture is a larger industry than finance, insurance, and real estate.

ANSWERS ARE ON PAGE 322.

WRITING ACTIVITY 4

Do you accept or reject the belief that a certain level of unemployment in the U.S. is acceptable? State your position in two to three sentences and then write two to three paragraphs to support your position.

ANSWER IS ON PAGE 322.

GED Practice

ECONOMICS

Questions 1 and 2 are based on the following table.

AVERAGE WEEKLY WAGES	
Child-care worker	$154
Cleaning person	$191
Cashier	$219
Waiter	$222
Bartender	$251
Teacher (pre-K through high school)	$561
Firefighter	$636
Registered nurse	$662

Source: Bureau of Labor Statistics

1. Which of the following is documented by the information in the table?

   (1) Occupations that require specialized education or skill receive higher wages than those that do not.
   (2) Nursing is a respected occupation.
   (3) Firefighting can be a dangerous job.
   (4) Many students earn money as waiters.
   (5) The actual wage of a cleaning person depends on the place of employment.

2. The average wage of child-care workers is most probably based on which of the following assumptions?

   (1) Child care requires little skill.
   (2) There is little demand for child care.
   (3) Child care is a much-needed service.
   (4) Child-care workers are well trained.
   (5) Child care is tax-deductible.

Questions 3 and 4 are based on the following passage.

In a recent report about consumer debt, one magazine included information about a special type of charge card. When a customer makes a purchase with a *debit card*, the money is immediately deducted from the customer's checking account.

According to *U.S. News and World Report*, "The retailer gets an immediate OK, through an electronic terminal at the checkout counter, that the cardholder's bank account can cover the purchase. Older cards, like credit cards, involve only a signed receipt. And anyone with a checking account at a participating bank can get one. Fees for debit cards, if any, vary by bank; some charge 10 cents per transaction, or $1 per month."

3. Which of the following is implied about debit cards?

   (1) Debit cards are harder to get than credit cards.
   (2) Debit cards can help consumers stay out of debt.
   (3) Debit cards are more popular than credit cards.
   (4) Debit cards are difficult to use.
   (5) Debit cards are not accepted by many retailers.

4. Which of the following would be the most likely result if the federal government was required to spend as if it were using only a debit card?

   (1) Government spending would be limited.
   (2) Government spending would increase.
   (3) The national debt would be eliminated.
   (4) The national debt would increase.
   (5) The government would no longer be responsible for the national debt.

Questions 5 and 6 are based on the following passage.

Most small businesses are owned in one of two ways. *Individual proprietorship* exists when the business is owned by one person. That person manages the business, is responsible for all its debts, and receives all its profits. *Joint partnership* exists when a business is owned through a contract between two or more persons. The profits are shared through arrangement. Each partner is responsible for any debts incurred by the business.

5. Which of the following would happen if one of three partners in a pet shop were unable to pay her share of the store's bills?

   (1) Neither of her partners would be held responsible for paying the shop's bills.
   (2) Only one of her partners would be responsible for paying the shop's bills.
   (3) Both of her partners would be responsible for paying the shop's bills.
   (4) No one would be responsible for paying the shop's bills.
   (5) The partnership would have to be dissolved in order for the bills to be paid.

6. Which of the following is an example of a business held in individual proprietorship?

   (1) a lumberyard owned by three brothers
   (2) a repair shop owned by a married couple
   (3) a bookstore owned by a retired schoolteacher
   (4) a flower shop owned by two friends
   (5) a factory owned by its workers

Questions 7 and 8 are based on the following passage.

Most home buyers finance their purchase with a mortgage and make monthly payments that include interest. When interest rates go down, people often refinance their mortgages in order to make lower monthly payments.

Usually only about 15 percent of loan applications are for refinancing. However, the Mortgage Bankers Association reported that refinancing applications made up to 65 percent of loan applications in 1992.

7. Which of the following is implied in the passage?

   (1) Refinancing can save homeowners money.
   (2) People apply for refinancing only when they cannot afford their monthly mortgage payments.
   (3) Mortgage payments automatically change when interest rates change.
   (4) Refinancing does not affect interest payments.
   (5) Refinancing eliminates interest payments on mortgages.

8. Which of the following conclusions is supported by information in the passage?

   (1) Interest rates went down in 1992.
   (2) Interest rates went up in 1992.
   (3) Interest rates remained stable in 1992.
   (4) The number of general loan applications went up in 1992.
   (5) The number of general loan applications went down in 1992.

ANSWERS ARE ON PAGE 323.

Social Studies Post-Test

Directions: This Social Studies Post-Test will give you the opportunity to evaluate your readiness for the actual GED Social Studies Test.

This test contains 64 questions. Some of the questions are based on short reading passages, and some of them require you to interpret a chart, map, graph, or political cartoon.

You should take approximately 85 minutes to complete this test. At the end of 85 minutes, stop and mark your place. Then finish the test. This will give you an idea of whether or not you can finish the real GED Test in the time allotted. Try to answer as many questions as you can. A blank will count as a wrong answer, so make a reasonable guess for questions you are not sure of.

When you are finished with the test, turn to the evaluation chart on page 277. Use the chart to evaluate whether you are ready to take the actual GED Test and, if not, what areas need more work.

POST-TEST ANSWER GRID

1 ① ② ③ ④ ⑤	17 ① ② ③ ④ ⑤	33 ① ② ③ ④ ⑤	49 ① ② ③ ④ ⑤
2 ① ② ③ ④ ⑤	18 ① ② ③ ④ ⑤	34 ① ② ③ ④ ⑤	50 ① ② ③ ④ ⑤
3 ① ② ③ ④ ⑤	19 ① ② ③ ④ ⑤	35 ① ② ③ ④ ⑤	51 ① ② ③ ④ ⑤
4 ① ② ③ ④ ⑤	20 ① ② ③ ④ ⑤	36 ① ② ③ ④ ⑤	52 ① ② ③ ④ ⑤
5 ① ② ③ ④ ⑤	21 ① ② ③ ④ ⑤	37 ① ② ③ ④ ⑤	53 ① ② ③ ④ ⑤
6 ① ② ③ ④ ⑤	22 ① ② ③ ④ ⑤	38 ① ② ③ ④ ⑤	54 ① ② ③ ④ ⑤
7 ① ② ③ ④ ⑤	23 ① ② ③ ④ ⑤	39 ① ② ③ ④ ⑤	55 ① ② ③ ④ ⑤
8 ① ② ③ ④ ⑤	24 ① ② ③ ④ ⑤	40 ① ② ③ ④ ⑤	56 ① ② ③ ④ ⑤
9 ① ② ③ ④ ⑤	25 ① ② ③ ④ ⑤	41 ① ② ③ ④ ⑤	57 ① ② ③ ④ ⑤
10 ① ② ③ ④ ⑤	26 ① ② ③ ④ ⑤	42 ① ② ③ ④ ⑤	58 ① ② ③ ④ ⑤
11 ① ② ③ ④ ⑤	27 ① ② ③ ④ ⑤	43 ① ② ③ ④ ⑤	59 ① ② ③ ④ ⑤
12 ① ② ③ ④ ⑤	28 ① ② ③ ④ ⑤	44 ① ② ③ ④ ⑤	60 ① ② ③ ④ ⑤
13 ① ② ③ ④ ⑤	29 ① ② ③ ④ ⑤	45 ① ② ③ ④ ⑤	61 ① ② ③ ④ ⑤
14 ① ② ③ ④ ⑤	30 ① ② ③ ④ ⑤	46 ① ② ③ ④ ⑤	62 ① ② ③ ④ ⑤
15 ① ② ③ ④ ⑤	31 ① ② ③ ④ ⑤	47 ① ② ③ ④ ⑤	63 ① ② ③ ④ ⑤
16 ① ② ③ ④ ⑤	32 ① ② ③ ④ ⑤	48 ① ② ③ ④ ⑤	64 ① ② ③ ④ ⑤

Questions 1–4 are based on the information below.

The world's five climate regions are:

tundra—land frozen solid most of each year with very short periods of thawing

rain forest—area of heavy vegetation and almost continual rain and heat

Mediterranean—region of little rain or temperature change, except during the rainy part of the winter

desert—territory of little rain along with quick evaporation and much heat

continental—region of extreme seasonal changes and much moisture year-round

1. Southern California has hot, dry summers and mild, wet winters. In which region is it located?

   (1) tundra
   (2) rain forest
   (3) Mediterranean
   (4) desert
   (5) continental

2. The central Corn Belt of the United States has warm, wet summers and cold, damp winters. In which region is it located?

   (1) tundra
   (2) rain forest
   (3) Mediterranean
   (4) desert
   (5) continental

3. The Amazon River basin is hot and rainy and contains an abundance of plants and trees as a result. In which region is it located?

   (1) tundra
   (2) rain forest
   (3) Mediterranean
   (4) desert
   (5) continental

4. Death Valley is an arid area of southeast California. It is scorching hot during the day and extremely cold at night. In which region is it located?

   (1) tundra
   (2) rain forest
   (3) Mediterranean
   (4) desert
   (5) continental

Questions 5 and 6 are based on the following cartoon.

"All right, deep down it's a cry for psychiatric help—but at one level it's a stick-up."

© *Punch*/Rothco

5. Based on the robber's response, you can tell that the man who is being robbed
   (1) has been robbed many times before
   (2) is trying to analyze his attacker
   (3) does not have any money with him
   (4) does not realize he is being robbed
   (5) has refused to cooperate with his attacker

6. This cartoonist is saying that psychiatrists

   (1) blame criminals' social misbehavior on a need for attention
   (2) believe that criminals cause their own problems
   (3) do not really understand the motivation of criminals
   (4) are just as socially maladjusted as criminals
   (5) are not a very intelligent professional group

Questions 7 and 8 are based on the following chart.

U.S. CITIES WITH FASTEST-GROWING POPULATIONS, 1980–1990		
(Ranked from highest to lowest in population percentage growth)		
Rank	City	1980–1990
1	Mesa, AZ	89.0
2	Rancho Cucamonga, CA	83.5
3	Plano, TX	77.9
4	Irvine, CA	77.6
5	Escondido, CA	68.8
6	Oceanside, CA	67.4
7	Bakersfield, CA	65.5
8	Arlington, TX	63.5
9	Fresno, CA	62.9
10	Chula Vista, CA	61.0

7. According to the chart, what general trend is occurring in U.S. population?

(1) a move to the Midwest and Northeast
(2) a move to the North and East
(3) a move to the South and West
(4) a move away from the North and West
(5) a move away from the Southeast and East

8. Based on this trend, which of the following cities would you *not* expect to be on a list of places ranked 11 through 20 in fastest-growing population?

(1) New York City, NY
(2) Modesto, CA
(3) Glendale, AZ
(4) Las Vegas, NV
(5) Mesquite, TX

9. From the end of the Civil War until the Spanish-American War in 1898, most Americans would have identified themselves as isolationists. What was most likely the cause of such widespread desire for withdrawal from international affairs?

(1) the lack of information about events taking place in foreign lands
(2) the desire to expand the U.S. boundaries farther across the continent into Canada and Mexico
(3) the disillusionment with foreign allies who had refused to take sides during the Civil War
(4) the preoccupation with reconstruction and industrialization after the Civil War
(5) the resentment toward the new immigrants flooding this country

10. The passing of the Federal Reserve Act in 1913 was one of the most significant contributions of the Wilson administration. The law remedied almost all the ills of American banking and currency of the time. Without this act, the country would not have been able to adjust to the financial strains of World War I.

What implication has the author made about the significance of the Federal Reserve Act for the World War I years?

(1) It helped keep the U.S. out of involvement in World War I.
(2) It helped absorb the shock of the expense of World War I.
(3) It helped keep down our expenses during World War I.
(4) It helped prevent individuals from going bankrupt during World War I.
(5) It helped keep bankers honest during World War I.

POST-TEST

Questions 11 and 12 are based on the following passage.

When Cesar Chavez began the United Farm Workers in 1963 with his famous grape boycott, he and his fellow workers were receiving 90 cents an hour. By 1985, they earned up to $5.00 an hour.

In July 1984, another grape boycott was called for by Chavez. However, it was less successful than the first. In fact, membership in the UFW had decreased from almost 100,000 in the late 1960s and early 1970s to about 25,000 by 1984.

11. Which of the following is the most likely explanation for the dramatic rise in wages for the members of the UFW?

    (1) The federal government forced the growers to pay the workers more money.
    (2) The growers were pressured to raise wages because they had lost sales.
    (3) Inflation over the two decades caused everyone's wages to increase that much.
    (4) The farm workers accepted more responsibilities in turn for more money.
    (5) The pressure tactics of the UFW backfired on them.

12. What hypothesis would best explain the drop in membership in the UFW?

    (1) The members of the UFW were not happy with the slow progress made for them since the 1960s.
    (2) There were far fewer farm workers during the 1980s than there were during the 1960s and 1970s.
    (3) Boycotts by buyers do not work on the same kind of product more than once.
    (4) The farm workers were not motivated to join the UFW once they began receiving fairer wages.
    (5) The people of the 1980s were much more conservative than people of the 1960s and 1970s.

Questions 13 and 14 are based on the following passage.

Progressivism thrived during the early years of the twentieth century, and the inspiration for much of its spirit and purpose was President Theodore Roosevelt. He was only forty-two when he became president, and, as the youngest chief executive in American history, he brought joy and excitement to the office. Intelligent, energetic, ambitious, and adventurous are words often used to describe "Teddy," but his success in office was due as much to his political savvy and sense of fairness as it was to his more colorful attributes. He was known as a trustbuster and champion of labor, yet he supported growth of industry as natural and beneficial, and he insisted on the open shop for government workers and optional union membership for private industry.

13. In the passage, Teddy Roosevelt is described as a trustbuster. *Trust* in this sense refers to

    (1) faith in the character and ability of others
    (2) property held by one person for the benefit of another
    (3) a bank that administers funds or property
    (4) a combination of corporations that control a single market
    (5) an office or position of responsibility

14. Which of the following opinions of Theodore Roosevelt would the author of the above passage support?

    (1) Roosevelt was an unpopular president because of his reputation as a bully.
    (2) Roosevelt did not handle the labor issue well despite his skill in other areas.
    (3) Progressivism contributed little to the nation's growth and development as an industrial nation.
    (4) Roosevelt was successful because he did not cater to either workers or big corporations.
    (5) Roosevelt's popularity may be attributed more to his young age and personality than to his actions.

Questions 15 and 16 are based on the paragraph and map below.

"The world must be made safe for democracy." On April 2, 1917, Woodrow Wilson spoke these words to a special session of Congress called by him to ask that they declare war on Germany. Congress did so on April 6, 1917.

THE EUROPEAN POWERS AT WAR

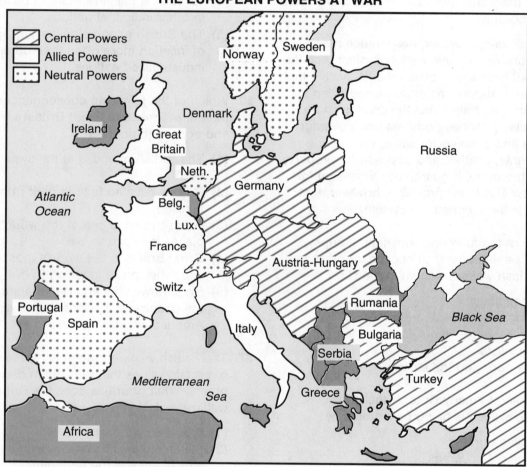

15. By declaring war on Germany, the U.S. was also declaring war on

  (1) Norway, Sweden, and Spain
  (2) Russia, France, and Italy
  (3) Austria-Hungary, Bulgaria, and Turkey
  (4) Italy, Greece, and Turkey
  (5) Africa, France, and Russia

16. By declaring war on Germany, the U.S. was also aligning itself with which major European powers?

  (1) Norway, Sweden, and Switzerland
  (2) Great Britain, Italy, France, and Russia
  (3) Austria-Hungary, Bulgaria, and Turkey
  (4) Italy, Greece, and Turkey
  (5) Great Britain, Norway, and Sweden

Questions 17–21 are based on the passage below.

Public assistance, or welfare, has been a much-used system for helping needy citizens in the U.S. since the Great Depression.

Most of the help has been in the form of direct payments, but during the 1960s the welfare programs were expanded to include job training, preschool programs, hot lunches, and many more diverse programs.

Great Britain, however, has a much more extensive cradle-to-grave welfare system than the U.S. In 1948, the British established a system that provides such support as extra money when a child is born and help when the dead must be buried. It also provides good medical coverage, free meals and clothing for some, vitamins, college grants, utilities, and payment for property taxes. Furthermore, it guarantees a pension for retirees. It is this latter provision, however, that many feel is bankrupting the system.

17. Which of the following American groups would be most likely to oppose introducing the British welfare system to the U.S.?

(1) communists
(2) progressive Democrats
(3) conservative Republicans
(4) socialists
(5) the poor and the elderly

18. According to many Britons, the British welfare system is being bankrupted by

(1) college grants
(2) medical coverage
(3) property taxes
(4) retirement pensions
(5) burial allotments

19. Which of the following is most likely to be true of the British economy, with its generous welfare system?

(1) Taxes in Britain are likely to be higher than in other industrial nations.
(2) More Britons are out of work than in any other industrial nation.
(3) The British government always operates at a deficit.
(4) Taxes in Britain are likely to be lower than in other industrial nations.
(5) The British economy experiences periods of inflation more often than other industrialized nations.

20. Which of the following consequences could be a direct result of Great Britain's welfare and economic policies?

(1) The British pound is at its lowest level ever.
(2) Britons have no faith in their prime minister.
(3) Great Britain is one of the world's worst places in which to live.
(4) Great Britain is the world's most expensive place in which to live.
(5) Britain's wealthy entertainers are leaving the country and choosing to live in America where taxes are lower.

21. The British welfare system is representative of certain values that the British place above others. What priorities does the British welfare system represent?

(1) lives over property
(2) full employment over government interference in the economy
(3) concern for the welfare of its citizens over concern about government spending
(4) balancing the nation's budget over caring for its nation's poor
(5) sensitivity to world opinion over excessive government spending

22. Which of the countries listed below has the most generous welfare program?

(1) Mexico
(2) Japan
(3) Sweden
(4) France
(5) India

Questions 23–26 are based on the following passage.

The Great Wall of China is reputed to be the only man-made feature visible from the moon. Although it was once thought to have been built entirely during the Ch'in Dynasty between 221 and 208 B.C., it is now believed to have been started earlier.

The 15-foot-high, 25-foot-wide, 1,500-mile-long structure was undoubtedly erected to keep out invading barbarians. To the common people of the empire, who had been forced to build the wall, it was not worth it, however. The wall, and other public works accomplished by the Ch'in Dynasty, had taken a great toll on the wealth and human life of the country. As a result, an indignant population rose up in rebellion against the Ch'in Dynasty, and in 207 B.C. the Han Dynasty began.

Because of its rich history and magnificent appearance, the Great Wall attracts tourists, scientists, and historians to this day and will continue to do so for generations.

23. According to the author of this passage, the Han Dynasty was able to come into power because

(1) barbarians were not effectively prevented from invading the empire
(2) it had started the work on the wall and really controlled it all along
(3) the common people rebelled against the empire that had forced them to work on the Great Wall
(4) the Ch'in emperor lost all his personal wealth in the creation of the Great Wall
(5) the Great Wall had become famous and attracted many tourists

24. The main idea of this passage is that

(1) the emperor of the Ch'in Dynasty was a slave driver
(2) invading barbarians were a problem in ancient China
(3) the common people of ancient China were very poor
(4) modern man has overestimated the importance of the Great Wall
(5) the human achievement of the Great Wall is widely appreciated

25. With which of the following opinions would this author most likely agree?

(1) The building of the pyramids of Egypt was not worth the human sacrifice it involved.
(2) The pyramids of Egypt are also intriguing to modern man because of the human effort they represent.
(3) The pyramids of Egypt would probably be visible to a human standing on the moon.
(4) The human significance of the pyramids of Egypt is greater than that of the Great Wall.
(5) The human significance of the pyramids of Egypt is not as great as that of the Great Wall.

26. The writer has not directly stated, but would support, the opinion that

(1) astronauts have taken a personal interest in the history of the Great Wall of China
(2) the common people of the Ch'in Dynasty were the ones who provided the labor in constructing the Great Wall
(3) work on the Great Wall was started before the Ch'in Dynasty came into existence
(4) the Great Wall of China is a great human achievement and was probably worth the effort it took
(5) the common people of today's China still resent the use of forced labor to build the Great Wall

Questions 27 and 28 are based on the following graph.

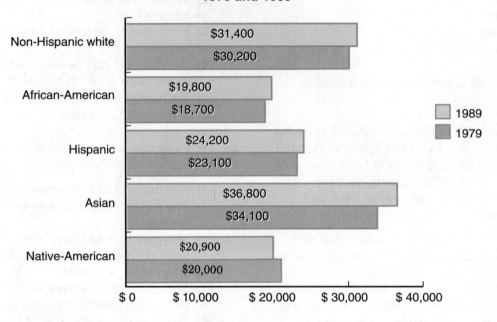

**Median Household Income by Race and Ethnicity
1979 and 1989**

Non-Hispanic white
$31,400
$30,200

African-American
$19,800
$18,700

1989
1979

Hispanic
$24,200
$23,100

Asian
$36,800
$34,100

Native-American
$20,900
$20,000

$ 0 $ 10,000 $ 20,000 $ 30,000 $ 40,000

Note: 1979 income expressed in 1989 dollars
Source: 1980 and 1990 Censuses of Population and Housing

27. Immigrants typically are a low-income group, but Asian-Americans are exceptions to this rule. Which factor, apart from level of educational attainment, might best account for Asian immigrants' high median household income?

(1) their willingness to learn the language more quickly than other immigrants
(2) their decision to relocate to areas that have a high cost of living
(3) their decision to live within their own neighborhoods in large cities
(4) the high level of financial resources many bring to the United States
(5) their greater dependence on two incomes to maintain their lifestyles

28. Of the five racial and ethnic groups represented, which shows the smallest increase in median household income?

(1) Non-Hispanic white
(2) African-American
(3) Hispanic
(4) Asian
(5) Native-American

Questions 29 and 30 are based on the following graph.

ABORTIONS IN THE UNITED STATES BY REGION

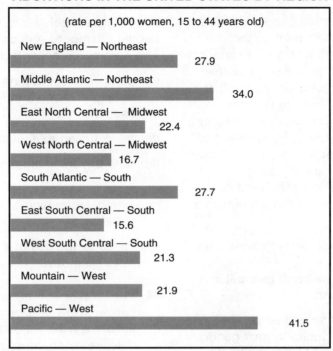

(rate per 1,000 women, 15 to 44 years old)

New England — Northeast 27.9

Middle Atlantic — Northeast 34.0

East North Central — Midwest 22.4

West North Central — Midwest 16.7

South Atlantic — South 27.7

East South Central — South 15.6

West South Central — South 21.3

Mountain — West 21.9

Pacific — West 41.5

29. Based on the information in the graph,

(1) New England women don't practice birth control

(2) the higher the education level of the population, the higher the abortion rate

(3) the higher the income level of the population, the lower the abortion rate

(4) women in the Middle Atlantic states have large families

(5) women in the Pacific—West tend to have abortions more frequently than others

30. According to the graph, the East South Central—South (Kentucky, Tennessee, Alabama, Mississippi) has the lowest abortion rate. Which of the following most likely accounts for this fact?

(1) Women in these states often cannot afford the cost of abortions.

(2) These states advocate women's rights.

(3) Large families are needed in these states to work on farms.

(4) Families in these states are rich and can afford to have large families.

(5) Women in these states tend to have a low pregnancy rate.

31. Anti-imperialists and isolationists have opposed American involvement in international affairs, but for very different reasons. For example, an anti-imperialist would say that American involvement in Vietnam was wrong because it was an attempt to dominate Vietnam. An isolationist, however, would say that American resources should be used at home.

Which of the following best explains the difference between anti-imperialists and isolationists?

(1) Anti-imperialists are against improper interference in other countries' affairs; isolationists are against making diplomatic and military commitments to other nations.

(2) Anti-imperialists are racially motivated; isolationists are not concerned with racial matters.

(3) Anti-imperialists are educated and concerned people; isolationists are selfish and lazy.

(4) Anti-imperialists are world travelers; isolationists have never left their own country.

(5) Anti-imperalists are powerful and influential people; isolationists are the common people.

POST-TEST

Questions 32 and 33 are based on the following passage.

"The male form of a female liberationist is a male liberationist—a man who realizes the unfairness of having to work all his life to support a wife and children so that someday his widow may live in comfort; a man who points out that commuting to a job he doesn't like is just as oppressive as his wife's imprisonment in a suburb; a man who rejects his exclusion, by society and most women, from participation in childbirth and the engrossing, delightful care of young children—a man, in fact, who wants to relate himself to people and the world around him as a person."

—Margaret Mead, "Some Personal Views"

32. The writer's opinion about role reversal in American society is that

(1) males and females should remain in those roles that are best suited to their gender
(2) women should work outside the home and men should stay at home with the kids
(3) women should make fewer demands on men
(4) males can take on all of the roles of females
(5) men and women both should be able to perform roles not traditionally assigned to them by society

33. What is the source of much frustration for modern men, according to the writer?

(1) demands that they reverse roles with women
(2) pressure to assume only traditional male roles and responsibilities
(3) employers who do not pay them enough to allow their wives to stay at home
(4) their own inability to relate to others as a person
(5) the lack of excitement and thrill in their lives

Questions 34–36 are based on the following information.

Defense mechanisms are means by which people attempt to reduce frustration and anxiety. Five common mechanisms are described below.

compensation—offsetting a feeling of inferiority or failure in one area of life by achieving in another area

denial—refusing to accept some hurtful truth

fantasy—daydreaming; imagining a world of one's own

regression—retreating to early forms and patterns of behavior

sublimation—the use of a substitute activity to satisfy a motive

34. The mother and father of a child dying of cancer show no signs of stress, as they truly believe a cure will be found in time. The defense mechanism used is

(1) compensation
(2) denial
(3) fantasy
(4) regression
(5) sublimation

35. A husband who has lost an argument about buying a new sports car pouts and refuses to eat the dinner his wife has prepared. The defense mechanism used is

(1) compensation
(2) denial
(3) fantasy
(4) regression
(5) sublimation

36. Teddy Roosevelt was very small and sickly as a child; however, as an adult, he became an enthusiastic boxer, hunter, politician, and soldier, leading the Rough Riders during the Spanish-American War. The defense mechanism illustrated in Roosevelt's case is

(1) compensation
(2) denial
(3) fantasy
(4) regression
(5) sublimation

Questions 37 and 38 are based on the following cartoon.

America's Problem Child   —By Hungerford

37. This cartoonist attributes the cause of delinquency among children today to

    (1) bad attitudes toward adults
    (2) poor education in the school
    (3) the increased number of divorces
    (4) low morals in society
    (5) the child's lack of purpose in life

38. What belief of the cartoonist is shown in this cartoon?

    (1) The need to keep our jails uncrowded is more important than teaching a child a lesson.
    (2) Children who turn to crime should not be given the same concern as those who are victims of broken homes.
    (3) Divorce is wrong when it starts victimizing the children and the society they belong to.
    (4) Older people and children are the least deserving of, but most vulnerable to, harmful effects of crime.
    (5) Children are our most valuable resource and do not belong in prison.

Questions 39 and 40 are based on the following passage.

The Noble and Holy Order of the Knights of Labor was organized in 1869 for all workers, regardless of race, sex, nationality, craft, or skill level. They believed that organized labor could meet the force of big business.

The Knights were opposed to strikes, except as a last resort, and child and convict labor. They favored a federal bureau for labor statistics, equal pay for both sexes, and an eight-hour workday.

The organization peaked at over 700,000 members but quickly lost its strength after the Haymarket Square riot in Chicago in 1886. The riot started during a meeting to protest police brutality against striking Knights. Violence erupted when a bomb was thrown into a police-controlled crowd. Seven policemen and ten workers were killed, and 117 people were injured. There was no proof that the Knights caused the violence, but public opinion turned against them.

39. The cause of the downfall of the Noble and Holy Order of the Knights of Labor was

    (1) spontaneous revolts by its members
    (2) the Haymarket Square riot in 1886
    (3) police brutality toward its strikers
    (4) the amount of work time lost by its members on strike
    (5) the ineffectiveness of its leaders in meeting the organization's goals

40. Which of the following is supported by the information given in the passage?

    (1) The Knights of Labor succeeded in keeping peace among black and white workers.
    (2) The events of 1886 proved that the Knights of Labor were dishonest.
    (3) The Knights of Labor kept the growth of monopolies and other big businesses to a minimum in the 1880s.
    (4) The Knights of Labor's importance was in articulating the demands of laborers to big business.
    (5) The federal government established child labor laws as a result of the Knights of Labor's influence.

Questions 41 and 42 are based on the graph below.

AMERICA'S DEBT
Owing More Than It Makes

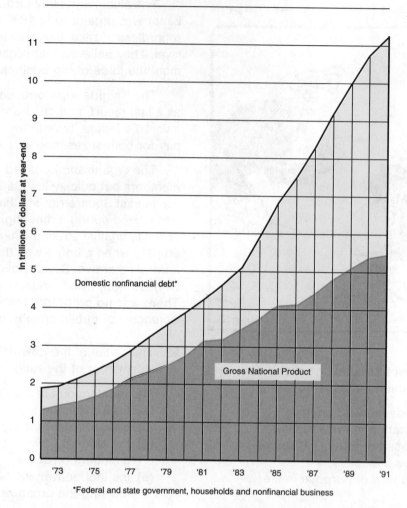

*Federal and state government, households and nonfinancial business

41. Which of the following statements is best supported by the information in the graph?

(1) The domestic debt is normally lower than the Gross National Product.
(2) The domestic debt increases and decreases from year to year.
(3) The domestic debt tends to decrease while the Gross National Product tends to increase.
(4) The domestic debt tends to increase more slowly than the Gross National Product does.
(5) The domestic debt increases at a faster rate than the increase of the Gross National Product.

42. In which of the following years was the amount of the domestic debt almost twice the amount of the Gross National Product?

(1) 1973
(2) 1978
(3) 1983
(4) 1985
(5) 1991

Questions 43–45 apply to the following definitions.

Governmental systems are classified according to the way in which authority is held and exercised. Defined below are five types of governmental systems that operate in the world.

absolute monarchy—a system in which a royal family has the final authority in all governmental matters

constitutional monarchy—a system in which the authority of a member of royalty is limited by rules set forth by the government's constitution

parliamentary democracy—a system in which the people elect the governing legislature which in turn elects the prime minister

totalitarian state—a system in which a central authority runs a government that subordinates the rights of individuals

theocracy—a system in which the head of state is considered to be guided by God and in which religion plays a prominent role in the government

43. Under this system, a vote of "no confidence" can be given by the legislature to the leader of the government. After such a vote, the leader will resign immediately or will ask the people to select a new leader. The form of government described is

   (1) an absolute monarchy
   (2) a constitutional monarchy
   (3) a parliamentary democracy
   (4) a totalitarian state
   (5) a theocracy

44. King John and his predecessors ruled England for many generations before the Magna Carta was instituted to make government more democratic. The form of government described is

   (1) an absolute monarchy
   (2) a constitutional monarchy
   (3) a parliamentary democracy
   (4) a totalitarian state
   (5) a theocracy

45. Vatican City is an independent state located within Rome, Italy. The Pope holds supreme legislative, executive, and judicial power. However, the administration of the state is delegated to a governor and his lower officials. The form of government in Vatican City most closely resembles

   (1) an absolute monarchy
   (2) a constitutional monarchy
   (3) a parliamentary democracy
   (4) a totalitarian state
   (5) a theocracy

Question 46 is based on the following quote.

"Please understand that we are not asking for a parade, a movement, or pity. But we do ask you to remember in your own way the 57,661 Americans who died in the war. Perhaps all of them died in vain."

These are the words of Al Santoli, a Vietnam veteran who recorded the verbal accounts of 33 veterans of the most unpopular war in U.S. history.

46. Which of the following statements would Santoli most likely support?

   (1) Vietnam veterans are heroes who should be honored as such.
   (2) Most Americans are unsympathetic to Vietnam veterans.
   (3) American soldiers sacrificed too much in the war.
   (4) The U.S. should have had welcoming parades and other signs of gratitude for returning Vietnam veterans.
   (5) Most Vietnam veterans were insulted by the monument built for them in Washington, D.C.

Questions 47–49 are based on the following chart.

JOB QUALIFICATIONS					
Examination announcements for Illinois civil service positions give information about the following qualifications.					
Qualification Requirements	*Office Clerk*	*Office Specialist*	*Electronics Technician*	*Maintenance Worker*	*Registered Nurse*
Written Test	yes	yes	yes	yes	no
Performance Test	no	yes	no	no	no
Education	high school	business college	technical school	—	nursing school
Experience	—	yes	—	yes	preferred
Monthly Salary	$1,306	$1,680	$2,010	$1,396	$2,066

47. By not requiring a written test for registered nurses, which of the following is the state of Illinois assuming?

(1) Nurses don't need to know how to write.
(2) Testing nurses would be too difficult.
(3) Graduation from nursing school is proof of knowledge about the job.
(4) Nursing experience is a substitute for education.
(5) Nurses are not trained to take tests.

48. From the information in the chart, you can conclude that

(1) nurses and electronics technicians earn about the same, so their jobs are the same
(2) training in nursing schools is considered to be more important than having had previous work experience
(3) office workers are underpaid for their skills
(4) maintenance workers are paid more than office clerks because maintenance work is more important
(5) electricians are more experienced than nurses

49. Which of the following is the most likely reason an office specialist is given a performance test?

(1) Office specialists are paid more than office clerks.
(2) It is the best way to test actual computer skills.
(3) Performance is important on any job.
(4) Extra experience is required for people who do poorly on the performance test.
(5) Office specialists are not required to have actual experience.

Questions 50–52 are based on the following graph.

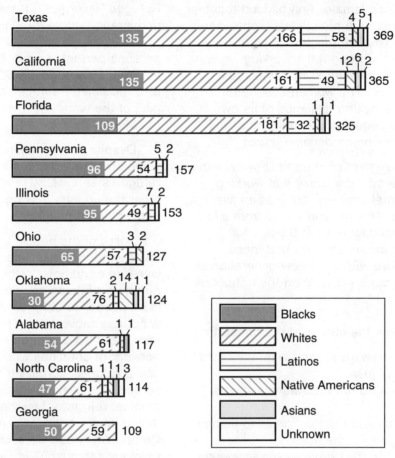

WHO IS ON DEATH ROW
Top 10 States — Number of Inmates by Race

Texas: 135 | 166 | 58 | 4 5 1 | 369
California: 135 | 161 | 49 | 12 6 2 | 365
Florida: 109 | 181 | 32 | 1 1 1 | 325
Pennsylvania: 96 | 54 | 5 2 | 157
Illinois: 95 | 49 | 7 2 | 153
Ohio: 65 | 57 | 3 2 | 127
Oklahoma: 30 | 76 | 2 14 1 1 | 124
Alabama: 54 | 61 | 1 1 | 117
North Carolina: 47 | 61 | 1 1 3 | 114
Georgia: 50 | 59 | 109

Legend:
- Blacks
- Whites
- Latinos
- Native Americans
- Asians
- Unknown

Source: "Death Row USA," July 1993, from NAACP Legal Defense and Educational Fund

50. Which of the following statements about capital punishment in populous states is best supported by the graph?

(1) Texas judges have been consistently harsher in sentencing minorities than in sentencing whites.
(2) A person convicted of a serious crime is more likely to be sentenced to capital punishment in Texas than in any other state.
(3) Texas is the most dangerous state in the U.S. for victims of violent crimes.
(4) There are no Asians on Death Row.
(5) Violent crimes are much less common among Latinos than among other minority groups.

51. Which of the following states has the most evenly balanced numbers of blacks and whites on Death Row?

(1) Florida
(2) Georgia
(3) Illinois
(4) Alabama
(5) North Carolina

52. Which of the following groups would most likely use this graph to support its position?

(1) the U.S. Supreme Court
(2) the Southern Governors' Conference
(3) the National Prison Guards Union
(4) the Texas State Legislature
(5) the Coalition Against the Death Penalty

Questions 53 and 54 are based on the following passage.

Women have been a growing force in the political world since females first banded together to demand equality with men in late-eighteenth-century France. The late-nineteenth-century industrial revolution brought the working woman to the forefront as "female" skills came into demand in factories. The women's liberation movement began making demands of its own in the early 1970s as equal pay, equal status, and "career" work for women became issues.

Despite many years of struggle, however, the most recent data available show that working women had been at their present jobs an average of only 3.3 years. This median varied from a low of 0.6 years for teenagers to 11.9 years for women 65 and older. It is hoped that these figures will improve with each new generation as women become more insistent on the rights due them.

53. In the passage, the author has assumed that

(1) women will want to remain on their jobs as long as men
(2) employers do not discriminate against women
(3) females should not join forces to demand equal rights for themselves
(4) working for one employer for an average of 3.3 years is the women's choice
(5) females in their teens make up the least desirable category of employees

54. The author of the passage would agree with which of the following statements about the women's liberation movement?

(1) Its beginning in France helped women there make gains not seen in other countries.
(2) Its achievements in the U.S. have far exceeded those in other countries.
(3) It was helped by the industrial revolution when women gained higher status and pay in the work force.
(4) It has not made much progress in the two centuries since it began.
(5) There are many issues concerning working women that still have to be addressed.

Questions 55 and 56 are based on the following passage.

In 1953, the U.S. Congress passed the Refugee Relief Act. This act increased the immigration quota for victims of war and disaster. In 1980, Congress raised the total number of persons permitted entry into the U.S. under the act from 290,000 to 320,000 yearly. This latter act also redefined a refugee as a person fleeing any part of the world, not just communist countries or the Middle East.

Despite the revamping of the law, however, some still find it difficult to enter the U.S. with refugee status. Many resort to illegal means to enter the country, risking imprisonment and deportation if caught.

Some of the people entering the U.S. illegally are attempting to escape political persecution or war-torn conditions in their homelands. As the numbers of these people increased during the last decade, so did the number of members in the sanctuary movement in the U.S. The sanctuary movement consisted of American citizens and a network of churches who banded together to assist illegals in crossing the border, getting settled, and seeking official recognition as political refugees. Members of the movement defied immigration laws, mostly for victims of Central American wars, by declaring churches religious sanctuaries immune from the law.

55. Why might members of the sanctuary movement think they should receive immunity from legal prosecution?

(1) They are helping victims of Central American wars.
(2) They are risking their lives to help the aliens.
(3) They are a religious sanctuary network.
(4) They are a large, growing group.
(5) They are preventing the deportation of illegal immigrants.

56. The members of the sanctuary movement are most similar to which group in U.S. history?

(1) young men who resisted the draft
(2) Underground Railroad for runaway slaves
(3) Vietnam war protestors
(4) immigrants seeking religious freedom
(5) civil rights activists

Questions 57 and 58 are based on the following passage.

Behaviorist psychologists have spoken highly of the benefits of positive reinforcement for much of the twentieth century. As a result, they have greatly influenced, for the better, education and parenting.

Teachers and parents are now more scientific and controlled in their approaches to teaching and child rearing and are therefore much better at these tasks than their counterparts were in past centuries.

57. The author's main point in this passage is that

(1) education and parenting are improved when positive reinforcement is made a part of each
(2) positive reinforcement has no place in the field of teaching and parenting
(3) behaviorists are basically educators and parents seeking better ways to do their jobs
(4) all other forms of psychology have had negative effects on education and parenting
(5) behaviorist psychology has a long historical tie to education and parenting

58. The basic assumption underlying this passage is the author's belief that

(1) punishment is detrimental to the education and raising of children
(2) parents and teachers in past centuries did not use methods of positive reinforcement
(3) parents and teachers today are worse than those of the past
(4) the problem with parents of the past is that they lacked control
(5) behaviorist psychology has worked wonders with unruly children

59. In the period following World War I, many Americans opposed American entry into the newly founded League of Nations and World War II. What belief were these Americans exhibiting?

(1) patriotism
(2) nationalism
(3) isolationism
(4) racism
(5) militarism

60. Between the years 1935 and 1957, America's birthrate had risen from 16.9 to 25 per thousand people. In 1967, 40 percent of the U.S. population was under 21 years of age, 46.5 percent under 25, and more than half under 30.

The most likely cause for this "baby boom" was

(1) the return of the young American soldiers from war in Europe and the Pacific
(2) the growth of the urban/suburban areas after World War II
(3) the increased mobility of the American family
(4) the continuing expansion of the middle class and its new, inflationary wealth
(5) the relaxing of moral sanctions against the use of artificial means of birth control

61. Mark Twain and Charles Dudley Warner's book *The Gilded Age* satirized the political corruption and hustle for the fast buck that characterized the post–Civil War years in the North. These writers were probably most critical of which of the following developments during this period?

(1) a larger, more efficient railroad
(2) the increased use of technology in farming
(3) a growth surge in the steel industry
(4) the spreading of materialistic attitudes
(5) the spreading of anti-imperialism

POST-TEST

Questions 62–64 are based on the following paragraph and map.

Zebra mussels originated in Europe. They first appeared in American waters around 1985. They breed quickly and live in large colonies by clinging to hard surfaces. Zebra mussel populations clog the pipes of industrial plants and boats. They also create an imbalance in the food chain for native fish.

NORTH AMERICAN RANGE OF THE ZEBRA MUSSEL as of July 4, 1993

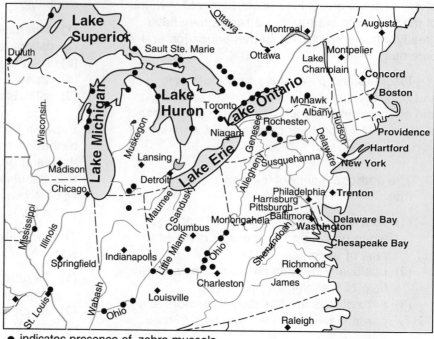

● indicates presence of zebra mussels

62. The Ohio River and Lake Michigan are shown to have a heavy zebra mussel population. Which of the following is most infested with zebra mussels?

(1) Lake Superior
(2) Delaware Bay
(3) Chesapeake Bay
(4) Mississippi River
(5) Lake Ontario

63. The paragraph and map best support the statement that zebra mussels

(1) live only in salt water
(2) are a problem that is spreading further than the Great Lakes
(3) do not pose a problem for rivers in the United States
(4) do not spread easily
(5) are harmless

64. Which of the following is the most likely effect of ignoring the zebra mussel infestation?

(1) an improved fish population
(2) little change in U.S. waterways
(3) a reduction in the levels of fish in affected waters
(4) a natural reduction in the mussel population
(5) improved conditions in U.S. waterways

ANSWERS BEGIN ON PAGE 275.

Post-Test Answer Key

1. (3) Southern California is mild and dry most of the year, which best fits the Mediterranean description.

2. (5) The temperature changes and the cold winters indicate that the Corn Belt is located in the continental region.

3. (2) Hot, rainy weather all year is typical of rain forests.

4. (4) Dryness and extreme heat are typical of deserts.

5. (2) The robber's response and the look on his victim's face indicate that the victim is trying to explain the robber's own actions to him.

6. (1) The cartoonist is using this incident to show his opinion about psychiatrists. He shows that the psychiatrist is blaming the robbery on the robber's cry for psychiatric help.

7. (3) The top ten cities in growth are all located in the South and the West.

8. (1) New York is not in the South or the West. All the other choices are in those fast-growing areas.

9. (4) Reconstruction and industrialization after the Civil War required the nation's complete attention.

10. (2) The reform of the banks and the currency of the U.S. helped to maintain balance in the economy during World War I. The author's reference to "adjust to the financial strains" refers to "absorbing the shock of the expense."

11. (2) The farm workers' successful boycott had led to reduced profits and unfavorable publicity. As a result, the growers were forced to give in to the farm workers' wage demands.

12. (4) With fairer wages, farm workers were less motivated to join the union.

13. (4) Because Roosevelt was a reformer, we can infer that *trust* in this context refers to a combination of corporations that control a single market.

14. (4) The passage says that Roosevelt was a trustbuster and champion of labor, yet he supported growth of industry as natural and beneficial. This suggests that he did not cater to either workers or big corporations.

15. (3) Germany, Austria-Hungary, Bulgaria, and Turkey comprised the Central Powers (represented by diagonal lines).

16. (2) Great Britain, Italy, France, and Russia made up the major Allied Powers (represented in white) with which the United States aligned itself.

17. (3) Conservative Republicans is the group listed that would be the most opposed to the kind of government spending that the British welfare system requires.

18. (4) The passage states, "It is this latter provision [a guaranteed pension for retirees] . . . that many feel is bankrupting the system."

19. (1) The welfare system must be supported by some revenue; taxes are the most likely source for this financial support.

20. (5) Many wealthy Britons have left the country, choosing to live in the U.S. where the tax burden is not as great as that in Great Britain.

21. (3) By choosing a "cradle-to-grave" welfare policy, the British have shown that they place the welfare of their citizens over a concern about government spending.

22. (3) Sweden is the only industrialized nation represented that has a socialist form of government that provides generous welfare benefits to its citizens.

23. (3) The passage states that the Ch'in Dynasty lost all its power when the people who were forced to work on the Great Wall finally rebelled.

24. (5) Choice (5) is the main idea of the passage. The other points are details and facts from the passage.

25. (2) The author is enthusiastic about the Great Wall, despite the suffering it caused. Therefore, he would probably feel the same about the pyramids of Egypt.

26. (4) Even though the author states that the people who built the Wall did not feel it was worth the effort, he states also that the Great Wall holds great fascination for modern man.

27. (4) Of the five choices, only (4), Asian immigrants' high level of financial resources, adequately explains their high median household income. Willingness to learn the language, (1), has no direct relationship to earnings; the decision to relocate to areas that have high costs of living, (2), presumes that Asians already have the financial ability to do so; (3), the decision to live in their own neighborhoods has no relationship to their high level of income; and (5) is not true since Asians don't depend on two incomes to a greater degree than the other groups represented.

28. (5) Of the five choices, Native-Americans experienced the smallest increase in median household income: $900. Non-Hispanic whites gained $1,200; African-Americans and Hispanics gained $1,100; and Asians gained $2,700.

29. (5) The only choice supported by the figures in the graph is that women in the Pacific—West tend to have more abortions than in other regions.

30. (1) These states have very low per capita incomes, so women might not be able to afford the cost of abortions. The other choices are not based on possible causes.

31. (1) Choice (1) gives the correct definitions of an anti-imperialist and an isolationist; the others do not.

32. (5) Men staying home to care for young children is a reverse of their usual role, just as women working outside the home is a role reversal for them. The writer makes it obvious that both reversals are their rights.

33. (2) The writer implies that men are frustrated because of society's confining rules regarding appropriate behavior.

34. (2) The parents are denying the seriousness of their child's illness.

35. (4) Pouting and refusing to eat dinner is a regressive form of childhood behavior.

36. (1) Teddy Roosevelt compensated for his feeling of physical inferiority by becoming physically active.

37. (3) The increased number of divorces (and the resulting broken homes) is seen by the cartoonist as the cause for delinquency among children.

38. (3) The cartoonist is blaming divorce for increased delinquency among children, victimizing them and society.

39. (2) The Haymarket Square riot was the most direct cause of the downfall of the Knights of Labor.

40. (4) The Knights served an important purpose in stating clearly the goals of organized labor. The passage does not provide enough information for us to conclude anything else.

41. (5) The line for the domestic debt rises much more quickly than the line for the GNP. The rate of increase in both lines does not support the other choices.

42. (5) In 1991, the GNP was about 5.5 trillion dollars. Domestic debt was slightly over 11 trillion, about twice as much. These amounts were not equaled by any of the earlier years shown.

43. (3) Under a parliamentary democracy the legislature elects the leader of the government.

44. (1) Under an absolute monarchy a royal family rules and has final authority in all governmental matters.

45. (5) Under a theocracy the head of the government is considered to be guided by God and has supreme authority.

46. (3) The author states that perhaps all the American soldiers died in vain in Vietnam. That was a tremendous sacrifice for what he sees as little gain.

47. (3) A nursing school diploma is considered a certification of a nurse's knowledge about the job, so a written test would not be necessary. The other choices are not logical assumptions.

48. (2) Graduates of nursing schools receive a very thorough education and are well trained enough without prior experience on the job.

49. (2) The ability to use a computer would be difficult to determine with only a written test. The type of test does not depend on salary, (1). Choice (3) is too general. The other choices are not suggested by the data.

50. (2) The graph shows that Texas has the most convicted criminals on Death Row.

51. (4) Alabama has 54 blacks and 61 whites on Death Row.

52. (5) The large number of inmates on Death Row could be cited by a group that opposes the death penalty.

53. (1) The writer assumes that women want to remain on their jobs longer than 3.3 years.

54. (5) The second paragraph indicates that the author believes that there are still many issues concerning women in the workplace that need to be addressed.

55. (3) The last sentence in the passage tells us that these people have declared their churches to be religious sanctuaries. Therefore, they believe they are immune from prosecution.

56. (2) The sanctuary movement members break the law to assist illegal aliens who are fleeing persecution and oppression. This activity is similar to that of members of the Underground Railroad who transported and hid slaves.

57. (1) The main idea expressed in the passage is that education and parenting are improved when positive reinforcement is made a part of each.

58. (2) In making the point, the writer assumes that parents and teachers in past centuries did not use methods of positive reinforcement.

59. (3) Only choice (3), isolationism, refers to many Americans' desire to withdraw from international conflicts and concerns.

60. (1) Quick marriages after soldiers returned from war most likely caused the surge in births. The other choices given here are either not relevant or not significant.

61. (4) The statement in the passage, "the . . . hustle for the fast buck," implies a criticism of spreading materialism.

62. (5) Lake Ontario is the area listed that shows the heaviest mussel infestation.

63. (2) The map shows that mussels have spread beyond the Great Lakes. The paragraph indicates that the mussel population is a problem.

64. (3) The paragraph says that mussels create an imbalance in the food chain for native fish. If fish don't have sufficient food, they can die, reducing their levels in affected areas. In that mussels negatively affect the fish population and waterway conditions, (1) and (5) are wrong. The information suggests the opposite of (2) and (4).

Post-Test Evaluation Chart

Use the answer key on pages 275–276 to check your answers to the Post-Test. Then find the item number of each question you missed and circle it on the chart below to determine the reading skill and content areas in which you need more practice. Pay particular attention to areas where you missed half or more of the questions. The reading skills are covered on pages 25–88. The page numbers for each content area are listed below on the chart. Both types of skills are absolutely essential for success on the GED Social Studies Test. The numbers in boldface are questions based on graphics. For those questions that you missed, review the skill pages indicated.

Skill Area/ Content Area	Comprehension	Analysis	Application	Evaluation
U.S. History (pages 91–143)	10, 13, **15**, **16**, 24	9, 23, 31, 39	14, 26, 59, 61	25, 40, 46
Political Science (pages 145–175)	**51**	55	43, 44, 45, **52**, 56	**50**
Behavioral Sciences (pages 177–209)	**5, 6**, 32, 33, 57	**37**, 53, 58	34, 35, 36	**38**, 54
Geography (pages 211–231)	**7, 62**	**29, 30**, 60	1, 2, 3, 4, **8**	**63, 64**
Economics (pages 233–255)	18, **27, 42**	11, 12, 19, 20, **28, 47, 49**	17, 21	22, **41, 48**

Social Studies Practice Test

Directions: This Social Studies Practice Test will give you a second opportunity to evaluate your readiness for the actual GED Social Studies Test.

This test contains 64 questions. Some of the questions are based on short reading passages, and some of them require you to interpret a chart, map, graph, or political cartoon.

You should take approximately 85 minutes to complete this test. At the end of 85 minutes, stop and mark your place. Then finish the test. This will give you an idea of whether or not you can finish the real GED Test in the time allotted. Try to answer as many questions as you can. A blank will count as a wrong answer, so make a reasonable guess for questions you are not sure of.

When you are finished with the test, turn to the evaluation chart on page 297. Use the chart to evaluate whether you are ready to take the actual GED Test and, if not, what areas need more work.

PRACTICE TEST ANSWER GRID

1 ① ② ③ ④ ⑤	17 ① ② ③ ④ ⑤	33 ① ② ③ ④ ⑤	49 ① ② ③ ④ ⑤
2 ① ② ③ ④ ⑤	18 ① ② ③ ④ ⑤	34 ① ② ③ ④ ⑤	50 ① ② ③ ④ ⑤
3 ① ② ③ ④ ⑤	19 ① ② ③ ④ ⑤	35 ① ② ③ ④ ⑤	51 ① ② ③ ④ ⑤
4 ① ② ③ ④ ⑤	20 ① ② ③ ④ ⑤	36 ① ② ③ ④ ⑤	52 ① ② ③ ④ ⑤
5 ① ② ③ ④ ⑤	21 ① ② ③ ④ ⑤	37 ① ② ③ ④ ⑤	53 ① ② ③ ④ ⑤
6 ① ② ③ ④ ⑤	22 ① ② ③ ④ ⑤	38 ① ② ③ ④ ⑤	54 ① ② ③ ④ ⑤
7 ① ② ③ ④ ⑤	23 ① ② ③ ④ ⑤	39 ① ② ③ ④ ⑤	55 ① ② ③ ④ ⑤
8 ① ② ③ ④ ⑤	24 ① ② ③ ④ ⑤	40 ① ② ③ ④ ⑤	56 ① ② ③ ④ ⑤
9 ① ② ③ ④ ⑤	25 ① ② ③ ④ ⑤	41 ① ② ③ ④ ⑤	57 ① ② ③ ④ ⑤
10 ① ② ③ ④ ⑤	26 ① ② ③ ④ ⑤	42 ① ② ③ ④ ⑤	58 ① ② ③ ④ ⑤
11 ① ② ③ ④ ⑤	27 ① ② ③ ④ ⑤	43 ① ② ③ ④ ⑤	59 ① ② ③ ④ ⑤
12 ① ② ③ ④ ⑤	28 ① ② ③ ④ ⑤	44 ① ② ③ ④ ⑤	60 ① ② ③ ④ ⑤
13 ① ② ③ ④ ⑤	29 ① ② ③ ④ ⑤	45 ① ② ③ ④ ⑤	61 ① ② ③ ④ ⑤
14 ① ② ③ ④ ⑤	30 ① ② ③ ④ ⑤	46 ① ② ③ ④ ⑤	62 ① ② ③ ④ ⑤
15 ① ② ③ ④ ⑤	31 ① ② ③ ④ ⑤	47 ① ② ③ ④ ⑤	63 ① ② ③ ④ ⑤
16 ① ② ③ ④ ⑤	32 ① ② ③ ④ ⑤	48 ① ② ③ ④ ⑤	64 ① ② ③ ④ ⑤

Questions 1–3 are based on the following information.

Socialization is the process by which members of a society learn about norms and patterns of behavior through social interaction. Five of the major institutions that influence a person's behavior are:

family—set of close relatives who help form a person's attitudes, personality, goals, beliefs, prejudices, and self-image

religion—organized set of practices related to a person's belief in a higher power

politics—system of government with policies that affect a person's life on local, state, and national levels

economics—system of production, distribution, and consumption of goods and services in a society

education—instructional system that teaches a person the language, skills, and knowledge needed to function in society

1. More mothers than ever before are joining the work force. Many mothers have found that their family's basic needs cannot be paid for from the father's income only. Which institution has most influenced this decision?

   (1) family
   (2) religion
   (3) politics
   (4) economics
   (5) education

2. People voted in greater numbers in the 1992 presidential election than they had in any previous year. More people wanted a say in determining governmental policies. Which institution most influenced this increase in voting?

   (1) family
   (2) religion
   (3) politics
   (4) economics
   (5) education

3. Many employers are paying for training their workers so that their companies can operate more efficiently. Which institution has most influenced this decision by employers?

   (1) family
   (2) religion
   (3) politics
   (4) economics
   (5) education

Questions 4 and 5 are based on the following cartoon.

NO ONE EVER SAID PRESERVING THE AMERICAN WAY OF LIFE WOULD BE EASY...

GUN LOBBY

ANOTHER VICTIM OF A SENSELESS SHOOTING SPREE

CAM CARDOW
Courtesy Regina Leader Post

4. The cartoonist assumes that the "senseless shooting spree"

   (1) could have been easily prevented
   (2) is part of the American way of life
   (3) is the fault of the gun lobby
   (4) is the fault of the U.S. government
   (5) represents a fundamental civil right

5. The conflict depicted in this cartoon is most similar to which of the following conflicts?

   (1) sexual harrassment vs. freedom from gender bias
   (2) pro-choice advocates vs. anti-abortion activists
   (3) private schools vs. public schools
   (4) private insurance vs. a public health-care system
   (5) school segregation vs. school integration

PRACTICE TEST

6. The focus of the U.S. work force has changed over the last 150 years. According to the Department of Commerce, 68.6 percent of the labor force was engaged in farming in 1840. The number had fallen to 31 percent by 1910. Farm occupations were held by 1.6 percent of the working population in 1990. These data support which of the following conclusions?

(1) Farming is not profitable.
(2) Farming is no longer necessary.
(3) Most farming is done by large corporations.
(4) Farming has become more popular as an occupation.
(5) Farming is no longer a major American occupation.

7. The U.S. Constitution does not specifically provide for the power of judicial review. *Judicial review* is the ability of a court to declare a law invalid because it is unconstitutional. The power of judicial review was not established until the Supreme Court's decision in the case of *Marbury* v. *Madison* in 1803.

This information supports which of the following conclusions?

(1) All laws are constitutionally valid.
(2) All laws undergo judicial review.
(3) The framers of the Constitution did not approve of judicial review.
(4) *Marbury* v. *Madison* was a masterpiece of judicial strategy.
(5) *Marbury* v. *Madison* was a landmark decision.

Questions 8–10 are based on the following information and pie chart.

Certain agencies in Illinois are required by law to report cases of child abuse. This chart shows the sources of child abuse reports in 1989.

CHILD ABUSE — in Illinois
Source of Reports by Type
(Fiscal Year 1989)

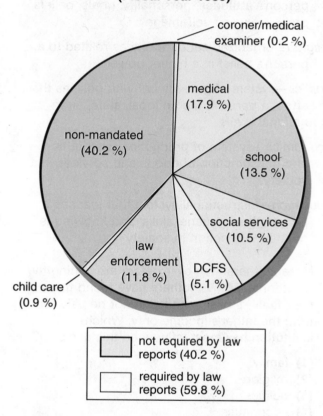

coroner/medical examiner (0.2 %)
medical (17.9 %)
non-mandated (40.2 %)
school (13.5 %)
social services (10.5 %)
law enforcement (11.8 %)
DCFS (5.1 %)
child care (0.9 %)

not required by law reports (40.2 %)
required by law reports (59.8 %)

8. According to the chart, child abuse reports in Illinois are submitted

(1) only by social service agencies
(2) mainly by physicians
(3) through a variety of sources
(4) more by schools than by medical agencies
(5) more by DCFS (Department of Children and Family Services) than by law enforcement agencies

9. Which of the following statements is supported by the data in the chart?

   (1) The law requires all child abuse cases to be reported.
   (2) Schools are more concerned about reporting child abuse cases than are daycare facilities.
   (3) Many children die from abuse.
   (4) People report child abuse cases even when not required by law to do so.
   (5) When not required by law, people are reluctant to report child abuse cases.

10. Why might so few reports of child abuse come from child-care facilities?

    (1) Child abuse does not occur in child-care facilities.
    (2) Abused children are not accepted by child-care facilities.
    (3) Parents of abused children tend not to take their children to child-care facilities.
    (4) Child-care facilities are afraid of being sued for child abuse.
    (5) Child-care facilities are not required by law to report child-abuse cases.

Questions 11–13 are based on the following passage.

   On June 14, 1777, the Continental Congress adopted the first version of the Stars and Stripes as the official flag of the United States. The flag's design incorporated thirteen stars on a field of blue in the upper left-hand corner of thirteen red-and-white stripes. When Kentucky and Vermont were admitted as states in 1794, two new stars and two new stripes were added. In 1818 the format of the flag was changed to limit the number of stripes to represent the thirteen original states and to add a new star to the blue field each time a new state was admitted. The flag now has fifty stars, representing each of the fifty states.

11. What did the original thirteen stars and thirteen stripes represent?

    (1) the Continental Congress
    (2) the number of states in 1818
    (3) the number of years between 1781 and 1794
    (4) the original thirteen states
    (5) the limitations of the flag

12. Which of the following values is suggested by the use of individual stars to represent each state in the union?

    (1) pride in space exploration
    (2) belief in freedom of expression
    (3) pride in the federal governmental structure of the United States
    (4) pride in capitalism
    (5) respect for the Continental Congress

13. It has been proposed that the District of Columbia be given status as a state. In fact, the voters of the District of Columbia have already elected two "shadow senators" to the U.S. Senate. Based on the information in the passage, which of the following would occur if Washington, D.C., were to become a state?

    (1) A fourteenth star would be added to the flag.
    (2) A fourteenth stripe would be added to the flag.
    (3) The flag would be completely redesigned.
    (4) A fifty-first star would be added to the field of blue.
    (5) No change would be made to the flag.

Questions 14–17 are based on the following information.

Federal, state, and local governments levy taxes to raise money for their operations. Most people in the United States pay at least one of the following taxes:

income tax—a percentage of wages, profits, and other income paid to federal, state, and local governments

social security tax—a percentage of wages paid into a public insurance fund that can be drawn on upon retirement

capital gains tax—money paid to the federal government out of profits from the sale of land, buildings, stocks, and other capital assets

property tax—money paid (usually to a local government) by the owners of real estate

sales tax—money paid to federal, state, or local governments on the purchase of goods or services

14. When people purchase groceries or household goods in most states, they pay an additional percent of the subtotal. What kind of tax are they paying?

   (1) income tax
   (2) social security tax
   (3) capital gains tax
   (4) property tax
   (5) sales tax

15. Every year, homeowners have to pay money to the county in which they live. What kind of tax are they paying?

   (1) income tax
   (2) social security tax
   (3) capital gains tax
   (4) property tax
   (5) sales tax

16. The Rodriguez family had lived in the same house for the past ten years. Recently they sold the house for twice as much as they had paid for it. What kind of tax did they have to pay?

   (1) income tax
   (2) social security tax
   (3) capital gains tax
   (4) property tax
   (5) sales tax

17. Manoli Reed retired at age 65. Soon he began to receive monthly checks from the federal government. What kind of tax had Mr. Reed paid that entitled him to this money?

   (1) income tax
   (2) social security tax
   (3) capital gains tax
   (4) property tax
   (5) sales tax

─────────────────────────

18. The foreign policy of the United States began to change when the Cold War ended in 1991. An example of the change was the humanitarian mission Operation Restore Hope, when U.S. soldiers helped to ensure the delivery of food and medicine to starving people in Somalia. The purpose of the humanitarian mission was to

   (1) stop the Cold War
   (2) engage in battle
   (3) help needy people
   (4) support a foreign government
   (5) keep soldiers busy

Questions 19 and 20 are based on the following passage.

Since the early 1900s, Mexico City has tried to reduce its high level of air pollution. According to *Time* magazine, "Since 1982, the amount of contaminants in the air has more than tripled, to 7 million tons. Because the capital lies 2,240 m (7,347 ft.) above sea level, fossil fuels do not burn efficiently, producing more ozone than normal. During calm winter months, the mountains that encircle the city trap the polluted air close to the ground in atmospheric sandwiches known as thermal inversions."

19. Which of the following conditions do *not* contribute to Mexico City's air pollution problem?

    (1) altitude of the city above sea level
    (2) burning of fossil fuels
    (3) surrounding mountains
    (4) season of the year
    (5) status of Mexico City as the world's most populous city

20. Which of the following is *not* stated in the passage?

    (1) location of the problem
    (2) type of problem
    (3) partial causes of the problem
    (4) time frame of the problem
    (5) solution for the problem

Questions 21–23 are based on the following map.

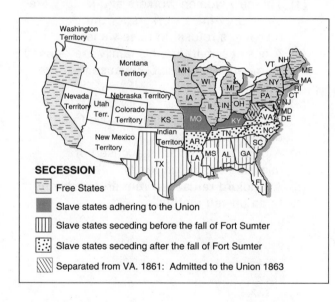

    The map shows how the United States was divided by the Civil War. States that seceded from the Union joined the Confederacy. Kentucky, Delaware, Missouri, and Maryland were called border states.

21. The map provides evidence for which of the following facts?

    (1) The capital of the Confederacy moved from Montgomery, Alabama, to Richmond, Virginia, after the battle at Fort Sumter.
    (2) The border states did not secede.
    (3) Southern Illinois was a destination for runaway slaves from the South.
    (4) Fort Sumter is in South Carolina.
    (5) The Union won the battle of Fort Sumter.

22. The map supports which of the following facts?

    (1) Not all slaveholding states seceded from the Union.
    (2) The decision to secede from the Union was made quickly by all slaveholding states.
    (3) Slavery was the only issue dividing the North and South.
    (4) Civil war can even affect family loyalties.
    (5) Kansas secretly supported the right to secede.

23. Based on information in the map, which of the following was a direct result of the secession of the Southern states?

    (1) addition of the border states to the Union
    (2) elimination of slavery in Kansas
    (3) establishment of new territories
    (4) establishment of more slaveholding states
    (5) formation of West Virginia as a new state

PRACTICE TEST

24. When Columbus sailed across the Atlantic Ocean, he was looking for a new sea route to Asia and the East. He did not realize that he had found islands off the coasts of North and South America. This mistake explains why Native Americans as a group

   (1) were misnamed "Indians"
   (2) welcomed European settlers
   (3) were forced from their lands
   (4) fought against the British
   (5) recently have objected to Columbus Day celebrations

Questions 25–27 are based on the following passage.

African-American lawyer Thurgood Marshall won the landmark *Brown* v. *the Board of Education of Topeka* decision, which established the legal basis for school desegregation. In 1967, President Lyndon Johnson surprised many Americans by appointing Marshall to the U.S. Supreme Court. During his long tenure on the Court, Marshall continued his support of civil rights.

25. With which of the following statements would Justice Thurgood Marshall most probably have agreed?

   (1) Separate but equal is the best policy.
   (2) Separate but equal is not truly equal.
   (3) Government is best that governs least.
   (4) The president is above the law.
   (5) Affirmative action gives unqualified people an unfair advantage.

26. The author of this passage assumes which of the following?

   (1) Many Americans were not expecting the appointment of an African American to the Supreme Court.
   (2) Marshall was a good friend of President Johnson.
   (3) Marshall was a token appointee.
   (4) Many Americans were in favor of Marshall's appointment.
   (5) Marshall was willing to ignore the U.S. Constitution.

27. Which of the following opinions is supported by the facts in this passage?

   (1) Marshall was probably the greatest Supreme Court judge.
   (2) Justice Clarence Thomas can't live up to Marshall's reputation.
   (3) Marshall interpreted the Constitution to suit his own ends.
   (4) Marshall's decisions have probably influenced many lives.
   (5) The Supreme Court needs more justices like Marshall.

28. A *scapegoat* is a person or group of people unfairly blamed for the troubles of another. Which of the following is an example of scapegoating?

   (1) The new women workers at a factory are blamed by male workers for the manager's refusal to raise wages.
   (2) A businessman and his family are refused membership in a club because they are Jewish.
   (3) Several members of a city police force are accused of using excessive force during an arrest.
   (4) A popular politician is accused of misusing campaign funds.
   (5) A landlord refuses to rent an apartment to an unwed mother.

Questions 29 and 30 are based on the following passage.

Americans celebrated the end of Operation Desert Storm with a three-month party. The parades began on March 8, 1991, when the first soldiers returned from the war in the Persian Gulf. In only forty-three days, American and Allied troops had forced Iraqi leader Saddam Hussein to withdraw his army from neighboring Kuwait. U.S. President George Bush was able to declare victory.

Two years later, just as President Bill Clinton's inauguration was being planned, Saddam declared that Iraq had actually won the war and that the cease-fire was over. He refused to comply with UN resolutions. Baghdad was closed to UN weapons inspectors, and Iraqi troops raided the borders of Kuwait for arms. Even after an Allied air strike on Iraq, Saddam threatened to renew hostilities, but he soon agreed to another cease-fire. After Clinton became president, Iraq, under the leadership of Saddam Hussein, continued to be problematic in its relationship with the United States.

29. The American victory celebrations were based on which of the following assumptions?

    (1) The Iraqis had acknowledged defeat.
    (2) America will never go to war again.
    (3) Saddam Hussein was no longer the leader of Iraq.
    (4) Renewed war in the Persian Gulf could be avoided.
    (5) Saddam Hussein would ignore the UN resolutions.

30. Which of the following is an *opinion* stated in the passage?

    (1) American soldiers returned home in March.
    (2) The United States and its allies were declared the victors.
    (3) Iraq had actually won the war.
    (4) Iraq renewed hostilities two years after the Persian Gulf War.
    (5) Two U.S. presidents had to deal with Saddam Hussein.

31. Eastern European, Asian, and Hispanic immigrants to the United States often make their first homes in large groups in low-rent city neighborhoods. The neighborhoods, or "urban villages," are often known by ethnically oriented nicknames such as Little Italy and Germantown. Which of the following best explains why newly arrived immigrants are drawn to the urban villages?

    (1) Immigrants don't speak English well enough to do anything else.
    (2) Immigrants want to separate themselves from all memories of what they left behind.
    (3) Urban villages help immigrants to blend in quickly with mainstream America.
    (4) Urban villages provide the cushion of a familiar cultural background within a larger, unfamiliar city.
    (5) Urban villages provide excellent business opportunities.

Questions 32 and 33 are based on the following passage.

According to information provided by *Consumer Reports*, "The National Credit Union Administration is an independent agency of the U.S. Government which regulates, charters, and insures credit unions. Like the FDIC, it insures accounts for up to $100,000. If a person has more than one account in the same credit union, those accounts are generally added together and insured up to $100,000. Joint accounts are insured separately from individual accounts, to a maximum of another $100,000. Individual retirement accounts are also insured separately up to $100,000." Credit union members can use this information to decide if their accounts are adequately insured.

32. The main idea of this passage concerns

    (1) how a credit union is regulated
    (2) how to choose a credit union
    (3) a comparison of NCUA with FDIC
    (4) the amounts of insurance provided by the NCUA
    (5) NCUA charters

33. What conclusion does the author draw in this passage?

(1) Credit union members can find out if they are adequately insured.
(2) The NCUA provides better insurance than the FDIC.
(3) The NCUA is a government agency.
(4) Joint accounts and individual accounts are insured separately.
(5) Retirement accounts are insured up to $100,000.

---

34. A presidential candidate is elected by a majority of the vote in the electoral college, even if he or she receives less than a majority of the popular vote. A winning candidate who receives less than half of the popular vote is called a minority president. Which of the following presidents could *not* be called a minority president?

(1) John Kennedy, with 49.7 percent popular vote and 56.4 percent electoral-college vote
(2) Abraham Lincoln, with 39.9 percent popular vote and 59.4 percent electoral-college vote
(3) Richard Nixon, with 43.4 percent popular vote and 56.1 percent electoral-college vote
(4) Ronald Reagan, with 59 percent popular vote and 97.6 percent electoral-college vote
(5) Woodrow Wilson, with 41.8 percent popular vote and 81.9 percent electoral-college vote

35. Bill Clinton, a Democrat, was sworn in as the forty-second president of the United States in January 1993. For the previous twelve years, the presidency had been occupied by Republicans Ronald Reagan and George Bush. This information supports the hypothesis that

(1) Americans were ready for a change in party leadership
(2) Americans are mainly Democrats
(3) Republicans are poor politicians
(4) Democrats can solve the country's problems
(5) The two-party system is no longer working

36. Many of the geographic regions in the United States have nicknames. One section of southern Louisiana is called the Sugar Bowl. A section stretching from Nebraska to Ohio is called the Corn Belt. The Bread Basket includes states from North Dakota to Kansas. Which of the following nicknames is based on the same idea as those just mentioned?

(1) the Sun Belt
(2) the Cotton Belt
(3) Silicon Valley
(4) the Dustbowl
(5) the Coal Belt

37. A newspaper reports "amazing" similarities between a set of identical twins separated at birth. It says they both read poetry, are left-handed, and drink bourbon. But it adds that the same could be true of any two people selected at random. Scientists say it is more important to know in what ways separated twins are different. The logic of the press report is faulty because it

(1) doesn't give the reason for the twins' separation
(2) doesn't mention the twins' favorite foods
(3) falsely assumes that twins should have nothing in common
(4) overemphasizes traits that are common to many people
(5) assumes these are the only similarities the twins have

38. For centuries, the Bushmen of the Kalahari Desert were a hunting and gathering people. Recently, a French television film crew paid some Dzu Bushmen to change from their usual Western clothing into traditional loincloths. They were also directed to pretend they were hunting. Details of this event suggest that

(1) Bushmen still follow ancient traditions
(2) television always portrays the truth
(3) Bushmen have adapted to outside ways
(4) hunting and gathering is no longer practiced
(5) Bushmen want to move out of the Kalahari Desert

Questions 39–41 are based on the following graph.

JOB CREATION AFTER THE PAST THREE RECESSIONS

Recession that ended:

Nov. 1982

March 1975

March 1991

New Jobs (in millions)

Months of Recovery

Source: DIR/McGraw Hill

39. According to the graph, which of the following best contrasts the recoveries from the three recessions?

   (1) The first two recessions recovered more slowly than the last.
   (2) All three recoveries happened at about the same rate.
   (3) The last recovery produced the fewest new jobs.
   (4) The earliest recovery produced the most new jobs.
   (5) The last recovery produced the most new jobs.

40. The rate of job creation during March 1991 resulted in many Americans believing that

   (1) prosperity was just around the corner
   (2) the economy had never been better
   (3) the recession had not really ended
   (4) they didn't have to worry about losing their jobs
   (5) job creation always follows a recession

41. During which three-month period was the number of new jobs created nearly the same for the recessions ending in November 1982 and March 1975?

   (1) eighteenth to twenty-first month
   (2) fifteenth to eighteenth month
   (3) twelfth to fifteenth month
   (4) ninth to twelfth month
   (5) third to sixth month

Questions 42 and 43 are based on the following graph.

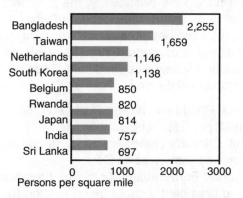

World's Most Densely Populated Countries — 1991

Country	Persons per square mile
Bangladesh	2,255
Taiwan	1,659
Netherlands	1,146
South Korea	1,138
Belgium	850
Rwanda	820
Japan	814
India	757
Sri Lanka	697

Note: Figure excludes densely populated countries with population below 5 million
Source: Bureau of the Census

42. Which of the following would you expect to find in each of the countries listed?

   (1) large tracts of empty land
   (2) wide, open ranges for grazing
   (3) huge national forests
   (4) widespread poverty
   (5) many cities

43. Which of the following statements is proved by the information on the graph?

   (1) Japan is densely populated because it is an island.
   (2) The growth rate of Bangladesh is expected to double by 2020.
   (3) Bangladesh, China, and the Netherlands have reached their population limits.
   (4) Bangladesh is the most densely populated country in the world.
   (5) The countries listed have population densities over five times the worldwide average.

PRACTICE TEST

44. Sociologists classify crowds in several ways. One classification is the mob, in which a crowd "explodes into generalized violent and destructive behavior." Which of the following crowds fits this description?

    (1) the Los Angeles rioters of 1992
    (2) people at the 1993 presidential inaugural parties
    (3) students in a lecture hall
    (4) people gathered on the sidewalk to watch a parade
    (5) the freedom marchers of the 1960s

45. The U.S. Constitution provides for an orderly succession to the presidency. If a president dies or steps down from office, the vice president becomes president. If the vice president dies or steps down, the president can appoint a new vice president. These provisions explain why

    (1) Vice President George Bush won the 1988 presidential election
    (2) Bill Clinton's choice for a vice presidential running mate was Al Gore
    (3) Gerald Ford became both vice president and president without being elected to either office
    (4) Gerald Ford lost the 1976 presidential election
    (5) Vice President Spiro Agnew had to resign

46. Jeanette Rankin of Montana was the first woman elected to Congress. She voted against U.S. participation in both world wars. In 1968, Rankin led a protest march against the Vietnam War. Rankin's record indicates that she placed a high value on

    (1) public opinion
    (2) military intervention
    (3) pacifism
    (4) civil rights
    (5) victory

47. Before Prohibition, Carry Nation lectured across the United States, speaking against alcohol use. She also was arrested for breaking up saloons with a hatchet. Eventually, Nation became a symbol for the temperance movement. Carry Nation's fame is most similar to that of

    (1) Susan B. Anthony, a militant advocate of women's rights, arrested for voting
    (2) Betsy Ross, the woman who is said to have made the first American flag
    (3) Eleanor Roosevelt, a president's wife and outspoken civil rights advocate
    (4) Charlotte Parkhurst, a woman who disguised herself as a man and went to work as a stagecoach driver
    (5) Geraldine Ferraro, the first woman nominated for vice president by a major party

Questions 48 and 49 are based on the following graph.

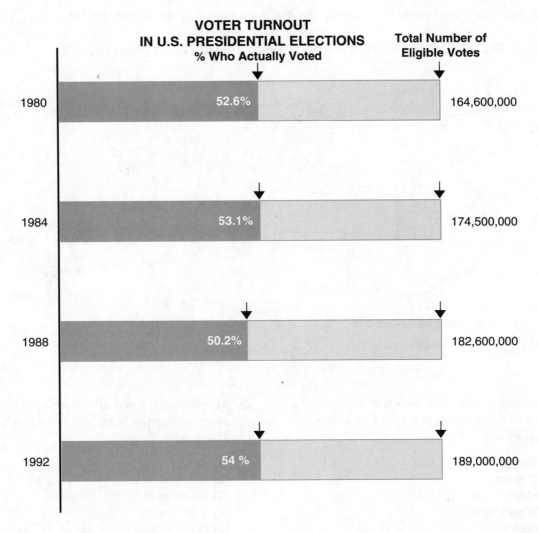

**VOTER TURNOUT
IN U.S. PRESIDENTIAL ELECTIONS**
% Who Actually Voted

Total Number of
Eligible Votes

1980	52.6%	164,600,000
1984	53.1%	174,500,000
1988	50.2%	182,600,000
1992	54 %	189,000,000

48. The information on the graph supports which of the following conclusions?

(1) The overwhelming majority of Americans are politically active.
(2) Americans are becoming less and less interested in voting.
(3) Many Americans are not politically active.
(4) Young Americans are not interested in voting.
(5) Elections don't really mean anything.

49. Which of the following is a likely result of continued low voter turnout?

(1) an increase in the number of third-party candidates running for president
(2) presidents being elected without a clear majority of votes
(3) the breakdown of the American political system
(4) special interests influencing presidential decisions
(5) difficulty in getting candidates to run for political office

Questions 50–52 are based on the following information and map.

Wetlands make excellent habitats for waterfowl that feed primarily on freshwater fish.

DISTRIBUTION OF WETLANDS OF HIGH VALUE TO WATERFOWL

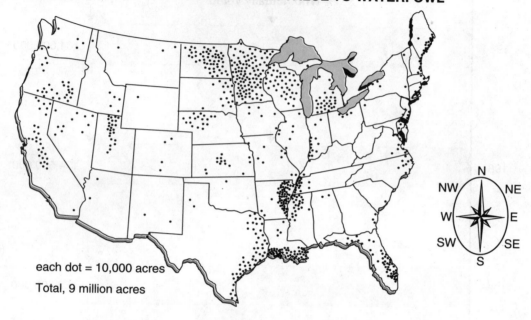

each dot = 10,000 acres

Total, 9 million acres

50. According to the map, which of the following states has the greatest amount of wetland acreage?

(1) Illinois
(2) Missouri
(3) Minnesota
(4) Washington
(5) Idaho

51. Which of the following situations would be least damaging to waterfowl in a wetland area?

(1) a decade-long drought
(2) drainage of swamps
(3) water pollution
(4) heavy snowfall
(5) hurricanes that drive saltwater inland

52. According to the map, which part of the country has the least amount of wetland acreage?

(1) north
(2) south
(3) southwest
(4) northeast
(5) southeast

53. The breakup of the Soviet Union in 1991 resulted in the formation of fifteen independent countries. Apart from political changes, which of the following was affected?

(1) location of natural resources
(2) time zones
(3) agricultural resources
(4) national boundaries
(5) agricultural products

54. To Americans, male and female behavior in Iran might seem to be reversed. Iranian men read poetry and hug each other in public. Men react emotionally; however, women act practically and logically. This information is an example of which of the following hypotheses?

(1) Iranians are overly emotional.
(2) American men should be more like Iranian men.
(3) Iranian women are stronger than Iranian men.
(4) Men and women behave the same all over the world.
(5) Expectations of male and female behavior vary from culture to culture.

55. In the 1840s, hundreds of wagon trains headed west on the Oregon Trail for Oregon and California. Following the doctrine of Manifest Destiny, thousands of migrant pioneers sought to extend U.S. borders to the Pacific, even though much of the land had been claimed by Britain and Mexico. Believers in Manifest Destiny acted on which of the following assumptions?

(1) Americans had the right to claim the land.
(2) Americans would become British or Mexican citizens.
(3) The price of land would be low.
(4) Americans could create a whole new nation.
(5) America no longer needed them.

Questions 56 and 57 refer to the following cartoon.

56. According to the cartoonist, Congress has a reputation for

(1) moving too quickly
(2) increasing its spending
(3) cautious driving
(4) wasting time
(5) spending too much time traveling

57. The cartoonist holds which of the following opinions?

(1) Congress will continue to spend wisely.
(2) Congress doesn't spend enough.
(3) Congressional representatives are like used car salesmen.
(4) Congressional spending should be slowed.
(5) The 103rd Congress will do better than the 102nd Congress.

PRACTICE TEST

Questions 58–60 are based on the following passage.

Lyndon Johnson established a number of welfare programs during his presidency. He was inspired by the government-run relief and reform programs of Franklin Roosevelt's New Deal. In his vision of a "Great Society," Johnson saw a nation "where no child will go unfed and no youngster will go unschooled; where every child has a good teacher and every teacher has good pay, and both have good classrooms."

If he were asked today, Johnson might add "and where every child has access to good health care." By 1992, Americans were faced with a health-care crisis. Health-care spending equaled almost 14 percent of U.S. gross national product, and health-care costs continued to rise. Many people couldn't afford even basic medical insurance. Americans appealed to the federal government for help.

Johnson's "War on Poverty" helped some people but failed to eliminate poverty. George Bush declared himself the "Education President," but when he left office, the nation's schools were still in trouble. Can government really find a workable way to provide health insurance for every American? This is a question that the Clinton administration, which has made health-care reform a priority, will have to answer.

58. Johnson's programs were based on the assumption that

(1) government has the ability to solve social problems
(2) education is more important than good health
(3) social problems are not the concern of government
(4) poverty is not an important problem in America
(5) Americans can't help themselves

59. Which of the following best states the writer's opinion about the future of health care?

(1) The health care problem will resolve itself.
(2) The government may not be able to solve the health-care crisis.
(3) Health-care costs will go down, but insurance will be harder to get.
(4) Government intervention will make the problem worse.
(5) The government will be able to provide a sound national health-care system.

60. Which of the following would most likely occur if the poor and unemployed were covered by a publicly funded health insurance program?

(1) Private insurance companies would raise their rates.
(2) Private insurance companies would lower their rates.
(3) Taxes would go up.
(4) Taxes would go down.
(5) The medical community would lower its fees.

Questions 61–63 are based on the following information.

Workers and employers can't always agree on wages or working conditions. The following terms identify processes involved in labor disputes.

collective bargaining—meetings in good faith between representatives of employers and employees to discuss and attempt to agree on conditions of employment

mediation—use of an impartial go-between to help reach an agreement between two sides of a labor dispute when the two sides cannot agree on their own

picketing—stationing of striking workers in front of a business to protest conditions or to dissuade workers and customers from entering the business

sit-down strike—planned work stoppage in which employees stop work but do not leave the workplace until an agreement is reached with management

walk-out strike—planned work stoppage in which employees stay away from the workplace until an agreement is reached with management

61. Metal workers at the Ucan factory want a raise of $.50 an hour. Two of their representatives and an attorney meet with Ucan's owners and their attorney. Ucan offers the workers a $.25 raise. The workers and the owners are engaged in

    (1) collective bargaining
    (2) mediation
    (3) picketing
    (4) a sit-down strike
    (5) a walk-out strike

62. Coal miners at Old Ben 52 refuse to go back into the mine unless the bosses agree to provide an on-site doctor. The miners are engaged in

    (1) collective bargaining
    (2) mediation
    (3) picketing
    (4) a sit-down strike
    (5) a walk-out strike

63. Representatives of the machine operators at Boxboy have been meeting for a week with company representatives. They have agreed to improved pension benefits, but they cannot agree about which benefits would be affected. To settle the dispute, the next process would most likely be

    (1) collective bargaining
    (2) mediation
    (3) picketing
    (4) a sit-down strike
    (5) a walk-out strike

64. Psychologists have found that mood can affect how people perform on multiple-choice tests. A person who is depressed or anxious is more likely to change correct answers to wrong answers. A person with low anxiety or with a positive attitude tends to change fewer answers. This information supports the generalization that

    (1) self-confidence is an element of success
    (2) multiple-choice tests are unfair
    (3) multiple-choice tests are accurate measures of knowledge
    (4) anxiety sharpens the intellect
    (5) anxiety always results in failure

ANSWERS BEGIN ON PAGE 294.

Practice Test Answer Key

1. **(4)** Although mothers are working more for the sake of their families, the need for more money, or economics, is most influencing mothers to join the work force. Religion, politics, and education are not mentioned.

2. **(3)** More people are realizing how much politics and government influence their everyday lives. The other institutions are not referred to in the passage.

3. **(5)** Employers see the need for education in helping their employees to learn the basic skills needed on the job.

4. **(3)** By including the figure of the gun lobby, the cartoonist indicates that it is the gun lobby's opposition to gun-control laws that allows irresponsible people to have guns. Therefore, the cartoonist is assuming that the fault lies with the gun lobby, not the government.

5. **(2)** Some people believe that strict gun-control laws would reduce violent crime. Others feel that gun-control laws violate their right to bear arms. This conflict is like that between the belief in a woman's right to abortion and the belief in an unborn child's right to life. Each side of both issues could possibly be protected by the Constitution.

6. **(5)** Because of the decline in the percentage of the labor force involved in farming, farming is no longer a major U.S. occupation. The figures do not refer to profits, the need for farming, or who does the farming.

7. **(5)** The *Marbury* v. *Madison* decision established a legal precedent for decisions about potentially unconstitutional laws. According to the decision, a law can be unconstitutional, although few laws have been reviewed by the courts. The framers of the Constitution did not mention judicial review, nor is there evidence for any "strategy" behind the decision.

8. **(3)** According to the chart, reports come from social service, educational, medical, and other sources. Choices (4) and (5) are not true.

9. **(4)** The chart supplies data indicating that 40.2 percent of reports come from voluntary (non-mandated) sources. None of the other choices are supported by the figures on the chart.

10. **(3)** Parents who use child care would probably be more concerned about their children's welfare. Neglectful or physically abusive parents would probably avoid child-care facilities. Abuse sometimes occurs in poorly run child-care facilities. Child-care agencies are required to report suspected abuse, but that does not prevent them from accepting abused children.

11. **(4)** The number of stripes is stated to be limited to the number of original states—thirteen. There were more than thirteen states in 1818. The other choices do not refer to what the stripes represent.

12. **(3)** Pride in the federal governmental structure is suggested by the fact that each new state is visibly represented as one part of a growing union. At the time of the designing of the flag, space exploration was unheard of. Choices (2) and (4) refer to values of basic rights and economic freedom, not to governmental structure.

13. **(4)** Because each state is represented by a star on the flag, one more would bring the total number of stars to 51. Based on the information in the passage, none of the other choices would apply.

14. **(5)** When people purchase products, they usually pay a sales tax. The other choices do not involve the retail sale of ordinary goods.

15. **(4)** The money paid out is based on the ownership of real estate, so the tax is a property tax. The other choices do not involve the continued ownership of real estate.

16. **(3)** Because the Rodriguez family made a profit on the sale of real estate, the money paid out was a capital gains tax. The other choices do not involve the sale of real estate.

17. **(2)** Because Mr. Reed had been paying a social security tax on his earnings, he was entitled to payments from this fund after retirement. None of the other taxes result in benefit payments.

18. **(3)** The purpose of the Somalia mission was to help feed people. So, a humanitarian mission is designed to help needy people.

19. **(5)** All but the fact that Mexico City is the world's most populous city are mentioned in the passage as contributing factors.

20. **(5)** All aspects of the problem except its solution are mentioned in the passage.

21. **(2)** The border states were slave states but remained in the Union. Although the other choices are facts, the map does not provide information about the location of the Confederate capital, the aim of runaway slaves, the location of Fort Sumter, or who won the battle there.

22. (1) Four slaveholding states—Missouri, Kentucky, Delaware, and Maryland—did not secede. The decisions to secede came over several months, not quickly. If slavery were the only issue, Missouri, Kentucky, Delaware, and Maryland probably would have seceded. The map gives no information on family loyalties or on support of secession in Kansas.

23. (5) The only effect supported by the map is the division of Virginia into Virginia (which joined the Confederacy) and West Virginia (which stayed in the Union). The border states already were in the Union, and more slaveholding states were not created.

24. (1) The reason that Native Americans were mistakenly called Indians is that Columbus thought they were natives of the Indies. The other choices do not involve Columbus's mistake about where he had landed.

25. (2) School segregation was based on the argument that separate schools for blacks and whites were equal. Marshall disagreed, insisting that segregated schools were inherently unequal.

26. (1) The author uses the word "surprised" in reference to Marshall's appointment to the Supreme Court. So he assumes that this was an unexpected event.

27. (4) Justice Marshall's action in the *Brown* case and his later acts on the Supreme Court upheld laws and established many legal guidelines. These facts support the opinion that many people's lives were influenced by Marshall's decisions.

28. (1) The women are not responsible for the manager's decision. They are the victims of prejudice, being used as scapegoats for the frustration of the male employees. Choices (2) and (5) are examples of other types of prejudice. Choices (3) and (4) are simply accusations of misconduct.

29. (1) The presumption of victory was based on Saddam's withdrawal of Iraqi troops and on the surrender of Iraqi soldiers. Although Americans might have hoped for no more war, this desire was not the basis of the celebration. Choices (3) and (4) are not facts. Choice (5) would not have been a basis for celebration.

30. (3) Saddam Hussein's belief that Iraq won the war is the only opinion listed. The other choices refer to facts mentioned in the passage.

31. (4) Immigrants would be attracted to areas in U.S. cities that provide them with something familiar. Many immigrants speak English, so the language problem would not be a deciding factor. Urban villages would help immigrants adapt to the new culture but not help them blend in quickly or offer any particular business opportunities.

32. (4) Most of the passage describes how accounts are insured in credit unions by the NCUA.

33. (1) The last line of the passage expresses the author's opinion. There is no basis for the second choice. The other three choices are supporting facts.

34. (4) Reagan is the only president listed who received over 50% of the popular vote.

35. (1) The election resulted in a change of party leadership. Nothing specific is stated about the effectiveness of either party. There is no evidence that anything is wrong with the two-party system.

36. (2) The nicknames in the passage are all based on agricultural products. Cotton is the only choice that is an agricultural product.

37. (4) The similarities could occur in a randomly selected population. Therefore, the findings can't be described as amazing. The fact of the separation or the neglect of favorite foods would not add to the logical conclusion.

38. (3) The Bushmen are described as having worn Western clothing, a sign that they have adopted outside ways. Their compliance with the television crew also suggests adapting to outside ways. Choice (2) is not always true. Choices (4) and (5) are not mentioned.

39. (3) By the twenty-first month of the recession ending in 1991, a substantial number of jobs still has not been created. None of the other options reflect the figures on the graph.

40. (3) Because there was no significant job creation in March 1991, many Americans saw no sign that the recession had ended. The lack of new jobs would not encourage any of the other beliefs.

41. (5) During the third- to sixth-month period the lines for the recessions ending in November 1982 and March 1975 coincided, signifying that the number of new jobs created in each period was about equal. For the other three-month periods, the two lines are far apart.

42. (5) Such dense populations would most likely indicate large numbers of cities but would not necessarily result in poverty. The first three choices would be in countries with much sparser populations.

43. (4) The proof lies in the heading of the graph and the placement of Bangladesh at the top of the list with 2,255 persons per square mile. Information about Japan's island status, potential growth rates or limitations, or the average population density is not given.

44. (1) The Los Angeles disturbances were violent and destructive with no clearly established goal except the expression of anger against the Rodney King verdict. People who attended inaugural parties, student lectures, parades, and freedom marches were all focused and peaceful.

PRACTICE TEST

45. (3) Ford became vice president by appointment, not election, when Spiro Agnew resigned. When President Nixon resigned, Ford became president. Ford's loss of the next election had nothing to do with the constitutional provision. The other choices are not explained by the process for presidential succession.

46. (3) Rankin opposed three different wars, all fought for different reasons. Her votes against the two world wars went against prevailing public opinion and showed that she was against military action. Her stance on civil rights is not mentioned.

47. (1) Like Nation, Anthony advocated an initially unpopular cause. Both were arrested for supporting the cause. Both were seen as symbols of women's movements. Ross and Parkhurst had no real political impact. Roosevelt and Ferraro were neither arrested for their convictions nor representatives of specific movements.

48. (3) In the four elections listed, only slightly more than 50 percent turned out to vote. The percentage of active voters has remained about the same, not decreased. There is no information about the age of the voters or the importance of the elections.

49. (2) Newly elected presidents will not represent the interests of a majority of people.

50. (3) The dots indicate a high concentration of wetlands in Minnesota. The dots in the other choices indicate few wetlands.

51. (4) All of the conditions except snowfall could have a negative effect on a wetland.

52. (3) The dots indicate fewer wetlands in the southwest.

53. (4) The Soviet Union was cut up into many smaller countries, so there were new national boundaries. All of the other choices were unaffected and remained the same.

54. (5) The information that Americans would see sex roles as reversed and the description of male and female behavior in Iran support the hypothesis that sex roles vary between cultures, the opposite of what is suggested in (4). The facts do not support the other three choices, all of which are opinions.

55. (1) Despite other countries' claim to the West, believers in Manifest Destiny were not deterred, suggesting they believed it to be their right. There is no question of a change in citizenship or formation of a new nation; they were extending U.S. borders.

56. (2) The car represents Congress's spending (not the tendency for its members to travel). The salesman is assuring the customer that the car can go faster and faster. There is no support for the ideas that Congress acts quickly, drives cautiously, or wastes time.

57. (4) The customer's question about brakes suggests that there should be a way to slow spending. Congress spends too much, not wisely nor too little. No mention is made of the 102nd Congress.

58. (1) Johnson believed that the reform programs of the New Deal had been effective. He saw government as being responsible for and being able to guarantee the welfare of citizens. There is no evidence that his programs ignored good health.

59. (2) The writer has doubts about the ability of government to resolve the health-care crisis. These doubts are backed up by mention of continuing economic and education problems.

60. (3) The money for a publicly funded program has to come from somewhere, usually from taxes. The rates of private insurers and the medical community would not be affected by a program geared for the currently uninsured.

61. (1) Labor and management are negotiating for a wage agreeable to both. This is not a process limited to management or to the union. As both sides seem willing to work out an agreement, there is no need for mediation, a strike, or picketing.

62. (5) The proposed action by labor means that work will stop because no one will be in the mines. A sit-down strike would require the miners to stay in the mine. There is no mention of discussion between labor and management, or a need for mediation at this point.

63. (2) While in the process of collective bargaining, labor and management have deadlocked. The advice of a third party (mediation) could help them reach an agreement.

64. (1) Self-confident people would probably not be overly anxious or depressed and so would tend to avoid second-guessing or doubting themselves. The example does not provide information about the fairness or accuracy of measurement provided by multiple-choice tests. Anxiety appears to impair rather than improve intellect, but it does not necessarily result in failure—only a tendency to do less well.

Practice Test Evaluation Chart

Use the answer key on pages 294–296 to check your answers to the Practice Test. Then find the item number of each question you missed and circle it on the chart below to determine the reading skill and content areas in which you need to do the most work. Pay particular attention to areas where you missed half or more of the questions. The reading skills are covered on pages 25–88. The page numbers for each content area are listed below on the chart. Both types of skills are absolutely essential for success on the GED Social Studies Test. The numbers in boldface are questions based on graphics. For those questions that you missed, review the skill pages indicated.

Skill Area/ Content Area	Comprehension	Analysis	Application	Evaluation
U.S. History (pages 91–143)	11, 18, **22**, **23**	**21**, **24**, 26, 29, 30, 55	13, 25, 47	12, 27, 45
Political Science (pages 145–175)	**4**, **56**	46, **57**, 58, 59	**5**, 34, 60	7, 35, **48**, **49**
Behavioral Sciences (pages 177–209)	**8**, 38	**9**, **10**, 31, 54	28, 44, 64	1, 2, 3, 37
Geography (pages 211–231)	20, **50**, **52**	19, 53	36, **51**	**42**, **43**
Economics (pages 233–255)	32, **39**, **41**	14, 15, 16, 17, **40**	61, 62, 63	6, 33

Answer Key

CHAPTER 1: COMPREHENDING

EXERCISE 1
page 26

1. **(4)** The main idea is that there was much abuse of power during the Nixon administration, a point stated at the end of the passage. Choices (1) and (3) are neither stated in nor supported by the passage. Choices (2) and (5) are ideas that support the main idea.

2. **(3)** The passage refers to John Dean's testimony, which led to formal charges against former president Nixon. The passage neither states nor implies that Nixon was found innocent (1), or was convicted (2). It is obvious that he was not executed (4). Because the former president resigned from office to escape impeachment proceedings, choice (5) is incorrect.

EXERCISE 2
page 28

1. **(2)** The point of the graph is to show the variety of methods this business uses to advertise. The title of the graph, "Advertising Spending for One Business," is a clue to the main idea. The other choices are either details, judgments, or facts not supported by the graph.

2. **(2)** Choice (1), the print media, with 57 percent, spends more than the other media on advertising. Choices (3), (4), and (5) are supported by the graph.

EXERCISE 3
page 31

1. **(4)** The passage says, ". . . a primary target is the American citizen." Choices (1), (2), (3), and (5) are not stated in the passage.

2. **(2)** The passage says, "sustain communication among hostages as much as possible." This means communicate as often as possible with other hostages. Choices (1), (3), (4), and (5) are not stated in the passage.

3. **(2)** The article says that you should not even appear to be capable of providing valuable information to the terrorists. This could put you in danger.

EXERCISE 4
page 33

Your answers may vary slightly; take Midlothian Road north to Peterson Road. Turn right on Peterson Road and drive east until you reach State Highway 45. Turn left on 45 and drive north to Gages Lake Road. Turn right on Gages Lake Road and follow it to Wildwood.

EXERCISE 5
page 34

1. **(5)** If the middle income group spends 2 out of every 10 dollars on wants and the upper income group spends 6 out of every 10 dollars on wants, then the implication is that as one's income goes up, one has more money to spend on wants.

2. **(1)** When the author says, "At best, they have just enough food and shelter to stay alive," he is implying that the poor cannot even provide for their basic needs.

3. **(4)** The upper income group could most afford to spend money on excess wants (superfluities) and not just on needs.

EXERCISE 6
page 36

1. **(2)** Since the average cost of tuition, fees, and room and board has continuously risen from 1980 to 1990 for both private and public colleges, the implication is that this trend will continue in the future. There is no indication of the capacity of institutions of higher education, so (1) does not apply. No figures are given to support (3), (4), and (5).

2. **(2)** In 1990, the cost of public colleges was a little over $4,000, while the cost of private colleges rose to $12,000. The other choices are not supported by the graph.

CHAPTER 2: APPLYING

EXERCISE 1
page 38

1. **YES** Busing children would quickly desegregate schools.
2. **NO** African-American history courses do not address the problem of separate and unequal facilities.
3. **NO** The United Negro College Fund program provides funding for colleges where the vast majority of students are black.
4. **YES** Minority quotas would help desegregate colleges quickly.
5. **YES** "Magnet" schools, open to students from all racial backgrounds, are known for their excellence in education.

EXERCISE 2
page 39

nurture—Verbal stimulation would be part of an environmental effect.

nature—Cooing and crying are natural activities and do not involve the environment.

nurture—Our attitudes toward people affect our actions toward them; this is an example of environmental influence.

nature—Chemical makeup comes from nature.

nature—Brain structure differences stem from nature.

EXERCISE 3
page 40

1. **(4)** This is the only choice that involves a violation of the Sherman Anti-Trust Act—price-fixing.
2. **(1)** Choice (1) is a government-sanctioned monopoly, whereas the other choices involve price-fixing or other illegal forms of monopoly.

EXERCISE 4
page 41

1. **(2)** The propaganda technique described is glittering generalities since the manufacturer speaks in general and vague terms. The statement does not tell us what the "leading product on the market" is.
2. **(4)** The propaganda technique used is bandwagoning. The announcer advises the residents to subscribe to the paper because practically everyone else does it.
3. **(3)** The propaganda technique used is transferring. The candidate expected the power or respect of the leader of the fundamentalist Christians to "rub off" and favorably impress the voters.
4. **(1)** The term "tax-and-spend liberal" is an example of the propaganda technique known as name-calling.

EXERCISE 5
page 43

(3) Boris Yeltsin is blamed for the poor economy. In U.S. history, Herbert Hoover, president during the Depression, was blamed for the country's economic problems. He was voted out of office and replaced by Franklin Roosevelt. Reagan (1) and Kennedy (5) were popular presidents and were not voted out of office. Nixon (4) resigned the presidency but not because of a poor national economy.

EXERCISE 6
pages 44-45

1. **(1)** Deal making is an old tradition of American politics. In both cases, historians believe that a deal was struck that enabled both men to become president. Prior knowledge would tell you that neither the Supreme Court nor the House of Representatives has the authority to choose a president.
2. **(1)** Conflicts between religious authority and governmental authority are described historically as issues of church vs. state.
3. **(2)** Prior knowledge of history would tell you that New Zealand is the only choice listed that is a British possession and that Maoris are natives of New Zealand.

EXERCISE 7
page 46

(3) This is the only choice that is based on physical features as described in the passage.

EXERCISE 8
page 48

1. **(3)** This requires prior knowledge of Leif Ericson's place in history.
2. **(2)** To answer this you would have to know that the North Sea is located off the coast of Norway and that Leif Ericson was a Norwegian.

CHAPTER 3: ANALYZING

EXERCISE 1
page 51

1. The *causes* are extended drought and extreme overpopulation, since they contributed to severe famine (the *effect*).
2. The *effect*, population growth in the Sunbelt states, has come from companies relocating (the *cause*).
3. The *effect*, emigration of the first Pilgrims, was prompted by religious persecution (the *cause*).
4. The *cause*, unfair employer practices, brought about the establishment of labor unions (the *effect*).

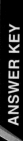

EXERCISE 2
page 51

1. (d) The passage states that the tornado series of 1965 caused $300,000,000 in property damage.
2. (c) According to the passage, the combination of location, population density, and development leads to a greater potential for tornado damage in the Chicago area.
3. (b) Rotating air masses cause tornadoes. This is stated at the beginning of the passage.
4. (a) The tornado series of 1925 killed 740 people in five states. This is stated at the end of the first paragraph.

EXERCISE 3
page 52

1. (5) The passage says in the third paragraph that U.S. automakers were able to improve quality, increase automation, and reduce manufacturing costs; this means that the automakers have become more competitive.
2. (1) The fact that Japanese manufacturers were able to make cars more cheaply than U.S. manufacturers implies that Japanese-made cars sold for less than U.S.-made cars. The 1992 figures show a reverse, with American cars selling for less than Japanese cars, the opposite of (4). There is no information to support the other choices.
3. (2) California voters realized that to improve the quality of their schools they would have to pay higher taxes.

EXERCISE 4
page 53

(2) The drop in interest rates helped the overall sales of new cars in spite of the higher unemployment rate.

EXERCISE 5
page 57

1. (2) According to the passage, the main source of stress for controllers is poor labor-management relations. Choice (2) is the only one that involves labor-management relations.
2. (1) This is the only choice given that can be proved with data. The other choices either are not true or are opinions.

3. (3) This answer is based on the quote "Controllers who were interviewed complained that their recommendations for providing safety backups and other measures were not being considered by their employers or the Federal Aviation Administration."
4. (5) According to the passage, the more conscientious, or careful, workers were most prone to experience stress.

EXERCISE 6
page 59

1. (2) The house, located on the moon, with a "for sale" sign, is looked at longingly by the family. The father is holding a sign that says "new-house cost doubles in 10 years," indicating that home ownership is threatened by increasingly high costs.
2. (5) Because of rising costs of homes each year, many Americans who would like to purchase a new home are unable to do so because they cannot afford one.

EXERCISE 7
page 60

(1) The U.S. had a long history of making loans to the Allied Powers. The graph shows a very strong financial commitment. Choices (2), (4), and (5) cannot be derived from the graph, and choice (3) would not affect the decision to align with all the Allied Powers.

EXERCISE 8
page 61

Exact words may vary.
1. The writer assumes that socialism is harmful for developing countries and that capitalism is better.
2. The writer assumes that Kennedy won the presidency in 1960 because he was more attractive on TV than Nixon was.
3. The writer assumes that before westernization, China had a dreary past.
4. The writer assumes that there usually is trouble at a rock concert but not at a Christian rock festival.
5. The writer assumes that there are cheats in the welfare system and that doing volunteer work would stop their cheating. Also, the writer assumes that those on welfare do not already perform volunteer work in the community.

EXERCISE 9
page 62

Statements (c), (e), and (f) are the assumptions made by the author. Statements (a) and (b) are stated directly in the passage. Statements (d), (g), and (h) are the opposite of what the author implies.

EXERCISE 10
page 63

1. (4) The governor says that private corporations would be good at running prisons because they are running hospitals effectively. The assumption is that privately run prisons would require management skills similar to those needed by privately run hospitals.

2. (2) "Doing well" means making a profit. "Doing good" means doing good works for society.

3. (3) Alexander believed that if prisons were run like businesses, they would be more efficient and cost effective.

4. (5) Making a profit is one of its chief goals. The other choices are contradicted in the passage.

EXERCISE 11
page 66

1. (3) By showing the bird full and proud in the beginning and featherless and weak at the end, the cartoonist assumes that, as government has grown larger over the years, it has eroded or taken away personal freedoms.

2. (3) The cartoonist views America as less powerful than it once was because big government has infringed on people's personal freedoms.

3. (4) The cartoonist would probably be against government-mandated school integration.

EXERCISE 12
page 68

1. (1) Since borrowers must choose between high fixed-interest rates and rates that can fluctuate (go up or down), the conclusion is that borrowers must be prepared to choose between different mortgage options.

2. (2) Parents have the ultimate responsibility for the proper development of their children (since parental neglect is punishable by the state).

3. (1) Because many examples of the use of computers in the workplace are given, the conclusion that may be drawn is that computers will be present in almost all aspects of the workplace.

EXERCISE 13
page 69

1. (3) By requiring businesses to give a year's notice before plant closings or layoffs, several community groups have given some employees a chance to plan their futures.

2. (4) The company in (4) has been given tax incentives to remain in Vacaville, and yet it is moving out of the area. The other choices do not involve employers subject to the agreement.

3. (1) Because the 1920s, like the 1980s, saw a large rise in wealth concentration, they must have been boom years for the rich.

4. (1) Since the net worth of the top 1 percent of American households rose from 31 percent in 1983 to 37 percent in 1989, you can infer that the gap widened between the super-rich and the rest of American households.

EXERCISE 14
page 72

1. Y Snow and temperature patterns in the Northeast suggest that this is a forecast for a winter day in the U.S.

2. Y The map indicates that only a small portion of the country has rain or snow.

3. Y The temperatures increase in 10-degree increments as you travel south.

4. N There is no snow in the Pacific Northwest on this map.

5. N Rain is indicated for some parts of the East Coast, but not enough to warrant fear of flooding.

6. Y Showers covering central Pennsylvania are shown on the map.

7. N Florida is shown to be in both the 60- to 70-degree ranges.

EXERCISE 15
pages 73-74

Exact wording may vary.

1. This speaker probably feels that social activism in Central America is the missionary's responsibility or obligation.

2. This speaker probably admires Japan's ability to produce cheaper cars.

3. This speaker probably resents or dislikes Six Flags Great America Amusement Park.

EXERCISE 16
page 74

1. (2) You can infer this from the last sentence, "Fortunately, Thurmond's filibuster did not prevent passage. . . ."

2. (5) A clue to the meaning of the word *filibuster* is that Thurmond "talked for more than twenty-four hours to purposely delay the vote. . . ."

EXERCISE 17
page 76

1. (4) If the men want to store nuclear waste in a citizen's garage, it can be inferred that nuclear waste disposal is "getting too close for comfort."

2. (3) Because of the men's protective garb, you can infer that nuclear waste is dangerous to handle.

CHAPTER 4: EVALUATING

EXERCISE 1
page 78

1. **NO—5** In this case, there can be no legal contract because illegal activity has taken place.
2. **YES** In this case, there is a legal contract. The attorney is a representative of the seller and accepts the $5,000 check from the buyer. The buyer will receive the property after the deal is settled.
3. **NO—2** The buyer seems to have made a clear offer, but the seller has not accepted; therefore, no settlement can be made.
4. **YES** The agreement is in writing and the valuables exchanged in the arrangement will be labor for room and board. The exchange of room and board for services performed is a perfectly legal exchange.

EXERCISE 2
pages 78-79

1. **(3)** Montagu's race has no bearing on the believability of the hypothesis.
2. **(3)** How long Montagu has had the theory adds nothing to its believability.
3. **(2)** The fact that the term *race* is still widely used and accepted tends to dispute Montagu's theory.
4. **(2)** There appear to be valid reasons for classification by race based on physical features.
5. **(1)** Montagu has strong credentials in the anthropological field.
6. **(1)** Other noted professionals support Montagu's theory.

EXERCISE 3
page 80

1. You should have written *patriotism* or *responsibility to his country*, since he chose to serve his country over getting married and settling down.
2. You should have written something like *principles* over his *career*, since he refused the project despite its prestige.

EXERCISE 4
pages 80-81

1. **(5)** The value of concern for lives and property after the sinking of the battleship *Maine* was the deciding factor in the United States' decision to enter the war.
2. **(3)** The passage states, "For good or ill, the U.S. became less nationalistic." None of the other choices are stated directly or implied in the passage.

3. **(3)** The viewpoint that the U.S. is an imperialist nation would be held by someone who believed that the invasion of Grenada was an act of aggression.
4. **(4)** The fact that the United States had an isolationist policy did not contribute to the start of the Spanish-American War. All the other choices cite factors that did play a role.

EXERCISE 5
page 83

1. **(3)** The statement to the effect that the ERA was not given enough time is the conclusion made, but there are no facts to support that conclusion.
2. **(1)** The last sentence of the paragraph says that a majority of American citizens supported the ERA. Since feminist organizations supported the amendment heavily, and since the government failed to pass the ERA, we can infer that organizations working for the ERA have more popular than governmental support.

EXERCISE 6
page 85

1. adequate
2. adequate
3. inadequate—weather map would show this better
4. adequate
5. inadequate—population and world map would show this better
6. adequate

EXERCISE 7
page 86

1. **(1)** Russia straddles Europe and Asia. Choice (2) is untrue according to this map. None of the other choices are represented adequately on this map.
2. **(4)** There is no key to use to determine mountain height.

EXERCISE 8
page 88

1. **(1)** There is no logical connection made by the writer between laws restricting the freedom of blacks and the bias shown against them by European immigrants.
2. **(3)** There is no logical reason to believe that if these laws did not exist there would not be racial bias.
3. **(3)** Slavery was for life, whereas indentured servitude lasted only for a limited time. The other choices are not factually correct.

CHAPTER 5: U.S. HISTORY

EXERCISE 1
page 93

Understanding Ideas
1. **(2)** According to the passage and the map, France and England became rivals in the establishment of some settlements in the New World.
2. **(4)** The map on page 92 shows that France had made the most claims for land in North America by 1689.
3. **(5)** The map shows that the French held little territory in the thirteen colonies. Choices (1), (2), and (3) cannot be supported by the map; and choice (4) is not true.
4. **(2)** According to the passage, the Proclamation Line of 1763, which showed the lands in which the English and the French claimed "ownership," proved to be meaningless.

EXERCISE 2
page 94

Evaluating Ideas
(1) and **(4)** The chart says that New England has dense forests and rocky soil. These conditions are not desirable for farming. Also, the abundant rainfall, warm temperatures, and suitability for farming encouraged the emergence of the southern plantation system (4).

EXERCISE 3
page 96

Understanding Ideas
1. **(2)** The passage states that the purpose of the first Continental Congress was to demand the colonists' rights as British citizens.
2. **(2)** The information states that "by the time of the second Continental Congress in May 1775, hostile encounters had already taken place between the English soldiers and the colonists."

Applying Ideas
3. **(2)** The struggle of India for its independence from Great Britain is the only event that can be compared to the American colonists' fight against Great Britain since both ultimately won freedom and established democracies. The other choices are not examples of anticolonial wars.
4. **(3)** After the French and Indian War in 1763, Great Britain needed to pay its huge war debt. It passed the Stamp Act of 1765 and the Townshend Acts of 1767 to help pay for the war.

Writing Activity 1
page 96

Your answer might include the following points:
- The American Revolution proved that a small number of inspired people can overthrow a large and powerful nation.
- The American Revolution represented an experiment in government that symbolized the fundamental ideals of many people throughout the world.

EXERCISE 4
pages 98-99

Applying Ideas
1. **A** This represents an anti-Federalist viewpoint that states and territories should have sovereignty.
2. **F** The Federalists believed that the national government should have the power to coin money.
3. **F** The Federalists held that only the federal government should have authority to regulate trade.
4. **A** The anti-Federalists held that the states themselves should have the right to form their own local militias.
5. **F** Those who believed in a strong national government believed that only the federal government should have the right to make treaties with other nations.

EXERCISE 5
page 99

Understanding Ideas
1. **(1)** Hamilton was a Federalist who believed in a centralized government for the thirteen separate states.
2. **(4)** As shown on the chart, the "Great Compromise" involved the creation of a two-house federal legislature to allow for fairness in representation.
3. **(1)** Counting slaves as only three-fifths of the population penalized the southern states because it meant that they would have fewer representatives in the House of Representatives.
4. **(3)** The Bill of Rights was an important addition to the Constitution because it guaranteed rights to the colonists.

Analyzing Ideas
5. **(5)** From the quote we can infer that Washington believed that ratification of the Constitution by the United States was surprising given the many differences among the states. None of the other choices are stated or implied in Washington's quote.

Writing Activity 2
page 100

Your answer should include the fact that had slaves been counted as part of the population, the South would have had greater representation in the House of Representatives. Thus, a majority of the legislators would have been sympathetic to the needs of the South and would have voted accordingly.

EXERCISE 6
page 101

Analyzing Ideas

1. **(3)** Based on the passage, you can tell that Jefferson believed that the Constitution did not specifically allow for the president to expand the territory of the U.S. Choices (1), (2), (4), and (5) are facts that are stated in the passage, not opinions.

Understanding Ideas

2. **(4)** This is stated directly in the passage. The passage states that Lewis and Clark established friendly relations with the Indians, not that relationships improved greatly, choice (1). Choices (2) and (5) are not true, and although choice (3) is true, the fact had little to do with the American belief in Manifest Destiny.

Evaluating Ideas

3. **(4)** Only choice (4) is supported by the passage that says Jefferson was reluctant to go beyond powers stated directly in the Constitution. However, when he did go along with the Louisiana Purchase, he laid the basis for future presidents to use implied powers.

EXERCISE 7
pages 102-103

Understanding Ideas

1. **(2)** According to the passage, the forcing of American seamen to join the British navy was proved and contributed to the War of 1812.

Analyzing Ideas

2. **(3)** The death of the British ally Tecumseh marked the end of the united Indian resistance in the Midwest and South, thus directly affecting the outcome of the War of 1812.

Understanding Ideas

3. **(1)** The information states that one result of the war was that "U.S. dependence on Europe was broken" since the war had forced the U.S. to learn to do without Europe's economic and political help.

4. **(3)** The takeover of Canada by the United States was a major aim, but there is no proof that it would have happened if the U.S. had won the War of 1812.

EXERCISE 8
page 104

Applying Ideas

1. **(2)** and **(4)** The only situations listed that represent attempts to enforce the principles of the Monroe Doctrine are the American opposition to the Spanish control of Cuba and the American blockade of Cuba. In both cases, the United States was trying to prevent European involvement in the Western Hemisphere.

EXERCISE 9
page 106

Understanding Ideas

1. **(c)** Virginia split in two over the issue of secession, with the western part loyal to the Union. This was the origin of the state of West Virginia.

2. **(d)** Texas seceded from the Union despite the fact that only the eastern part of the state voted to do so.

3. **(a)** Kentucky was a border state that remained in the Union despite being a slave state.

4. **(b)** Mississippi is a solidly southern state that voted overwhelmingly to secede from the Union.

5. **(e)** Of the states listed, Maryland was located closest to the nation's capital.

EXERCISE 10
page 107

Analyzing Ideas

1. **(2)** Lincoln did not issue an order for emancipation for the entire country out of loyalty to the four border states that remained with the Union despite the fact that they were slave states.

2. **(3)** Of the states listed, only Missouri was not part of the Confederate states.

EXERCISE 11
pages 108-109

Applying Ideas

1. N
2. S
3. S
4. N
5. S
6. N
7. N
8. B
9. N
10. S

EXERCISE 12
page 109

Analyzing Ideas

1. (5) The passage says, " As a result of this [Emancipation] proclamation, the Union Army's ranks were swelled by 180,000 former slaves who fought against the Confederacy."

Applying Ideas

2. (2) Catton said that "we move to make a living reality out of the great ideal of equality of all Americans. . . ." Based on that, you could assume that Bruce Catton would most likely support the actions of the civil rights workers of the sixties.

Evaluating Ideas

3. (2) Bruce Catton repeatedly points out that the Civil War obligates Americans to promote freedom at home and abroad.

Applying Ideas

4. (2) The other main event in U.S. history that forced women to become equal partners in the work force was World War II. As was the case for the Civil War, women entered the work force to replace the men who had to go to war.

EXERCISE 13
page 111

Applying Ideas

1. (4) The Freedmen's Bureau Act, whose function was to provide food, education, and work in the Reconstruction South, is sometimes regarded as the nation's first federal welfare system.

2. (3) The Fifteenth Amendment guaranteed voting rights to all citizens and is a logical basis for opposition to discriminatory voting requirements.

3. (1) As a result of the Emancipation Proclamation, slavery was abolished (Thirteenth Amendment).

EXERCISE 14
page 112

Understanding Ideas

1. (5) One of the most important aspects of the industrial revolution was the ability to mass-produce goods. Factories that adopted the method of using interchangeable parts were able to produce more goods than before.

2. (5) The U.S. had more miles of railroad than all of Europe and Russia and was recognized as the industrial leader of the world. Based on that, you can see that dependable transportation is a key to mass production and sale of goods.

Analyzing Ideas

3. (2) The maps show more dots in the North than in the South. Moreover, the larger population centers are shown to be in the North. Since industry was related directly to population growth, you can infer that there was more industry in the northern states than in the southern states during the period 1870–1900.

Understanding Ideas

4. (4) From the maps it appears that industries and the cities that grew up around them were usually established near bodies of water such as the Atlantic Ocean, the Great Lakes, and the Mississippi River.

EXERCISE 15
page 113

Applying Ideas

The actions that represent economic activity without government intervention are:

(1) Major airlines engage in a price war, setting competitive prices for air fares.

(2) The absence of a usury law, a law that sets the maximum interest rate that can be legally charged for a loan.

(5) Banks charge whatever rate of interest the market will bear on passbook savings accounts.

EXERCISE 16
page 114

Analyzing Ideas

1. (2) Based on the quotes ". . . big business grew without restrictions," and "This policy often resulted in economic and social abuse . . ." you can infer that big business grew in the U.S. at the expense of public welfare.

2. (2) Carnegie, Morgan, and Rockefeller were called robber barons because of their unscrupulous and unfair business practices.

EXERCISE 17
page 115

Understanding Ideas

1. (3) The only statement that is true and may be proved by reading the graph is that the trend at the turn of the century was for immigrants to come to the U.S. from eastern, central, and southern Europe in greater numbers than twenty years earlier.

2. (3) Of the regions listed, northwest Europe experienced a reduction in the numbers of immigrants coming to the U.S. It is the only region shown in which the bar for the period 1891–1910 is substantially shorter than the bar for the period 1871–1890.

3. (3) Of the regions listed, Southeast Asia is the source of the greatest number of immigrants coming to the United States at the present time.

Writing Activity 3
page 116

Your answer might include the following points:
- Naturalized Americans today do not always accept today's "new Americans" as readily as our ancestors did; overt discrimination may not be as widespread today as it was during the nineteenth century, but it still exists.
- "New Americans" are competing with native Americans for America's dwindling number of jobs.
- Many of today's "new Americans" are coming from Mexico, India, the Middle East, and southeast Asian countries.
- Many of today's "new Americans" are not as motivated to learn English and therefore persist in speaking their native language, thus creating a need for bilingual programs in schools.

EXERCISE 18
page 117

Evaluating Ideas
1. (5) Based on Plunkitt's definition of "honest graft" and "dishonest graft," you should have arrived at the judgment that political bosses appeared to have no sense of right and wrong.

Understanding Ideas
2. (4) According to the information in the passage, another name for "honest graft" as described by Plunkitt might be profiting from inside information on government purchases. Choices (1), (3), and (5) are described as "dishonest graft." Choice (2) is not mentioned by Plunkitt.
3. (4) Of the choices listed, only blackmailing tavern owners (saloonkeepers) is described as "dishonest" graft.

EXERCISE 19
page 119

Understanding Ideas
1. (3) In his statement, Riis says, "The greed of capital that wrought the evil must undo it."

Evaluating Ideas
2. (5) In his statement, Riis points out, "The greed of capital that wrought the evil must undo it. . . ." By capital, he means private industry. Riis would likely agree with the position that private industry is morally responsible for helping to correct social problems.

3. (3) Riis believed that justice should come from the public conscience, as represented by private citizens who established settlement houses. Choice (1) is incorrect because the "Four Hundred" do not represent the public conscience. Choices (2) and (5) are incorrect because machine politicians and businessmen who believed in social Darwinism are the very ones Riis attacked for creating the conditions. Choice (4) is incorrect because Riis says legislation cannot undo the evil.
4. (3) The Progressives believed that through legislative reforms Americans' lives would be improved.
5. (2) The Progressives believed that businesses would be improved with governmental controls.

EXERCISE 20
page 121

Applying Ideas
1. (4) An example of American imperialist policy is the U.S. control of most of the Panama Canal Zone, because it is a case of the U.S. controlling a foreign territory.
2. (1) In making his decision, President Grover Cleveland was abiding by the principles of rule by "consent of the governed" put forth by the Declaration of Independence.

EXERCISE 21
page 122

Analyzing Ideas
The events that most directly contributed to the U.S. entering the war on the Allied side were:
(4) Germany's attack on the passenger ship the *Lusitania*
(5) threats to U.S. neutrality

Writing Activity 4
page 123

Your answer might include the following points:
- Both the twenties and eighties were dominated by conservative politics, with the Republicans in power.
- As in the twenties, the Reagan administration cut taxes for the rich with the belief that economic benefits would "trickle down" to the poor.
- Also, as in the twenties, social programs have been cut, hurting the poor and middle classes.

EXERCISE 22
page 124

Analyzing Ideas
(1), **(2)**, and **(5)** The statements that reflect assumptions by this writer are: (1), (2), and (5). Choice (3) is incorrect because the writer felt that American society was hurt by its young artists and writers flocking to Paris. Choice (4) is incorrect because the writer believed that young people's striving for individuality and self-expression represented a breakdown in America's moral fabric.

EXERCISE 23
page 125

Analyzing Ideas
1. **(4)** The rise in unemployment from 4 million in 1930 to 11 million by 1932 is a result of the Depression, not a cause. The other choices are causes that are stated in the passage.
2. **(3)** Of the presidents mentioned, Reagan was most similar to Hoover in his conservative approach to government.

EXERCISE 24
pages 126-127

Understanding Ideas
1. **(3)** The entire passage compares and contrasts the two men's policies and personal styles.

Analyzing Ideas
2. **(5)** When, in the last paragraph, the author says, "Opinions are sharply divided," she is expressing the opinion that the verdict is still out on Reagan's stature as president.
3. **(2)** While it is obvious that the author has respect for both men's personal styles, her positive references to the New Deal reveal an admiration for Roosevelt's policies.

Writing Activity 5
page 127

Your answer might include the ideas expressed below.

Franklin Roosevelt and Ronald Reagan appealed to the American people because both:
- were reassuring in their style, manner, and way of speaking
- were very experienced politicians
- knew how to use the media—radio and television—to their best advantage
- had immediate popular support for the programs needed to correct America's problems

EXERCISE 25
page 128

Understanding Ideas
1. **T**
2. **F**
3. **T**
4. **F**
5. **F**

EXERCISE 26
page 129

Applying Ideas
1. **(5)** The passage says, "Six million others were slaughtered by the Nazis for no other reason than that they were Jewish and thus considered to be racially inferior to Germans."
2. **(2)** The writer shows concern for the concentration camp inmates and is upset by "man's inhumanity to man."

Understanding Ideas
3. **(3)** Only choice (3) is mentioned as a reason for why the author's life was not taken.
4. **(4)** Choice (4) is correct because an internationalist believes in maintaining good relations with other nations. Choice (1) is incorrect because Roosevelt says that we can't isolate ourselves from the rest of humanity. Choices (2) and (5) are incorrect because the quote makes no mention of one country controlling or not controlling another. Choice (3) is incorrect because Roosevelt's language is not warlike.
5. **(5)** Acting on a policy of isolationism, the United States tried to remain neutral, or uninvolved, as the Allies fought against the Axis Powers.
6. **(4)** Roosevelt showed the trait of realism when he stated that from now on America must no longer be isolated from the rest of the world.

Writing Activity 6
page 130

You might argue one of the following points:
- President Truman was justified in dropping the bomb because the action ended a long, bloody war and saved American lives.
- President Truman was not justified in dropping the bomb because there can never be any justification for taking another human life.
- President Truman was not justified because the action opened the door for nuclear war and the ever-present threat of the destruction of mankind.

EXERCISE 27
page 131

Applying Ideas

(1), **(2)**, and **(4)** The situations that represent modern-day attempts to enforce the principles of the Truman Doctrine are: (1), (2), and (4). Choices (3) and (5) do not represent the U.S. support of free peoples who resist attempted control by armed minorities or outside pressures. The Soviet Union, friendly to Cuba, sought to establish missile bases there, (3). Duvalier was forced out of Haiti because of his abuse of political power, choice (5).

EXERCISE 28
page 133

Applying Ideas

1. (4) The undeclared war in Vietnam most closely resembled the situation in the Korean War. Both were undeclared wars that resulted from the U.S. policy of containing communism.

Understanding Ideas

2. (3) The decision in *Brown* v. *the Board of Education of Topeka* is significant today because it said that there could not be "separate but equal" educational facilities. This serves as the legal basis for school busing to achieve desegregation.

Analyzing Ideas

3. (1) The passage stresses that Dwight Eisenhower was a war hero. The other choices either are not true or do not account for such great popularity.

4. (2) Communism was not overthrown during the Eisenhower era. In fact, it grew during that period.

EXERCISE 29
page 134

Understanding Ideas

1. (2) This choice summarizes the Kennedy administration's participation in the Peace Corps and Vietnam abroad as well as in civil rights issues at home.

Analyzing Ideas

2. (4) From the reading, it may be assumed that Cuba, a communist nation, was an ally of the Soviet Union.

Writing Activity 7
page 135

You might argue either of the following points:
• President Kennedy was justified in trying to overthrow Castro because Castro's friendliness toward the Soviet Union threatened, indirectly, our national security.
• President Kennedy was not justified in trying to overthrow Castro because no country has the right to meddle in the political affairs of another country.

EXERCISE 30
page 136

Understanding Ideas

1. (2) The information outlines the contributions that former president Johnson made in the areas of civil rights and economic opportunity.

2. (5) Because of his inability to achieve victory in the Vietnam War, and because U.S. involvement in the war caused such dissent among the American people, Johnson decided not to seek reelection in 1968.

3. (5) The information shows how the Vietnam War and the protests against it disrupted American society.

Evaluating Ideas

4. (4) The thrust of the material is that the war in faraway Vietnam had a big impact on American society.

EXERCISE 31
page 137

Evaluating Ideas

1. (5) The opinion best supported by the evidence presented in the material is that "the president of the United States is not above the law." It was President Nixon's involvement in the cover-up of the break-in and the subsequent impeachment action that led to the first presidential resignation in U.S. history.

2. (3) Of former president Nixon's foreign policy initiatives, history will likely credit him most for reestablishing relations with the People's Republic of China.

EXERCISE 32
page 140

Evaluating Ideas

1. (3) This choice illustrates Carter's commitment to peace. Choice (1) is incorrect because it is not very historically significant. Choices (2) and (4) are incorrect because many Americans did not agree with Carter's policies toward the shah of Iran and Somoza. Carter likely will be remembered unfavorably for his failure to gain the hostages' release, choice (5).

Understanding Ideas

2. (1) Reagan's foreign policy is characterized generally as one of anticommunism. None of the other choices reflect this foreign policy emphasis.

Evaluating Ideas

3. (3) The passage shows that, despite his high approval ratings during the Persian Gulf War, President Bush lost favor because of economic troubles in the U.S.

4. (1) Although Carter was a Democrat and Reagan and Bush were Republicans, all three did better with foreign policy than with America's domestic problems.

EXERCISE 33
page 141

1. (2) According to the passage, Clinton "was faced with more problems than he had expected." His experience as a governor (1) did not necessarily make him a better president. Clinton has had problems with foreign affairs (3) and has had more than a few surprises (4). With (5), the opposite is true.

2. (5) As a candidate, Clinton could think about tomorrow's problems without solving them, but as president he had to act. Clinton's solutions do not always please the public (1) or immediately solve the country's economic problems (3). He has appointed many women to public office (2).

U.S. HISTORY
pages 142-143

1. (3) Lincoln's quotation refers to a line in the Declaration of Independence that asserts a basic principle of American political belief. The Know-Nothings did not want to allow any but their own kind to enjoy equality. The other choices are the opposite of what the Know-Nothing party advocated.

2. (2) Some people believe that immigrants take jobs from Americans because they work for low wages. Just as they had objected to immigrants, the Know-Nothings would want to keep undocumented immigrants out of the country. They would not be likely to support any statement that encouraged immigration.

3. (5) Jackson appealed to the ordinary voter because he seemed, like them, to be from a simple background. His political stance was unlike the party line. The passage doesn't mention the campaign at all and refers only briefly to Jackson's time as a soldier.

4. (3) Before Jackson, the political base of democracy was focused on property owners. By supporting the role of average people, Jackson encouraged a large group to become politically active. This change was welcomed by many people.

5. (5) The date is provided in the map title. The names and locations of tribes and cultural areas are written on the map. No numbers for Native American population are given.

6. (3) The name of the Sioux is found in the center of the map in the Plains Group.

7. (3) Tribal groups are shown in almost every section of the country. The clear definition of cultural areas supports the conclusion that culture was well established. There is no support for conclusions about forests or Native American occupations.

CHAPTER 6: POLITICAL SCIENCE

EXERCISE 1
pages 146-147

Applying Ideas

1. O A system of government in which decisions are made by a "few top men" in the People's Republic of China is an example of an oligarchy.

2. DI A system in which one man overthrows the previous ruler and has complete control of an island is a dictatorship.

3. M A system of government headed by a king and in which power is passed down within the family is an example of a monarchy.

4. DI A system in which one man rules a country with absolute power is a dictatorship.

5. **DE** A system of government in which a prime minister heads the legislature and cabinet is an example of a parliamentary democracy.
6. **M** Authority to rule that is inherited and that was justified by a God-given right is an example of an absolute monarchy.
7. **DI** A system of government in which one person has total control and who usually comes to power after a revolution is an example of a dictatorship.

EXERCISE 2
page 148

Applying Ideas
1. **C** The power to declare war is stated in the Constitution.
2. **C** The power to approve presidential appointments is stated in the Constitution.
3. **E** The Constitution states that Congress has the power to provide and maintain an army and navy. At the time the Constitution was written, there could not be an air force. Therefore, the establishment of an air force is an application of the elastic clause.
4. **C** As the passage states, the power to impeach a president is stated in the Constitution.
5. **E** The authority to advance Daylight Savings Time is not significant enough to be stated in the Constitution and, therefore, represents an application of the elastic clause.
6. **E** This goes beyond the powers stated above.
7. **C** The power to admit states is granted in the Constitution.

EXERCISE 3
page 149

Analyzing Ideas

(1) and **(3)** Choices (1) and (3) are logical conclusions that can be drawn from the information on the map. According to the reading, the Supreme Court decided that redrawn legislative districts must be proportional to the population. The fact that the Ninth Congressional District is so much smaller than the others implies that its population is the densest. Also, you could conclude that if the districts had been drawn to equalize land area, the population apportionment would not have been fair.

EXERCISE 4
page 151

Understanding Ideas
1. **(3)** Presidents until FDR followed Washington's precedent. As defined by this section, a precedent is an earlier action that serves as a justification for a later action.
2. **(3)** The history section of this book states that President Roosevelt created a number of agencies to deal with the state of the economy. Washington's presidency was too far removed, in years, from the Kennedy and Johnson administrations, and President Truman did not create as many agencies as had Roosevelt.

EXERCISE 5
page 151

Understanding Ideas
1. **(b)** Just as Polk had done in Mexico, Johnson escalated the buildup in Vietnam without Congress's declaration of war.
2. **(c)** The national emergency that prompted Roosevelt's extensive use of executive power was the Great Depression; the national emergency that forced Lincoln to expand his authority was the Civil War.
3. **(a)** Carter's assumption of the role of mediator in the Middle East can be linked to the precedent set by Teddy Roosevelt in his mediating between Russia and Japan.

EXERCISE 6
page 152

Applying Ideas
(5) In the section, the term "strong president" is used to describe one who dominates the legislative branch. The description of Andrew Jackson best fits that definition.

Writing Activity 1
page 152

Your answer might include the following points:
Direct Election
● The president and vice president of the United States should be elected by direct vote because the principle on which the electoral college operates is unfair; a candidate who loses a state by a narrow margin also loses the state's electoral votes.
● Electors may cast their ballots as they choose because they are not legally bound to vote for the winner of the popular vote.
Electoral College
● The system should not be changed because the Founding Fathers intended for the president and vice president to be elected by the electoral college.

EXERCISE 7
page 154

Understanding Ideas
1. (4) The only issue common to all five decisions is the defending of an institution's or individual's civil liberties. Choices (1), (2), and (3) are not illustrated by the cases, and choice (5) is the opposite of the Supreme Court's intent.

Analyzing Ideas
2. (3) The *Miranda* case affects police procedures during an arrest. None of the other cases have anything to do with the mechanics of local law enforcement.

Writing Activity 2
page 154

Your argument might include either of the following points:
YES
- The president's appointing Supreme Court justices who agree with his political philosophy is an abuse of power because the Supreme Court should be as independent as the Constitution intended it to be. A lack of independence hurts its ability to serve as a check on the executive branch.

NO
- The president has the right to appoint whomever he desires to the Supreme Court in order to have the court support his administration's policies.

EXERCISE 8
page 155

Applying Ideas
1. (1) Of the choices, only choice (1) was the result of actions of the judicial branch. The other choices were the result of actions of either the legislative branch or the executive branch.
2. (5) According to the passage, the Voting Rights Acts outlawed restrictions on voting. Choices (1), (2), (3), and (4) did not involve the issue of literacy tests for voters.
3. (5) The Voting Rights Acts of 1965 and 1970 stopped the use of literacy tests for voter qualification. This led to greater opportunity at the ballot box and in the workplace.

EXERCISE 9
page 157

Understanding Ideas
(2) Choice (2) is supported by the part of the chart that shows that a bill must go to a conference committee for compromise. The chart does not indicate that a bill may be introduced directly by the president (1). As you read in Chapter 3, a filibuster is an acceptable means by which a vote on a bill may be delayed (3). Bills introduced by either house may be amended as shown in the illustration (4). Bills may become law without the president's signature (5).

EXERCISE 10
page 157

Understanding Ideas
2. legislative, executive
3. legislative, executive
4. legislative, executive
5. judicial, legislative
6. executive, legislative

EXERCISE 11
page 159

Applying Ideas
1. (4) According to the reading, the Fifth Amendment includes the "right to remain silent," one of the rights read to an accused. The Sixth Amendment gives the accused the right to call a lawyer.
2. (3) The quote refers to the First Amendment, the guarantee of freedom of speech. An American citizen is guaranteed freedom of speech as long as this freedom does not infringe upon the rights of others.

Writing Activity 3
page 159

Your argument might include either of the following points:
YES
- Schools that censor their student newspapers deny students freedom of the press. Freedom does not exist when students are told what to write—and what not to write.

NO
- Schools have the right to make sure that student newspapers live up to the school's standards. The newspaper is owned by the school, and students often get academic credit for working on the newspaper staff.

EXERCISE 12
page 161

Understanding Ideas
(1) Democratic Party; controlled the presidency from 1933 to 1953
(2) Republican Party; controlled the presidency for twelve terms
(3) Answers will vary.

Writing Activity 4
page 161

Your answer might include the following points:
YES
• The Republican party was once a third political party. Such a political shift could happen again. If the third party represents enough people, it could succeed.
NO
• Third parties historically have not succeeded in gaining control of the presidency, so it is unlikely that they will do so in the future.
• The two-party system in the U.S. is rooted in tradition; therefore, a successful third party cannot be established.

EXERCISE 13
page 162

Applying Ideas
1. (5) Because the speaker advocates a return to an earlier policy (arming oneself as in the Old West), the speaker is classified as a reactionary.
2. (2) Because the speaker advocates social improvement through governmental action, the speaker may be considered a liberal.
3. (4) Because the speaker advocates maintaining the existing order (the law should remain the way it is), the speaker may be considered to be a conservative.
4. (3) Because the speaker believes in avoiding extreme changes based on the belief that current laws on the books need only to be enforced, the speaker may be considered a moderate.
5. (1) Because the speaker advocates stopping the manufacture of guns immediately, the speaker may be considered a radical.

EXERCISE 14
page 164

Analyzing Ideas
(1), (2), and (4) The fact that Truman won the election even though Dewey was predicted to win suggests that voters might have changed their minds between the time of the surveys and the time of the election, choice (1). The fact that the voters were not as committed to Dewey as the pollsters were led to believe [choice (2)] is a second hypothesis that may be drawn since Truman defeated Dewey. A third hypothesis that can be drawn based on the poll results is that the sampling of voters might have been too small or that the pollsters didn't ask the right people, choice (4). Neither choice (3) nor choice (5) can be supported by the information in the chart.

EXERCISE 15
page 165

Evaluating Ideas
1. (1) The best choice is (1), which is based on the hypothesis that the early announcements of Reagan's victory discouraged Carter's supporters from voting.

Understanding Ideas
2. (3) According to the passage, showing the exit poll results before the voting ended influenced the way some people voted.
3. (5) According to the exit polls, the vote for Perot made the difference. The votes for the Democrats did not change substantially, but the votes for Republicans dropped.

Writing Activity 5
page 165

Your answer might include some of the following points:
YES
• The job of the television news departments is to report the facts as they see them; if this means predicting election outcomes, then the television networks have that right.
NO
• It is unfair for television news stations to predict the outcome of an election before all votes are cast because the practice discourages potential voters from voting for the losing candidate.
• Television, in predicting the outcome of an election, influences the outcome; this practice hurts the electoral process in a democracy.

EXERCISE 16
page 168

Understanding Ideas
1. **(3)** Choice (3) is an infringement of the freedom of the press, a right guaranteed by the Constitution.

Evaluating Ideas
2. **(3)** The most likely reason for forbidding states to grant titles of nobility is that doing so would violate one of the key principles on which the American Revolution was based, that "all men are created equal."

EXERCISE 17
page 168

Understanding Ideas
1. **B**
2. **B**
3. **F**
4. **F**
5. **S**
6. **S**

EXERCISE 18
page 169

Understanding Ideas
1. **(3)** According to the section, circuit courts, county courts, district courts, and superior courts handle civil cases that involve greater monetary rewards; personal injury suits usually involve large monetary rewards.

Applying Ideas
2. **(4)** Because the murder case has already gone to trial, and the accused has been sentenced, the decision must be appealed and referred to the state appellate court.

EXERCISE 19
page 171

Analyzing Ideas
1. **(4)** County B has a greater concentration of children because of the larger proportion spent on schools (75% vs. 10%).
2. **(4)** Because the proportion of money spent for law enforcement in County A is higher than that spent for law enforcement in County B, there must be a greater need for law enforcement services in County A. Also, the proportion of money spent for law enforcement in County A is the second-highest expenditure after general and public assistance.

Writing Activity 6
page 172

Your answer should include one of these four types: weak mayor-council plan, strong mayor-council plan, commission form, and council-manager form.

EXERCISE 20
page 173

Understanding Ideas
1. boxes
2. affordable housing
3. winter

EXERCISE 21
page 173

Understanding Ideas
1. **(3)** The people in the cartoon are apparently homeless because they can't find affordable housing in the suburbs.
2. **(4)** The problem of homelessness is no longer confined to the cities but is now prevalent in the suburbs also.

POLITICAL SCIENCE
pages 174-175

1. **(1)** The figure on the left represents the government. The knife it holds represents the cuts it intends to make on the figure on the right. The "food," or money, will come from entitlements.
2. **(2)** The entitlement figure is drawn as a hog and represents overfeeding, or overfunding. By representing the U.S. government as Uncle Sam holding a knife, the cartoonist is expressing the opinion that entitlements have grown too much.
3. **(2)** The total number of male members in both the House and Senate is much greater than the total number of women. These figures support the conclusion that the proportions are not in balance. The charts give no figures concerning the total number of new freshmen, the number of women who ran for office, or any other information about the elected women.
4. **(5)** The House had 48 women and the Senate 6, a total of 54.
5. **(3)** The author made a judgment about the importance of the document. It cannot be proved or disproved. The other choices are facts.
6. **(2)** The quotation emphasizes the idea that people have natural rights and that government exists to protect those rights. Jefferson may have valued freedom of religion and truth, but they are not the focus of the document.

7. (1) The fake bills would fall under the Secret Service's function to prevent counterfeiting. Investigation of the other situations would belong to either the CIA or the FBI.

8. (3) A problem with a foreign government would be looked into by the CIA. The other situations would be investigated by either the Secret Service or the FBI.

CHAPTER 7: BEHAVIORAL SCIENCES

EXERCISE 1
page 178

Applying Ideas

1. *biologist*—A biologist studies humans and their physical functions.
2. *sociologist*—A sociologist studies societies of today.
3. *anthropologist*—An anthropologist traces a culture from its earliest origins.
4. *psychologist*—A psychologist studies a person's personality and mental capabilities.

EXERCISE 2
page 178

Analyzing Ideas

The order of the steps is:
4. carrying out an experiment or research
2. hypothesizing about the problem
5. drawing a conclusion and doing further research
1. observing a situation
3. designing an experiment or developing a method of research

EXERCISE 3
page 180

Applying Ideas

1. cultural anthropologist—The sentence says that Turnbull studies every aspect of their unique life; a cultural anthropologist studies a people's culture.
2. physical anthropologists—The sentence states that the Leakeys analyzed skeletal remains dug up in Africa; a physical anthropologist studies the development of human physical characteristics.

EXERCISE 4
page 181

Analyzing Ideas

2, 5, 1, 3, 7, 6, 4

EXERCISE 5
page 182

Analyzing Ideas

1. **(4)** According to the passage, art was created because people had more time for leisure since they did not need to focus as much on basic survival. Choices (1), (2), (3), and (5) are not stated in the passage.

Understanding Ideas

2. **(4)** According to the passage, the development of goods and the trade between villages and towns created the need for written records of transaction. This led to the development of written language.

Evaluating Ideas

3. **(5)** According to the passage, goods created a demand that contributed to the development of villages and towns around trading centers. The other choices are either not referred to or are contrary to what the passage says.

Writing Activity 1
page 182

Your description might include one of many ethnic subcultures within the U.S.—Mexican, Polish, East Indian, etc. You might write about distinctive foods introduced by these cultures as well as family relationships—nuclear or extended.

EXERCISE 6
page 183

Applying Ideas

1. **(5)** When an American woman describes European women's refusal to shave their legs as "masculine," she is being ethnocentric. Clean-shaven legs are an American standard of beauty, and European women are being judged by an American cultural standard. None of the other choices show the act of judging one culture by the standards of another.

Evaluating Ideas

2. **(3)** Choice (3) is the only objective assessment of the Hindu rite of cremation shown. Choices (1), (2), and (4) are value judgments and therefore are not objective. Choice (5) reflects an argument in favor of the practical benefits of cremation, not the cultural aspect.

EXERCISE 7
pages 184-185

Understanding Ideas

1. (2) The only example of cultural diffusion shown is the Pygmies' use of prefabricated materials to build their houses. Choice (1) led to cultural diffusion, choices (3) and (5) have no relationship to the process of cultural diffusion, and choice (4) is a result of cultural diffusion expressed in the passage.

Evaluating Ideas

2. (3) The passage states that "the group is weakened when the rules begin to bend or are ignored" and that "once primitives come into contact with the outside world, an innocence and unquestioning contentment is lost." These words suggest that the author thinks that the effect of cultural diffusion on the Pygmies has been negative.

3. (5) The author's emphasis on the words *civilized*, *advanced*, and *primitive* indicates an effort to avoid being ethnocentric; this attitude suggests that cultures described as civilized, advanced, and primitive may not be what we think they are.

4. (5) According to the passage, "handicrafts are produced less for use by home and society than for sale to tourists."

5. (1) According to the passage, "since rituals and religions reinforce group solidarity and dependence on one another, the group is weakened when the rules begin to bend or are ignored."

6. (4) According to the passage, Pygmies "wear few articles of clothing, if any, until they learn to feel ashamed by tourists from more 'advanced' cultures."

7. (5) According to the passage, of the choices mentioned, only the need for hunting and gathering has remained unchanged.

EXERCISE 8
page 186

Analyzing Ideas

(1), (2), and **(4)** That Pygmy camps are smaller than plantations, choice (1), is obvious. Since all of the Pygmy camps represented begin with the word *Apa*, it must refer to "camp" or "tribe," choice (2). No villages are shown outside of plantations, choice (4).

EXERCISE 9
page 188

Applying Ideas

1. S
2. S
3. S
4. P
5. S
6. S
7. S
8. P
9. S
10. P

Writing Activity 2
page 188

Your description should include your family, friends, work group or members of a club or team. You should explain how the degree of intimacy between you and other group members determines whether the group is a primary or secondary one.

EXERCISE 10
page 190

Applying Ideas

1. N Because the couple move away from their in-laws, the situation describes a nuclear family.

2. E Because the law requires the husband and wife to live in the same compound as other relatives, the situation describes an extended family.

3. E Because family members other than the immediate family are involved in the rearing and care of the children, an extended family is described.

4. E Because the elderly live with their children who are required to support them, the situation described is that of an extended family.

5. N A single-parent family is an example of a nuclear family.

EXERCISE 11
page 190

Analyzing Ideas

1. (2) Because the mother is the head of the Seminole household, the mother's brother is more important to the family structure than the father, who is not a blood relative. Choices (1), (3), (4), and (5) are not supported by the facts in the passage.

2. (2) Because the passage states that inheritance and lines of descent are through the mother's side of the family and that women are the heads of their households, we can infer that women are central figures in both the nuclear and extended families.

Writing Activity 3
page 191

Your description should indicate whether or not your family is nuclear or extended and whether or not it is headed by one or both parents, and it should describe the degree of interaction between the members.

EXERCISE 12
page 192

Applying Ideas

1. Claude—The mother traditionally stays at home with the kids, so Claude is reversing roles.
2. Dr. Scott (woman); Nurse Davis (man)—Men are predominantly the doctors and women the nurses; qualities of warmth and caring are usually attributed to female, rather than male, nurses.
3. Jimmy (home economics); Betty Sue (auto mechanics)—Traditionally, a girl is expected to take home economics classes and a boy is expected to take auto mechanics.

EXERCISE 13
page 192

Applying Ideas

1. ascribed—One is born into a racial category; therefore, being a member of the mongoloid race is ascribed status.
2. achieved—One must undergo training to become a policeman, so the status is achieved.
3. ascribed—Because age confers a special status on members in certain cultures, becoming a senior citizen is an example of an ascribed status.
4. achieved—Obtaining a GED certificate is an achievement.
5. ascribed—One is born into royalty; it may not be earned.

EXERCISE 14
page 194

Evaluating Ideas

1. (3) The reading states, "money is not the only criterion that determines status in our society. . . . The degree of formal education also contributes to social status in America." The other choices are neither stated in nor supported by the reading.

Applying Ideas

2. (3) The occupation of brain surgeon is the only one shown that indicates high earnings along with a high level of formal education; therefore, it would be considered to have the highest status in American society today.

EXERCISE 15
pages 194-195

Analyzing Ideas

(1), (3), (4), and (5) In the quote, the "replacements" the writer describes are members of the working class and include more Hispanics and blacks than did his previous middle-class students, choice (1). Working-class people moving into a formerly middle-class neighborhood represent social mobility, choice (3). The quote states that the "replacements were more often working class . . . took achievement tests less well," choice (4). According to the quote, the "replacements . . . collected more welfare," choice (5).

Writing Activity 4
page 195

Your answer might include the following points:
YES
- People are still able to improve their lot with education and hard work.
- The middle class is constantly growing.
NO
- Illegal immigrants are competing with native Americans for fewer jobs.
- The poorer class is growing larger every day.
- Big business, by taking over smaller firms, is making it hard for the small businessman to succeed.

EXERCISE 16
page 197

Applying Ideas

1. The *hunger drive* represents the id in the case described because the reading states that id consists of all the basic drives and instincts we are born with.
2. Lenny's *limiting himself to five cookies* represents the functioning ego. The reading states that the ego "keeps us from having 'too much of a good thing.'"
3. The *guilt* Lenny experiences represents the superego because, according to the reading, the superego acts as the conscience.

EXERCISE 17
page 198

Applying Ideas

1. **(3)** Conditioning involves the use of positive or negative reinforcement to encourage a certain behavior (work). Human nature is not a psychological explanation for human behavior, choice (1). Conditioning is explained by behavioral theory, not psychoanalytic theory, choice (2). Choices (4) and (5) are incorrect because conditioning involves both negative and positive reinforcement, not just one type of reinforcement.

2. **(4)** This is the only choice that represents the use of a positive reinforcement (a reward) to encourage good behavior. Choices (1) and (2) are punishments. While choices (3) and (5) are intended to help the child with his grades, they do not reward good behavior.

EXERCISE 18
page 199

Applying Ideas

1. **P** Psychoanalytic theory attributes adult behavior (Kevin's stubbornness) to childhood influences (Kevin's difficulty in toilet training).

2. **B** Behavioral theory involves conditioning (David's waking up on his own in response to the negative reinforcement of the alarm clock).

3. **B** The reward for Lillie's losing weight is the applause of fellow members of Weight Watchers; therefore, she is conditioned to remain on her diet. Conditioning is an element of behavioral theory.

4. **P** The linking of adult behavior (Al's smoking) with a childhood occurrence (lack of oral stimulation) is a feature of psychoanalytic theory.

5. **B** The reward of a "smiley face" appearing on the computer screen conditions Johnny to strive for the correct response. Johnny is being conditioned, an element of behavioral theory.

Writing Activity 5
page 199

Answers will vary according to individual experience.

EXERCISE 19
page 201

Analyzing Ideas

1. avoidance-avoidance—José has a sore tooth, the pain of which he wants to avoid, but he also wants to avoid the dentist who can take care of the problem.

2. approach-approach—Keisha wants to go out with Lionel, to whom she is attracted, but she also wants to be with her best friend on her birthday.

3. approach-avoidance—Hal needs a new car, a goal that attracts him, but is repelled by the idea of getting deeper into debt.

4. approach-approach—Their dream vacation to Hawaii attracts Kim and Lee, but so does Kim's parents' anniversary celebration, which is taking place at the same time.

5. avoidance-avoidance—Tina is unhappy about her weight problem, but she doesn't want to give up the food she loves to eat.

Writing Activity 6
page 201

Answers will vary according to individual experience.

EXERCISE 20
page 202

Understanding Ideas

1. **(b)** One is caught between two undesirable choices—the devil and the deep blue sea.

2. **(c)** One is attracted to honey but at the same time is repelled by the bee's sting.

3. **(b)** One is caught between two undesirable choices—a rock and a hard place.

4. **(c)** One is attracted to the rose because of its beauty but repelled by the thorn it carries.

5. **(a)** One wants two things but cannot have both—having the cake and enjoying the pleasure of eating it.

EXERCISE 21
page 203

Applying Ideas

1. **(3)** The dishonest politician is assigning a bad trait of her own to another person, her opponent.

2. **(5)** The man's reaction (joining a campaign to have X-rated films banned) is the opposite of his true feelings (he enjoys watching them).

3. **(4)** In his mind, the man is transferring his aggression toward his coworkers to the bowling pins.

ANSWER KEY

Writing Activity 7
page 204

Answers will vary.

EXERCISE 22
page 206

Understanding Ideas

1. Because Phobic Phil and Immaculate Isabel's neuroses are linked to childhood experiences, the psychoanalytical theory of psychology would best explain their actions.
2. If Claude receives attention only when he complains about being ill, his behavior is conditioned. The behaviorist theory of psychology would best explain his actions.

EXERCISE 23
page 206

Applying Ideas

1. (3) obsessive-compulsive—George is obsessed with order. Keeping his record albums in special groupings is a compulsion.
2. (5) fugue state—Sylvia left her home and responsibilities and doesn't remember doing so. decision to do so.
3. (2) conversion-reaction—Lavonna's sickness is a reaction to the guilt of having an affair with her husband's friend.

Writing Activity 8
page 207

Your description should be based on one of the following disorders:
• phobia
• conversion-reaction
• obsession-compulsion
• depressive reaction
• fugue state

EXERCISE 24
page 207

Evaluating Ideas

(3) This is the only choice that suggests a biological basis for the development of schizophrenia. Because identical twins develop from a single egg, it would follow that both members of a set of identical twins would be much more likely to be schizophrenic than two non-twin siblings.

BEHAVIORAL SCIENCES
pages 208-209

1. (1) According to Lindemann, women are security-conscious and less likely to take risks than men. They aren't shown to be passive or hesitant, but they do seem to approach marketing realistically.
2. (1) By making marketing decisions based on opportunity and potential gain, men show the positive belief they have in taking chances. When people are competitive, they think about taking risks, not about being secure. A person who acts moderately is usually cautious and would not take risks.
3. (2) Lindemann herself suggests that combining a conservative attitude with a competitive attitude can result in a strong decision. The other arguments fail to account for the importance of the contrast between the attitudes.
4. (2) The college pennant and the fur coat are long-time symbols of the "big man on campus," the popular man. By dressing a bottle of alcohol in a pennant and fur coat, the cartoonist is saying that drinking alcohol is popular and is an accepted activity.
5. (4) College students often are subject to peer pressure, which can influence their behavior. None of the other choices alone can explain the popularity of drinking on college campuses.
6. (1) Drug abuse in high school is the only choice that is also about harmful behavior caused by peer pressure.
7. (2) People expect to find major cultural differences in other countries. But it is missing the little things—like toilet paper and Kleenex—that makes a person feel out of place.
8. (4) Americans expect their food to be dead and preferably cooked when it is brought to the table. Being presented with a live fish would make the average American feel uncomfortable. Riding an unusual bus or seeing an elephant are expected activities in an adventure. The other choices would be reassuring and familiar to an American.

CHAPTER 8: GEOGRAPHY

EXERCISE 1
page 213

Analyzing Ideas

1. (2) Sardes is located exactly in the center of Herodotus's world.

Understanding Ideas

2. (3) Ethnocentrism is the judging of another culture based on one's own cultural values. Since Herodotus and others like him believed their country was at the center of the world and that other countries were located around them, this belief is similar to the concept of ethnocentrism.

3. (4) The fact that Herodotus and the people of his time believed that the earth was flat and that the Black Sea and the Mediterranean Sea were at the center of the earth contributed to their narrow view of the earth's geography.

4. (4) According to Herodotus's map of the world, the largest body of water was the Mediterranean Sea.

EXERCISE 2
page 218

Understanding Ideas
1. (3) North Africa
2. (1) The North Atlantic Ocean
3. (2) the United States

EXERCISE 3
page 220

Applying Ideas
1. (2) Since San Francisco lies in the Pacific time zone, which is two hours behind Chicago, which lies in the central time zone, it would be 10:00 P.M.

2. (3) Since Salt Lake City, Utah, lies in the mountain time zone, which is two hours behind New York, which lies in the eastern time zone, it would be 2:00 A.M.

EXERCISE 4
page 221

Analyzing Ideas
1. (2) Since there is an even distribution of population in Iowa, as shown on the map, it can be inferred that lowlands allow for an even distribution of population. None of the other conclusions are supported by the map.

Applying Ideas
2. (3) West Virginia is the only state represented that is not primarily flat; therefore, the distribution of its population would be most unlike Iowa's.

Writing Activity 1
page 222

Answers will vary based on students' locations.

EXERCISE 5
page 223

Evaluating Ideas
1. NO The opposite is true; based on the information in the graph, the population of undeveloped countries exceeds that of developed countries.

2. YES The graph shows more dramatic increases for undeveloped nations than for developed nations from 1750 to 2000.

3. YES In 1750, the world population for both developed and undeveloped countries was nearly 1 billion; by the year 2000 it will be about 6½ billion. This figure represents more than a five-fold increase.

4. YES According to the graph, the population of developed countries has lagged behind that of undeveloped countries since 1750.

EXERCISE 6
page 224

Evaluating Ideas
1. (2) Brazil is an underdeveloped nation with a large population. Canada, Germany, Australia, and France are all developed nations. None have a problem with large growth rates, as do Brazil and India.

2. (2) Of the five choices, England has the most in common with Japan—it is an island, it is heavily industrialized, and it is densely populated.

EXERCISE 7
page 226

Evaluating Ideas
1. (5) The prediction based on the graph does not take into account the possibility that new technologies for finding, processing, or transporting fresh water supplies will be found by the year 2020.

2. (4) Since the predicted water shortage is less severe with a two-child average family size than with three-children families, it stands to reason that the water shortage would be further reduced with an even smaller average family size.

3. (5) The Southwest, which includes the desert areas of Arizona, New Mexico, parts of southern California, and Nevada, would have the most limited supply of water.

Writing Activity 2
page 226

Your answer might include the following points:
YES
- Few alternatives exist for those states that need electrical energy; therefore, dependence on nuclear power plants is worth the risk they pose to small numbers of people.
- Technological progress brings some risks with it; to abandon using nuclear-power plants is to stand in the way of progress.
- The threat of nuclear-power plants to human life is being blown out of proportion; most nuclear power plants are operating safely.

NO
- Events like the Three Mile Island and Chernobyl disasters prove that nuclear-power plants threaten human life and health.
- America has an abundance of coal reserves that have been relied on in the past to produce the electrical energy needed to run our industries and homes.
- Safe forms of power, such as solar energy, should be explored fully before risking the potential dangers of nuclear energy.

EXERCISE 8
page 228

Understanding Ideas
1. **(1)** Illinois, with 13, has the greatest number of nuclear power plants.
2. **(3)** For the most part, the states that have the largest numbers of nuclear plants are also the states that have the largest populations and greatest amount of industrial production. Therefore, they are higher users of energy than states with smaller populations.

Evaluating Ideas
3. **(1)** Montana is the only state listed that is not highly industrialized and has no nuclear plants. Nebraska is also not highly industrialized, but it does have a couple of plants.

EXERCISE 9
page 229

Understanding Ideas
1. Japan—Great Britain and Japan, being island nations, have few natural resources. Both import the raw material needed to manufacture goods they sell in the world market.
2. Saudi Arabia—Saudi Arabia and South Africa both have abundant supplies of natural resources—petroleum and gold, respectively—which they export in exchange for the basic goods required by their populations.
3. the U.S.—The U.S. has, and the former Soviet Union had, an abundance of mineral resources that helped establish their positions as world powers.

GEOGRAPHY
pages 230-231

1. **(3)** The white 1992 bar is longer than the black 1989 bar for all papers but the Chicago *Sun-Times*.
2. **(4)** The main idea is that already-used products be turned into a base material for use again in a second product. The other choices refer to other types of environmental programs.
3. **(3)** By placing the burden of proof on the home owners, the insurance companies are assuming that such proof exists. Proof would consist of maps and records of the location of the mine tunnels. If such records had not been kept, they could not be used as evidence of mine subsidence. The requirement does not imply blame or attempt at fraud. The requirement is aimed at eliminating other possible causes in order to compensate for damage.
4. **(2)** The decrease in large city population and the dramatic increase in that of nearby small cities suggests that residents are moving from one to the other. As the population of the state has doubled, there is no evidence of people leaving the state.
5. **(3)** Both Seattle and Spokane have decreased in population. If this trend continues, they will both lose residents.
6. **(5)** The map shows that the Colorado River flows through or along the borders of five states, all of which benefit from its water.
7. **(5)** The drainoff from the five dams and several aqueducts would divert more water than the natural drainage into the Colorado River and its tributaries. The drying up of the Gila and the erosion of the Grand Canyon are effects, not causes of the problem.

CHAPTER 9: ECONOMICS

EXERCISE 1
page 233

Applying Ideas
1. e
2. c
3. a
4. b
5. d

EXERCISE 2
page 236

Understanding Ideas
1. communist—Under the communist system of government, the state controls the economy.
2. capitalist—A capitalist economy is based on the system of free enterprise with very little government interference.
3. socialist—Under socialism, the government regulates many economic activities with the goal of equalizing the distribution of wealth.

Writing Activity 1
page 236

Answers will vary based on the topic selected.

EXERCISE 3
pages 240-241

Understanding Ideas
1. (4) The supply and demand curves intersect at .60; therefore, this would be the market rate for painting houses.

Analyzing Ideas
2. (3) According to the information, in general, when prices fall, demand increases. Therefore, demand for painting houses would increase. Choice (1) is the opposite of what the passage states. Choice (2) is unlikely, since some house-painting companies would have to exist to satisfy demand. Choices (4) and (5) are incorrect because there is no basis for them in the information.
3. (3) The situation describes a case in which increased labor costs (hiring of more workers) did not result in increased profit (return on investment).

Understanding Ideas
4. (4) The company became less efficient when it took eight workers to do the same job that it previously took only six workers to do.

Writing Activity 2
page 241

Your answer might include the following points:
OIL PRODUCERS
- Raising of oil prices will bring more money into developing economies of Third World nations.
- If industrialized nations can get good prices for the goods they export to oil-producing nations, oil-producing nations should be able to get good prices for their product.

CONSUMERS
- With a reduced supply of imported petroleum, the price of oil and oil-derived products such as gasoline would increase.
- With increased petroleum prices, demand, or consumption of gas and other oil-based products, probably would fall.
- With increased imported petroleum prices and lowered demand, gas stations might become unprofitable.
- With increased imported petroleum prices, domestic (U.S.-based) oil companies might recover from financial difficulty and supply more oil than they had in recent years.

EXERCISE 4
page 243

Understanding Ideas
1. F The chief role of the Fed is to regulate the nation's supply of money and credit.
2. T
3. F The discount rate, not the prime rate, is the interest rate that the Fed charges member banks to borrow from it.
4. F The Fed neither coins money nor sets the prime rate to influence the money supply. It sets the reserve ratio and the discount rate.
5. T

EXERCISE 5
page 244

Applying Ideas
1. (5) When too much money circulates, the Fed follows a tight money policy by increasing the reserve ratio and the discount rate. Both measures take money out of the hands of consumers.
2. (4) When too little money is in circulation, the Fed follows a loose money policy by lowering the reserve ratio and discount rate. Both measures put more money in the hands of consumers.

Analyzing Ideas
3. (3) According to the quote, Will Rogers admires a central banking system (the Federal Reserve System). The Fed keeps the economy on a steady course during unstable economic times. Choice (1) is incorrect because the system is not regarded to be foolproof. Choices (2) and (4) are incorrect because the system did not exist since colonial times or since the beginning of human civilization. Choice (5) is critical of a central banking system.
4. (5) The items for sale were originally priced at ridiculously high prices, which suggests the military consistently paid more for items than ordinary Americans pay. Choices (1) and (3) suggest the opposite.

EXERCISE 6
page 246

Analyzing Ideas

(1) This is the only statement that justifies and supports the idea that a federal deficit may be acceptable. Choice (2) contradicts the quote. Choice (3) is not supported in the passage. Choices (4) and (5) are unrelated to the facts presented in the reading.

Writing Activity 3
page 246

Your answer might include the following points:
YES
- National expenditures for the poor are being cut while expenditures for defense are on the rise.
- The poor have no lobbyists who have been effectively pleading their case for the saving of social programs.
- There has been a perceptible shift away from concern about social services for the nation's poor.

NO
- The money spent for social programs during the 1960s has contributed greatly to the nation's budget deficit.
- Many of the programs established in the 1960s have failed so it is a continued waste of the taxpayers' money to continue to support them.
- It is the states' responsibility to provide for their poor, not the federal government's.

EXERCISE 7
pages 248-249

Analyzing Ideas

1. (1) The CPI rose 13.5 percent between 1979 and 1980, not 2 percent (choice 3). A sharp increase in a major commodity price would result in a sharp increase in the overall CPI.

2. (3) Based on the information in the right-hand column of the table, prices have generally risen since 1970.

Evaluating Ideas

3. (3) In the cartoon, the "flying carpet" is a credit card. This suggests that Americans' spending habits have not been curtailed by inflation but have been supported more and more by credit.

4. (1) The mythical flying carpet rides high. By comparing a credit card to a flying carpet, the artist is suggesting that American consumers think they are "riding high," or experiencing financial success because of the ability to finance purchases with credit.

EXERCISE 8
page 251

Applying Ideas

1. (4) The situation of construction workers being unemployed for part of the year is an example of seasonal unemployment.

2. (2) The situation of computers gaining importance in the workplace is an example of structural unemployment—unemployment caused by a rapid change in technology that changes employment needs.

3. (1) The situation of construction workers being laid off because of a slow economy and rehired when the economy improves is an example of cyclical unemployment.

EXERCISE 9
pages 252-253

Understanding Ideas

1. (1) The displacement bar for construction reaches higher than that for any other industry listed.

2. (5) The bar for services reaches 33 percent of employed workers, higher than any of the others.

3. (5) Government had only three percent of displaced workers during 1990–1991.

4. (3) The mining industry employed only one percent of workers from 1990 to 1991.

Evaluating Ideas

5. (3) Worker displacement bars exist for the major industries. There is no evidence for increase or decrease of actual employment (1). Several industries show a lower increase in displacement than mining (2). Agriculture is a much smaller industry than finance, insurance, and real estate (5).

Writing Activity 4
page 253

Your answers might include the following points:
ACCEPT
- There will always be poor and unemployed people; we can never employ all the people in this country.
- Some people don't want to work in spite of any effort to make them employable.

REJECT
- Full employment is a worthy goal to strive for; to accept any level of unemployment is to weaken the resolve to reach the goal.
- It is government's responsibility to see that every person contributes to society by engaging in meaningful work.

ECONOMICS
pages 254-255

1. **(1)** The figures show that occupations requiring special education or skill receive significantly higher wages than those that do not. The other choices are not shown in the table.

2. **(1)** The less skill required for a job, the less the wage tends to be. The rising demand for child care should bring higher wages. The other choices may be true, but they are not assumptions that would dictate a low wage.

3. **(2)** The debit card can draw only on available funds, which suggests that the user cannot run up a debt with the card. There is no support for the other choices.

4. **(1)** The government would be able to spend only the money it actually had, thus limiting spending. Neither spending nor debt would be increased. A national "debit card" might keep the debt in check, but it wouldn't save enough to make the debt go away or reduce the government's responsibility.

5. **(3)** According to the definition of joint partnership, the remaining partners would have to pay the shop's full debt. The partnership itself isn't affected by the problem in payment.

6. **(3)** The bookstore is the only business listed that is owned by an individual. The others are owned by two or more people.

7. **(1)** A reduction in interest payments because of refinancing would save money. No amount of refinancing would get rid of interest payments altogether.

8. **(1)** The dramatic increase in applications for refinanced loans in 1992 suggests that interest rates went down because refinancing often takes place when interest rates are low. The percentage of loan applications refers only to refinancing, not to the number of general loans.

Index